THE SOUTHERN INDIANS
AND BENJAMIN HAWKINS
1796–1816

The Southern Indians
and Benjamin Hawkins
1796–1816

by Florette Henri

We seem to have Forgotten altogether the rights of the Indians. They were treated as tenants at will—we seized on the lands and made a division of the same as possessing allodial rights.

BENJAMIN HAWKINS, PRINCIPAL TEMPORARY AGENT
TO THE INDIANS SOUTH OF THE OHIO

UNIVERSITY OF OKLAHOMA PRESS : NORMAN AND LONDON

BY FLORETTE HENRI

Kings Mountain (New York, 1950)
For Love of Martha (New York, 1956)
Bitter Victory (New York, 1970)
George Mason of Virginia (New York, 1971)
The Unknown Soldiers: Black American Troops in World War I (New York, 1974)
Black Migration (New York, 1975)
The Southern Indians and Benjamin Hawkins, 1796–1816 (Norman, 1986)

Library of Congress Cataloging-in-Publication Data

Henri, Florette.
   The southern Indians and Benjamin Hawkins, 1796–1816.

   Bibliography: p. 359.
   Includes index.
   1. Indians of North America—Southern States—
History. 2. Hawkins, Benjamin, 1754–1816. 3. Indians
of North America—Government relations—1789–1869.
4. Southern States—History—1775–1865. I. Title.
E78.S65H46   1986   975'.00497   85-40945
ISBN 0-8061-1968-3 (alk. paper)

For Raymond

Contents

Illustrations

Preface

THE Constitution gave to the Congress of the United States the power to regulate intercourse with the Indian tribes. How this was to be done, however, according to what policy, and with what consideration for the rights or desires of the states and individual citizens, were not spelled out by the Constitution. These remained matters for experimentation and challenge right from the start, especially in the South, where the tribes were sufficiently at peace with the United States to make possible regular relations with them.

These southern tribes lived in what was then the "Southwest," the area south of Tennessee and west of Georgia, from the frontiers to the Mississippi: the Cherokees, Creeks, Chickasaws, Choctaws, and the Creek splinter group called Seminoles. The government had several agents with the tribes, but in 1795, President Washington entrusted to Benjamin Hawkins, a distinguished North Carolinian, the job of supervising the affairs of all five tribes.

The twenty years of Hawkins's agency, from 1796 to 1816, are of prime significance in the development of Indian-white relationships; they were the formative years of United States Indian policy, during which benevolent attitudes and programs collided with the urgent needs and emerging goals of the nation and its citizens. When Hawkins became agent, the southern tribes held communal rights to huge lands, on which they pursued their hunting life with considerable freedom if not with any stable prosperity. By 1816, when Hawkins died, Indian lands had been eroded by cessions of millions of acres, Indian freedom was more form than substance, and the tribes were being prepared to accept removal to unknown, hostile country west of the Mississippi River.

It is ironic that Hawkins should have been the shepherd to lead the southern Indians toward those barren new pastures, because to an unusual degree he respected and liked the Indians, and guarded their welfare as sternly as that of white men. He was also, however, an informed and dedicated patriot, fully cognizant of the need of his nation eventually to contain the Indians and absorb their enormous hunting grounds. How to do justice to the Indians and yet serve his government was Hawkins's constant dilemma. His hope was that both goals might be accomplished by teaching the Indians the advantages of the white economy, which was based on private property, and of industry, from which capitalist accumulation would result and rescue them from the feast-or-famine pattern of their hunting economy. He further hoped to make them happier people by inculcating the principles of Anglo-American government, law, and justice, which to him were beautiful and perfect concepts. In these ambitions he was supported by the "benevolent plan of government" to bring the Indians the benefits of "civilization"—the federal program that he was appointed to administer. Success would have required a great deal of time and the cooperation of both red men and white men, but as white Americans were rushing forward to become a rich and powerful nation, the Indians were hanging back, wishing, to Hawkins's repeated frustration, to remain Indian.

Through exertions almost unbelievable for a man of middle age and delicate health, Hawkins pressed toward his goal, opposed by the expanionist ambitions of the states and by a series of disruptive plots to seize Indian land and evict the "tenants at will," as Hawkins called the tribes. Although he built a somewhat reluctant following among the older chiefs, the young Indians vehemently rejected his interference in their traditional life. Indian nationalism increased proportionately to white intrusion on Indian land and culture. Indian resistance to further treaties and land cessions grew absolute, while government pressure for more and greater cessions grew stronger. The fatal blow to Hawkins's hopes, a civil war between the conservative and radical factions among the Creeks, was perhaps precipitated by Hawkins's insistence on the capture and punishment by the Creek Nation of Indian murderers of white people, a process necessary and just according to Hawkins's philosophy, but foreign and intolerable to the Indians, especially the younger ones. The civil war and its causes dwindled into insignificance, however, when white leaders injected themselves into the Creek struggle, which then became an expansionist and punitive campaign against the rebellious red men by Andrew Jackson and other white men leading white troops and a substantial number of Indian friendlies.

The end of that war was effectively the end of the southern Indians east of the Mississippi; but their end was bound to come soon, by whatever means, because the survival and growth of the United States required it. The cession of twenty-three million acres of land, exacted by Jackson at the end of the war, ignored tribal boundaries, ignored distinctions between Indians who had fought alongside white troops and those who had fought against them, ignored every consideration except the interests of the southern states and of land speculators, made nonsense of Hawkins's twenty-year labor to bring about a just, peaceable relationship between Indians and whites, and established a pattern of war and land rape that displaced the benevolent program of twenty years earlier.

The main purpose of this book is to give reality to the time, the place, the people, and their acts, especially the Indian people, who too often in historical reconstructions are as silent and lifeless as chess pieces, giving an illusion of animation because they are moved about but endowed with neither intelligence, emotions, volition, nor the internal conflicts and anguish all human beings must suffer. I have attempted to show the Indians as they were living and had long lived; the frontier as it was; the lives of red, white, and black people in or on the edge of Indian country; the trading that brought them peaceably together; and the drinking, boredom, and explosions of violence that punctuated monotony. And I have tried to present this living material against the background of changing Indian cultures and of the needs, policies, and relations with other nations of the emerging United States.

FLORETTE HENRI

Yonkers, New York

PART ONE

Treats

They told me they did not understand the plan, they could not work, they did not want ploughs, it did not comport with the ways of the red people, who were determined to persevere in the ways of their ancestors. They saw no necessity why the white people should change the ways of their ancestors, it had been time out of mind custom with them to give presents to the Indians of Cloathing, Salt, and provisions, & they expected it would be continued. They said it had always been customary, when a great Chief or Warrior was mad and threatened to go on the frontiers to do mischief, to pacify them with presents. That these things were more necessary now than ever as the game was gone, the people were naked, & had not any other resources but in the presents expected to be offered by the white people. . . . To all beggars the answer was no.

BENJAMIN HAWKINS TO
SECRETARY OF WAR JAMES MCHENRY, JUNE 24, 1798

CHAPTER 1

Bear, Deer,
Turkeys and Indians

When the woods are not burnt for a year or more, the [whortle-berries] are on dwarf bushes, grow larger, and in great abundance. The dwarf saw palmetto, when the woods are not burnt, in like manner bears a cluster of berries on a single stem, which are eaten by bear, deer, turkeys, and Indians.

BENJAMIN HAWKINS, *Sketch of the Creek Country*

Indians met us on the way, playing upon Flutes; which is a token that they come in peace.—

SAMUEL PURCHAS, *Pilgrimage*, c. 1615

THE land of the southern Indians was very large and vague in outline; the tribes who lived there could draw accurate maps but made no exact surveys of their individual tribal holdings. Together the Cherokees, Chickasaws, Choctaws, and Creeks (with their Seminole offshoot) considered as theirs, to live on and hunt over, all the land from above the Tennessee River in the north and from the Oconee in the east to the Mississippi in the west and the gulfs of Mexico and Florida in the south. All their frontiers, however, were challenged. Settlers in the Cumberland and Franklin regions of the Southwest Territory claimed for themselves the Tennessee Valley and were pushing southward. Georgia—although its settled portion was merely a hand's breadth along the Atlantic coast from the Savannah River south to the Saint Marys, narrowing to a finger's width as it pushed northwestward—claimed by charter the whole vast area from the coast to the Mississippi. Spain claimed the southern portion of the Indian country, from the Mississippi to the

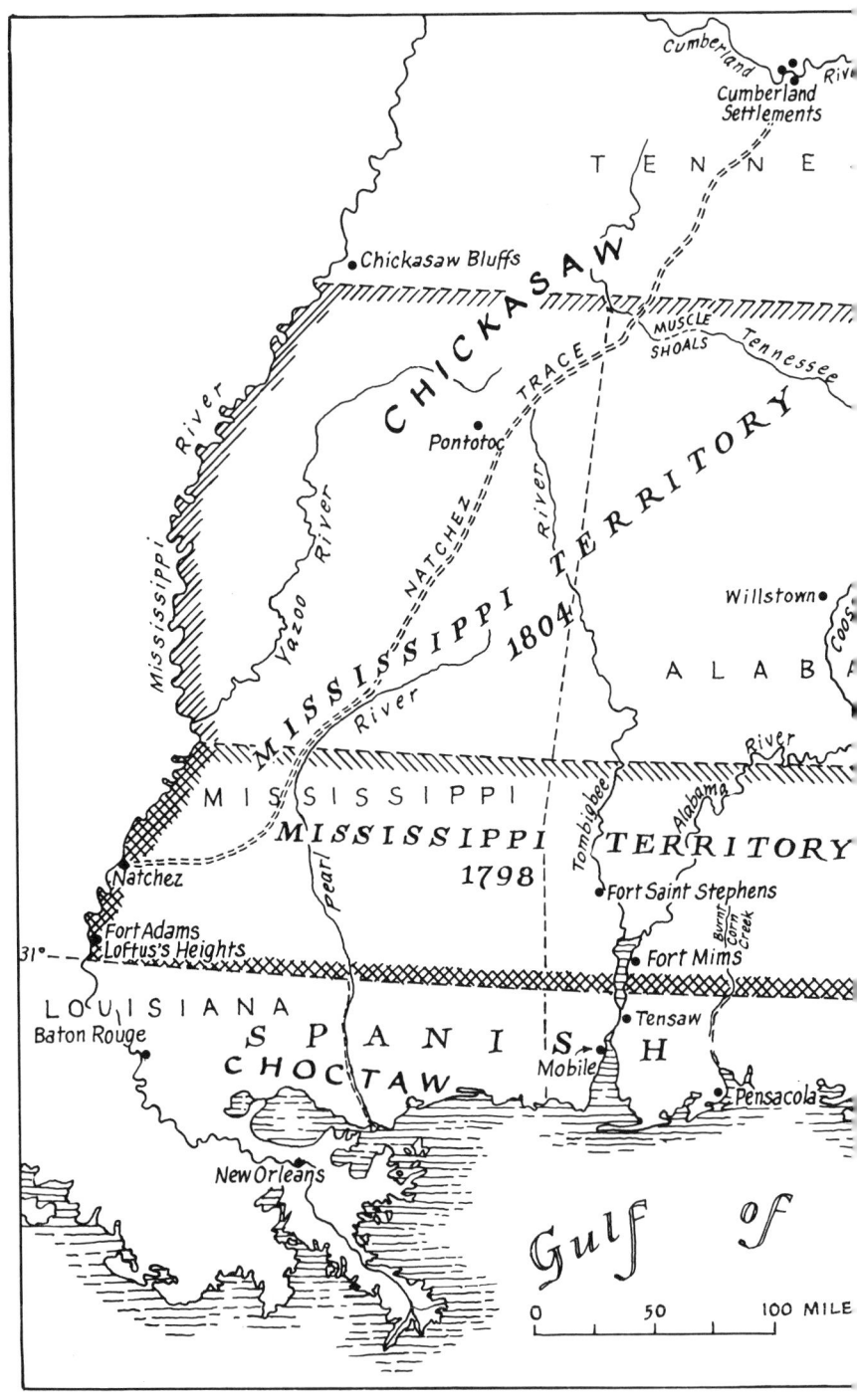

Indian Country Southeast, 1796–1816

Atlantic, an area that included Louisiana, the West Florida strip along the gulf, and the rest of the peninsula, East Florida.[1]

Choctaws ranged the southern Mississippi Valley from towns on the Pearl River. The Chickasaws were located farther to the north and west. Cherokees were mostly concentrated in the Tennessee Valley, their westernmost villages colliding with the easternmost villages of the Chickasaws. The Creek Nation claimed the whole middle part of Georgia's western lands, and the Seminoles had retreated to the swamps of Florida as being safer than contact with either the Spaniards or the Americans.

The Indian lands, more than two hundred miles from north to south and three hundred miles across, were temperate in climate in the north with occasional sharp winter frosts, and subtropical at their southern extremity. They comprised every kind of terrain and soil to be found in those latitudes. But whether forest or savannah, bottomland or mountain range, the common quality of the Indian country was openness, space; and no traveller described the land as other than beautiful. To Christian Gottlieb Priber, who lived the Indian life with the Indians in the 1730s, their land was "Paradice." And this is how it looked to the naturalist William Bartram, forty years later:

> The birds sung merrily in the groves, and the alert roebuck whistled and bounded over the ample means and green turfy hills. After leaving our encampment, we travelled over a delightful territory, presenting to view variable sylvan scenes, consisting of chains of low hills affording high forests, with expansive savannas, cane meadows, and lawns between, watered with rivulets and glittering brooks.

That was in Creek country; here he speaks of the land of the Cherokees:

> The mountains recede, the vale expands; two beautiful rivulets stream down through lateral vales, gliding in serpentine mazes over the green turfy knolls, and enter the Tanase nearly opposite to each other. Straight forward the expansive green vale seems yet infinite; . . . an expanded wing of the vale spreads on my right, down which came precipitately a very beautiful creek, which flowed into the river just before us; but now behold, high upon the side of a distant mountain overlooking the vale, the fountain of this brisk-flowing creek; the unparalleled waterfall appears as a vast edifice with crystal front, or a field of ice lying on the bosom of the hill.

As for the Chickasaws, trader-historian James Adair said two decades before Hawkins's time that they "live in a region, as happy as any under the sun," temperate and fertile.[2]

In the late 1790s, Benjamin Hawkins set out to acquaint himself with Creek country, a part of the territory whose affairs he was to administer as principal agent to the Indians south of the Ohio. He looked at nature less romantically than Bartram, noting the pine barrens along with the cane meadows, and the stiff, gravelly soil as well as the green turfy knolls, because one of his chief duties was to bring nature under cultivation, to tame it. He was an agriculturist, not a naturalist. In general, however, what he saw was good. He reported: "The Coosau has its source high up in the Cherokee country. . . . The [Indian] settlements are generally on rich flats of oaks, hickory, poplar, walnut and mulberry. The springs are fine; there is cane on the creeks, and reed on the branches." For thirty miles down the Tallapoosa River to the Alabama, and then for another thirty miles down that river, he found grassy plains: "They are waving, hill and dale, and appear divided into fields. In the fields the grass is short, no brush; the soil in places is a lead color, yellow underneath, within the abode of ants, and very stiff. In the wooded parts the growth is generally post oak, and very large, without any underbrush, beautifully set in clumps. Here the soil is a dark clay, covered with long grass and weeds, which indicates a rich soil."

The mountains of Cherokee country also pleased Hawkins: "This pass is a difficult one, ascending or descending, and I recommend to all travellers to take the other rout, unless they are pleased with mountain scenes and will exchange for the plague and fatigue of climbing for them as I have done."[3]

The land, when Bartram and other early travelers saw it, was host to a large population of wild life, although their numbers had thinned by Hawkins's time. Bartram saw "herds of sprightly deer, squadrons of the beautiful fleet Seminole horses, flocks of turkeys." Several years after Bartram's journey, Louis LeClerc Milfort claimed to have seen, in Choctaw country, many wild oxen and a herd of four thousand buffaloes stampeding out of caves in the bluffs over the Mississippi. According to Lt. Henry Timberlake, in his travels in Cherokee country in 1761 he saw an "amazing quantity of buffaloes, bears, deer, beavers, geese, swans, ducks, turkeys and other game," and also raccoons, opossums, rabbits, squirrels, partridges, and pheasants. At a peace talk with the Indians at Chota (in what is now Tennessee), chief town of the Cherokees, Timberlake was served a feast "consisting chiefly of wild meat; such as venison, bear, and buffalo."[4]

Indian country was a treasury of vegetable as well as animal riches. The waterside meadows, or savannahs, grew succulent cane and grasses, excellent range for deer, horses, and cattle. The woods provided great store of hickory nuts, walnuts, and acorns. In the forests of Cherokee mountain country the nineteenth-century botanist Asa Gray found 136 varieties of trees and 174 species of shrubs and flowers—more different kinds within a day's walk, he said, than are native to all Europe. In the southern part of the land grew wild oranges, limes, and papayas, and farther north, wild peaches, plums, and cherries, along with fox grapes and muscadines, persimmons, haws, chestnuts, blackberries, and some strawberries. Bees made great quantities of honey from the wild flowers. The bog potato and the China briarroot provided emergency rations for hunters. Ginseng and many other plants produced medicinal roots, leaves, bark, buds, and flowers.[5]

Up and down and across, Indian country was striped with rivers. Flowing north and south were the Oconee, Ocmulgee, Apalachicola, Flint, Chattahoochee, Tallapoosa, Alabama, Tombigbee, Pearl, Yazoo, and finally the Mississippi. Across the northern part flowed the Clinch, Cumberland, Duck, Elk, French Broad, and the great Tennessee. The rivers, with their countless tributary creeks and the many lakes and ponds, were as fecund as the land. The shad came in hundreds and thousands in spring, and there were sturgeon, rockfish, trout, perch, catfish, and suckers. Otters and beavers thrived on the well-watered land. Bartram rhapsodized about Florida lake as a "paradise of fish." Furthermore, the tortoises of the swamps, he observed, provided flesh and eggs that were much esteemed as food.[6]

The beasts and vegetables were the principal known treasures of the earth and its waters in the Indian South, not precious metals or gems, although some gold, silver, and copper had been found in the Cherokee country, and semiprecious amethyst and aquamarine. There were also some iron ore, lead, saltpeter, and clay for pottery. Benjamin Hawkins noted the potential of Bartram's brisk-flowing creeks and waterfalls to power gristmills and sawmills. But to harness the streams and mine the earth required a kind and degree of labor not appropriate in "Paradice," nor congenial to its aboriginal inhabitants.[7]

The Indians were keenly aware of their land's wealth of all kinds. In negotiating treaty terms, they pointed out the lasting value of natural fruitfulness in contrast to the ephemeral trade goods offered them in exchange for the land. The earth would keep producing grass; the trees, acorns and hickory nuts; the bushes, blackberries. The trees, the water, and the fertile land would yield indefinitely, they said; "the good that will arise from the land will have no end."[8]

With little labor, a mere scratching of the top crust of soil, the fertile earth could be made to produce in addition to its wild fruits big crops of beans, potatoes, Indian corn, pumpkins, melons, and tobacco—plants indigenous to the country—and from imported European seed better crops could be grown than in their native climate, Timberlake said. True, the Indian method of cultivation without systematic fertilizing wore out the land, but there was so much of it that old fields could always be abandoned for new fields.[9]

The Indians felt about the gifts of the earth more than gratitude, rather a mystical identification. A comment in a recent study of Pueblo Indians was probably as true for the Indians of the Southeast: "If a Pueblo eats beans it becomes a part of him and he becomes a part of the soil and a part of God." Such a sense of communion explains much that whites did not understand about the bond between Indians and their land. Anyone who suggested to Indians that they part with land risked rude insults; "The bare mention excites very disagreeable emotions," Hawkins wrote. They would not mind giving up personal property, "but land they say should not be touched."[10]

Land was property like any other, Hawkins tried to convince them, and could be used to satisfy damages or debts if a man had no other property with which to pay. But to the Indians land was property unlike any other. It had been given into their keeping by the Master of Breath; they regarded it "as their blood and their life," wrote James White in 1787, when he was agent to the southern Indians. They were also aware, it seems, that the untouched land was synonymous with their freedom, so that if they saw trees being felled and land cleared, they were alarmed lest a fort was to be built and themselves enslaved. As James Adair had noted, "their darling passion is liberty"; and as the Shawnee chief Tecumseh warned them fifty years later, their liberty resided in their land, and once the land was gone so also would be their ancient freedom. The land was the Indian's whole being, his flesh, blood, and spirit; as long as he kept the land, he could not be subjugated. It was both himself and his power. However passionate the attachment of a white American to the fields, woodlots, and wilderness acres to which he held title, it was different in kind from the Antaean oneness of the Indian with the unbounded earth beneath his feet. Indians were aware of nature in the way that they were aware of the limbs of their own bodies. When they talked, nature's preeminence in their minds suggested similitudes with natural phenomena to express and emphasize abstractions, and they were able to choose their metaphors well not only because they lived in nature but also, it seems, because they had observed it with unsated appreciation. "When we approached the shore," wrote Francis Baily in describing a passage through the land of the Chickasaws, "there were a number of them sitting on the banks, and others standing at the top of the hill, enjoying the mildness of the evening and the beauty of the setting sun."[11]

The bounty of the land around them in a lavishment of animals, fishes, trees, and herbs, and the ease of coaxing corn from the land for their bread and gruel, produced in the Indians a feeling about labor very different from that of whites. "Six days shalt thou labor" was the command of the Judeo-Christian God; Indians felt God in their food, but not in their sweat. Food was there to be taken, respectfully and thankfully; why labor?

A Christian indignation at this heathen philosophy comes through in the words of Lewis Cass, later Andrew Jackson's secretary of war: "There can be no doubt that the Creator intended the earth should be reclaimed from a state of nature and cultivated; that . . . a tribe of wandering hunters . . . have a very imperfect possession of the country over which they roam." And even more plainly was the same conviction expressed by a congressman who supported the Cass-Jackson stand: "Jacob will forever obtain the inheritance of Esau. The earth was given for labor, and to labor it belongs." [12]

In the thinking of the Indians, however, the Master of Breath had given them the earth not to enslave them but to free them to enjoy it. They were Adam, not Jacob. "They consider labor not merely as an evil, but as a disgrace," wrote Alexis de Tocqueville; "so that their pride contends against civilization as obstinately as their indolence. . . . [The Indian] considers the cares of industry as degrading occupations; he compares the plowman to the ox that traces the furrow; and in each of our handicrafts he can see only the labor of slaves." Let an Osage tell it: "You whites possess the power of subduing almost every animal to your use. You are surrounded by slaves. Everything about you is in chains, and you are slaves yourselves. I hear I should exchange my presents for yours. I too should become a slave. . . . For myself, I was born free, and wish to die free. I am perfectly content with my condition." [13]

Slavery was not merely an abstract concept to the Indians. Black slaves worked the plantations of white men in Indian country; the more prosperous Indians and part-Indians themselves owned black slaves. And it is not more paradoxical for the freedom-loving Indian to own slaves than for the white American who had fought a war to defend the proposition that all men were born free and equal. Indians themselves had been, and still occasionally were, held in slavery, so they knew its horrors at first hand. In the early eighteenth century, out of South Carolina's total population of 9,580 there were 2,900 black slaves and 1,400 Indian slaves. Since Indians knew so well how ill a man could be esteemed and treated who had lost his liberty, which to them was identified with their land, it is not surprising that the southern Indians were incited by the plea of Tecumseh the Shawnee in 1811 that they fight to keep what land was left them. His words stung: "Do they not even now kick and strike us as they do their black-faces? How long will it be before they will tie us to a post and whip us?" The young Creeks who heeded Tecumseh were not mad or possessed, although they chose a path to death; they acted on the simple proposition that death was preferable to servitude.[14]

An Indian not only abhorred selling land, but in fact could not sell it, because it was not his but the tribe's. Settlers and speculators from Georgia and Tennessee who invaded Indian country to make private deals with individual Indians were furious to find they had bought nothing; no such purchase could be honored. Where only a handful of chiefs had turned out to act for the tribe, even official federal treaties were repudiated; treaties had to be approved by the entire tribe in council. The great Creek chief Alexander McGillivray went in fear of his life because in 1790 at the treaty of New York he and twenty-three other chiefs and warriors had sold land that belonged to all the Creeks.[15]

Ownership in commonalty was recognized from the start by white authority as a chief stumbling block in "civilizing" the southern tribes. Secretary of War Henry Knox, who in 1789 recommended a law declaring that, as prior inhabitants, "the Indian tribes possess the right of the soil of all lands within their limits," added wistfully that, "were it possible to induce among the Indian tribes a love for exclusive property, it would be a happy commencement of the business "of civilizing them." But was it possible to induce such a love? Edward Price, the first factor at the United States government store in Georgia, wrote Hawkins that "their ideas of the sacredness of the rights of property as established in civilized nations are in embryo." What Price and so many others mistook for childishness, or simple-minded savagery, was a confirmed attachment to freedom. Labor was slavery. If a man owned a little piece of land, he must labor to live; if he shared equal rights in the vast tribal lands, he could support himself without what he considered labor—and labor to him had none of the dignity with which it was endowed by Christian doctrine. Therefore, private ownership would reduce him from freedom to slavery, he believed.[16]

The argument here illustrates not only the Indian's equating of land with liberty, but his definition of labor as work done by slaves, or at best, inferiors, such as captives or women. The long winter hunt of Indian men was not considered labor, although it was both arduous and compulsory. The men had to provide food and clothing for themselves and their families until the next hunt. They roamed far from their homes and wives; they not only killed but also skinned, butchered, dried, and packed home their kill (one horse load being the dried meat of ten deer); during the hunt they risked cold, hunger, thirst, fatigue, sickness, accident, and failure. Yet this they did not consider labor. True, tasks of the hunt were not repetitious or monotonous, and perhaps those qualities are specific attributes of labor. Moreover, hunting was the very acting-out of freedom; the winter hunt reestablished annually the right of the Indians to great open spaces of land, as a white landowner establishes his title to a customarily public right-of-way through his property by blocking it once a year.[17]

Benjamin Hawkins, describing Indian resistance to a treaty invitation in 1801, said it was caused "by a panic terror, springing from the apprehension that they are soon to be pressed for further relinquishment of Lands."[18]

The lovely, fertile land, described purely in terms of waters, soil, flora, and fauna, misleadingly gives the impression of virgin wilderness. There were, indeed, great unpeopled stretches of hunting ground, nurseries of the game on which the southern Indian economy was based, but for a true picture of Indian country one must also envisage the habitations of men that made the region far from a desert. In 1790 between 60,000 and 70,000 Indians made their homes in the region—small numbers, but not for that part of America at that time, where there were only 35,691 inhabitants, white and black, in the Tennessee country, 73,677 in the Kentucky country, and 82,548 in the state of Georgia.[19]

The southern Indians were no mere disembodied essence of liberty but a very lively, vocal group, of whom 10,000 to 15,000 were warriors, and the other 50,000 to 60,000 were women, children, and men too old to fight.[20] Of the four tribes (Seminoles are included with Creeks in this study except where otherwise noted), the Choctaws were the most numerous, with about 6,000 warriors, and their Mississippi Valley region was the most

densely inhabited. Next came the Creeks, with about 5,500 warriors; then the Cherokees, with 2,000 or less; and last the Chickasaws, with 1,000 or less.

In 1796, when Hawkins became their agent, the Creeks
claimed they could cede no more land and yet feed their
people, because they were increasing just as the whites were.
Hawkins's estimate of 1803, however, showed a drop in the
number of Creek-Seminole warriors to 4,500, and in 1805 he
lowered that figure to 4,000. Hawkins may have underestimated deliberately, to depreciate the potential danger posed by
the Creeks and thus protect them; the estimate of the Spanish
agent, Capt. Pedro Olivar, was more than double Hawkins's,
possibly because it suited his purpose to make the Creeks seem
more formidable than they were. How many of those included
as Indians were of full Indian ancestry is impossible to say with
any certainty, but even by 1800, after long contact with black
and white men, full bloods undoubtedly formed a majority.
There was, however, a significant number of part-Indians,
some of whom held important tribal positions while others
chose to live like white men, as farmers and traders—but not as
citizens, because they could not get citizenship.[21]

Within the four tribes were subtribes, and although some
were closely related, others were quite different in origins, culture, and language. What united them were the proximity of
their lands and the fear of losing them, and certain physical
characteristics pointing to a common stock.

In appearance, the Indians in the South were apparently
enough alike to be described as a whole; the Choctaws' flat
heads were a cultural, not a genetic, phenomenon—they
weighted their babies' foreheads to achieve this admired feature. Bartram claimed that the southern Indians had the
perfect human form, and his hyperbole here seems justified
by common agreement. The complexion of the men was generally a more or less bright copper color, while some were of an
olive cast, they were sturdily built and erect in posture; "strong,
well proportioned in body and limbs, surprisingly active and
nimble," Adair wrote. Timberlake described the Cherokee men
as of middle height, but Bartram said they were very tall, the
tallest men he had ever seen. All observers agreed that the

southern tribesmen in general were of a good height, and the disagreement between Timberlake and Bartram may indicate only that Timberlake himself was tall, and Bartram short. The women were described as small, with childishly tiny hands and feet, but like the men they were well formed. Generally they had lighter skin than the men; some were nearly as fair as Europeans, Bartram said. He also described them as modest, bashful, beautiful, loving, and expert in the use of those charms; whereas Hawkins described Creek women as mulishly stubborn, except "when they are amorous, and then they exhibit all the amiable and gentle qualities of the cat." Perhaps here, too, as between Timberlake and Bartram on the men's height, the difference lay more in the observer than the observed.[22]

The everyday clothing of the men consisted of a loin cloth or flap, a blanket or shirt, or both in the cold weather, leggings and moccasins. Women wore a short petticoat to just below the knee, and sometimes over it a shift, or chemise, opening in front and quite short so that a child could easily be put beneath it to suckle, and in cold weather a blanket, mantle, or cape over all, with moccasins on their feet. A wealthy woman might fasten her shift with silver and bead brooches, her ears might be fringed with numerous earbobs, and she might wear necklaces of silver beads and bobs. Still, she would be far outshone by a chief at a treaty or council meeting or ceremonial visit to the United States capital—the contexts in which most whites saw Indians. An assembly of dozens, hundreds, sometimes thousands of red men in their formal dress must have been a dazzling spectacle. Envisage row upon row of large, muscular men in silver gorgets and medals, hung with gold and silver neck chains, bracelets, and earbobs of metal wire and feathers; faces painted awesomely with designs of vermilion; heads shaved shiny except for the central comb, *en brosse* in front, in back long and adorned with ribbons, feathers, silver quills, beads, and colored stones. On their bare breasts and arms, the bulging muscles bore a picture book of beasts, flowers, sun, and stars, tattooed in a bluish tint. Their hips and thighs were naked except for the loincloth with its pendant flap in front accented with beads and metallic lace. They wore cloth leggings, fine deerskin moccasins on their feet, and short or long cloaks of scarlet or blue draped from their shoulders. And every one of these articles of clothing was a riot of bells, beads, lace, ribbons, and fringes. Some of the chiefs and warriors would top their costumes with broad headbands, from which feather plumes stood upright; and others would be wearing turbans made of yards of fine cloth wound round their heads with a frontispiece of plumes springing from a brooch.[23]

Inwardly as well as outwardly, the several southern tribes had basic similarities, although environmental and experimental differences overlaid these with individual traits. A recent sociological study has pointed to qualities that the author found common to all Indians and enduring: they prefer quiet observation and deliberate consideration of a problem to direct, quick action; they dislike hurry and pressure; they are more present-minded than future-minded; they are more patient and pragmatic, less competitive, aggressive, and materialistic, than white people; they are more likely to feel shame than guilt when they have done wrong; and their religion is not a separate department of life but woven into its entire fabric. Creek Indians listened attentively when two Moravian missionaries in Hawkins's agency told them about the love of God through Jesus Christ, and when asked if they understood they said, "Yes." "This is their answer to all matters spiritual," the missionaries complained; "They are most anxious to say 'yes' followed by a 'yes, yes, I know.' When asked whether they really understood, it is 'yes, yes' as always." The Moravians did not understand that Christian theology had no appeal for people who felt God everywhere, in the earth and its fruits. Alex Cornells, an outstanding half-Creek chief, told the missionaries: "But I have heard much of it from the old chiefs, the same word of God of which you spoke here. The Indians know it without a book; they dream much of God, therefore they know it."[24]

The southern Indians who had been longest and most intensively in contact with white Americans were the Cherokees, because they lived nearest to the Carolinas and Virginia, and so were the most accessible to traders from an early date. The Cherokees were described by most commentators as having made the greatest progress in farming, stock raising, and the industrial arts, although they were still great warriors, as they had shown in the French and Indian wars. In the 1790s, the Cherokee warrior John Watts again demonstrated Cherokee potential for ferocity in retaliation for slaughters of his people by Tennessee Indian fighters. But, unprovoked, they were probably the most admirable of the southern tribes for moral character and disposition, by Indian or white standards; Bartram found them notably grave, dignified, circumspect, deliberate, honest, cheerful, and humane. Timberlake agreed, adding that they were soft-spoken, gentle, and friendly. Both observers were sure of one characteristic: the high value that the Cherokees set on their land and liberty; they were implacable enemies to any who tried to restrict these, said Timberlake; and Bartram confirmed that they were willing to sacrifice "even their blood, and life itself, to defend their territory and maintain their rights."[25]

The Choctaws, less vulnerably situated than the Creeks, were generally characterized as mild people. Hawkins spoke of them as "humble, friendly, tranquil, pacific people" who, astonishingly and commendably, he said, refused gifts of whiskey, and who were better disposed towards whites—"more tractible and less sanguinary"—than other tribes; however, he added, the tribe "has been long buried in sloth and ignorance." Bartram had described the Choctaws as ingenious, sensible people, brave but peaceable, good farmers but slovenly about their persons and dress.[26]

Another tribe peaceable toward whites, probably because their location had spared them much contact or intrusion, were the Chickasaws. Hawkins reported the Chickasaw boast that they had never spilt the blood of a white man, but they had engaged in a long, bitter war with the Creeks, despite their close relationship (they said they were "of the same fire" with the Lower Creek town of Cusseta). The Chickasaws were a little slow in learning the "civilized" arts, Hawkins said in 1801, but seemed to be catching up and even to be developing a taste for private property.[27]

Most important of the southern tribes in this period, and most adamantly opposed to United States westward expansion, were the Creek Indians. Without some understanding of the Creeks it is difficult to follow the complicated, often murky events of the decades from 1780 to 1820, and certainly not possible to comprehend or evaluate their own part in those events, which precipitated the removals west of the southern Indians. The Creeks are not easy to understand, however, because although this group was treated officially in its relations with the United States government as a tribe, actually it was a conglomerate of many bands of Indians of different ancestries with different geographical origins and different languages, traditions, and laws. Within the tribal area were towns and villages demonstrating those differences by a wide range of character traits, living styles, and economies. The entire group, calling itself the Creek, or Muskogee, Confederacy or Nation, consisted of two geographical sections. The Upper Creeks lived just south of the Cherokees and the Tennessee country. Their twenty-five or twenty-six towns and sixteen associated villages were sprinkled along the banks of the Coosa, Tallapoosa, and Alabama rivers. The Lower Creek country was southeast of the Upper Creeks, bordering on Georgia and Florida. The twelve Lower Creek towns and twenty-four villages were mostly along the Flint and Chattahoochee rivers.[28]

The dominant element in the population called themselves Muskogees and spoke the Muskogee, or Creek, language. In Lower Creek country the two most important bands of this Muskogee stock were the Cowetas and the Cussetas, who had probably moved into the area at some early date from across the Mississippi. The Cowetas' town was the "red town" of the Lower Creeks, where war tactics were planned, and the Cussetas' town was their "white town," where all other public matters, including declarations of war, were debated and decided. Cusseta, the largest of the Creek towns, with its satellite villages had a population of less than 1,000, of whom about 180 were gunmen, as Hawkins called the warriors. In Upper Creek country the dominant Muskogee group was the Coosas, who were settled in towns and villages along the Coosa and Tallapoosa rivers; the Coosas' ancient town Tuckabatchee in Hawkins's time had about 600 people.[29]

Attached to those leading groups were smaller bands, many of them nomads from west of the Mississippi. The Alabamas, for example, had moved eastward and had arrived in Creek country late in the seventeenth century; some stayed in Upper Creek country, some wandered on to Mobile (in present Alabama), or to Florida. Of still another derivation were the Uchees, an independent, aggressive people who had moved southward into Creek country along with a splinter group of Shawnees.

A few miles south of the Uchees were the Oosoochee settlements; the two groups were much alike in background and temperament. Shortly before Hawkins's arrival the Uchees had suffered dreadfully in a raid on their village of Padgeeligau by a Capt. Benjamin Harrison, in which seventeen of their warriors had been killed and the village destroyed. After that incident they were "very cross," "recalcitrant," and "trouble-makers," in the opinion of whites. Officially, the retaliatory depredations of the Uchees and Oosoochees were not sanctioned by the leaders of the Creek Nation. As for the Uchees and Oosoochees, in but not of the Creek Nation, they held themselves aloof and retained their own language, traditions, and laws. Other unrelated bands drawn into the Creek Confederacy included the Hitchitis, Koasatis, and Natchez.[30]

All the Creek bands were known as formidable warriors, as they needed to be, living between the Spanish and American jaws of a nutcracker. Some families and bands of Muskogees, Uchees, Shawnees, and other Creek subgroups had thought to escape from their perilous situation by migrating to the rich lands, plentiful game, and natural fortress of Florida's impenetrable swamps and forests. Hawkins called these people "Sim e no luh gee," which he translated as "wild people"—not because they were wilder in character than other Indians but because they had left established towns to pitch irregular settlements in a wild country. Because the seven Seminole towns were in Spanish territory, outside the jurisdiction or control of Creek government or United States Indian agents, they became a nursery for intrigues planted by Spanish and British agents, American Loyalist refugees, vagabonds, and adventurers. The Seminoles therefore were often at the center of some kind of trouble, and their name came to signify people wild and ferocious in character. Hawkins, however, wrote that "notwithstanding their name I have found them as decent and orderly as any of the Creeks."[31]

The heterogeneity of the Creeks makes it difficult to assign them a national character, but they did have certain qualities not so noticeable in other tribes. Pride must be mentioned first, because the word is so frequently used to particularize the tribe. The Creeks were a proud, haughty, arrogant race, said Bartram; even to Hawkins, in general their admirer, they were on occasion a "proud, haughty, lying, spoiled, untoward race" or "the most numerous, proud, haughty and ill behaved Indians in the agency South of Ohio." They apparently not only felt but also showed they felt themselves superior. "It is a well-known trait in Indian character," wrote John Wheeler in commenting on the Creek War of 1812 to 1814, "that whenever war is waged in their vicinity their belligerent and restless temper will cause them to take a part" (though, in fact, many Creeks proved extremely reluctant to fight in that war). Adair also had called the Indians naturally pugnacious, but pointed out that it was usually the white traders who prompted them to make war; and that when they did fight, few were killed, and the survivors purged themselves afterwards in a religious ceremony of atonement for the shedding of blood. War did not mean the same thing to Creeks or other Indians as it did to white men, John Swanton said; and Indian "war" was "merely a small raid, depending on secrecy and surprise"; the war party was satisfied by taking a scalp or two, but considered their war a failure if two or three men died. Some Creeks must have committed atrocities, as some whites did; but Tennessee Governor Willie Blount's generalization about Creeks in 1813 as "monsters in human shape" and "infuriated hell-hounds" is scarcely compatible with other, better informed and less self-serving descriptions of their character. What may have misled white observers into a belief that Creeks were always looking for a fight was that their small wars or raids in retaliation for some injury occurred frequently—indeed, almost continuously—but these were blood feuds, rather than warfare in the white man's sense.[32]

"As moral men," Bartram wrote, "[the Creeks] certainly stand in no need of European civilization." An examination of the Creek social and economic systems will explain the absence of avarice and covetousness: in their communal economy individuals had no need to accumulate wealth, and in fact, the man who hoarded his resources earned not distinction but shame. As Swanton explained: "The pull upon which we [whites] rely is acquisitiveness and our push is starvation, while the pull of the Creeks was social position and popular esteem, and their push contempt and ridicule."[33]

Benjamin Hawkins, sent to the Creeks to bring them changes that they resisted, admired and liked the tribe except when they frustrated him beyond his endurance in the performance of his duties. He found them trustworthy, loyal, and capable of training, industry, frugality, good husbandry, and especially good housewifery. In individual cases he valued and loved them, characterizing particular men as candid, intelligent, responsible, and bold in expressing themselves. When Alexander Cornells died, for example, Hawkins wrote the secretary of war mourning "a great national loss. . . . We have not his equal among us."[34]

Confounding the stereotype of the impassive, taciturn Indian, Creeks were great talkers. At treaties and councils chiefs gave long, often impassioned speeches that sometimes bored white listeners but earned the orators high esteem in the red community. The Speaker of the nation was one of the highest officials among the Creeks; oratory was his business, and men who hoped one day to succeed him vied to demonstrate their skill in speaking. John Innerarity, a trader present at a Creek council to collect money owed his company by the Indians, complained bitterly about how endlessly they all talked, day after day. Hawkins held treaty conferences with the Creeks at which the talks went on for weeks and even months. But if they were indeed prolix to exhaustion, painstakingly careful in unfolding an argument in every complexity, repetitious, and as one critic of Creek oratory holds, unimaginatively metaphorical, it should be born in mind that at these treaties the Creeks were being pressed to cede land, their blood and their life; it was incumbent upon them to be at least as deliberate and cautious as delegates at, let us say, the treaty of Paris at the conclusion of the Revolutionary War or the treaty of Ghent at the end of the War of 1812, both of which negotiations dragged on for half a year and more. It seems and may be true that Creek diplomats at treaties enjoyed the sound of their own voices; that was probably true also of white diplomats at Ghent and Paris.[35]

There is much evidence that on social occasions the Creeks were extremely convivial, talkative, lively people. They loved to eat, drink, gamble, joke, play games, dance, and sing. When they were guests, they expected the same hospitality that they as hosts extended to visitors. Hawkins complained that Creeks crowded his house and flocked to his table, and truly they must have eaten well, because his household food cost almost $1,500 a year although he grew much of what was consumed. When Creeks went to the government store to trade, they considered it a social as well as a business occasion, and they lingered on after their trading was done, drinking if they could get drink, and expecting to be fed at government expense. At the Creek council meeting Innerarity was at first pleased to have some of the chiefs come to dine with him, but as they came every evening in greater and greater numbers, and kept him awake with noisy talk afterwards, he got very cross.[36]

Hospitality was built into Creek life perhaps even more integrally than into the life of tidewater planters. For both, sharing one's table with visitors was a road to respect and advancement in life, although possibly more formalized among Creeks. The Creeks had a call on Innerarity's hospitality because he had been generously dined at Indian homes on his way to the council meeting: once on fine turkey soup, venison, potatoes, and *saufkee*, or hominy; and again on roasted beef, corn, soup, potatoes, and peas. Creeks shared according to their means, and sometimes beyond their means. Hawkins knew a chief in Tuckabatchee, a very poor man except in cattle, who could have lived better if he had occasionally sold off one of his animals, but instead he slaughtered a couple of them every fortnight to entertain his friends. This brought him far more respect than being able to buy a new shirt or blanket. We are poor but hospitable, was a Creek boast. Hawkins, stopping at the home of an ordinary Creek, was served a meal of bean bread and dumplings, hickory nut oil, and milk; at a similar house, he got potatoes, hickory milk, pumpkin, beans, ground peas, and chestnuts. At Christmas dinner with more prosperous people

he ate pork and greens, a pair of fowls, ducks, rice, and potatoes, washed down with rum and water; and two days later,
Alexander Cornells's wife served him venison, pork steaks, and
coffee, apologizing because she was not properly prepared.[37]

Indians were considered stoics because, although they ate
enormously when food was available, they also suffered fasting
with patience. But feast and fast were the essence of their ceremonial life, and also of their economy, in which putting by for a
rainy day was thought ridiculous.

Qualities often admired in Creeks by whites, to which Hawkins
frequently alluded, were their judiciousness, discretion, reserve, and secrecy about important matters. For their part, they
admired in Hawkins his fairness in examining both sides of a
complaint—"like an old chief," they wrote the president. The
Creeks were alert and well informed about events that concerned them. For example, they had been expecting war between Spain and Britain, Hawkins said, a good while before it
finally broke out in October 1797, and were busy figuring out
how best to gain an advantage from it. They were well aware of
the activities of various foreign agents, speculators, and dissidents among and around them, and were able to supply
Hawkins with intelligence through spies, infiltration, and inter-
cepted letters. Flattery and promises did not deceive them.
They knew that intruders on their lands, although formally
prohibited by treaty terms, were being allowed to settle within
Creek country, and that a large part of that country was claimed
by land jobbers. Not all observers, however, agreed that Creeks
had foresight and the ability to plan ahead. In spite of the so-
phistication they so often demonstrated, they were likened to
children. Tocqueville, for example, spoke of their "childish
carelessness of the morrow," and said that they "wait for the
near approach of danger before they prepare to meet it." Indian agent Return J. Meigs wrote the secretary of war that
Creeks, like all Indians, were "unstable as water, & . . . acted on
from the impulse or pressure of the moment without the pain
of anticipating consequences." Meigs was, however, a biased
commentator. He seems to have been involved in various land
schemes and was an early advocate of moving the southern Indians west of the Mississippi. And Tocqueville sometimes wrote

profoundly of matters with which he had superficial acquaintance. Hawkins and others who knew the Indians well, and were unmotivated by self-interest, did not see them as careless or impulsive.[38]

The Indians had need to be careful and wise in the ways of non-Indians. For hundreds of years the prospect of profit had beckoned traders of many different nationalities to the lands of the Indians. In the early and middle eighteenth century traders had been licensed for specific towns, men of respectable character like James Adair and Ludowick Grant. A few were representatives of large commercial houses with headquarters in Pensacola, Florida, or in the Bahamas, and the rest tended to be reasonably permanent, fairly prosperous businessmen. Adair claimed that the Indians were "easy in their minds and peaceable because of the plain, honest lessons daily inculcated on them" by decent and responsible traders. These early traders were also the geographers and cartographers, the archaeologists, anthropologists, and historians of Indian country and the Indians; further, they functioned as an intelligence arm of their colonial governments, reporting frequently on the temper and activities of the Indians, and serving as special agents in times of crisis.[39]

Such men were many cuts above the fly-by-night "skin catchers" who came piling in when licensing was relaxed before and during the Revolutionary War. Indiscriminate licensing, not for specific towns, brought in men of bad character who were out for profit by any means. According to Adair, Indian country then swarmed with white people, generally the dregs and off-scourings of the colonies. These "lewd and idle white savages," by getting the Indians drunk on contraband spirits, managed to buy furs and skins "at four and five hundred percent cheaper than the orderly traders"; and the lessons these skulking peddlers taught the Indians were "obscenity and blasphemy."[40]

After 1790 United States law again required that traders be licensed for particular towns or villages, generally one for each settlement, which may have eliminated some of the worst characters. Still, the factor at the government store among the Creeks complained that traders were "the outcasts of civil so-

ciety," and it was a fighting insult to call anyone "Indian trader."
Hawkins said there was at least one trader, sometimes with an
assistant, in each of the almost fifty Creek towns and a few of
the villages, all up and down the rivers. There seem to have
been many more, because in his letters and reports he mentions
by name about one hundred. Probably half of these were white,
many of them family men who had Indian or black wives and
numerous children. A sampling of traders' surnames shows
most as Scottish in origin, such as McCartney, Lovat, McClung,
McKee, and McQueen. There were also many English names,
such as Barnard, Wilson, Clark, and White; and a few Irish,
like Paddy Lane. There was also a sprinkling of other extrac-
tions: Michael Ehlert, who was literate in a strange, marvellous
German-English; Juan Anthony Sandoval, alias Wany Tawny
the Spaniard; the Frenchman James Darouzeau and a DuJong,
Zuzan, or Jujong whose name gave scribes a lot of trouble; and
Jews, such as Solomon Marks and Abraham Mordecai, and possibly William Mizell. Some of these were half or more than half
Indian, despite their names; and there were also half-Indian
traders who had Indian names. A few of the traders whom
Hawkins mentioned were full-blooded Creeks; two were women
of prominent Creek families; and at least one trader and the
assistants of several of the others were black men. Of forty-four
traders listed at one time by Hawkins as living in Creek country,
he described eighteen as decent and honest, eleven as infamous,
and five as drunkards. Presumably the same proportions held
among traders who served the Cherokees and the other tribes.
Bad traders were an endless source of trouble and anxiety to
the Indians, who occasionally demanded the banishment of especially pernicious ones.[41]

There were among the bad traders not only drunks but horse
thieves, slave thieves, and fugitives from justice in the States,
and also "white men who run after your women . . . and would
sell their fathers, their mothers, or their country for a wench."
Such traders could have created only hostility toward white
men. In addition, many were rumormongers, some probably
only to relieve their boredom, but others deliberately set on
by British or Spanish agents to arouse anti-American feeling
among the Indians. Yet, for all the harm traders did, they could

not be eliminated, because the Indians insisted on, and by then needed, trade.[42]

At least as great an evil as the traders were the "Indian countrymen," an amorphous category of white Americans dwelling in Indian country and living like the Indians, who were not mainly traders, horse thieves, or agents of foreign governments, but most of them a little of each. Almost all had been Tories during the Revolutionary period and had fled for safety among the Indians. Some of them led war parties in guerrilla raids on American settlements, while others simply settled down to what Hawkins called a life of crime, taking Indian wives and teaching their families to be as lawless as themselves. The Indian countryman was, "with but few exceptions," Hawkins wrote, "a lazy, idle, craving, thievish animal," so degraded that the Indians contemptuously treated them like slaves. He added that they were completely ruled by their Indian wives, who increased their humiliations by cuckolding them. The exceptions were a few men who lived with the Indians because they found Indian life congenial; they behaved in a style less rude and uncouth than the others. Illiteracy was common among whites in Indian country, whether traders or "countrymen"; many were unable to write their names and, like the Indians, signed official papers with their marks. There was, however, at least one Indian countryman of good character: Timothy Barnard, a man whom Hawkins liked and respected, who labored to keep his half-Creek sons from being corrupted by the undesirables. There is no count or estimate of the number of Indian countrymen; but one of the more scoundrelly border characters, John Chisholm, who recruited an armed force of Tories to help in a secret, treasonous plot, claimed to have rounded up 1,500 of them. Chisholm was a notorious liar, however; and the figure is perhaps grossly exaggerated.[43]

So the hills and vales that in Bartram's nature story seem to echo with emptiness begin to crowd up with human personae. To the red and white men one must add an uncounted but certainly considerable number of black people for any true picture of Indian country.

Many of the blacks were held in slavery by prosperous Indians, traders, and government employees. Some of those in slavery to Creeks had been given by British agents to those Indians during the Revolutionary War in payment for their military aid against the Americans; those slaves called themselves "King's gifts," Hawkins said. Among other blacks in slavery, some had been bought, some captured in raids on white settlements, some seized by red or white slave catchers after escaping from Georgia and other nearby states; a few were free blacks who had been impressed again into slavery despite manumission papers. Among the Indians the status, treatment, and prospects of black slaves were on the whole better than in the States. Their relationship to their Indian masters in some cases was more that of serf than slave; they made regular money payments to their owners, and in return had considerable freedom, with their children slipping easily into free status. Georgia claimed that the Creeks had committed themselves by treaty in 1783 to return escaped slaves, but the Indians denied this and refused to cooperate.[44]

Other black individuals and families, who had successfully escaped from slavery in the States or who, free and therefore unwanted in Georgia or other states, had migrated farther south for safety and better opportunities, managed to live in comfort and sometimes plenty among the Indians. Intermarriage between blacks and Indians was common. Mrs. Sophie Durant, a sister of Chief Alexander McGillivray, was married to a mulatto, and many blacks lived nearby in Upper Creek country. At Christmas, Mrs. Durant entertained whites, Indians, and blacks at "a proper frolic of rum drinking and dancing." Seminole country seems to have offered blacks the happiest and safest environment. There they mingled and intermarried most freely. With the advice and help of the Seminoles, some blacks became prosperous farmers and stock raisers on Florida lands given them by Spain. Others found sanctuary and a measure of prosperity in the southermost country of the Creeks, on the Tombigbee and Chattahoochee rivers, where, it was claimed, they lived better than the whites on the Georgia frontier.[45]

Wherever they lived in Indian country, blacks are seldom mentioned in the records as involved in troublesome or illegal activities. Hawkins, in his *Sketch of the Creek Country*, made two comments about blacks in Indian country which, from him, were the highest praise: "where they are, there is more industry and better farms"; and "the negroes are all of them, attentive and friendly to white people, particularly to those in authority." It is worth noting that, however industrious and friendly blacks might be, *negro*, in Hawkins's *Sketch* and consistently in other records, is spelled with a small *n*, whereas *Indian* is practically always capitalized, as are the names of tribes and languages of Indians. Nowhere does a more slighting appellation occur for Indians than "red gentry," and that expression is used very seldom. There are a number of possible reasons, but none is completely satisfying. Was it perhaps because *Land*, frequently capitalized, earned uppercase respect for its owners, the Indians?[46]

One class of dweller in Indian country that enormously complicated its human problems was the military. In the mid-1790s there were two federal forts, one in Cherokee country and one in Creek country, adjoining the government factories at Tellico and Colerain. At the start each had a garrison of 150 to 200 soldiers and officers from nearby states, and by 1801 the Cherokee fort had 700. The forts served important functions, but Hawkins said that they were a constant source of trouble because of "the sinister intrigues and connexions of a licentious soldiery, and a neighborhood formed principally of camp followers." Camp followers averaged one for each soldier. It was impossible to control the behavior of this large number of underpaid, bored, often drunk and unruly men, and their women and children. The soldiers ran up debts with the factories, they bartered privately with the Indians—a trouble-breeding practice prohibited by the regulations—and they stole anything they could lay hands on, including Indian horses and the fort's hospital stores. Yet they seem less wicked than desperate when one considers that a private soldier's pay was as little as $4 a month and scanty rations. Discontent and drunkenness were endemic in the forts, where the men had very little to do of a military nature and considered civilian tasks, such as chores at the factory, beneath their dignity. The combination of conditions led to brawls of incredible ferocity between soldiers and civil employees, in which eyes were gouged and noses bitten off; and occasionally a drunken soldier would beat up an Indian.[47]

Hawkins, in various communications, mentioned by name about thirty women of Indian country. Some of them were white women, some black, and a few were Indians of importance. Since there were also nameless hundreds of camp followers, about thirty thousand indigenous red women, and hundreds or thousands of black women, it is apparent that females were not scarce in that man's country. Of women named by Hawkins, some were wives or daughters of civil or military officers, of traders, or of Indian countrymen. One was the matron of the fort's garrison hospital, one helped out in the Creek factory, one was a white woman captured in childhood by Indians who had chosen to remain with them, and a few were women proficient in spinning and weaving whom Hawkins had imported to teach Indian housewives those arts as part of the program of "civilization."

Now the peopling of Indian country is complete except for one small but influential group, the little aristocracy created by official United States activities. In addition to the officers of the garrison commanded by Lt. Col. Henry Gaither, there were the civil servants and their salaried employees: Principal Agent Benjamin Hawkins with his subordinate agents among the four tribes and their assistants, interpreters, and clerks; and the factors at the Creek and Cherokee government stores, with their clerks and helpers. Next came a few skilled craftsmen, such as carpenters and blacksmiths, black or white, who worked in Hawkins's agency. At the bottom of this group were the drovers and wagoners, skin beaters, and other manual laborers employed in clearing and building—a generally rough and illiterate assortment who were nonetheless part of the frontier aristocracy because they were paid money for fairly regular employment. The military officers and top civil servants were white; from there down, complexions were the tricolor of Indian country.

From this untaken census it is clear that Bartram's sylvan scenes, Adair's "happy region," Priber's "Paradice," were populated, if not populous. In this southern melting pot an extraordinary variety of human ingredients seethed in the blood of frontier savagery and the milk of government intentions; the fire beneath it was fed by international rivalry for control of the tribes and the lust of Americans, rich and poor, for a little piece of Eden. From his home at the Creek agency, deep in Indian country, Hawkins wrote his friend Thomas Jefferson in 1800 that "at the moment I am writing I hear the language of Scotch French Spanish English Africans Creeks and Uchees, and all in peace considering themselves as forming one family." But melting pot is a concept of the cook, not the ingredients. The Creeks and Uchees, last named in Hawkins's happy family, did not wish to be one with Europeans and Americans, something Hawkins could never totally comprehend. What they wanted were the bears, deer, and turkeys, their own old manner of life, and their lands.[48]

CHAPTER 2

"That Ingenious Gentleman, Benjamin Hawkins"

I likewise send a shorter specimen of the language of the Southern Indians. It was procured by that ingenious gentleman, the Hble. Mr. Hawkins, a member of Congress from North Carolina, and lately a Commissioner from the United States to the Indians of the South.

GEORGE WASHINGTON TO THE MARQUIS
DE LAFAYETTE, 10 JANUARY 1788

AT another time, he might have been accounted a prodigy. President Washington described him as an ingenious gentleman, but he lived in a period of ingenious gentlemen, whose clever improvisations brought their country through its first fifty years. From the beginning of the War of Independence until the United States demonstrated full sovereignty at the end of the War of 1812, citizens were called on to do all kinds of tasks for which they had not been trained and which they could not have anticipated. They had to be, seriatim or simultaneously, fighting men, businessmen, legislators, administrators, explorers, diplomats, and statesmen—the architects and masons of a government without precedent—and its lexicographers, memorialists, and eulogists. Considering that most of them had been farmers, especially those of the South, their sprouting so many worldly talents, so quickly, and to such a degree of excellence, is matter for wonder.

Hawkins was, in accomplishments, one of the smaller of this generation of giants, although he had greatness. Perhaps his trouble lay in his being too old for a young time, too old not in years but in philosophy: he was an eighteenth-century man of unbending logic and justice whose culminating work came in the more pragmatic, therefore more flexible nineteenth century, when the wish easily fathered the thought. The wish that Indians would give up their land turned with the century into the thought that they must; and Hawkins's plea, in the name of the Indians, that the government "will assist us here, to preserve the birthright portion of the planet we inhabit," had time against it. His advocacy of Indian rights accompanied, to Hawkins without any inconsistency, a deep love of his country. In the nineteenth-century spasm of national growth, however, the two were incompatible.[1]

In 1785, when Hawkins first visited the southern tribes as a federal treaty commissioner, he was just over thirty years old. His father, Philemon Hawkins, a Virginian, had moved to North Carolina when he married Delia Martin, settling in Bute County (later renamed Warren County), where he raised four sons and two daughters: Joseph, John, Benjamin, Philemon, Delia, and Ann. Benjamin was born in 1754. It was the comfortable-size family of a self-made, industrious, and comfortable tobacco planter. The paterfamilias drew his reward for piety, virtue, and political acumen by seeing his sons become legislators of their state and nation, and by having a grandson, William Hawkins, elected governor of North Carolina in 1811. Benjamin Hawkins and his brothers seem to have remained rather close in adulthood, and at least two of Benjamin's nephews came to work for him while he was agent to the southern Indians.[2]

Benjamin, his brother Joseph, and their neighbor Nathaniel Macon went to the College of New Jersey at Princeton, members of the class of 1777; but in November of their senior year, as British troops bore down upon the town, the college was abandoned. That was the end of Hawkins's formal education, which, as he later demonstrated, had been a very good one. For example, President John Witherspoon of Princeton, an advanced educator, had brought French into the curriculum, in addition to the conventional Latin, Greek, and Hebrew, justifying the rather daring innovation of a modern language by the circumstances "that there are multitudes of Frenchmen come over. . . . I am often employed as interpreter to those who come to Congress, and have many visits from them." From this it appears likely that the traditional allusions to Hawkins's proficiency in French and allegations that he served for a time on General Washington's staff as a French interpreter may be true.[3]

A more important result of President Witherspoon's enthusiasm for language studies, and perhaps of the way languages were taught at Princeton, was Hawkins's abiding curiosity about all tongues and his philologic foundation for learning them. His voluminous letters and reports from Indian country, in the collection published by the Georgia Historical Society, are led off by this language lesson:

How many were killed?
Hungau humgot humgotcan istornin acunnan wocgregescan.

How many were wound[ed]?
Iste unnutulgee natchomau.

Are you wounded?
Achenuttau.[4]

As early as 1786, Hawkins, just returned from his first assignment in Indian country, was able to write Jefferson: "I shall send you a vocabulary of the Cherokee and Choctaw languages extended only to the most common objects in nature," and to comment that Choctaw and Chickasaw were "radically the same." His interest in languages provided him, through twenty years as agent among the Creeks, with sorely needed intellectual stimulation. When he had been there only a short time, he wrote a friend: "I have made some progress in learning their language, and its an amusement to me the few moments of leisure I have. I began with writing words, names, then dialogues; as my knowledge increased, I corrected my errors. I am preparing a treat for our friend, Mr. Jefferson. I expect in one year to give him an extensive vocabulary of the tongues of the 4 nations; the Creek will be my work, and it will be well done." In a letter to the secretary of war about learning to speak to the Creeks in their own tongue, he observed what every traveller in a foreign country learns: "This I find is flattering to them."[5]

Love of and respect for words show clearly in Hawkins's writings, and this too may have been a Princeton legacy, because Dr. Witherspoon was determined to inculcate in his students "a taste for the study of the English Language," its grammar, punctuation, and orthography. Punctuation was not yet standardized, and Hawkins's is as erratic as most; his orthography is painfully crabbed; but the words fit the thoughts with precision, and fit each other with music. In his great mass of writing—letters, reports, journals—there is scarcely a clumsy, ambiguous, or cacophonous sentence, a truly amazing feat considering that he rarely had time for revision, or paper if he had the time.[6]

This is not to claim that Hawkins was extraordinary in his unique generation. What should be remembered about Hawkins is that he did his major work while living deep in Indian country, among men of a different culture and the rough breed of Indian traders and Indian countrymen. While his brilliant colleagues had each others' similar minds upon which to sharpen their logic and wit, Hawkins thought and wrote in intellectual solitude in an Indian-style log house, surrounded by chattering and laughing Indian guests, his mind its own whetstone. Some of his Indian friends were excellently endowed with intelligence, and he recognized it and enjoyed locking minds with them at treaties and council meetings; but their thinking was formed by a quite different culture and background, so intellectual comradeship existed only within a very limited framework.

Without books, Hawkins might not have retained his sharpness of mind during his long exile, but he did have books, a library that was then almost certainly unique among Americans south of the Tennessee River and west of the Savannah. Out of nearly two hundred books, only a handful were the professional paraphernalia of an Indian agent: technical volumes on bookkeeping, arithmetic, cooking, medicine, architecture, farriery, surveying, and agriculture. The largest category consisted of works on government, law, and jurisprudence, including the Constitution and the laws and acts of Congress of the United States. History was also well represented, as were biography, philosophy, and literature. Hawkins had the natural history of Georges Louis Leclerc, comte de Buffon and about twenty-five other works in French, and for classical refreshment he could pick up Horace or Ovid, Xenophon or Demosthenes. On America there were Jefferson's *Notes on Virginia*, Adair's *His-*

tory of the Indians, Bartram and other travel journals, geographies, gazeteers, atlases, and maps. Hawkins's collection included also a surprising number of English dictionaries, a Spanish dictionary, and some books on grammar and spelling.[7]

Unfortunately, Hawkins's physique did not measure up to the tough, athletic mind one perceives in his writing and reading. Delicate health plagued him from, at latest, his first journey into Indian country in 1785, when he was just over thirty. His endurance of physical hardships for the rest of his life is especially remarkable in that he was chronically ill with rheumatism and gout, often with what he described as "gout of the stomach," and seemed particularly susceptible to fevers. The great amount of travel required by his responsibility for the whole southern Indian area and by his assignments to run treaty lines was particularly trying. Most of it had to be done on horseback, and at the end of the day's ride there was often no shelter available, no comfort but a campfire and a blanket in wet weather or dry.[8]

Hawkins's character, however, was as unyielding as his mind. He was firm, courageous, humorous, conscientious, punctual, and prodigiously patient. The Indians admired his honesty and perseverance, but what he took most pride in was his incorruptible fairness. In cases brought before his court—one of his many functions as agent was to hear complaints civil and criminal—he undoubtedly pursued the course he set forth in the following memorandum:

> That the evidence of any person, red, white or black, shall be allowed and admited in all cases, the right of which evidence being seriously considered and compared with all other circumstances attending the case, shall be left to the court.[9]

From 1776, when war interrupted his studies at Princeton, Hawkins pursued a career of public service. After some experience in battle (according to tradition), in 1778 he was elected to represent his country in the North Carolina legislature. Two years later, as aide and commercial agent to Governor Nash, he directed shipments of tobacco to Europe and the West Indies, and the purchase and shipment of war supplies with the proceeds. In those transactions he put his personal credit at the disposal of his state and country, risking his fortune in ships and cargoes endangered by British men-of-war.[10]

Beginning in 1784, Hawkins had served four one-year terms in the Continental Congress under the Articles of Confederation adopted in 1781. In 1788 he declined to run for reelection, perhaps because his support of both the Constitution and the cession of western lands was unpopular in North Carolina, and perhaps also because he could not afford another term. His private fortune, like so many others after the war, was at a low ebb. Although in 1789 he owned 4,000 acres and nineteen slaves, he was short of cash money, and remittances from the North Carolina treasury to its congressional delegates for salary and expenses were always months in arrears, if indeed they ever came. In 1783, Hawkins had appealed monthly to the governor for assistance, saying in June, "I am now living on credit. . . . I shall be in a very disagreeable as well as disgraceful situation in a short time"; in September, "I have for some time been absolutely without as much money as will support me one day except what I borrow and perhaps not be able to repay"; and in October, "We are now and have been for some time without one Shilling of money."[11]

During those years and later as a United States senator, Hawkins's only pay, almost, was the opportunity to work with and become acquainted with practically everyone important in American politics and government, such men as Thomas Jefferson, Alexander Hamilton, James Madison, James Monroe, and Henry Knox. He also knew the minds of John Adams, John Jay, and Benjamin Franklin, who were the negotiators of treaties sent to Congress from abroad for ratification. Hawkins had probably earlier known his fellow North Carolinians in Congress, but there perfected his acquaintance with William Blount, Hugh Williamson, and others of wealth and influence.[12]

Hawkins's life-long preoccupation with Indians, their rights, and their lands, began during his first years as a national legislator, when he served on Indian affairs committees. Much more momentous in 1783, however, was the need of the United States for a way of escaping bankruptcy, Congressman Hawkins fled to Princeton from Philadelphia with angry unpaid troops snapping at the heels of a legislature helpless to satisfy them. "Congress could only give one month's pay in money to the Army and three months pay in notes by anticipation," Hawkins wrote Governor Martin of North Carolina. "They have been told that . . . the glorious war they have supported would consign them to ruin." That was only a few weeks after the signing of the treaty ending the war, in Paris on September 3, 1783, a costly war that left the victors penniless—except in land.[13]

Land would satisfy the debts owed the Revolutionary War veterans and other persons, groups, and nations, and there was a vast plenty of unappropriated lands in the west of the states of New York, Virginia, the Carolinas, and Georgia, clear to the Mississippi. Although it was obviously impossible for any single state to administer and protect such a huge area, there was no rush to place it under federal jurisdiction; the states hoped first to use parts of their western lands to pay their own debts, as well as, in some instances, to enrich land speculators.

Virginia and New York had overlapping claims, which they finally both agreed to cede. The Carolinas and Georgia, however, procrastinated. "Our Army is extremely impatient to obtain the lands that were promised to them," Hawkins wrote in September 1783. By 1786 all state land claims north of the Ohio had been ceded to the federal government, but the southern states still held out. "The Eyes of every State to the Northward are now turned towards the Carolinas and Georgia and expecting from them liberal cessions," Hawkins reported home. William Blount, a leading North Carolina Federalist who had earlier been a member of Congress, that year sat in his state's legislature to press for cession of its western lands, but his efforts were frustrated by a rival political coalition. Hawkins and his fellow delegate Hugh Williamson were put in the embarrassing position of explaining in Congress why their state delayed. North Carolina needed to pay its own soldiers, they said; and it feared that by the time Congress had accepted its offer, the land speculators would have reaped a rich harvest; therefore the state would open its own land office at once. The explanation was weak, and Hawkins was ashamed that his state should profit by the cessions of others while giving nothing themselves.[14]

In this sense of nationhood, and of the obligations of the states to a centralized national entity, Hawkins showed a tendency toward Federalism, favoring the centralization of power in the federal government. In addition, he indicated some conservative and typically Federalist attitudes in favoring the payment of prewar debts of Americans to British creditors, and in supporting the Society of the Cincinnati headed by Washington and Knox. He opposed the admittance of the public to congressional debates and voted to force a printer to reveal the source of a letter that he had printed. Although not a Federalist, Hawkins shared the general affection and respect for the Federalist leader, Washington, almost to the point of reverence.[15]

Actually, Hawkins had much more in common with Jeffersonian than with Federalist ideas. His relationship with Jefferson, who would soon emerge as the anti-Federalist, or Republican, leader, was most friendly and affectionate. The two men were very close in tastes, interests, and philosophy. And while Washington was old enough to be Hawkins's father, Jefferson was of an age to be his elder brother, which perhaps explains why Hawkins was on such easy terms with him. Like Jefferson, Hawkins was an agrarian, had a deep interest in horticulture and languages, and like the young Jefferson was convinced of the rights and capabilities of the Indians. Also, while he supported federal power, Hawkins clearly thought of himself as a southerner and a North Carolinian. He was concerned, for example, that the southern states "keep up respectable representations in Congress until their *rights* are perfectly *secured*," and he worked to have the nation's capital located on Chesapeake Bay. He was, in addition, very much a westerner, determined to gain for western settlers the free use of the Mississippi River, their economy's lifeline; to prevent preemption of western lands by speculators who would line their wallets at the expense of nation, state, and individual planters; and to keep peace with the Indians and protect the frontiers from violence. In international relations Hawkins shared the Jeffersonian anti-British and pro-Democratic French attitudes. In the Senate he voted increasingly with Jefferson, Madison, and Monroe, while managing to keep unimpaired his excellent relationship with Washington.[16]

Probably because Hawkins was acceptable to both parties, and because he had worked on congressional committees dealing with frontier problems, in March 1785, he was selected to head a commission to treat with the southern Indians. He won the votes of eleven out of twelve states, a notable achievement since the northern states were in general suspicious of the motives of the southern states toward the Indians.[17]

Hawkins was thirty-one when he was sent with three other federal negotiators to try to bring order to a chaotic situation in the Indian South, a tangle of claims and counterclaims exacerbated by intrigue, rumor, and propaganda, in which land speculators, foreign agents, adventurers, Indians, and frontiersmen were tightly knotted. The stand of the Indians was that they were there, had always been there, and meant to stay.

At the treaty of Paris, Great Britain and the United States had privately agreed that, if the Floridas were to be returned to Great Britain, the southern boundary of the United States would fall at 32°30′ north lattitude, but if Spain should acquire Florida, the line would be farther south at the thirty-first parallel. Spain gained possession of the Floridas (to the great dismay of the American Loyalists who had taken refuge there), but would not accept the thirty-first parallel as the line. The United States insisted it was indeed the line. Uncertainty about where the boundary was to fall created continual disputes and confusion.[18]

Spain claimed jurisdiction over Choctaws, Lower Creeks, and Seminoles and kept its agents in their villages. Spanish control was assured by a monopoly of trade with these Indians through the house of Panton, Leslie, and Company, in which the Creek chief Alexander McGillivray was a shareholder, and by giving McGillivray a commission, with stipend, in the Spanish army. Additional trouble for the United States was made by British subjects and Tory refugees in Florida, men who, Hawkins said, "were instructed to turn loose the Indian fury against the frontiers." The position of Georgia in this controversy becomes clear from a glance at a map of the period; the state was determined to expand into the vast western lands included in its charter, from which the Indians were somehow to be dispossessed.[19]

Georgia had no right—no state or individual had the right—to deal directly with the Indians for land. Article 9 of the Articles of Confederation had reserved to the federal government alone the right to act in matters concerning the Indians. This did not, however, deter the efforts of Georgians and western Carolinians, frontiersmen whose passion to have land of their own had gone unfulfilled both in their European past and as immigrants in the crowded eastern seaboard. They tried desperately to snatch chunks of Indian land before these lands were ceded to the federal government, which would make land acquisition much more difficult and costly. Until federal authority should be imposed, it was fairly easy for a small force of armed men from Georgia or transmontane Carolina to raid Indian villages and extort thousands of acres from a few bribed, liquored-up, or terrified chiefs as the price of peace.

The first postwar land grab of this kind started as a private deal between Cherokees and two white men, Gen. Andrew Pickens of South Carolina and the Georgia freebooter Elijah Clarke. Pickens had been fighting pro-British Cherokees throughout the Revolutionary War, and in 1781 he was on orders to patrol the Cherokee border looking for destructive bands of Tories. With Indian fighter John Sevier of Tennessee and others, Pickens destroyed thirteen towns of the Lower Cherokees, killing forty and taking as many prisoners. In 1782, Pickens got permission from the governor of South Carolina for another foray, ostensibly to break up a Tory camp at Long Swamp Creek. Elijah Clarke joined him in the campaign. They did not find the Tory leader they were seeking, but they wrought great damage in Cherokee and Creek towns along the Etowah River. In the peace negotiations that followed at Long Swamp in October, 1782, the treaty commissioners prized from the Indians a big tract of land between the upper Oconee River and the Tugaloo, a northern branch of the Savannah. In the following year the cession was extended and formalized by Georgia treaty commissioners and a very few Creeks as the treaty of Augusta.[20]

The Augusta treaty, begun in May 1783 and carried over to November, expanded the Long Swamp cession; enough territory was secured to form two new Georgia counties and pay off many war veterans of the state in land bounties. Significantly, the roster of Augusta commissioners reads almost like a list of the counties of Georgia: (Lachlan) McIntosh, (Edward) Telfair, (John) Twiggs, (John) Martin, (William) Few, and Clarke. Title to the land near the Tugaloo River, around the upper reaches of the Savannah, was in dispute between Cherokees and Creeks, and the Creeks vehemently denied the right of the Cherokees to sell it to Georgia, as they had privately done before the treaty opened. Bartram brings the scene to life:

> The Creeks, nettled and incensed at this, a chief and warrior started up, and with an agitated and terrific countenance, frow[n]ing menaces and disdain, fixed his eyes on the Cherokee chiefs, and asked them what right they had to give away their lands, calling them old women, and saying they had long ago obliged them to wear the petticoat; . . . . And moreover, these arrogant bravos and usurpers carried their pride and importance to such lengths, as even to threaten to dissolve the congress and return home, unless the Georgians consented to annul the secret treaty with the Cherokees, and receive that territory from them [the Creeks], as acknowledging their exclusive right of alienation.

The Creeks won the argument; to be sure, all they gained was the right to be the losers, but they saved their pride. Soon they opened hostilities again, giving Clarke an excuse for still another expedition.[21]

Thus began a period of hasty land grabbing by Georgia—of all states probably the poorest at the end of the Revolutionary War—and of Indian reprisals. It was clear that, if such a succession of events were not to perpetuate itself, the federal government would have to take command of relations with the Indians. Early in 1785, therefore, Congress elected that first federal commission, headed by Hawkins, to go to Georgia and try to bring order in Creek country, at the same time securing confirmation of the land cessions at Long Swamp and Augusta in order to pacify Georgia.

The first treaty was to be held with the Creeks at Galphinton on the Ocmulgee River, deep in Creek country. In addition to federal commissioners Hawkins, Lachlan McIntosh, Joseph Martin, and Andrew Pickens, Georgia sent its own commissioners to protect state interests: Edward Telfair, William Few, and James Jackson—land speculators all. The Georgia state government did everything possible to hold up and, it hoped, prevent the federal commissioners from meeting with the Indians, including halting Hawkins and Martin at Savannah by not remitting its share of the treaty expenses. North Carolina advanced funds, and the commissioners were able to proceed, but federal status had been damaged. Chief Alexander McGillivray, speaking for the Creek Nation, bluntly rebuked Congress for its long delay in taking the Indians under its protection. "We want nothing from you but justice. We want our hunting grounds preserved from encroachments," McGillivray wrote to Pickens; he and his people were willing to meet the federal commissioners whenever they received notice "that every matter of difference will be made up and settled, with that liberality and justice, worthy the men who have so gloriously asserted the cause of liberty and independency."[22]

A final effort by Georgia to spike the treaty was the circulation of a rumor among the Indians that the purpose of the Galphinton meeting was merely to reconfirm the Augusta treaty and arrange for running the lines it had set. As a result, McGillivray and all of the other Creeks stayed away except for two chiefs, Fat King and Tallassee King, and about eighty warriors, representing only two of the hundred or so Creek towns.

Hawkins and his colleagues decided that a treaty with only two towns would not be legally binding. They held one meeting with the Creeks, to explain why they had come, and left almost immediately on November 12. Next day the Georgia commissioners concluded their own treaty with the Indians present, confirming and vastly extending the Augusta cession to take in land from a line north of Oconee to the headwaters of the Saint Marys far to the south. They assured the Indians that Creeks were citizens of Georgia—a lie—and promised to prosecute white men who robbed or murdered them. In a provision most important to Georgians, the Creeks by this treaty agreed to return runaway slaves. Not only did the Georgia commissioners dare to make this quite illegal treaty, but they protested the one meeting the United States commissioners had held with the Indians, nonsubstantive though it had been, denying the right of Congress to hold treaties with the Indians except to cement peaceful relations.[23]

Hawkins and the other federal commissioners proceeded northward to Hopewell, South Carolina, where General Pickens lived, for a treaty with the Cherokees, Chickasaws, and Choctaws. Here the same contest of authority took place between state commissioners and federal agents. Georgia commissioners came along, because the eastern line to be set with the Cherokees would be common with Georgia's western boundary. The commissioner sent by North Carolina was William Blount, Hawkins's sometimes fellow delegate to Congress. Blount was at Hopewell to protect his land investments in the Great Bend of the Tennessee River—Cherokee land.[24]

Blount's object at the treaty of Hopewell was to coerce the Cherokees and Chickasaws to accept the Tennessee River as their northern boundary. "Across it they must not come," he commanded Joseph Martin, one of his land partners, who happened to be one of the federal commissioners. Blount meant, in fact, to have not only lands lying north of the Tennessee, but some to the south of it as well. He and James Robertson, a blunt, semiliterate frontiersman who perhaps because of his rough-diamond qualities, had acquired a reputation for forthright honesty, in 1783 had made a business agreement by which Blount was to buy as many military land warrants as possible, 50,000 or even 100,000 acres, of which Robertson, in return for locating and surveying them, was to get a 25 percent cut. Furthermore, by this agreement Blount had promised Robertson that he would at once enter 40,000 acres on the south side of the Tennessee, indisputably Cherokee land, and again Robertson for the same services was to get his 25 percent.[25]

The Hopewell treaty was crucially important to Blount and his partners, who included John Sevier, by now an Indianfighting folk hero, "Nolichucky Jack." Blount for his land company had engineered purchases from the Chickasaws and Cherokees in the fertile bends of the Cumberland and Tennessee rivers; the Tennessee River lands, at Muscle Shoals, were particularly valuable. Blount always preferred to act within the law, by creating law to suit his acts; so in 1783 he had tried to persuade the North Carolina legislature to cede the state's western lands in order to put his company's holdings under the protection of the federal government, which had promised to honor any titles existing before cession. It did not at all suit Blount's purposes when, the cession act balked, angry westerners were played upon by rival politicians and speculators to split off from North Carolina and, in 1784, to establish the transmontane state of Franklin. However, Sevier took charge there by getting himself elected governor of the new state.[26]

The Cherokees, Chickasaws, and Choctaws turned out for the Hopewell treaty as the Creeks had not, 918 of them, a spectacular gathering in their ceremonial regalia. These tribes, especially the Cherokees, had given substantial aid to the British during the Revolutionary War, and they could not afford to be as haughty toward the victorious United States as the more neutral Creeks. In fact, the Cherokees were humble at the treaty. Chief Chescoenwhee said: "Being under the protection of the United States, I shall return satisfied. . . . The talks of the Commissioners are the most pleasing to us, as they do not want any lands. . . . I am in hopes you will adjust and settle our limits, so that we may be secured in the possession of our own. I will abide by what hitherto has been said on this subject, but cannot cede any more lands." Cherokee chief Tassel drew a map of Cherokee country, and asked that the commissioners appeal on behalf of the tribe to Congress to force removal of intruding whites from Cherokee hunting grounds within the fork of the Holston and French Broad rivers. Discussions proceeded amicably through late November. On November 28, 1785, a draft treaty was read aloud and interpreted.[27]

Most of the terms were desirable or at least unobjectionable to Blount and the Georgians. They provided for return of runaway or stolen slaves, recognition of United States sovereignty, and punishment of Indians or whites for capital crimes. Article 12, which would later be a source of trouble, seemed innocent enough: "That the Indians may have full confidence in the justice of the United States, respecting their interests, they shall have the right to send a deputy of their choice, whenever they think fit, to Congress." But Article 4 laid out the boundaries of Cherokee hunting grounds with such a liberal hand that Blount must have been confounded; the northern line was not the Tennessee, but considerably to the north of it, leaving in Indian country the Blount faction's speculations in the Great Bend. Also, to the confusion of the Georgia men, the Cherokees' eastern line ignored white claims and was set much farther east than in earlier Georgia treaties. Blount and the Georgians immediately lodged protests; the Indians declared themselves satisfied. Presents worth $1,300 were distributed by the federal commissioners, and rations for the Indians' homeward journey.[28]

Hawkins forwarded the treaty to Congress with the comment that the Cherokees were glad to be protected from land speculators by the United States. He stated without comment: "Colonel William Blount, an agent for North Carolina, is with us, and he has entered a protest against the treaty." Rumors were rife that Blount had attempted through Martin to force the Cherokees into accepting his boundary, and that he was actually making private purchases from the Indians while the treaty took place. If Blount made any attempt to influence Hawkins in favor of his interests, it has escaped the records. Yet it must have been a tense, unpleasant confrontation between the two North Carolinians. Possibly because of the strain, Hawkins fell ill and was unable to travel for a few months. When he did arrive in New York in June, 1786, he wrote jubilantly to Jefferson in France:

> You will see by the Treaties which I enclose how attentive I have been to the rights of these people; and I can assure you there is nothing I have more at heart than the preservation of them. It is a melancholy reflection that the rulers of America in rendering an account to Heaven of the aborigines thereof, will have lost everything but the name. The interposition of Congress without the co-operation of the Southern States is ineffectual, and Georgia and North Carolina have refused by protesting against their authority. The former will not allow that the Indians can be viewed in any other light than as members thereby [probably], and the latter allows a right of regulatory trade only without the fixing of any boundary between the Indians and the citizens, as they claim all the land Westward according to their bill of rights and that the Indians are only tenants at will.[29]

To this Jefferson replied:

> The attention which you pay to their rights also does you great honour, as the want of that is a principal source of dishonour to the American character. The two principles on which our conduct to-

wards the Indians should be founded are justice and fear. After the injustices we have done them, they cannot love us, which leaves us no alternative but that of fear to keep them from attacking us. But justice is what we should never lose sight of, and in time it may recover their esteem.

Fifteen years later Jefferson, risen from minister to France to president, had to modify the noble thoughts here expressed. Perhaps he still thought them but might no longer express them, because as president it was his job to separate the Indians from their rights, to impress upon them that they were only "tenants at will" on land that the United States was destined to possess.[30]

Hawkins must have warmed to this reassurance from his respected friend, especially because the treaties and he himself were already under attack. Alexander Outlaw, one of Blount's mixed bag of associates, had a reputation for brutally murdering Indian women and children, and for having "done everything in his power to drive the Indians to desperation"; he castigated the commissioners for depriving the frontiersmen of their "just Right." The speculators were determined by any means to hold the Cherokees to private land purchases as far south as the Cumberland River, purchases that predated the treaty of Hopewell, although Chief Tassel disclaimed any such agreements. As for the Creeks, as soon as they returned from their winter hunt in the spring of 1786, McGillivray at once hurled them against the Georgia frontiers and Cumberland, and the Muscle Shoals where a small settlement had been begun. That little colony was wiped out, and raids and murders occurred at other points on the frontiers. The obvious reasons for the spurt of violence were the intrusions of whites on lands that the spurious Galphinton treaty had promised to the Creeks and the Creeks' refusal to honor a treaty to which only two chiefs had agreed. But James White, another Blount man in Congress, who was appointed the first superintendent of Indian Affairs for the Southern District in October 1786, threw the onus on Hawkins, reporting that the warfare was the result of the sudden interference by United States commissioners with the treaties of Georgia, which perplexed the Indians; and of an impression given by the commissioners that the United

States would take a soft, nonpunitive attitude toward Creek hostilities.[31]

This was the first of many allegations throughout Hawkins's career that he favored the Indians over his fellow citizens. It was not true; he simply tried to ensure the Indians justice.

Throughout 1786 and 1787, Alexander McGillivray unintentionally aided Blount by sending war parties against one or another intruder on Creek land, so that Blount was able to protest a few years later that "if the citizens of the United States do not destroy the Creeks, the Creeks will kill the citizens of the United States; the alternative is, to kill or be killed." McGillivray was doubly gratified by violence against the intruders; first, he hated Americans, and second, the deployment of his troops as a general exercised his intelligence and fed his vanity and ambition, none of which qualities must be underestimated if one is to understand this extraordinary man.[32]

Although Hawkins at Hopewell had not brought peace to the South, two articles of the treaty looked toward a better future in Indian-white relations. Article 8 called for the trial and punishment of malefactors, to replace the Indian custom of retaliation, which often resulted in the punishment of the innocent and merely perpetuated hostilities. Article 9 said, "For the benefit and comfort of the Indians, and for the prevention of injuries or oppressions on the part of the citizens or Indians, the United States in Congress assembled shall have the sole and exclusive right of regulating the trade with the Indians, and managing all their affairs in such manner as they think proper." This article laid the groundwork for the federal factory system that was established ten years later, which Hawkins believed would correct many abuses complained of by the Indians and help greatly in bringing peace to the South.[33]

Late in the summer of 1786, Hawkins returned to Congress. He served there that year and the next with William Blount, frequently traveling with him from and to North Carolina. There was no sign of ill will between the two, despite the clash at Hopewell. Both men worked to get federal aid to protect their state's western citizens and to secure free use of the Mississippi. During periods of separation in those years and for several years thereafter, Hawkins corresponded with Blount in a perfectly friendly way, inviting him to stop by at the Hawkins home when passing.[34]

Whatever chicanery, bribery, and subversion Blount may have resorted to in building a land empire, his political fortunes at that time suffered no harm. In April 1790, he at last succeeded in getting North Carolina to give the nation its western lands, thus putting his speculations under federal protection. To cap his triumph, he was named by President Washington governor of the district created by the cession, the Territory South of the Ohio.

Hawkins was properly congratulatory, and another year went by before he began gently to expostulate with Blount, whose speculations by then can have been no secret, concerning the danger and impropriety of claiming land within the Indian country, and to express his disagreement with Blount's claim that the Indians were the aggressors on the frontier, when in fact "those encroachments on our part are the true cause of the hostilities on theirs." Hawkins explained his frankness by adding, "I am very desirous that you should stand well with the southern tribes."

In May 1791, Hawkins tried to warn Blount tactfully that his actions were arousing suspicion, though "all your friends have the utmost confidence in your integrity." That November, although still assuring Blount, the Federalist leader of the West, that "your character is as you wish it. . . . You are to have no anxiety you have buoyed yourself . . . above party considerations," Hawkins nevertheless did begin to hint that Blount was in trouble politically, as the anti-Federalists, or Radicals, were gaining in power. Hawkins said in the same letter, "Your brother Thomas Blount wrote me a letter singularly rude," which suggests that Blount had dropped the guise of friendship. The following spring Hawkins was still being agreeable, assuring Blount that the president was well pleased with him; but he also firmly expressed his conviction that people claiming title to lands within the Indian boundary "cannot be put into possession but by extinguishment of Indian claims."[35]

Neither Georgians nor Tennesseans, however, had any intentions of giving up their claims. In September 1786, Alexander Outlaw declared that, treaty or no treaty, the land on both sides of the Tennessee River would soon be settled. The Georgians were equally ruthless concerning Creek claims. George and John Galphin, half-Creeks influential in the Lower Towns, claimed that they tried to bring peace to the frontier but peace was impossible because the Georgians "always bully [rather] than treat with the Indians." In November "peace" was declared by the treaty of Shoulderbone, an insignificant meeting attended by only a few Indians and shunned by McGillivray. For another year murders and retaliations continued to mount. With McGillivray demanding "life for life," Creeks ravaging the Georgia frontier, and Elijah Clarke of the Long Swamp adventure again leading a punitive expedition, in which, he said, he killed thirty or forty Creeks.[36]

Georgia officials again insisted, in the same words James White had used, that the surge of violence was the result of United States interference with Georgia treaties, an explanation that confused the Indians; and the Georgians demanded that Congress enforce peace by validating the cessions made at Augusta, Galphinton, and Shoulderbone.

By 1789 the frontier situation had so deteriorated that Congress decided it must try once more to end the violence. Accordingly, federal commissioners (not including Hawkins) were instructed to go to the Rock Landing on Georgia's Oconee River and negotiate a treaty with the Creeks led by McGillivray which would acknowledge the legality of the earlier Georgia treaties and cessions. Knox instructed the commissioners to guarantee the Creeks that their remaining territory would be protected by a line of federal military posts, and to tell them, "The United States do not want Creek lands; they desire only to be friends and protectors of the Creeks and to treat them with humanity and justice." If kind words alone did not suffice to win McGillivray's cooperation, the commissioners were to offer him a rank in the United States Army one grade higher than his rank in the Spanish army, with a commensurate annuity, if he would resign the Spanish commission.[37]

The careful preparations for a meeting in June 1789 turned out to be only the windup for a humiliating pratfall. The commissioners met their engagement at the Rock Landing, but McGillivray sent word that his people were in too angry a mood for a treaty. It is more likely, however, that this experienced Indian diplomat believed a delay would give the Spanish time to become alarmed at the prospect of a Creek–United States understanding and thus persuade them to renew interrupted shipments of war supplies to the Indians. A new treaty date was set for September 1789.[38]

A new group of commissioners arrived at the Rock Landing in September with a boatload of presents and further per-suaders in the form of a United States Cavalry escort. This time McGillivray came, drank the commissioners' liquor, and lis-tened agreeably to their proposals of United States Army rank and pay. But it seems that David Humphrey, one of the commis-sioners who wined and dined McGillivray, annoyed the sophisti-cated Creek by crude, patronizing efforts at flattery and intim-idation. Besides, McGillivray's hand was strengthened by word just received that the Spanish would renew war supplies. When the draft treaty was presented, and McGillivray found that it merely confirmed cessions allegedly made at Long Swamp, Au-gusta, and Shoulderbone, he and his escort of 2,000 chiefs and warriors quietly melted away.

A few days later he wrote the commissioners that the draft treaty was unacceptable, but that he did not close the door to future conversations. To his friend Panton he wrote more heat-edly, possibly for the eyes of the Spanish officials, that "by G——, I could not have such a Treaty cram'd down my throat."[39]

The outraged commissioners insisted that the earlier treaties were perfectly legal and binding, and itemized the damage that the Creeks had done in defiance of those treaties—82 people killed, 140 taken captive, and 2,000 head of livestock killed or seized. They recommended that "the Creek nation ought to be deemed the enemies of the United States and punished accordingly."[40]

Cooler thinking prevailed, however. An occasion was planned that could scarcely fall short even of McGillivray's appetite for compliments. Col. Marinus Willett, once one of George Washington's most trusted military aides, was dispatched to invite McGillivray to New York for a treaty, where he would meet the president and everyone of consequence in the govern-ment. Willett also carried a letter from Hawkins, who had met

McGillivray and had been impressed by him at the Hopewell treaty. The letter urged McGillivray to attend the New York treaty and suggested, that "the U States have the means of estimating properly the value of your character." Colonel Willett and McGillivray evidently struck it off well together. Willett commented on McGillivray's "open, candid, generous mind . . . good judgment and very tenacious memory," and McGillivray agreed to accompany Willett to New York with an escort of twenty-three other Creek chiefs.[41]

In New York, from late May well into summer, McGillivray was entertained by the great and feted beyond the endurance of a constitution weakened, it is said, by sexual indulgence and drinking. He collapsed from pleasure, but by early August was well enough again to sign a treaty, along with the other twenty-three Creek chiefs, ceding land in the name of the entire Creek Nation. Secretary of War Knox himself signed for the United States. Hawkins, an observer at the treaty, was deceived by his characteristic optimism into the belief that the lands ceded by McGillivray would satisfy the Georgians, win the friendship of the Creeks, and "greatly conduce to keeping the other tribes quiet," as he wrote to Blount. But the cession fell far short of what Georgia insisted it had gained by earlier treaties, and far more than the Creeks were willing to grant for the promised annuity of $1,500.[42]

One part of the agreement, however, reiterated a promise of things to come that deeply interested Hawkins: a controlled Indian trade with the United States and, in Article 12, a program for "civilizing" the Indians. According to the latter, the United States proposed to send agricultural equipment and domestic animals, "that the Creek nation may be led to a greater degree of civilization, and become herdsmen and cultivators, instead of remaining in a state of hunters." This federal program was not, in its motive, mainly altruistic, although a few Americans, like Hawkins, had high hopes of what might thus be accomplished in the interest of the Indians. The policy behind the program did not differ in its ends from that of William Blount, John Sevier, or the Georgians; both they and the federal government knew that the Indians must be persuaded by one means or another to yield up their hunting grounds for the peace, growth, and security of the United States. The difference lay in the means. Washington, Knox, Jefferson, and Hawkins hoped to accomplish national policy by teaching the Indians that an agricultural economy would bring them greater benefits than a hunting economy, from very much less land. But such a change from hunting to husbandry would necessarily take time. Blount's way was an immediate shrinkage in the extent of Indian hunting grounds.[43]

That was the year, 1790, when Hawkins was elected to the United States Senate and Blount, with Hawkins's recommendation, was appointed governor of the Southwest Territory. Doubtless a primary reason for Blount's appointment was his staunch Federalism at that time; and even if his grandiose land schemes were suspected, as they certainly were by Hawkins, they would quite possibly have been a recommendation for the office of governor, on the theories that the man who has most to protect will protect best, and that as governor, Blount would match his conduct to the respectability of his position.[44]

For the first time in their government careers, Hawkins and Blount found themselves in different branches, the legislative and the executive respectively. Blount, in an executive role, was jealous of legislative control and supervision of trade in his territory: he did not want congressionally appointed commissioners treating with the Indians; he did not want Indians going off to Congress to complain about his treatment of them, as they were entitled to do by the treaty of Hopewell. What Blount wanted was a quick, large cession of Indian lands on which to locate his claims.

Blount lost no time after his appointment in summoning the Cherokees to a treaty at the Holston River. Before the treaty Hawkins had warned Blount that to try for the Tennessee River as a boundary would "rouse the resentment of the Cherokees, give serious alarm to the Chickasaws and risk cause of suspicion to the Creeks and Choctaws," because part of the land to be asked for was considered hunting ground common to all the tribes. Moreover, there were already settlers on the lands between the Holston and French Broad rivers, although the Indians at Hopewell had unequivocally refused to cede these lands. "Those encroachments on our part are the true cause of hostilities on theirs," Hawkins wrote Blount, a point he had made before and would insist on for the next fifteen years, "and as long as the first is suffered the latter may be expected."[45]

In beautiful spring weather, the Holston treaty was held with full pomp and protocol. The scene on the riverbank, where the leaves were unfolding on the trees, must have been gorgeous. Governor Blount, a handsome man of commanding presence, was seated near his marquee. About him were the members of his entourage, his interpreter, James Carey, and a gathering of interested onlookers. In front of him sat an assemblage of forty-one chiefs and one thousand two hundred warriors vivid with paint and ceremonial adornment. Blount was prepared with the expected gifts—shirts, blankets, shoes, feathers, hats, beads, scarlet cloth, looking glasses—all of which were worth less than $100. Beyond that, he had permission from Congress to offer the Cherokees an annuity of $1,000 for the relinquishment of specified lands. As Hawkins had warned, the Indians were obdurate in their resistance to ceding land south of the Tennessee River, except for a small bulge that was not nearly enough to satisfy the Tennessee claimants, many of whom were already occupants. Blount did, however, get one important concession: permission from the Cherokees to put a road through their territory to link East and Middle Tennessee. In July the treaty was signed by Blount and the chiefs.[46]

Hawkins was a member of the Senate committee charged with study of the treaty. In its report of November 9 to the Senate the committee commented that the boundary was little changed except for the bulge already being farmed by settlers. Although the treaty was promptly ratified, as Hawkins advised Blount in a letter of November 14, it was an agreement that satisfied no one, and it was to cause trouble for years to come. White settlers at once violated the terms; Cherokees retaliated by a raid on a stockade outside Nashville and an attack on the territorial capital at Knoxville. Sevier hit back with an invasion of Cherokee country. There seemed no way of ending the hostilities deriving from the treaty. As President Washington said, "the difficulty of deciding between lawless settlers and greedy Speculators on one side, and the jealousies of the Indian Nations and their banditti on the other, becomes more and more obvious every day; and these, from the interference of the Spaniards (if the reports we have be true) and other causes . . . add not a little to our embarrassment." (The "other causes" will be examined in the following chapter.)[47]

For the next treaty in this early series, and by far the most important one, Hawkins headed the federal commissioners. He, George Clymer of Pennylsvania, and again Andrew Pickens were to meet Creek delegates for treaty negotiations in the spring of 1796 at Fort Colerain, on the Saint Marys River in southern Georgia.[48]

Hawkins, as usual, was the first to arrive, followed by Pickens and Clymer and several Georgia "observers." The Georgians, who arrived with a shipload of presents and an armed militia guard, were determined to get land from the forks of Ocmulgee and Oconee to the headwaters of the Saint Marys, which they claimed by the treaty of New York. Just as determined were the Creeks not to yield what McGillivray assured them he had not granted at New York. It is entirely probable that the talks at New York had been conducted in English, McGillivray's first language, and that the other chiefs did not know precisely what he had promised. The federal commissioners, for their part, were determined to fulfill their orders to come to a just and peaceful understanding with the Creeks.[49]

Word had spread among the Creeks that the Georgia militia would be waiting for them at the treaty grounds. Whether for this reason or because, as Timothy Barnard said, they used the threat of a treaty meeting to go to Florida and beg presents from the Spaniards, few of the Creeks came to Colerain.[50]

Through the last week of May and the first of June, Hawkins handled a delicate situation firmly and carefully, enforcing his regulations with the aid of the commandant and garrison of the fort. He set a guard outside the Indian encampment to prevent the Georgians from tampering with the Creeks or making private land deals with them, which nevertheless occurred. He forbade the landing of the Georgia militia and the carrying of firearms by unauthorized persons; and he prohibited whites from visiting the Indians, or giving or selling them anything, above all spirits. The Georgians declared themselves insulted by these restrictions, but by soft answers Hawkins managed to assuage their anger without making concessions. Indians at last began drifting in, until finally about four hundred chiefs and warriors were present. Hawkins was also scrupulous in safeguarding the rights of the Georgians present, although clearly he thought the Indians conducted themselves better. Commenting on a dinner to which he had invited some of the chiefs, Hawkins wrote, "They on this, as on every other occasion, behaved decently." His measures for safeguarding the Indians seem to have quieted their fears, and everyone was very polite and proper for several days. Then somebody somehow smuggled liquor to the Indians and "upwards of 20 Indians were drunk in camp last night," Hawkins reported.[51]

When at last the several parties met for serious negotiation, the Indians were sober, again well behaved, but absolutely unyielding to demands for land. When the Georgians cited Creek violations of earlier treaties, Big Warrior sarcastically requested a long roll of paper so that the Indians could set down Georgian violations. Bird King made it plain they had come not to meet Georgia commissioners, but three of George Washington's "beloved men," the three federal commissioners. In a long address he listed many examples of white intrusion and trespass on Indian land; in the course of his talk he invoked the name of George Washington twenty-one times, each time with respect and affection, indicating the reliance of the Creeks on the federal government and its head. "George Washington told us," said Bird King, "a father will speak to his children . . . if there should happen to be a cloudy day over us, we must look about, and see how to dispel it, that we may have a clear day to live in . . . you see, and I see, the rivers; when they run dry, and the mountains disappear, we shall cease to talk of peace and quietness, and there will be an end of all things."[52]

The metaphorical language of Bird King is typical of treaty rhetoric. Yet the question remains, are these the actual words he spoke? How reliably bilingual was the translator? How accurate and literate was the transcriber who entered the speech in the records?

The Creeks had chosen as speaker, or linguister, to present their case, Oche Haujo, known to the white people as Alexander

(Alec, Alex, or Alecks) Cornells, who like McGillivray had a Scottish father and a Creek mother, and who became, after McGillivray's death, probably the most influential Creek chief. Faithful to his tribe, yet friendly to whites, Cornells was to be Hawkins's trusted deputy for the rest of his life. He was a moderate man, but at the time of the Colerain treaty he must still have been embittered by the senseless killing by white men three years earlier of his kinsman David Cornells and other Creeks who were carrying dispatches for the garrison at Colerain. Nevertheless, Oche Haujo presented the Creeks' case with restraint. The Creeks had accepted the line McGillivray told them he had agreed at the treaty of New York, Oche Haujo said, and were prepared to accompany the white commissioners in running that line; but then William Augustus Bowles, the Tory troublemaker from Florida, had come with his lies and dissuaded them, "and was a great obstruction to their performing their promise to the President of the United States."[53]

Cornells went on to speak of all the land the Creeks had already relinquished, and its perennial productivity of timber, grass, water power, and rich soil; even the dead pines on the land, he pointed out, yielded valuable tar. Yet see the shoddiness, the inadequacy of what the Indians received in return, Cornells said: "If they have had a little goods, in one or two seasons, they are rotten, and gone to nothing." When Cornells had finished his speech, one of the Georgians insultingly asked what the Creeks knew about making tar out of dead pines. We have watched you, we know all about it, Oche Haujo answered: "When the trees are dead, and nearly rotten, the white people take the light wood, cover it with dirt, burn it, and the tar runs out." However much the Indians have relinquished, intruders press still farther into their hunting grounds, Oche Haujo observed: "the woods are constantly full of white men, hunters, even going about in the night, hunting deer with fire light." Every cane swamp where the Indian hunters "go to look for a bear, which is part of their support, is near eat out with the stocks put over [the line] by the citizens of Georgia." McGillivray had given them to understand that the line would begin at the head of the northernmost branch of the Oconee, then run southeast to "the old line drawn by the British," then across the Altamaha River, continuing on the old British line to Saint Marys on the coast. Now, Oche Haujo said, the Creeks are being asked for lands south and east of that line "as far as the Oakmulgee river, and across, from the fork of the Oconee, and Oakmulgee rivers, to the head of St. Mary's. We are told that those lands are of no service to us, but still, we consider that, if we can hold our lands, there will always be a turkey or a deer, or, in the streams of water, a fish to be found, for our young generation, that will come after us. We are afraid that, if we part with any more of our lands, that at last the white people will not suffer us to keep as much as will bury our dead."[54]

So pleaded the prophetic Alex Cornells, "by far the most eloquent man in the Creek Nation," as Hawkins described him. "He is smaller than the ordinary standard of his tribe," Hawkins said, "but equally erect in his deportment." The genes of his white father had displaced the copper coloring, high cheek bones, and thick lips of his Creek mother's heritage; he retained his Indian dress, but acted like a well-bred white man. He spoke English with some ease, but could not read, nor write so much as his name, using instead an elaborate mark. In his own Muskogee language he was fluent. Hawkins admired his graceful gestures, sweetness of tone, and animation of countenance, and mentioned particularly that he spoke without the self-consciousness and desire for applause common to orators, but rather went straight to the point and concentrated on it the whole energy of his mind.[55]

Through Oche Haujo, the Creeks told the Georgians to keep their shipload of presents; the Indians would keep their land. This was a final answer, he said: the Indians would give no more land; further talk was useless. But Oche Haujo recognized the futility of this victory. "If you are determined to take the land," he concluded, "to drive us off, and make us poor, it must be so. If the sharp weapons of defence are to be taken from us, and as our dependence is on the white people, we must be driven from our lands, and made poor. We must, we suppose, submit." Hawkins answered: "You knew, some time ago, that this business, respecting your lands, rested entirely with yourselves; the President sent his talk to you, and told you, if you are willing to sell your lands, say so; if not, say so. There was no compulsion."[56]

They were not willing, and they said so. The Georgians, for the time being, desisted. A few more treaty terms were amicably discussed; the Creeks accepted the offer of two blacksmiths to work among them, agreed to permit trading posts to be built in their nation, but rejected schools for their young, on grounds that "Indians, when educated, turned out very worthless; became mischievous and troublesome." The long meeting was over. Hawkins left Colerain for Saint Marys on July 6 at five o'clock in the morning, travelled thirty-three miles before breakfast, and yet had the strength and interest to note in his journal "a bed of strawberries, in bloom, and full bearing, many of them quite ripe."[57]

By the year of the Colerain negotiations, the tired, old, beleaguered president sought some more lasting relief from the southern chaos than a treaty that would at once be broken. He needed a man who could firmly and honestly guide a program for trade with and "civilization" of the Indians, which he had been proposing since 1790, and toward which Congress was finally taking the necessary steps. Hawkins was available; he had not offered again for the Senate in 1794, possibly because a radical sweep of North Carolina put his reelection in doubt. In August 1796, when he returned from Colerain, Washington had been considering him for surveyor general of the United States, but within a short time the president's annoyance with the ineffectual conduct of "the Indian Agent to the Southward," James Seagrove, suggested a more useful role for Hawkins. On August 29 the president addressed a talk to the Cherokee Nation, introducing to them "the first general or principal Agent for all four southern nations of Indians, Colonel Benjamin Hawkins, a man already known and respected by you. I have chosen him for this office because he is esteemed for a good man; has a knowledge of Indian customs, and a particular love and friendship for all the Southern tribes."[58]

The appointment was formalized some time before the middle of November, when Hawkins left Philadelphia to join

Pickens for the running of the Hopewell treaty line. He may have been chosen for the job of principal agent because of Washington's concern that North Carolina and every other state should have its proper share of federal officers. It may have been at Hawkins's own request that he was called "Principal *Temporary* Agent." He tried several times to resign the job, from as early as 1798, when he wrote some Georgians, "My appointment Gentlemen is temporary, and I had determined to ask leave to resign it as soon as I had completed some negotiations."[59]

A more interesting question is, Why did Hawkins accept the appointment even temporarily? Why should an intellectual, prosperous, prominent man, who counted many of the great among his friends, interrupt his career to take on an obscure dead-end job? "Can such a man," he wrote playfully to his friend Mrs. Elizabeth Trist, "be in his senses?" The rest of his letter, he continued, would explain "this enigma." Then he recounted what he had learned about the Indians during his difficult winter journey through their country in 1797, especially about the hard life of Indian women. When Indians asked anxiously what would happen to them under his agency, "I explained the objects of my mission, my *love* [Hawkins's emphasis] for the red women and determination to better if practicable their situation." Playfulness aside, the answer to the enigma seems to be that his mission to improve the lives of the Indians and protect their rights meant more to him than the deprivations he might suffer.[60]

Hawkins's hope was that the southern Indians could be persuaded to give up land voluntarily, once they had been made to see that farming and simple industry would yield them a safer, richer life on small holdings than the hunting economy that required vast open lands for a very chancy survival. Thus and thus only could the Indians of the South defend themselves from the machinations of Georgian and other land speculators and from foreign troublemakers. In fact, thus only could they survive, Hawkins sincerely believed. What was needed was enabling legislation for an encompassing program of "civilization" of the Indians, with funds to establish and maintain it.

By coincidence, the night before Hawkins told the Indians at Colerain that they were under no compulsion to sell their land, he and the other commissioners were encouraged by receiving from the War Office copies of "An Act to regulate trade and intercourse with the Indian tribes, and to preserve peace upon the frontiers." This was probably the act approved April 18, 1796, an expansion of earlier acts. It specifically empowered the president to establish and regulate nonprofit trading houses in or near Indian country and appropriated for this purpose $150,000. The legislation assured Hawkins of the support of Congress and the president in his efforts to "civilize" the Indians, and put into his hands a powerful tool for accomplishing that end. The act was read aloud to the Creeks assembled at Colerain, and they liked the idea of trading houses, offering to point out the most advantageous locations. Hawkins must have been greatly buoyed in his hopes for the future.[61]

Angie Debo says of Hawkins: "He knew that white advance was inevitable, and he labored to prepare them [the Indians] to adjust to it. He held them at peace, he encouraged their economic progress in farming, homemaking, and commerce, and he tried—unwisely—to break down their communal life by undermining the towns and creating an artificial central government responsive to him." For all Hawkins's good intentions, John Mahon points out that he was a disruptive force in trying to turn the Creeks away from their traditional culture to a white mode of living. The Creeks kept trying to tell Hawkins where his mistake lay: "They told me they did not understand the plan," Hawkins wrote; "They could not work, they did not want ploughs, it did not comport with the ways of the red people, who were determined to persevere in the ways of their ancestors." Hawkins put forth an enormous amount of effort and ingenuity to save Indian lives, but the Indians were determined to save Indian life.[62]

CHAPTER 3

Separatists, Nationalists, and Adventurers

Our western citizens feel much alarmed for their situation. They will have less confidence in the justice of Congress and be disposed to carve for themselves.

BENJAMIN HAWKINS
TO THOMAS JEFFERSON, MARCH, 1787

I cannot help Joining in the General cry, of the Southern Indians in wishing the return of the British once more to the Floridas. . . . I am offered by the Spaniards the appointment of a Commissary of the Cherokee Nation but have not as yet accepted the offer.

JOHN MCDONALD, TRADER, TO JOHN MCKEE,
AGENT AT TELLICO, TENNESSEE, APRIL, 1794.

THE American Revolution was a long war fought over a large expanse of territory and involving several nations. Every great war ends in a revision of borders and sovereignties, and is therefore bound to be followed by confusion, unrest, migrations, nationalist and separatist movements, jurisdictional disputes, and a heyday for opportunists, mercenaries, and outlaws. Thus, for many years after the redefinitions of the treaty of Paris, chaos ruled along the perimeter of a United States that was too weak to enforce its treaty gains, providing opportunities for foreign powers, speculators, adventurers, freebooters, displaced persons, and Indian nationalists to create further trouble or to become rich and powerful.

In the Old Northwest the British managed to hold off evacuation of their military posts for a dozen years, creating an almost continuous state of warfare in which both British and Americans recruited aid from the northern Indian tribes. In the South the Spanish were still more dilatory in honoring treaty lines and in abandoning their forts along and east of the Mississippi River, similarly involving the southern Indian tribes and the many anti-American whites who lived among them.

Hawkins as agent to the southern Indians walked into a situation almost indescribably disorganized and demoralized. In 1796, Spain was still arguing the boundary; speculators from the Tennessee country and Georgia were thrusting deep into Indian country; former Tories, now refugees among the Indians, were collaborating with zeal in any actions promising discomfort for the United States. The southern Indians themselves, apprehensive of punishment for the aid many of them had given the British during the Revolution, were ready to accept any anti–United States propaganda. The tribes were also in extreme need, because the war had stopped the flow of trade upon which they had depended, and because the pressure of white settlements had diminished the game that was their chief resource for living and trade. Their allegiance could be bought by practically anyone for presents of food, clothing, or guns and ammunition. To win goodwill, the United States sent relief amounting to more than $13,000 in food, goods, and money in 1792, when drought wiped out the Creek corn crop.[1]

Spain kept its hold on such settlements as Natchez and Tensaw, although by the secret Anglo-American agreement at the treaty of Paris these were now in United States territory. In fact, for fifteen years after 1783, Spain continued to build posts north of its line, insisting that Great Britain had had no legal right to cede this land to the United States. From the early 1790s, American migrants were attracted to the Spanish settlements by promises of free land. In 1792, James Seagrove advised the secretary of war that official passes should be required of persons traveling through Creek country, because the Indians were complaining of a flood of whites going through their land. In 1798 and 1799, Hawkins issued an average of six or seven passes a month to parties on their way to Tensaw, Mobile, Pensacola, and other Spanish settlements, and the number increased in 1800 and 1801. Passport or no, many of these migrants through Indian country were robbed, and some were murdered. Those who did arrive at the settlements found rough, disorderly towns and confusion about land claims. Natchez in 1798 was reported as an abominable place roamed by drunken blacks and Indians, full of Spanish brigands and begging Choctaws, a wretched little outpost without a regular mail route, law officers, jails, or armed militia.[2]

The treaty of New York, by which in 1790 the United States had acquired from McGillivray a great deal more southern land into which to expand, alarmed both Spain and Britain. Both nations, therefore, through their agents pressed the Indians to nullify that treaty. The consequent Indian unrest and alarm was used by white Southerners, chafing under United States restrictions on both their legitimate and illegal activities, to gain their own ends.

Probably the most troublesome aspect of the Spanish presence to the greatest number of Americans was Spain's control of the Mississippi River and its vacillating policy under successive regimes in restricting American river traffic. In 1784, New Orleans was barred to American vessels, which were seized when they reached Natchez. This action infuriated American settlers and speculators on the Tennessee and Kentucky frontiers, because their livelihood and the value of their land depended on the right to deposit cargoes of such products as tobacco, corn, and lumber at New Orleans for transshipment to coastal and foreign markets. Yet in 1785, when John Jay was commissioned to negotiate a commercial treaty with Spain, he found himself so hampered by the vexatious Mississippi question that he recommended to Congress that the matter of river rights be dropped for twenty or thirty years until it became vital to a larger number of frontiersmen. Jay, New York born, was burned in effigy in the West; the Mississippi question was the first important sectional issue to arise in the United States.[3]

John Sevier, James Robertson, James Wilkinson, and other prominent Americans with western interests to protect began thinking of secession from the union and alliance with Spain; in 1788 their schemes were shared by a new arrival in the Tennessee country, Andrew Jackson. Feelers were cautiously put out to the Spanish government; a string of American settlements along the Cumberland River was named Mero District in phonic tribute to Estebán Miro, governor of Louisiana, who was reasonably friendly toward Americans and had tried to protect them from Indian hostilities. Despite the great risks involved, land speculations in the South flourished from the early 1780s. All were illegal, in that they involved lands as yet unrelinquished by the Indians. The Yazoo land companies, for example, claimed vast holdings in a swath reaching northeastward from Walnut Hills (the site of Vicksburg, Mississippi) to Muscle Shoals in the bend of the Tennessee River. Almost every man of the area important enough to be recorded by historians was a shareholder in one or another of the land companies. The prevailing wind on the frontier was toward the southwest. The coming of Hawkins in 1785 for the treaty of Hopewell and his pride in defending the rights of the Indians were threats to Sevier, Robertson, Blount, and all the other land jobbers; their overtures to foreign powers became more definite and organized.[4]

Contributing greatly to the disorderly situation in the South were the agents placed among the Indians by the Spanish governors of Louisiana and Florida. They became particularly active after the treaty of New York. The news that the Spanish pensioner Col. Alex McGillivray had become General McGillivray of the United States Army with an American pension greatly alarmed the Spanish government, which counted on keeping the Creeks as a friendly buffer between Spanish possessions and the United States. The busiest Spanish agent was Pedro Olivar, who had as his deputy and informant Louis LcClerc Milfort, McGillivray's brother-in-law and close associate. In 1792, Olivar was sent by the baron de Carondelet, who had just succeeded the more peaceable Miro as governor of New Orleans, to live in the Creek Nation, gather intelligence, and incite violence against Americans. Hawkins learned later from his friend Tustunnagan (or Tustunnugee) Emautlau of Tuckabatchee that the Spanish "constantly have Captain Oliver teaze us to fight them [Americans]" and to "take hair" from them, for pay. Instructed by the aggressive Carondelet, Olivar also urged the Creeks not to go to treaties with the Americans, not to give them a foot of land, but to unite and destroy the American settlers, Olivar's activities, of which Hawkins was quite aware, were totally in violation of the pact of peace and friendship between Spain and the United States reaffirmed in 1795 by the treaty of San Lorenzo, by which they were pledged not to incite the Indians against each other. Hawkins observed the pact to the letter.[5]

British agents and refugee Loyalists capitalized on any rumor or action that might damage the relations of the United States with the Indians. The agents were under instructions "to turn loose the Indian fury against the frontiers," Hawkins wrote, "and some of them accompanyed the war parties and urged them to an undistinguished destruction of all ages and sexes." The Loyalists joined in this warfare or served as guides. They married Indian women, and taught their wives' families "every species of cunning and theft," Hawkins recorded, and found markets for the horses that the Indians stole under their tutelage. To understand the Creeks and do them justice, Hawkins said, their background of systematic corruption by Loyalist refugees had to be remembered. "It will be sometime before the Creek young will get rid of the remains of that alloy," he wrote.[6]

Although not as pervasive a force for division in the South, the French contributed their share to the prevailing confusion in the Genêt affair, which created its own special turmoil starting in 1793. All but the most conservative among American patriots had been sympathetic toward the French Revolution. The newly declared French republic, at war or on the verge of war with practically every important European power, welcomed American friendship and promised to send a French fleet to liberate Louisiana and the Floridas from Spanish rule. Enthusiasm for this plan was unbounded in the South, and land values soared.[7]

The French minister to the United States, Edmond Charles Genêt, arrived in Charleston early in 1793 and was extravagantly feted. Pro-French groups, called Democratic, or Democratic-Republican, societies, sprang up in many cities that year and the next. In the South, separatist plots flared again; frontiersmen declared that if their government would not secure for them the navigation of the Mississippi, they would win it for themselves, with French support. Georgians, disappointed by failure of the Federal government to get relinquishment of Indian land claims, were also poised for the campaign westward. Genêt had no trouble recruiting volunteers.[8]

At the last minute, however, greed was tempered by discretion, in which the southern fear of free blacks and of a black revolt played a large part. Genêt had had a connection with the organization known as Amis des Noirs, which had been influential in stirring up a Santo Domingan revolt in which many French whites were massacred. Refugees from Santo Domingo had poured into the United States, including free light-colored blacks who were in as great peril as whites. The panic caused by this free-black influx was at its peak as Genêt was marshaling support for his expedition, and the allegation that he had helped incite the bloody island revolt cooled American feeling toward him. Then, just as his campaign was to start, President Washington demanded that his government recall him.[9]

The United States and Spain were both now aware as never before of frontier determination to obtain Mississippi rights and western lands. In July of the following year, 1795, Spain withdrew from its alliance with Britain to sign the treaty of Basle with France; rumors circulated that France was to get back Louisiana. A treaty negotiated by John Jay with Great Britain had just been ratified by Congress, and although in fact the treaty made no changes in the international situation, Spain feared that it might contain a secret Anglo-American pact endangering Spanish interests in America. In October, therefore, Spain signed the treaty of San Lorenzo, which was negotiated for the United States by Thomas Pinckney. Westerners were jubilant because Pinckney's treaty promised free use of the Mississippi River by American vessels and the rights of deposit and transshipment. Furthermore, the treaty reaffirmed the thirty-first parallel as the southern U.S. boundary, again called on Spain to surrender posts and land claims north of it, and pledged both parties to control the Indians within their jurisdictions. Spain was to delay ratification of the treaty, and it would be almost five years before Spanish posts were all evacuated. But in October, 1795, when the San Lorenzo instrument was signed, the future of the West looked very rosy. Land values boomed, land speculation increased, and separatist plots were, for the moment, set aside. Emboldened white settlers intruded on Indian land, and Indian reprisals grew furious.[10]

To understand the hostility of the southern tribes, one must bear in mind not only their corruption by Loyalists and foreign agents—which Hawkins pointed out—but also the white wrangles and plots for possession of the lands where the Indians lived, which they considered to be their own. As early as 1783, the year of the treaty of Paris, John Sevier and a few friends had been secretly perpetrating a huge land fraud by which they would claim title to four million acres of Indian land in the Tennessee River country. The fraud was so dramatic in scope, encompassing one-sixth of what later would be the state of Tennessee, that in accounts of it the drama of the victims tend to be overlooked. It was no mere pathetic story of naïve people swindled by promises that they ignorantly believed. It was, rather, a tragedy, because the Indians were quite aware of the plots to seize their land. They knew of the machinations of Blount and his group, including the ruffian John Chisholm; of the lawless intentions of Zachariah Cox to seize the Muscle Shoals land for Yazoo speculators; of the unreliability of the promises made at treaties that no further intrusions on their land would be tolerated. It was commonly believed that the Indians did not think about the future, nor care what the next day might bring. Such facile characterizations are popular because they fit a useful stereotype; but the Indians knew, cared, and tried by every means in their power to prevent the consequences not of their lack of prescience but their deficiency of power, their helpless dependence on white magnanimity material and ethical.[11]

Material generosity was traditional; every deal, every empty promise of the land-grabbers (the *ocunnaunuxulgee*, as the Creeks called them), had to be sealed by presents of food, clothing, and frippery. When the United States wanted Indian cooperation, and Spain wanted Indian opposition to the United States, as in running the boundary between the two powers, the requests of both powers were doubtless sweetened with presents. The Indians were entirely aware of the struggle between the white nations.[12]

Since the coming of the first white men, relations between southern Indians and whites had been based on force or presents: presents in return for land or promises of peace, or for restitution of captives or property. James Seagrove and all other Indian agents had dealt with the Indians by "temporary expedients only; and amongst the most powerful and persuasive, was the pressure of fear from without, and *presents*," Hawkins wrote in his study of the Creek Nation. Also, he observed, any suggestion for improving Indian life was opposed by the Indians at once and for "as long as there is hope to obtain *presents*, the infallible mode heretofore in use, to gain a point."

Hawkins detested a system that made beggars of capable people. Also, the practical weakness of such a system was that a promise extorted by bribes would be honored only until bigger bribes were offered. In the light of the Indians' attachment to their land and their awareness of white intentions, it seems obvious that promises made to speculators, arriving with armed militia behind them and gifts in their hands, would be as unreliable as the promises made by the speculators. The speculators and their agents dealt with chiefs at treaties, and it was the chiefs and head warriors, the elders, who got the presents, on the assumption that they would distribute the gifts throughout the tribe, town, or village. They apparently did not always do so, which caused resentment.[13]

The close of the Revolutionary War brought into notice one very large segment of the Indian population who neither compromised with the white speculators and treaty commissioners nor, probably, shared in their presents. This was the restless, rebellious, nationalistic Indian youth. All long wars leave behind them a turbulent generation suddenly bereft of the outlet for anger and hate provided by years of warfare, but still in the grip of those emotions. Or perhaps the turbulence of Indian youth during this period was as much cognitive as affective: perhaps they perceived that they had been used by whites as tools and that, now their usefulness was at an end, the white world meant to destroy them. Indian youths, unscarred by compromises, undazzled by presents, feeling their strength and confident of many years ahead in which to right wrongs, seemed to perceive reality more sharply than most of their elders. Whatever the reason or reasons, there is massive testimony from the Indian elders that their young people violently opposed white intrusion on ancestral tribal lands and vehemently espoused their ethnic culture.

This is not to say that none of the older Indians participated in the opposition; to put the blame for thefts and murders on youths alone permitted Hawkins, or Blount, and the chiefs to discuss malefactors in the third person, a useful diplomatic device.

Cherokee chief Doublehead begged territorial Governor Blount not to "get in a passion . . . if some of our mad young men should go and steal a horse from some of your people"; it would be returned. Blount told the Cherokees at a meeting in the winter of 1794–95 that they surely knew "too many of your young warriors" had gone with the Creeks to do "horrid murders and Thefts" in the Cumberland settlements, and that if their "foolish young People" continued to go with the Creeks, their towns would be destroyed. "The young and ambitious must be taught to respect the decisions of their wise and old chiefs. . . . If they will not be taught this, they may be assured, red and white, that their father will extend his arm, and correct," said Hawkins and his fellow commissioners at Colerain. A Cusseta chief admitted to Hawkins that he knew there were bad young men on both sides of the frontier who would commit violence, and promised he would supervise his young hunters. Hawkins hoped the Lower Creeks would "cooperate with me in restraining their imprudent young men," but he expected that "some of the ungovernable young men" would bring stolen horses back from the hunt. "Young, worthless fellows" were stealing horses, Hawkins complained; he could not decide whether to protest to the chiefs or the young men, he wrote Cornells in 1797, speaking about treaty violations, "as the latter seem determined on mischief and the chiefs unable to controll them." Among other misdeeds of Creek "young people" was their encouragement of black slaves in the United States to leave their masters and seek protection in Creek country—

where in fact, Hawkins said, they belonged to the first Indian who claimed them.[14]

There is plenty of evidence that the willful and wild young men did not all carry on their depredations purely from high spirits, a craving for excitement, or the urgings of foreign agents. Youths knew too much about white intentions to accept Hawkins's view that, if the young would be attentive to their chiefs, the Creeks would be a great people. The young men became more and more determined not to cede any part of their country, and, when pressures increased after Jefferson became president, the chiefs feared youths would forcibly resist cessions, overthrow the existing Creek government of chiefs, "and by some hasty and imprudent act involve their country in ruin."[15]

Hawkins had not been long with the Creeks before he was firmly convinced that Indian recalcitrance "is produced by a panic terror, springing from the apprehension that they are soon to be pressed for further relinquishment of Lands." He had advised often that Indian border violence originated from white intrusion on Indian land, but intrusion continued to be permitted, even covertly encouraged, by Blount and other speculators, and the War Department was lax in enforcing treaty terms. In 1797, Hawkins told the secretary of war: "The Indians on their part . . . charge their neighbors with trespassing on their rights, driving their hogs, horses and cattle to range on their lands, . . . surveying their lands and cultivating some of them; that this is a source of vexation to the whole nation and keeps their young men unruly." Two years later he reiterated the Creek complaints of whites' ranging stock, fire hunting, building fish traps, and settling on Indian soil, so that "the young men were alarmed for their situation and the chiefs did not know what to say or do." The pressures intensified for another decade; so also did the resistance. The Lower Creeks in 1812 were still bitterly protesting that white intruders on their land and white claims to timber, hunting, and fishing rights "rendered their young men ungovernable" and were the real cause of their depredations.[16]

Up to the mid-1790s the ungovernable young men could do little more than torment white intruders, occasionally killing one or two. They were angry, impatient, ready to fight—but leaderless; no one southern tribe, Blount's claims notwithstanding, had the numbers and power to destroy the United States citizens on the frontier. What Indian resistance required was an all-Indian confederation, such as the one of which Pontiac had dreamt a generation before. That dream never altogether ended. Northern and southern tribes kept open lines of communication by means of runners and delegations, who came by the many trails leading east and west, north and south, through the Indian territories. As early as 1785, Congress was alarmed by rumors that northern Indians had sent messengers to the southern tribes, urging them to joint warfare against the United States under British or Spanish auspices. In the early 1790s, Creeks and Cherokees were taken north to join some Shawnees who were fighting under the American generals Arthur St. Clair and Anthony Wayne against an uprising of other Old Northwest Indians allied with the British. In the fall of 1792, Andrew Pickens informed Blount that a Shawnee delegation had arrived among the Cherokees to promote a general Indian confederacy and a war against the United States. Creek and Cherokee delegates returned the visit the following summer and attended a "General Council of the Indians" sponsored by the British. Communications between northern and southern tribes became more frequent in the following year, and an Indian confederacy was much discussed.[17]

In April 1793, Creek chiefs, including Houthlie Opoi Micco and Cherokee chief Little Turkey, wrote the British agent at Detroit, Alexander McKee, that they had "taken the Talks of our Bretheren the Northern Indians" and had commended the war; that they approved of the talks of the Shawnees, "our Red Bretheren, who live about the Lakes." Let the British only give them arms, they wrote, and they would fight the Americans to the end. The Cherokee chief Glass was another vehement hostile; he had destroyed Zachariah Cox's blockhouse at Muscle Shoals, and his hatred for the Cumberland settlers was so ferocious, it was said, that he tore off their scalps with his teeth and hands.[18]

These were formidable individuals, no question. Certain chiefs were disillusioned with promises, finished with friendliness toward lying white men. Youths were almost unanimously full of rage and determination to expel the invaders of their land. All the tribes, northern and southern, were ready to unite in war. Yet it did not happen, and the chief reason was probably a lack of leadership, the kind that makes men willing to die.

Two men tried to harness the Indian fury and dash it against the Americans, but neither had totally pure motives, and neither was wholly an Indian. Alexander McGillivray, an opportunist, half or less than half Creek, chose to speak, dress, and live like a white man; and William Augustus Bowles, a white American adventurer, preferred to speak, dress, and live like an Indian. Both were undoubtedly motivated in part by a desire to liberate Indians from the power of the United States, but both had selfish motives as well, desires for wealth, power, revenge, or plain adventure. There was nothing in either man of the mystic, the evangelist, the parter of seas or walker through flames. A successful war under either of them would have brought to the Indians a return of easier times, without land-hungry Americans breathing on their necks, and with a plenty of presents, British or Spanish, in exchange for good behavior.

For such rewards Indians would make forays, but would not wage a war of extermination; as the missionary John Heckewelder wrote in 1819, "they will not fight with passion for the mere sake of a livelihood. . . . Their passions must be excited." The Indian god was "the preserver of breath," and Indian living was permeated by a respect for life; they would fight for liberty under leaders like Pontiac or the messianic Delaware Prophet, but those men offered Indian self-sufficiency and liberty, a return to the old way of life, not merely a change of masters and some handouts.[19]

McGillivray's father, Lachlan, a prosperous Scottish trader among the Creeks, had remained loyal to Britain during the Revolution, for which he had been banished. He had returned to Scotland with considerable wealth, but had left behind an estate worth $100,000, which Georgia had confiscated. By a part-Creek wife, Sehoy Marchand, Lachlan had fathered Alexander and other children, including Sophia Durant. Near the Durants lived a half sister of Sophia and Alexander, who married Charles Weatherford, a fair-skinned Creek trader and horse-breeder of dubious integrity. Charles's son William, of such light hair and coloring that he was often taken for a white man, became the great Creek nationalist hero Red Eagle. Many of Lachlan McGillivray's influential family connections lived along the Coosa River. Alexander's home was at the Hickory Ground (near present-day Wetumpka, Alabama), near which he had several plantations. These were large, slave-operated estates where he lived much in the manner of a white southern planter.[20]

As a young adolescent, probably when he was about fourteen, Alexander was sent by his father to an English school in Charleston, and then to Savannah for business training. At the outbreak of the Revolutionary War, then probably seventeen or eighteen, he was brought back to the Creek country. His intellectual gifts, developed by a good education, were frequently remarked. He was said to have excellent judgment and a tenacious memory; to be well-spoken and witty; to combine "the good sense of an American, the shrewdness of a Scotchman, and the cunning of an Indian"; and to be able to down a great quantity of liquor without faltering in logic or memory. He had the height and litheness, the dark, piercing eyes of a Creek. He did not, however, inherit the robust health of a typical Creek, and he abused his naturally delicate constitution with drink and venery; he was subject to chronic headache, and was often ill. His niece, or so-called niece, Rachel Walker, said McGillivray described himself as "in some sort a lone man, [who] had nobody about him to do things for him" despite all his wealth and power. He seems a good example of the alienation that contemporaneous observers found among educated Indians, who were accepted by neither whites nor reds: such a man, said missionaries Jeremy Belknap and Jedidiah Morse, would try to escape the contempt of his own people "in the inebriating draught, and when this becomes habitual, he will be guarded from no vice, and secure from no crime."[21]

McGillivray hated Americans and especially Georgians because of the confiscation of his father's property. During the Revolutionary War he had taken the British side and had formed a connection with the Scottish trader William Panton. But when the British at the treaty of Paris made no effort to protect their Indian allies, McGillivray turned away from them. By 1784, the year before Hawkins's first mission in Indian country, McGillivray was persuading the Spanish authorities in Florida that he was head of all the Creeks, and that he spoke for them in seeking Spanish protection. By this device McGillivray secured Spanish support for himself and for Panton's trading house, Panton, Leslie and Company. The Spanish gave Panton a monopoly of the Indian trade and made McGillivray the king's commissionary among the Creeks, with the rank of colonel and pay of $50 a month. Thus protected, McGillivray could afford to ignore the Galphinton meeting and the Hopewell treaty that followed. To crown his achievements, the Spanish yielded to McGillivray's pleas to supply the Creeks with arms. Although these were allegedly to be used only for defense, in arming the Creeks Spain violated its treaty of peace and amity with the United States. For two years Creek raiders, armed and urged by McGillivray, harassed frontiersmen of Cumberland and Georgia; and by the power of guns and ammunition, McGillivray became in fact what he had pretended to be in order to get them, the headman of the Creek Nation.[22]

Unfortunately for McGillivray, the Spanish policy changed at that point from harassing frontier Americans such as Sevier and Robertson to courting them and encouraging their separatist schemes. The Jay proposal to leave the Mississippi closed for many years was still being considered by Congress; and the West was ready to secede if it should be accepted. Spain had to act the sympathetic friend of western Americans, not the source of weaponry to murder them.[23]

McGillivray cast about for a different ally. First, he made a tentative offer to the United States to cede the sought-after Oconee lands in exchange for recognition of the Creek Nation as the fourteenth state of the union. When that proposal failed, McGillivray looked elsewhere for a remedy.[24]

The other contestant among the Creeks for the role of leader, hero, and messiah, William Augustus Bowles, was not a Creek and had no wealth or power. He was a Maryland-born white American, a few years younger than McGillivray, a Loyalist in the War for Independence, who joined the British Army but was cashiered from his regiment while it was stationed at Pensacola. Bowles then joined the Creeks in guerrilla actions against

Georgia frontiersmen. Loyalists were fleeing to New Providence Island (Nassau) in considerable numbers, and Bowles appears to have gathered together a theatrical company and voyaged with it to New Providence, where he had a brief career as impresario, and portrait painter. By dangling prospects of securing Creek trade and Creek allegiance against the Americans, he managed to impress Lord Dunmore, governor of the island, and the British trading firm of Miller, Bonnamy and Company, rivals of Panton who were headquartered there. Throughout his life Bowles could persuade others to believe the image he saw in his enlarging glass; it seems to have been a major factor in his fascination for all kinds of people. As events fell out, in the latter part of 1788, when Spain stopped supplying McGillivray with war materials, Bowles was able to promise a continuance of them from Miller, Bonnamy. So the two men entered into a collaboration, ostensibly in the interest of the Creeks.[25]

It would be difficult to invent two more different characters than McGillivray and Bowles. Here was the Creek chief, cadaverous, sickly, nervous, depressed, indolent, and hating trouble or violence; very rich, capable, and powerful, but aloof and lonely; an armchair general who did not inspire loyalty among the troops; an educated half-Indian living in two worlds and fitting neither of them. Then there was Bowles, a white man living with the Indians as an Indian, who moved as confidently at a reception given by Lord Dunmore as he did naked in a Seminole swamp; a big, handsome youth in the Anglo-American style, but choosing to wear Indian accoutrements of gorget, armlets, and plumed turban, and looking as if he were born to them; "a bold and daring adventurer, a good figure and address," Hawkins later described him. By the age of eighteen Bowles was said to have "grown out of recollection and in every respect like a savage warrior" who led the Indians in battle with reckless courage. He was everything to everyone. On a visit to London he exhibited Indians as a sideshow at Vauxhall, went about in Indian dress, promoted a dish called "fricassee des Cherokys," and devastated a highborn lady with his charm. The Creeks seem to have been infatuated with him, although he often failed them; the Cherokees hung his portrait in their houses. The "Director General of the Creek Nation," or "Ambassador from the United Nation of Creeks and Cherokees," or "General & Commr in Chief of the Muskogee"—as Bowles variously styled himself—was a strong stimulant, better than drink, although it appears he distributed that, on occasion, too. McGillivray, although not yet thirty when the two men met in 1788, was an old man in his addiction to quiet, ease, and comfort; Bowles, then about twenty-four, was quicksilver. When McGillivray at age thirty-four was reported to have gone into retirement, a Bowles follower remarked that "indeed it was time, as he was almost out of Date."[26]

The two men met in July 1788. Bowles gave McGillivray a present of ammunition that he had procured from Miller, Bonnamy, and he promised more in the autumn if McGillivray would join him. McGillivray promptly used this overture to induce Spain to resume arms supplies. In November, Bowles returned from a short trip to Nassau with some more presents of munitions from Miller, and he persuaded a rather small number of Creeks to follow him in an attack on Panton's stores on the Saint Johns River in Florida. The Indians were discouraged by bad weather and the rumor—false, as it happened—that a Spanish cavalry unit was approaching, and the expedition petered out, but not before it had alarmed Spanish officials.[27]

By spring 1789, Bowles had retreated to Nassau. By summer the Spanish resistance to resumption of supplies showed signs of softening, and in September, just before McGillivray went to meet the commissioners at the Rock Landing, he learned of the Spanish trade and arms concessions he had hoped for. Thus fortified, he was free to indulge his anger by walking out of the conference with his 2,000 Creeks. "Do you not see my cause of triumph," he gloated to Panton, "in bringing these conquerors of the old masters of the new world, as they call themselves, to bend and supplicate for peace at the feet of a people, whom, shortly before, they despised and marked out for destruction?"[28]

Creek border depredations surged, and McGillivray was about to reach his pinnacle of power over the conquerors at the 1790 treaty of New York. Panton tried to prevent his going to the treaty, but McGillivray was flattered, and his usually bitter mood had been sweetened by a recent offer by Georgia to restore to him his father's confiscated estate. At New York, McGillivray betrayed everyone. Not only did he pledge a large cession of Creek land, but he also agreed to a secret article that virtually promised control of the Indian trade to the United States, a piece of treachery that infuriated the Spanish. He apparently appropriated to himself a gift meant for distribution, saying flippantly that "'tis too much for the few that pretend to it, and too little for the many," and that the six chiefs for whom it was intended "are worthy men, and they get theirs in a way that others know nothing of." Upon McGillivray's return from New York the alarmed Spanish increased his pension to $2,000.[29]

McGillivray's triumph did not last long. He took sick that winter with fever and rheumatism. Word of his disloyalty at the New York treaty quickly spread. Then, to compound McGillivray's troubles, Bowles returned from travels in Canada and a visit to London where he had again been feted, this time because Britain feared imminent war with Spain and courted Bowles for his influence among the Creeks. But the war scare blew over, and neither Bowles nor the southern Indians held any further interest for the British government.[30]

In September, 1791, Bowles returned via Nassau to his Creek friends with a ship and some presents. He did not have much difficulty whipping up the Creeks' anger against the New York treaty and McGillivray, who was so terrified for his life that he fled to the Cherokees and, apparently under orders from Spain, offered $100 for Bowles's capture.[31]

Meanwhile Bowles had used up his presents, but could not organize the Creek uprising on which he had counted. In October, taking refuge among the Oosoochees from assassins whom McGillivray sent looking for him, Bowles had the audacity to profer peace feelers to United States officials, albeit in a stern and threatening tone. "We have retreated from the plain to the woods, from thence to the mountains, but no limits established by nature or compact have stayed the ambition, or satisfied the avarice of your people," he wrote. Warfare could be ended, he said, by a true compact, "not a Clandestine bargain with an unconnected individual, as this present pretended convention with Alexr McGillivray has been." To end bloodshed, Bowles wanted the Congress to send a commission to treat with

Creek chiefs in council at Oosoochee; but, he added, if this were not done with honest intentions, "KNOW that we have enough WARRIORS to stain your land with blood." This message was signed "Genl Wm a Bowles, Director of Affairs Ck Nn. By order of the Supreme Council."[32]

Although a promised arms shipment from Nassau did not arrive, Bowles had managed by January 1792 to round up some Creeks who were willing to try another raid on a Panton store. At the same time he made overtures for a peace meeting to Governor Carondelet in New Orleans. This time Bowles and his Indians completed their mission, investing the store and the Spanish fort at Saint Marks without much trouble. In late February, Bowles had a reply from Carondelet inviting him to New Orleans for discussions about the creation of a Creek state, of which Bowles was to be the head. Bowles should, perhaps, have sensed a trap; his friends warned him. Evidently, however, he found the Spanish governor's message intoxicating; and the manner of its delivery (by a ship of the governor's flotilla which came to pick him up, and on which he was wined and dined by the ship's officers while he made up his mind) gratified his taste for the luxurious. Bowles agreed to sail in the ship to New Orleans.[33]

Carondelet's move was, in fact, the culmination of plots by the United States and Spain, and by McGillivray and Panton, to remove Bowles. The United States, after receiving assurances (false) from Great Britain that it in no way supported Bowles, had promised its assistance to McGillivray in stopping this "bold adventurer, attempting to push his fortune by your destruction." McGillivray had sent his brother-in-law Louis Milfort to dispatch Bowles, but Milfort was instead talked round to Bowles's side. Panton had demanded that the Creek chiefs kill "that villain Bowls," but they would not; he had also written an associate to hire one John Miller to kill him: "I know he has a good gun & a steady hand. . . . If he rids me of that scoundrel he shall never be poor again as long as he lives."[34]

Where guns had failed, butter worked. Bowles had taken Carondelet's delicious bait, promising his Indian friends he would soon be back from New Orleans. The Creeks, left aimless and leaderless at Saint Marks, took what they fancied from

Panton's store and wandered back home. Bowles was seized when he reached New Orleans, and by April was on his way as a prisoner to Havana, whence he was taken to Madrid and finally to Luzon in the Philippines for a long captivity. He was still in prison there in 1796 when Hawkins took up his duties as Indian superintendent. The Indians, however, had not forgotten their friend.[35]

Bowles's capture came too late to help McGillivray, who by his own admission was a nervous wreck from trying to cope with his rival. Bowles had driven the Indians mad, McGillivray wrote Seagrove shortly after Bowles's capture, and "[I] am myself in the situation of a keeper of Bedlam, and nearly fit for an inhabitant." In July he went with Panton to New Orleans, where he and Carondelet made an agreement: McGillivray was to have the Creeks annul the huge cession made at New York, and Spain promised to supply arms enough so that the Creeks could drive the Georgians out of the Oconee River lands on which they had intruded. But this desirable agreement, accompanied by an increase of his pension, could not restore vigor in McGillivray. He was very sick and depressed that fall. In the winter, feeling somewhat better, he set out from his plantation to visit Panton in Pensacola, but was stricken, possibly with pneumonia, on the road. He died in Panton's house on February 16, 1793. Even the corpse of the half-Indian, despite education and wealth, remained between two worlds; Tim Barnard wrote Seagrove, "Our friend Mr. McGillivray has departed this life, and was interred in Mr. Panton's garden, as the Dons would not admit of his being laid in their burying ground." Bereft of both leaders, the Creek Nation and all of the southern Indians fell into a confused and violent mood.[36]

The struggle between McGillivray and Bowles contained elements of all the frontier problems—foreign plots, separatism, nationalism, and also the schemes of the big land speculators to a degree not yet entirely known. To the land speculators, influence with the Indians upon whose lands their claims encroached was a prime necessity. Early in 1790, McGillivray had received a most attractive offer from Alexander Moultrie, head of the South Carolina Yazoo Company, if he would use his good offices with the Creeks.[37]

Bowles, who was never fazed by uncertainty or illegality, probably got himself much more deeply enmeshed than McGillivray in the plots of land speculators and separatists. An aide of Bowles, William Cunningham, questioned by the Spanish to whom he deserted during the 1792 raid at Saint Marks, testified that the attack on the store and fort had been intended as the first offensive in seizing the western South and making it an independent state under British protection. Cunningham also testified that, from Bowles's papers, he had learned "that the whole of it was a plot of conspiracy from Lord Dunmore of Providence, General Clark of Georgia [Elijah Clarke], & Governor William Blunt & John Surveyor [Sevier]" and their fellow speculators "to take possession of Walnut Hill, the Yasoos, Tenesis, Pensacola, New Orleans &c. in order to open the navigation of the Mississippi River, & to make themselves independent of the United States & Britain with the support of the British merchants, for which the different Company's had bound themselves by the double oath of secrecy & performance, having raised about 18,000 mens for that purpose, this plan being formed upwards of three, or four years." Although Cunningham's testimony was self-serving—he had deserted Bowles, he claimed, when he learned of his anti-Spanish plot—and although Britain disclaimed aid to Bowles, everything Cunningham said fits neatly with more reliable and factual evidence.[38]

The most interesting revelation is that Blount, if Cunningham is to be believed, was mixed up in treasonous schemes as early as 1790, when he accepted appointment as governor of the Southwest Territory. Cunningham's testimony about Blount, Sevier, and the lot entirely bears out Hawkins's warning as early as 1787 that westerners must have the right to Mississippi navigation or they would "be disposed to carve for themselves."[39]

It is suggestive, although not proof, of a connection between Blount and Bowles that Blount received from his informants in Indian country communications about Bowles's doings. One correspondent wrote Blount, at the time of the raid at Saint Marks, that "a half pay British vagabond officer introduced himself among them [the Creeks] telling them that he was the man that would restore to them their ancient rights." Another of Blount's agents reported at about the same time on Bowles's status among the Indians; one Richard Justice, ran the report, possessed a painting of Bowles flanked by Cherokee chiefs and also "a number of dining cards, (copperplate) addressed to Bowles while in England, styling him 'commander-in-chief of the Creek Nation.'" When Bowles left Saint Marks to go to New Orleans, Blount passed that information along promptly to Daniel Smith, who with Blount was deeply involved in dubious speculations: "Its pretty certain Bowls has left the Creeks and that McGillivray is returning to that nation," Blount wrote Smith in April 1792. Certainly it is plausible that Blount might have used Bowles to alienate the Indians from the United States and Spain in furtherance of his own long, careful plot to separate the South with British aid, a plot similar to Bowles's except that its motive was profit. Is it also possible that Blount in 1797, as his own plans neared maturity, through Spanish connections and bribery procured Bowles's escape at that very time from Luzon? Bowles did escape, and it is almost inconceivable that without help he could have gotten off the island, made his way to Europe, from there to the British colony of Sierra Leone on the west coast of Africa, thence to the West Indies, and finally back to Creek country. Blount's plot was to be set in motion in the fall of 1797, by which time, with luck, Bowles could have been brought back to Florida to lead the Indians in an uprising vital to the success of the plan: "and if the Indians act their part," Blount wrote in April to his agent James Carey, "I have no doubt but it will succeed."[40]

Presumptive as are the arguments for a link between Blount and William Augustus Bowles—between a wealthy, well-connected United States senator and a half-pay vagabond British officer playing Indian—the known facts strongly suggest it and no known facts refute it; and relevant dates have a logical affinity. Very suggestive also is the fact that in 1795 Blount's brother, John Gray Blount, gave his fourth son a name new in the Blount family records, according to Wheeler's genealogy: William Augustus.[41]

This was the chaotic situation in 1796 among the southern Indians, torn by separatist factions, nationalistic youth, and adventurers for glory or gain, when Hawkins arrived in Creek country to take up his duties as principal agent. It took him a whole year to win the friendship of the Indians, to crack the system of presents that was an integral part of that corrupt era, and to convince the Indians that there could be an honest, just white man who was determined that the Indians should survive.

CHAPTER 4

"Civilization"

We are better clothed and better fed than heretofore, our little daughters have extended their petticoats from the knee to the ancle by their industry and in like manner have clothed some of them, our fathers and mothers. Labour is no longer a disgrace in our land, and our men lend a hand. Hunting has become insufficient to clothe and subsist us, and will soon be resorted to as an amusement for our young men. We shall in future rely on stockraising, agriculture and household manufactures.

BENJAMIN HAWKINS
TO JAMES MADISON, JULY 11, 1803

Never since the arrival in America of the first English colonists had coexistence with the Indians been a viable choice. The Indians would have to be dispossessed of their lands. All that remained to be decided was how this should be accomplished— a decision made particularly painful by the Anglo-American conscience.

An opinion of Chief Justice John Marshall, handed down in 1823, is enlightening. From the discovery of the New World, he said, European nations had agreed among themselves that discovery alone, without conquest, gave exclusive title to the government, or the grantees of that government, whose subjects had discovered a land; title would be perfected by possession. The land "discovered" was the land of the Indians, who were not a few uncivilized savages but numerous bands of skilled tribesmen who had lived satisfactorily before the white invasion. What rights were left to them? The legal situation was fuzzy. Under the law, said Marshall, Indians were conceded to have the limited rights of occupying and using the land, but not the right to dispose of it; use and occupancy rights could be extinguished by purchase or conquest by the sovereign nation—the United States—which held the exclusive, absolute title. By the treaty of Paris the United States had acquired the title by which Great Britain had claimed Indian country south and west of the settled portions of the colonies, and as Marshall stated, if the principle of title by discovery has been asserted and maintained, "if it be indispensable to that system under which the country has been settled," and if the property of the great mass of the community originates in it, then the principle becomes reasonable and cannot be rejected by the courts. Thus, according to Marshall, international conventions, custom, precedent, and necessity make defensible law out of debatable ethics.[1]

Marshall's decision somewhat clarified an earlier Supreme Court opinion, which might stand as a paradigm of ambiguity: "that the nature of the Indian title, which is certainly to be respected by all courts, until it is legitimately extinguished, is not such as to be absolutely repugnant to seisen in fee"—absolute possession—"on the part of the State."[2]

Article 9 of the Articles of Confederation, and its successor Article 1, Section 8, of the United States Constitution, gave to Congress the exclusive right to deal with the Indians. A proclamation of 1783 and later the Indian Trade and Intercourse Act of 1790 prohibited land purchases in Indian country except by authorization of Congress. Indian country in colonial times was generally taken to mean land, or territory, belonging to Indians, occupied by them, and recognized as areas where Indians have a right and title. Later, the self-assumed control by Congress became worked into the definition, so that Indian country was then defined as country within which Indian laws and customs, and federal laws relating to Indians, were generally applicable. Thus the rights of states like Georgia and Tennessee to legislate concerning Indian country south and west of federal treaty lines were restrained.[3]

The declared right of seisin in fee made shallow ceremonies of the picturesque Indian treaties, so far as the law was concerned. Payments for lands were no more than presents to sweeten the Indian mood and prevent hostilities. Secretary of War Knox said in 1787 that such payments, protection money as they plainly were, did not diminish the dignity of the United States. He completed the paradox by adding: "The Indians being the prior occupants, possess the right of the soil. It cannot be taken from them unless by their free consent, or by the right of conquest in case of a just war. To dispossess them on any other principle, would be a gross violation of the fundamental laws of nature, and of that distributive justice which is the glory of a nation."[4]

Knox here raised more questions than he answered. What constituted the "right of the soil"? Did that right necessarily imply the right to farm it or raise cattle on it? What was "free consent"? Was it the consent of one chief, several chiefs, or of all the people of the tribe? What was a "just war"? Would it have to be a defensive war against Indian aggressions, or would war be justifiable if, as Marshall later enunciated, the land in question "be indispensable to that system under which the country has been settled"—that is, by steady encroachment on Indian lands—if the Indians resisted further intrusion? What did Knox mean by "distributive justice . . . the glory of a nation"? Did such justice not depend on the interpretation of "free consent," "right of the soil," and "just war"? The concepts voiced by Knox had been current since early in the Spanish occupation of the New World, when the guiding principle was that the Indians were entitled to the land on which they lived and that it could not be taken from them except for remuneration or in case of that "just war."

Yet, if the twists in Knox's semantic pretzel are difficult for the modern mind to follow, they were perfectly plain to most ordinary people of Knox's time. Governments felt constrained to deal with the Indians in ways that would not damage their "national credibility," in S. Lyman Tyler's phrase. The frontiersmen were to be the villains who did the dirty work—deplored by government—of corrupting, cheating, terrifying, and extinguishing both the Indians and their claims. John Sevier, no scholar, aptly construed the wink given by Knox: "By the law of nations, it is agreed that no people shall be entitled to more land than they can cultivate. Of course, no people will sit and starve for want of land to work, when a neighboring nation has much more than they can make use of." Another expression of the lebensraum defense came from James Wilkinson, who told the Creeks that, if they would not sell the land sought by the United States, the president would be "under no obligation to extend his cares to a people, who withhold from others what they cannot themselves enjoy." So much for "free consent." Concerning "right of the soil," some white intruders in Chickasaw country complained to the president that in the huge tribal territory each individual Chickasaw averaged 100,000 acres, and all they used it for was "to saunter about upon like so many wolves or bares," while good white citizens "must be forsed even to rent poore stoney ridges to make a support to rase their families on." Such a situation, to their mind, was not "distributive justice," and anyway bears and wolves were not tax-paying citizens. A Kentucky pioneer asked if any reasonable person could believe it possible "to prevent the emigration from a barren country loaded with taxes and impoverished with debts, to the most luxurious soil in the world?" No, of course not. John Breckenridge's "Eden of America," James Robertson's "promised land," Andrew Jackson's "promised land that flows with milk and honey"—that land was destined to belong to white Americans. In the next century the inevitability of United States expansion into underdeveloped areas would be given the name "manifest destiny," but the practice had been recognized as such from colonial times.[5]

Thus did ordinary Americans gloss Secretary Knox. Yet, in spite of the vulgarity of popular interpretation of government rhetoric, there is no great difference between what settlers did and what Knox said. It is difficult to support the view held by some scholars that national policy consistently intended to observe treaties and recognize Indian rights to the land, but that this policy was frustrated by aggressive settlers. Rather, as Francis Paul Prucha says, treaty after treaty proves that the federal government meant to prevent intrusion "only up to a point. . . . The basic policy of the United States intended that white settlement should advance and the Indians withdraw." Arthur De Rosier says, "Evacuation of all eastern lands for a new home in the West was the real goal." Or, as Ronald N. Satz has expressed it, "The underlying assumption of American Indian policy was that the eastern tribes would continue to relinquish their land at approximately the same rate that whites demanded it." Government's appeals to natural law and distributive justice, its insistence on acquisition only through free consent or a just war, were backhanded invitations to the people of the frontiers privately to achieve ends that were not consonant with the national glory.[6]

Frontiersmen as a lot are aggressive, self-reliant, acquisitive, and prepared for hardship and violence, or they would not be frontiersmen. Such characteristics made them excellent administrators of a national policy that called for pushing back the Indians; they were useful scapegoats when they pushed too hard and trouble ensued. This is not to suggest that national policy was based on a national character of viciousness, greed, and deception, though the characters of many of the frontier administrators could be so described. National policy was based on sheer necessity. The country had to expand its borders or shrivel. It had to satisfy the pleas of its citizens for land, had to acquire public lands for both civilian and military claimants, had to have land to sell to pay its tremendous war and postwar debts—or become bankrupt. Under those circumstances, although the nation did not condone evil acts, it cultivated a useful skill at blinking them, even when land jobbers were the major gainers, not the nation as a whole nor its needy citizens. Land jobbers and speculators, in fact, were only mildly censured by government, if at all. There was enough milk and honey in the promised land for all to share.[7]

The land was enticing, and, according to white concepts, unused. "The tribes claimed it, and the white men wanted it," in Bernard Sheehan's succinct summation, and men who had thought most profoundly about the problem "knew that in the end the Indian must give up the land." That was the long and short of United States policy, although the means of achieving its goals changed from time to time, president to president. For the policy to succeed, however, it was necessary to change or remove or destroy the Indians, because they were one with their land.[8]

The southern Indians and their land had been the subjects of earlier attempts at change. The big open country had presented a vacuum, which nature and the Indians did not find abhorrent, but which seemed intolerable to white men. Sir Alexander Cuming, a Scotsman who migrated to South Carolina and thence to Cherokee country, had petitioned the British crown in 1748 to let him colonize the Southeast with Jews. At about the same time a utopian socialist Christian Gottlieb Priber had proceeded far enough in his plans for Indian independence to alarm the French and English colonial offices. Priber, a well-educated German, went out to "Paradice," as he called the Cherokee country, and lived with the Cherokees as one of them. All that is known of his plan is that he meant to make a communal state of what in fact was one, but with the addition of some radical reforms, such as equality of the sexes and state education of children. His influence with the Cherokees so alarmed the British colonial governors that, claiming he was a French agent sent to stir rebellion, they had him murdered.[9]

The next important Indian-changer was Hawkins, who was sent to "civilize" the southern Indians, changing them into people who farmed instead of hunting, whose laws, government, and system of justice would conform to Anglo-American practice, and who would eventually respect the institution of private property and cherish it as a privilege bestowed by God.

Hawkins owned Adair's *History of the American Indians*, and so we may assume that he knew about Priber, of whom Adair wrote. Hawkins's own philosophy, however, was not utopian nor socialist, but a combination of eighteenth-century rationalism and nineteenth-century capitalism. He had little or no interest in formal religion and made no attempt to convert the Indians to Christianity. He tolerated Moravian missionaries in his agency because they could improve the Creek economy by making useful objects, such as spinning wheels and butter tubs, but he did not encourage their efforts to bring the Indians the Christian gospel. Included in Hawkins's library was the key work of the new, radical philosopher William Godwin, whose hypotheses were that reason, not religion, could bring man to a state of perfection, and that character was not purely predestined but could be shaped by environment. These basic tenets may well have influenced Hawkins's thought, for he relied heavily on reason in dealing with the Indians, and his whole work was based on the assumption that their character could be changed by white civilization; that they would then no longer be Indians but rather red men with white values and characteristics.[10]

This raises the questions, What was the Indian character? Or what was it believed to be? What kind of men did Hawkins expect to encounter when he paid his first visit to the Indians?

There is persuasive logic in the thesis that to white men the Indian had no existence as a real person, but was rather an embodiment of white expectations, which in turn depended on white goals. The main goal was and always had been acquisition of land. From the minds of the earliest English colonists to arrive in Virginia and settle on Indian land, men who because of their own reverence for the institution of private property expected violent opposition to their intrusion, came the image of the Indian as an uncoooperative, hostile, savage, treacherous, murderous creature; and the Indians' disinclination to destroy the handful of colonists, but rather to shelter, feed, and aid them, was interpreted as proof of their guile. Revenge deferred was a favored explanation of the Indians' perplexing friendliness. This expectation gave rise to the characterization that they were "so malitious, that they seldom forget an injury." When Indians kept alive the few sick and starving Virginia settlers with gifts of corn and meat, it was reasoned that this kindness "probably boded the little colony a future harm." The colonists felt vindicated and relieved of unwanted love when the Indians finally struck back at them in a massacre that wiped out one-third of the Chesapeake colony: "Our hands, which before were tied with gentleness and faire usage, are now set at liberty by the treacherous violence of the Savages," reported the survivors. Plainly, a bad Indian character was essential for the realization of white goals. "Now their cleared grounds in all their villages . . . shall be inhabited by us," wrote the Virginia colonists. In New England, Indian kindness was an obstacle to the accomplishment of God's ends. John Winthrop wrote that an epidemic of 1617 was the Lord's work, and that the Indians "are neere all dead of the small Poxe, so the Lord hathe cleared our title to what we possess."[11]

The stereotypic bad Indian attracted to himself all sorts of undesirable traits and emerged in the records of the Virginia

Company as a creature "slothful and idle, vitious, melancholy, slovenly . . . lyers, of small memory, of no constancy or trust . . . sottish and sodaine, never looking what dangers may happen afterwards, less capable then children of six or seaven years old, and less apt and ingenious."[12]

Contrast these opinions of intruding settlers with those of men who had no designs on Indian land, and an opposite image emerges, that of Rousseau's noble savage. Francis Baily, a young English traveler, told of a party of Cherokees whom he had met along the way: "They advanced and shook hands with us, and accosted us with the title of 'good brothers'; . . . they appeared to commiserate our situation, laid their venison before us . . . and seemed to take a pleasure in being able to gratify us. . . . I could not but admire their simple mode of living. . . . They appeared to me perfectly happy in this their primitive state of man, and to enjoy all the pleasures which so simple a state, unsophisticated by the false refinements of life, seemed to afford." Vicomte François Auguste Chateaubriand, after a journey in 1791, spoke thus of the Indian life:

> Why does one find so much charm in the life of the wild? Why does the man most given over to thought forget himself when joyously in the tumult of the chase? To go through the woods, to pursue wild beasts, to build one's shelter, light one's fire; to prepare one's own meal near a spring is, indeed, a very great happiness. Thousands of Europeans have come to know this happiness and have wanted no other, while the Indian dies of grief if shut up in our cities.

James Adair, that trader extraordinary of the following century, knew the Indians too well to see them as all good or all bad. He described them as persevering, discreet, temperate, faithful to the tribe, but also crafty, and vengeful for the killing of a loved one "to a degree of distraction."[13]

One other observation of Adair's throws fresh light on the general low opinion of Indians among white Americans. Indians did not much esteem wealth, Adair wrote, considering it a transient thing, much better to share than to save. Antoine du Pratz, a historian of Louisiana, commented that Indians were more generous than some civilized people, who would not permit themselves to be compared with the Indians "for want of knowing or wishing to give things the values they deserve." For

most white men wealth was the highest value, and the Indians
dared insult it. Indian indifference to wealth was taken as either
stupidity or an intolerable assumption of superiority.[14]

John Lawson, an early eighteenth-century observer of Indians in North Carolina, commented on the Indians' extraordinary awe for life. Material losses were greeted with laughter, as
trivial misfortunes; but if a relative or friend was killed, they
went into long and deep mourning and became very pensive.
Indian improvidence, Lawson said, was actually generosity:
"They are really better to us than we are to them, they always
give us victuals at their quarters, and take care we are armed
against hunger and thirst; we do not do so by them, (generally
speaking) but let them walk by our doors hungry and do not
often relieve them." We look upon them with scorn and disdain,
Lawson observed, but in truth "for all our religion and education, we possess more moral deformities and evils than these
Savages do."[15]

Nurturing the image of the Indian as savage, not noble savage,
were the sensational stories so popular in Hawkins's time of persons who had been, or pretended to have been, held captive
by Indians. Earlier captivity narratives had been more or less
genuine, their tone one of pious gratitude for deliverance from
the savages; but in the period of the French and Indian wars
and the Revolutionary War captivity stories were often written
as propaganda against the Indians, who mostly sided with the
enemies of the colonists, French or British. They thus became
atrocity stories, stressing the guile, cruelty, and savagery of the
Indians, who were pictured as naked, lascivious people who co-
habited "like beasts without any reasonableness." By 1800 the
captivity story had become a literary form catering to a public
hungry for cheap sensationalism, and its incidents, far more
often invented than true; it was a native American contribution
to the Gothic literature that was immensely popular among
readers of fiction in the early nineteenth century.[16]

Purportedly scientific corroboration of Indian inferiority was
provided by the "deficiency" theory of the French naturalist
Georges Louis Leclerc, compte de Buffon, who claimed to have
proven that the flora, fauna, and aborigines of the New World

all showed the degenerative influence of that environment. In describing Indian men, Buffon contradicted the lascivious beast image projected by the captivity stories, claiming that Indian men were inadequate in sexual drive and performance due to the unusually small size of their penises. This accusation gave rise to rebuttals and explanations that were almost as titillating as the captivity narratives. All kinds of people—historians, travellers, traders—sprang to the defense of Indian lustiness. Jefferson was a staunch defender of Indian capability and of the equality or superiority of American plants and animals, of which he wrote glowingly in his *Notes on Virginia*. While Jefferson was in Paris in 1787, Hawkins sent him an assortment of American plants, in care of "M. Le comte de Buffon, intendant du Jardin du Roi," perhaps to be used in refutation of Buffon's calumny.[17]

After 1800 the myth of the bad Indian served a useful propaganda purpose for a white nation increasingly in need of the land where Indians lived and hunted. Jefferson as a young man, probably under the influence of Rousseau, had questioned the ethics of taking Indian land: "Whoever shall attempt to . . . reconcile the invasions made on the native Indians to the natural rights of mankind, will find that he is pursueing a Chimera, which exists only in his imagination, against the evidence of indisputable fact." If the Indians became "civilized," the whites believed, they would not feel invaded, but rather would welcome settlers to their lands. Hawkins described the civilization program as Jefferson's idea, calling it in a 1798 letter to Jefferson, "the benevolent plan devised by you for bettering the condition of the Indians in the southern part of the United States." But more than a dozen years earlier, at the Hopewell treaty, Hawkins himself had enunciated the germ of the benevolent plan. In 1807, after he had administered the plan for more than two decades with remarkable consistency, he described it as follows: "The plan I persue is to lead the Indian from hunting to the pastoral life, to agriculture, household manufactures, a knowledge of weights and measures, money and figures, to be honest and true to themselves as well as to their neighbors, to protect innocence, to punish guilt, to fit them to be useful members of the planet they inhabit."[18]

In November 1796, Hawkins left the civilized world of Philadelphia to undertake his mission as Principal Temporary Agent for Indians Affairs South of the Ohio. At last, after a month or more of hard travel slowed by illness, Hawkins was able to rest a few days at the home of Alex Cornells, whom he had come to know at Colerain.[19]

Very soon, however, he was on the move again, acquainting himself with the country and its people. He visited throughout the Creek Nation during that frosty winter, calling on trader Timothy Barnard on Flint River in February, but soon going on to Fort Fidius on the Oconee, which guarded the Georgia frontier. In March 1797 he received his commission to run the treaty lines between the Indian nations and the United States, and was off again to meet his fellow commissioners Andrew Pickens and James Winchester at the Tellico blockhouse in the Cherokee country. He was to run the line of Blount's Holston treaty, made with the Cherokees in 1791 and now protested by the tribe. Then, intermittently from 1797 to 1799, Hawkins was working with surveyor Andrew Ellicott to establish the line between Spanish and United States territory set by the Pinckney's treaty of San Lorenzo in 1795, his efforts constantly being frustrated by Spain and the Creeks. Bearing in mind all that travel meant riding through extremely rough country, in all weathers, by a man who was seldom in good health, Hawkins's perseverance and dedication to duty stand out as truly remarkable. He could even write, during a seizure of gout so disabling that for a week or more he was scarcely able to turn in his blankets: "I find my mind disposed to buoy itself above the whole, and I find some amusement in the certain progress of the benevolent views of government intrusted to my superintendency."[20]

It becomes apparent in overview that Hawkins was required to act as both anesthetist and surgeon on the Indians. Through treaties and the running of treaty lines, he used the knife to pare away Indian lands, and between times he dulled the pain of loss of "their blood and their life," as the Indians regarded their land, by teaching them the pleasures of husbandry, honest trade, and better living conditions. He got to know them as few government officers had, because he made his home among them; he despised the former agent, James Seagrove, who had operated from the safety and comfort of his seaside residence at Saint Marys, far from the Creek towns and forests.[21]

Trade, dependable and on favorable terms, was the most popular feature of the civilization plan with the Indians and the least dislocating to their traditional ways. Especially vital to them was a regular source of guns and ammunition; without these for the annual winter hunt, there could be no deerskins or furs to offer in trade. The two federal stores established by the Trade and Intercourse Act of 1796—one for the Cherokees at Tellico and the other for the Creeks at Colerain—after some early grumbling because the stores did not extend credit or give presents became welcome and essential parts of Indian life. When, in the summer of 1797, the Creek store was moved north to the new Fort Wilkinson on the Oconee River, a more convenient location for the Indians than the Colerain site in the far south of the Creek Nation, it was much frequented both for business and as a social meeting place. The old system of trade, depending on personal and international rivalry, had been notably unreliable, and the Indians had too often been at the mercy of traders, honest or dishonest, in their towns and villages. The government acts not only established the stores but also provided for strict licencing of traders; the Indians could ask and obtain the removal of any whom they felt were bad or dishonest.[22]

One of Hawkins's favorite parts of the plan of civilization was the opportunity it afforded to help the Indians produce better food and some of the other necessities of life by their own efforts and skill; he was a convinced Jeffersonian agrarian. The self-sufficiency of the Southern Indians had been deeply eroded by the ease of getting white trade goods for skins and gifts for promises of peace, but a number of skills had managed to survive the corrupting influence of trade. Creeks built sturdy-enough houses of wood and plaster, with bark or shingle roofs and chimneys of sticks and clay; Chickasaws made two-part houses joined by a covered passage. These techniques and designs, suitable to the climate and using plentiful materials, were imitated by white settlers throughout the South. The Indians made canoes, hunting and fishing gear, and big mortars and pestles for grinding corn, the staple crop. These were all men's tasks, as was the bringing in of game, which provided meat and skins for clothing. The Indians also knew how to tan and dress skins, but that was generally women's work. The women also spun thread by hand from plant fibers and animal hairs and could weave it into cloth on a frame sophisticated enough to produce patterns. Women did a lot of the gardening in the individual family gardens of vegetables, and the whole village turned out to work the big communal fields of corn. Among other necessities made by the women were pottery, moccasins, and clothing. If the southern Indian technology could not be called advanced, neither was it so primitive that the Indians could not deal pretty well with their life.[23]

But Hawkins was to bring them technological improvements to enrich their living. He introduced cotton culture, the spinning wheel, and modern looms, so that they could make quantities of their own homespun cloth instead of buying it. Iron ploughs and hoes; new improved strains of seed, plants, and fruit trees; modern methods of fertilizing and cultivating food crops; domesticated cattle to fatten on the fine grass and cane of Indian country—all these innovations brought by Hawkins made life more pleasant, secure, and healthy, and like the trading houses, they gradually became desirable to many of the Indians, although some of the younger warriors firmly held that to give up the traditional ways was to lose some of the ancient pride and freedom of their tribes.

They were, in fact, brushing the truth. The Indians' problem in the 1790s was not so much a slippage of skills as an expansion of needs. The simple requirements of their earlier living had grown accretions of all manner of desires, from dainty textiles to table luxuries such as coffee, cane sugar, and whiskey; such cravings could not but corrupt the ancient values and burden the ancient freedom born of self-sufficiency. Some of the young warriors held Hawkins responsible for the changes they saw happening, and, indeed, they were right. From the most conscientious and friendly motives, Hawkins's personal goal in dealing with the Indians was to reconcile them to a more re-strained way of life, a pastoral, cottage-industry way of life not too different from that of most white Americans of that time, which would reduce their need for land and prepare their minds "to accommodate the wishes of our fellow citizens."[24]

With game scarce and getting scarcer, and a crop failure spelling disaster, most Creeks were willing to accept Hawkins's technological improvements. But they rejected the civilization program where it demanded excision of distinctive features of Indian life and substitution of systems rooted deep in the Anglo-Saxon past that threatened the very core of Indian phi-losophy. One such part of the civilization program was the white system of private land ownership.[25]

Indian land was held in commonalty by the tribe, although each family was allotted a plot to work in the general planta-tion. Traditionally, a portion of the tribal produce was stored in a common granary for famine times or as war rations or for the relief of the needy and the aged; no Indian, therefore, was des-titute, unless all were. Shelter, food, and clothing could be taken for granted like air and water except in the event of natu-ral catastrophes. Accepting help brought no loss of face, because in the Indian economy there was no charity, only hospitality and sharing. The Indians were very conscious of the ever-present threat of need because of droughts, floods, or epi-demics human or animal, or because of old age, sickness, or be-reavement. To the southern Indians there simply was no choice between their communal land and mutual-support systems and what the white men—with their greater control of nature and disease and cultural pride in self-support—had to offer: a pri-vate, separate piece of land to live and die on.[26]

Yet, for the United States to achieve its goal, the change from communal to individual property had to be effected; it was the gate to the rainbow at the end of which lay the coveted pot of gold, Indian lands. The "civilization" process would, in the views of Washington, Jefferson, Knox, Hawkins, and many others, bring peace to Indian-white relations, but before it could succeed, the solid opposition of the Indians to giving up their ancient communal land system had to be breached. Secre-tary Knox thought a good way to start would be to give the chiefs presents of sheep and cattle, which would diminish the need for large hunting grounds and also encourage fencing off parcels of land, which in turn, it was hoped, would stir in the Indians an appetite for sole and exclusive ownership. Such a change, however, would cut right to the heart of Indian thought and religion. Indians conceived of themselves as joint tenants of hunting grounds that the Great Spirit had given their ancestors, which they were committed to leave to their offspring. The land was literally their blood and their life because of the wild animals with which the Great Spirit had stocked it for their sustenance. The Indian concept of heaven was a warm, pleasant country of forests and savannas, with plenty of game and fish—in fact, merely a glorification of their wild, earthly abode. Totally at odds were the white convictions, expressed by Lewis Cass in 1830, that "there can be no doubt that the Creator intended the earth should be reclaimed from a state of nature and cultivated" and that "a tribe of wandering hunters . . . have a very imperfect possession of the country over which they roam."[27]

Cass was of a later day, but the Indians had not changed. They still resisted selling land; content to live as their fathers had lived, they were not ambitious or emulative of others of greater substance. Therefore, Cass lamented, "the *fulcrum* is wanting, upon which the lever must be placed" to hoist the Indians out of their ancestral lands; they opposed accumulation of wealth and private ownership of land and were "clinging with a death-grip to their own institutions."[28]

Hawkins believed that the fulcrum for moving the Indians out of a savage state was not so much inculcation of love of wealth as respect for the Anglo-Saxon system of government. That institution called out Hawkins's passionate devotion. He had written glowingly of it, while he was in the Senate, to his friend Governor Blount: "You cannot, from anything heretofore known to you, form any, or rather but an imperfect idea of the dignity and respectability of our government."[29]

Hawkins would not, therefore, have seen anything absurd, outrageous, or arbitrary in imposing suddenly upon the Indians a system of government that was the accretion of centuries of experimentation by a people with totally different values, a system laboriously constructed, in fact, to protect property and life, and ultimate property. Hawkins believed that for peace on the frontier the absolute essentials were centralized authority, a congress of elders, accepted definitions of crime, and when individual guilt was determined, firm and fair-handed punishment of the criminal by the nation.

By great effort and attention Hawkins had some success in centralizing executive authority among the Creeks in a national council of chiefs, or *miccos*, representing the various towns. The council met in formal conclave once a year in the spring after the men had returned from the hunt. Here was another innovation not altogether new, because the Creeks traditionally had town councils, each headed by the micco, who with his counsellors and warriors met every day in the town square to discuss local matters.

As Hawkins described the national council several years after its inception, it was a model body of executive-legislative powers. No one member insisted on his own opinion, Hawkins said; everything was discussed and debated in an effort to reach consensus:

> The cessation of the debate becomes the signal of unanimity. No vote is taken in form among them; there is no numbering of the yeas and nays; but the chief simply pronounces in an interrogative tone of voice: "You are agreed then upon this measure?" if it be a question of war, the principal warrior addresses the chief, and demands: "Is it war?" The speaker answers, "It is war"—at that moment the warrior lifts up the tomahawk, and the question is supposed to be irrevocably decided.

Decisions of the national council, Hawkins said, become part of the common law; chosen rememberers, who are "the historical and legal libraries of the tribe," listen to the decisions of the council, so that they can recite them later and thus pass them on as part of the traditions, history, and law of their nation. Bartram was one of several observers who had commented on the excellent civil government, without coercive laws, of the Creeks.[30]

In attempting changes in the Creek systems of justice and punishment, however, Hawkins was working not with but against Creek traditions. He met stubborn opposition in trying to persuade the Indians to substitute Anglo-American practices of arrest, trial, and punishment by law for the ancient practice of personal retaliation, without due process, and often practiced on some innocent relative of the person deemed guilty if he himself could not be found. In a more peaceful time Hawkins's efforts might have been better received, but since the signing of Blount's Holston treaty in 1791, Tennessee frontiersmen had poured through the opening that the treaty claimed to have created, and the Cherokee borderlands were tumultuous with intruders and resistance. At the same time the Creeks, repudiating McGillivray's treaty at New York and encouraged to defiance of it by Bowles, were angrily opposing the intrusion of whites from Georgia. Violence remained at a peak for several years after the removal from the scene in 1792 and 1793 of the two contending leaders, Bowles and McGillivray, and was still running strong when Hawkins arrived. Complaints of thefts, scalpings, murders, and other atrocities committed by Indians in that period were quite possibly true; and there is much evidence that whites instigated the violence and retaliated in kind. It was an unfortunate time for any white man to attempt to teach the Indians white ways of dealing with crime and criminals.[31]

A count taken from the records seems to show that most of the serious crimes were committed by whites, not Indians, and that most of these were unprovoked except by the circumstance that the Indians were where whites wished to be. Indians killed almost entirely for revenge, if not in self-defense; in both cases, bloodily. Few of the white murders seem to have been crimes of passion or pure bloodthirstiness, although the names of David Morgan, Mike Fink, Simon Girty, and Alexander Outlaw became synonymous with senseless, horrid savagery. Even Alexander Outlaw was no simple homicidal maniac. In 1784 he had been an Indian commissioner and a militia officer of the State of Franklin, and he was its observer at the treaty of Hopewell in 1785. In 1789 he was the representative sent by North Carolinians to present to Congress their claims on Indian lands. It is interesting to note that when Joseph Martin wrote the secretary of war that Outlaw was murdering women and children in indescribably inhuman ways, doing all in his power to drive the Indians to desperation, Martin was defending himself against complaints by Outlaw. It was still more curious, however, that until 1788 both men had been working for William Blount's land interests; Martin held the title of agent to the Cherokees, but after that date he seems to have involved himself in the speculations of a rival land company, and by 1789 he was referred to as "the late agent to the Cherokees." Outlaw stayed with Blount and was still on his payroll the year of the Holston treaty, earning $146.92 for the year 1791. And he was a scourge to the Indians throughout.[32]

One purpose of the white violence on the frontier was to provoke Indian retaliation, in the hope of persuading the federal government to declare full-scale war against the southern tribes—Knox's "just war." The federal government, however, knew what was going on. Washington in 1792 said that a Colonel Alexander and other settlers were "with nefarious means" doing everything that they could to bring on war between the United States and the Creeks; as early as 1787, Alexander had deliberately killed seven Creeks of a small Cusseta village. Captain John Beard, hired most likely by Blount, crossed the Tennessee River in June 1793 and killed a number of unoffending Cherokees. John Sevier in 1792 and 1793 remorselessly pursued and killed many Cherokees and destroyed 300 head of their cattle to starve them into selling land. In July and August 1793, Sevier led out the Tennessee militia against the Lower Cherokees; and, also in August, colonels Doherty and McFarland took 180 volunteer riflemen and destroyed six Indian towns. Finally Sevier, who had been killing Cherokees since the early 1780s, was given cause for retaliation in November 1794, when Indians attacked the forted home of his brother Valentine, killing or wounding a number of Valentine's sons. Two years later, when he was governor of Tennessee, John Sevier cried for vengeance. He wrote the secretary of war that the tribes were licentious, "educated to a vagrant, lawless, debauched and immoral life"; and would be stopped by nothing but the certainty of "harsh and cruel" punishment. He cried out in the name of self-preservation for the War Department to "put the aggressors in such a condition as will prevent them in future from being guilty of like offences."[33]

The assaults on Indians never paused. In September 1794, James Robertson, with Governor Blount's acquiescence, ordered Major James Ore and the Tennessee territorial militia to prevent future aggressions of the Lower Cherokees by totally destroying their towns of Nickajack and Running Water, the two main crossing places of the Tennessee River from Indian country. Robertson is quoted as having said afterwards, "If I have erred, I shall ever regret it; to be a good citizen . . . is my greatest pride and to earn the approbation of the President."[34]

White aggressions were not in the nature of a battle with a limited objective and therefore a foreseeable end. As Washington wrote to Timothy Pickering, his second secretary of war, "I believe scarcely any thing short of a Chinese Wall, or a line of Troops will restrain Land Jobbers, and the Incroachment of Settlers, upon the Indian Territory." It is plain that almost all the white aggressions were for land, to settle or to sell, mostly the latter. The terrible destruction wrought by Captain Harrison upon the Lower Creek town of Padgeeligau was a bleeding wound in Indian memory when Hawkins took over the agency; in 1797, Indians were still retaliating murderously whenever they had a chance, and Hawkins's clerk, Richard Thomas, told him that they would not stop "until you had Harrison brought to the Fort & executed." When two unoffending white men, John Gentry and a Mr. Brown, were killed by Creeks, Hawkins said the cause was "that murderous business of Harrison." Harrison does not appear to have been punished any more than were Ore, Outlaw, Alexander, Beard, or any other of the assassins; all of them had a powerful protector, William Blount.[35]

Hawkins's efforts to teach the Indians respect for punishment by process of law were vastly handicapped by the example of whites constantly flouting the law with impunity. For example, Zachariah Cox, Blount's agent, whose previous efforts to seize land at Muscle Shoals had been frustrated by the Indians, made another sortie early in 1797, in outright violation of treaty lines. In August, Hawkins alerted Secretary of War Pickering, who took a hard line against intruders, and was able to call on federal troops to stop Cox's expedition; in November, Hawkins was still waiting to hear of Cox's arrest, trial, and punishment.[36]

Yet Hawkins, by extreme firmness and fair dealing, and by

setting troops to guard the Georgia and Tennessee borders against intruders, did at the outset of his career as agent make headway in curbing Indian crime and the system of retaliation. Horse stealing by the Indians was one of the commonest causes, or excuses, for white raids on Indian settlements, and Hawkins wisely concentrated at once on curbing this crime. He appealed to the Creeks to make their young men stop taking horses, even when the animals were ranging on Indian land, saying frankly to the chiefs that "every theft of a horse might be considered as the stealing of a plantation from the Creeks," and that unless they could put an end to the evil it would bring ruin on their land. Tennesseeans who had horses stolen got passports to go into Indian country in search of them, and, of course, trouble ensued, often "the stealing of a plantation." But Indians would go on taking horses as long as whites offered a ready market for the stolen animals. To stop illegal purchases, Hawkins instituted a system of special licenses issued by his department to anyone wishing to buy a horse. Anyone suspected of having stolen property could be required to produce his license, which was proof of legal purchase and showed from whom the horse had been bought. Also, all Indians with horses to sell were required to report them to the agent, and get from him a certificate describing the horse and naming the seller.[37]

To trace horses reported stolen, Hawkins employed Sackfield Maclin to travel the whole Indian country collecting all the stolen horses that he could find. Maclin did his job well, but the intricacies of it are evident from the history of one case, which undoubtedly was representative of many: John Galphin came before Hawkins and swore that a horse now in the possession of David Walker was the same horse that he, Galphin, had bought from Emautly Haujo of Coweta. Emautly Haujo had told Hawkins that the horse had been stolen from Peyton T. Smith of Greene County, Georgia; Galphin further swore that he had sold the horse to John Mulegan of Savannah, and Mulegan sold him to John Randolph of the Tensaw settlement on the Mississippi, and Randolph sold him to Lachlin Durrants, who sold him to his father Benjamin Durrants (the last step, from Benjamin Durrants to David Walker, was not accounted for). It is very unlikely that Hawkins, although a humorous man, found anything funny in this story. He had to stop the theft of horses, which he said, was "the source of endless mischief, and unless I can check it . . . will totally frustrate the benevolent plans of the government."[38]

Nonetheless, Hawkins's presence and obvious sincerity had great impact on the Creeks. They liked his living among them, either at the agency, near Timothy Barnard's on Flint River, or at Coweta on the Chattahoochee, the principle Lower Creek town, or at Tuckabatchee on the Tallapoosa River, among the Upper Creeks, near Alex Cornell's place. At the Creek National Council of 1799, notable progress was evidenced when the dignified Efau Haujo, then Speaker of the Creek Nation, and described by detractors as "a very turbulent fellow" because of his vehemence in opposing frontier intruders and dishonest traders, agreed to Hawkins's request that the chiefs try to stop their youth from stealing horses and punish those who did by severe beating. He told Hawkins, "It is for the good of our land, you have often wished it. You have a regard for our land and wish to see us in peace and quietness."[39]

The concept of punishment by the Creek Nation, instead of the traditional method of personal retaliation, continued to perplex the Creeks. In the fall of 1799, after a party of Creeks raided the camp of the commissioners who were marking the boundary between Spanish and United States jurisdiction, Hawkins sternly took up the matter of their punishment with the chiefs in council. They agreed to punish them, and they did so, most severely; so severely, in fact, that they feared retaliation upon themselves if death resulted from the punishment. Deeply troubled, they asked Hawkins:

> As this is the first time the nation ever undertook to punish and crop people, who violate their laws we want your advice and opinion respecting those who die under the punishment we inflict. Can any one be answerable for executing the orders of the nation in such case?

Hawkins answered:

> If the sticks are used by the Law of the whole nation and a man dies, it is the Law that killed him. It is the nation who killed him. It is not one man or one family. If any one complains and asks for satisfaction this is your answer, Your relation was a rogue and mis-

chief maker, the law says such people must have the sticks, and that is their pay. And if they are killed by the sticks that is their pay. It is the pay of the nation.[40]

Hawkins said that such was the law. The chiefs followed it without completely accepting it, and they went in fear of their lives each time they had to hunt down and kill a man. They did not, therefore, report crimes voluntarily, and they lagged in pursuing criminals. White people, even Hawkins, seemed unable to grasp this; the Creeks' promises to catch and punish criminals, unfulfilled for weeks or months, were considered examples of the lying and deceit of the Indian character. But whites' reasoning did not take into account that the Indians were profoundly troubled by the complex question of individual, as against national, guilt for the taking of life—a problem that has always troubled men's consciences, leading the executioner to beg forgiveness of his victim before bringing down the ax. The deep Indian reverence for life made the problem particularly anguishing.

Hawkins's efforts from early 1797 convinced both Indians and whites that he meant business, that he was no James Seagrove living in ease and giving out presents as life insurance. Timothy Barnard, whom Hawkins had named as one of his deputies, reported in March 1797 that the Indians had never been so peaceable. Some horses were still being stolen, Barnard said, but he was surprised that the situation was not worse, "as the woods on this side [of the Georgia-Creek line] is swarmed with hogs horses and cattle" sent by their white owners to range twenty or more miles within Indian country. A month later Barnard commented that "those red Gentrey has nearly got there eyes open," and that "the frontier Georgians begins to know they are to be under Government Since the troops have got there and your Collo Hawkins has given some of them his opinion." No hunting party could set forth without a pass from Hawkins to a reliable chief, who would take responsibility for the group's good behavior. Although there continued to be some incidents of lawlessness by both whites and Indians, Hawkins believed by the end of his first year as agent that he was making good progress.[41]

For every wise measure that Hawkins took to reduce frontier violence and to eliminate offenses that would bring in retaliation land grabs or outright warfare, equal and opposite measures were taken by others to ensure that Indian land would be seized, tribe would be set against tribe, and if at all possible, war would be declared against all the southern tribes by the United States.

The more honest among the Indian agents had always been complaining of provocation by whites. For example, Joseph Martin in 1789 had said, "There is a party that has such a thirst for the Cherokees lands, they will take every measure . . . to prevent a treaty." James Seagrove in 1793 had said that continued Georgian attacks on Creek towns would weaken the Indians' trust in the good intentions of the president, and they "will be irritated and soured to such a degree . . . a general Indian war is inevitable." Seagrove in 1794 reiterated that all efforts for peace were spoiled by the "outrageous doings of the lawless people of Georgia." Timothy Barnard in 1795 wrote Governor Blount that if encroachments on Indian lands between the Ocmulgee and the Oconee did not stop, it would be impossible to keep the Indians quiet. In 1795 Secretary of War Timothy Pickering, the man finally responsible for Indian affairs, told Blount, "Tranquility on the frontiers is not to be expected while we permit our Citizens to encroach on Indian Lands." [42]

The appeals to Blount by Barnard and the secretary of war were not worth their paper and ink, for Blount stood by his statement that, "if the citizens of the United States do not destroy the Creeks, the Creeks will kill the citizens of the United States; the alternative is to kill or be killed." The Creeks had not the numbers to present a real threat to American expansion, but Blount was determined that they should seem to. The intentions of Tennesseeans were apparent even to a foreign visitor; Louis Philippe, duke of Orleans, commented: "The system of pillage by the whites toward the Indians is always the same. The whites want the land the Indians have in Tennessee." [43]

While the location of the line between Tennessee's Cumberland district and the Cherokee-Chickasaw country was being argued, Blount saturated Congress with a record of Indian offenses within the outside Cumberland, to make his point that the Indians would not desist from killings no matter where the line was drawn. Blount had been preparing a dossier of Indian crimes since his appointment as governor of the Southwest Territory in 1790, from reports that he solicited from his aides, agents, friends, and other correspondents.

There was nothing necessarily sinister in such action by a chief executive, responsible for the welfare of people within his territory; but Blount welcomed the news of killings and scalpings, in many cases inspiring the Indian violence that he professed to deplore, by encouraging, even ordering, expeditions against unoffending Indians (as at Nickajack and Running Water) in order to provoke retaliation or scare the red people out of their homes. He advised James Robertson, his agent, that he wanted particulars on all Indian murders and thefts in Mero District, and minute reports of all Indian parties found on the frontiers, "even if such party does no mischief." Hearsay evidence of Indian depredations was acceptable to Blount. Andrew Pickens informed the governor that he had heard of several murders, all supposed to have been done by Creeks, and passed on a rumor from another agent of Blount's, Leonard Shaw, that a concerted blow would be struck against the Cumberland settlements by Cherokees, Creeks, and recently arrived northern Indians. James Carey, later employed by the Indian department as an interpreter, was in Blount's pay, and Blount's report to Congress in 1793 of Indian violence was based on information Carey provided. David Allison, Blount's man of business, wrote Blount that a party of twelve people moving to Kentucky from Virginia had been fired on by Indians, and two were killed. John Chisholm, the barely literate thug appointed by Blount as justice of the peace, had been deep in separatist and land plots since the earliest settlements in transmontane Carolina. He was one of the chief fomentors and reporters of frontier killings. Among Blount's other chief informants were John Sevier, Alexander Outlaw, and possibly William Augustus Bowles. By 1798, Blount's political and financial situation had taken a drastic downturn. To avoid bankruptcy he had to get possession of the Cherokee lands in which he had heavily speculated, and he continued to pour on pressure that practically maddened the Indians.[44]

In 1798, only months after the line of the Holston treaty had been run, the Indians were again summoned to a treaty meeting, whose purpose was to modify the line to accommodate whites who had already intruded over it. The Indians were angry and frightened. It was obviously an unpropitious time for Hawkins to teach them restraint and nonretaliation. All the gains of his first year as agent were threatened by this new white thrust. The meeting was to be held at Tellico in Cherokee country in the summer; months earlier rumors were spreading through Indian country that produced mistrust of all whites, including Hawkins. To many of the Indians, especially the nationalistic Indian youths, Hawkins was simply one of the feared and hated race of white men.

The mood of the annual Creek National Council meeting at Tuckabatchee at the end of May, just before the Tellico meeting, was tense and suspicious. It must have been particularly trying for Hawkins, who had suffered debilitating attacks of gout for the past three months, to hear his friend, Speaker Efau Haujo, set the keynote of complaints, demands, and rejections:

> The first thing I will mention is relative to the cattle ranging on our lands. . . . when they come over, people who own them must have time to hunt them. . . . When the people come over they must come without their arms. We wish you to discourage all you can the white people from driving their stock on our lands, or permiting them to come over, and we hope you will prevent it if possible. We wish not to encourage our young men to injure their neighbors . . . let them come without arms of any kind, guns or swords. . . . I have no other talk to give you; it is time for us to look about us, our land is small, game is scarce, the white people are on our hunting grounds, particularly near Cumberland and it's neighborhood.[45]

The chiefs complained of vagabonds and bad characters living as traders in the Creek Nation, and Hawkins promised to get rid of them. They complained of whites coming by boat down the Tennessee; Hawkins told them that the Holston treaty permitted this, but that any violations of treaty terms by red or white would be punished. Hawkins's patience was sorely tried by a long discussion among the chiefs about whether they would permit two blacksmiths to continue in the Creek Nation. The smiths were provided for them free of charge under the civilization program to repair and make weapons and tools, and Hawkins thought the discussion indicated insolent ingratitude on the Creeks' part. To these essentially Stone Age people, however, the smith with his fire and bellows, other tools, and skills might seem a kind of fearsome magician, and indeed the Tucka-batchees had killed a black man who worked for the smith, believing him a wizard. Also, jealousy for their land preoccupied the Indians constantly, and they objected to the blacksmiths because, in order to provide these workers with a vegetable plot, a field had been cleared around the smithy. This aroused suspicion, Hawkins's clerk Richard Thomas told him, and the Indians "grumble and groul about the trees that are cut down. . . . they say a fort is to be built there and they are to be made slaves of." At the National Council meeting the Indians talked also of how poor they were, possibly as a bid for presents. When Hawkins suggested that they were not poor while they had so much land that could always be used to pay their debts, the chiefs angrily repudiated the idea. They would pay their debts with anything else that they had, Hawkins observed at another time, "but the land they say should not be touched."[46]

The council meeting continued through the last days of May and the beginning of June, with the chiefs seeming responsive to Hawkins's demands that they prevent their young men from committing robbery and murder, and that they severely punish those who did. The young warriors were infuriated. Hawkins reported to the War Department: "In the evening [of June 3], an old chief called at my lodgings to inform me a large body of Indians armed with hostile views were coming up the river to me." Other chiefs came hurrying to tell him the war party was only five miles off. Hawkins reported the incident as follows:

> The Chiefs immediately ordered my horses to be brought from the woods and saddled. They sent runners to the neighboring towns and called on the Chiefs and Warriors to assemble at my lodging without delay. They then advised me to set out immediately to a place of safety which they named. I replied to the Chiefs, that if the Indians were coming here to find an enemy they would be mis-

taken. I was their friend. That if they were determined for War and mischief, I advised them to take a little time to collect all the rogues and rascals in the nation and march in a body. I would conduct them to Col. Gaither [at Fort Wilkinson] who would soon make them sick of War and mischief.

Hawkins then ordered his horses turned loose, and went to sleep. "In the morning," his report continued,

I found I had been guarded by some of the principal Chiefs of the Land, and this day I amused myself in my little farm and Garden. On the 5th I set out for Cowetuh and had not entered the square five minutes before we heard the War Whoop coming up the river after me in full speed. The town was alarmed, I retained my seat, the Messenger arrived and made his report. The head Warrior was ordered to call the warriors together . . . and declared their determination to defend me, they said they knew there were horse thieves who wished to bring trouble on their land to drive them and their children into the woods and swamps to perish.[47]

The attack on Hawkins was not consummated. The chiefs of the twelve towns on the Chattahoochee, who were present in the Coweta square, after consultation reported to Hawkins that the whole thing was a misunderstanding; the young warriors had meant simply to give him a rousing welcome to Coweta. Hawkins wisely accepted this explanation, and passed it on as fact to the War Department. But to his trusted agent among the Cherokees, Silas Dinsmoor, Hawkins admitted what he preferred not to have the War Department know, that he was having great trouble with the Creeks, and that military intervention might be needed to teach them to respect their neighbors.[48]

After what must have been a shocking experience for a far-from-robust man of forty-four, Hawkins proceeded at once to the appointed treaty meeting at Tellico and some very exasperating encounters with the intruders into Cherokee country, who tried by every trick they could devise, to make Hawkins set the Indian-Cumberland line where they wanted it. For his efforts to play fair with the Indians, he was "calumniated" by the Tennesseeans, who wanted desperately to have him removed from office because of the obstacle that he presented to their illegal speculations.

The pressures from both sides, first from the Indians and

now from his fellow citizens, although borne by Hawkins with patience and diplomacy, may have brought on the excruciating attacks of gout that at once laid him low, leaving him feeble in body and low in spirits. He was ready to resign as soon as he could be replaced. Especially was he disheartened by the Indian rebuff of his civilization program; after the attempt on his life at Tuckabatchee, he wrote to Colonel David Henley of the United States Army: "A proud, haughty beging spoiled untoward race . . . they demand anything they want from a white man, and feel themselves insulted, when refused. [They] think they confer a favour on the donor if they accept of clothes from him [when] naked, or provisions when hungry." Following the Tellico impasse created by settlers and Indians, he told Dinsmoor: "I find all my efforts are ineffectual and that I am left to devise other plans than those I first set out upon." To Sam Mitchell, newly appointed agent to the Choctaws, Hawkins bitterly repeated his indictment of the Creek character: "Having tasted of the sweets of good living and of being supplied by beging or Stealing it is difficult to restrain them."[49]

But Hawkins was ebullient by nature. As he recovered from his attack of the gout, he cheerfully took stock of the accomplishments of his program: the plough in use, new crops and better methods taking hold; cotton being raised from the green seed he had introduced, and spun and woven into cloth by Indian women taught by white women he employed. As for his personal achievements, although the nationalistic young Indians were opposed to him and the changes he wished to make, he stood high in the confidence of the most influential chiefs. The Indians were coming to depend on the government stores, known as factories, and were getting used to Hawkins's no-credit system of trading. Despite the increasing scarcity of game, they were able to bring in enough deerskins to pay for what trade goods they needed.

Life in the Indian agency had grown more pleasant. Hawkins could discuss Indian affairs with Robert Grierson, a very intelligent and progressive trader. He was on confidential terms with his assistants, Timothy Barnard and Silas Dinsmoor; and at the factory there was Edward Price, the factor, a young man of education, with whom Hawkins could talk or correspond about books, history, and philosophy. Also he had found an agreeable female companion. He had been seeking some capable woman to manage the complicated household that he maintained in his log house, with its constant stream of Indian visitors, and he had finally found her in Lavinia Downs, a good housekeeper, a teacher of the household arts to Indian women, and an agreeable companion for his bed.[50]

So he probably set out on his journey through the Creek country in good humor, despite recent troubles, following his own maxim: "Let us be happy when we can, and render others so." "I am going directly into the nation," he wrote after the Tellico meeting, "to visit all the towns, to examine into abuses of every description. . . . I shall omit no opportunity to render every service in my power." And so he did, enjoying the scenery and new experiences, enduring hardships without complaint. Edward Price wrote him from the factory: "Lavinia is with us sleeps alone & says she cannot help feeling her solitary situation these cold nights tis so cold and no glass in our windows."[51]

CHAPTER 5

Trade, Not Treats

Credit is the ruin of every project to better the condition of these people.

BENJAMIN HAWKINS TO MATHEW HOPKINS,
ACTING FACTOR, MARCH 1799

We ought also to recollect that were the Indians to become indebted for goods furnished them by the trading Houses, equal to the amount of their respective capitals, the United States must sooner or later be reimbursed therefore by a cession of land equivalent to the debt.

SECRETARY OF WAR TO HOUSE OF
REPRESENTATIVES, MARCH 1800

BY Article 8 of the treaty of Colerain, signed June 29, 1796, the Creeks agreed to the establishment of "trading or military posts on their lands" at the discretion of the president.[1]

President Washington had urged a trading system under federal military protection since 1790. He believed this was the only way to protect the Indians against "the continual pressure of land speculators and settlers on the one hand; and . . . the impositions of unauthorized, and unprincipled traders . . . on the other."[2]

Secretary of War Knox had strongly supported the president's pressure for a factory, or trading, system. It was, he felt, perhaps the only way to save the southern Indians from extinction as the nation's population inexorably moved westward: "It is a melancholy reflection that our modes of population have been more destructive to the Indian natives than the conduct of the conquerors of Mexico and Peru. . . . A future historian may mark the causes of this destruction of the human race in sable colors." Mingled with Knox's compassion for the aborigines and his constant concern for the glory of his nation, present and future, was his sense of the desperate need for peace on the frontiers. To achieve lasting tranquility, he knew that the influence of Spain must be canceled out, and that it was mostly through its control of trade through Panton, Leslie and Company that Spain was able to keep the Creek border country in an uproar. Knox told this to the president in 1789 and presented two solutions for the intolerable situation: either a punitive expedition against the Creeks, requiring 5,000 troops for two years at a cost of $1.5 million a year, or the much less costly and more effective method of federal stores scattered through Indian country and protected by military posts. The latter solution was preferable, Knox believed, because "the obligations of policy, humanity, and justice, together with that respect which every nation owes to its own reputation, unite in requiring a noble, liberal, and disinterested administration of Indian affairs." The object was to "civilize" the Indians, and although some persons claimed this to be an "impracticable" objective, Knox commented dryly, "This opinion is probably more convenient than just." If it were true, he said, society could not have progressed "from the barbarous ages to its present degree of perfection." Garrisons at the posts could not altogether prevent but would restrain intruders on Indian lands. If they were not restrained, Knox predicted, "in a short period, the idea of an Indian on this side of the Mississippi will only be found in the pages of the historian."[3]

Opposition to a federal factory system protected by troops came, as Knox undoubtedly anticipated, from intruders, speculators, and private traders. Major James Holland, a member of Blount's faction, wrote Blount from Congress before the final reading of the expanded 1796 version of a trade and intercourse act, that he did not believe federal stores would work, because of the "disaffection common to all that are engaged in business in which they are not principally interested." His letter concluded, "My heart is congenial to every motion [in Congress] that will contribute to your Happiness," making it clear that this motion would not. A year later, with the factories established, Governor Sevier of Tennessee wrote Tennessee senators Blount and William Cocke and Tennessee Representative Andrew Jackson that the traders, red and white, spoke of the Tellico factory "with much contempt, and reprobate and despise the measure, frequently calling the President and Congress pedlars and Indian traders. . . . They conceive the present mode of monopolizing the indian trade as a total prohibition intended against every trader in the nation; and in fact they cant well consider it in any other light. Red-headed Will . . . swore 'that Congress was scratching after every bit of a rackoon skin in the nation that was big enough to cover a Squaw's ———.'" The traders were made the scapegoats, but Sevier's real objection to the factory system was that it placed his land and his trading operations under surveillance. A year later he wrote the Tennesseans in Congress expressing his hope that this "infamous" act would not be revived. Sevier's militia officer, James Ore, wrote the governor: "Tellico Blockhouse is particularly offensive to a great number of the influential men of the nation." The blockhouse would certainly make it harder now to swoop down on and destroy Indian villages in the way Ore, with the nod of the Robertson-Sevier-Blount junta, had destroyed Nickajack and Running Water in 1794.[4]

Despite the clamorous opposition, Knox and Washington prevailed in passing and renewing the trade and intercourse act. At Colerain, Hawkins was able to tell the Indians that federal stores and posts would be established; that every item of goods would have a fixed price, which would be posted in every town; that weights and measures would be introduced so that a hunter would get accurate value for his deerskins at the store; and that the stores would stock a full assortment of goods at reasonable, nonprofit prices. The Cherokee factory at Tellico cost $2,005.20 to build and equip. The cost of the Creek factory was not recorded. Furthermore, the act of 1796 increased the appropriation for the Tellico and Colerain factories from the 1795 allowance of $50,000 to $150,000, of which the Creek store would get two-thirds. It was required that the stores should be self-supporting, and that this capital investment would not be diminished. Hawkins highly approved of the factories and the rules for running them. They were under his general charge and guidance, though he was not involved in the daily activities of the trade and did not intervene unless asked to do so by the factor.[5]

The first factor of the Colerain store was provided with a set of detailed instructions on how to carry out his functions and on United States policy in regard to trade and intercourse with the Indians. He was to sell at prices based on cost plus only a third markup to cover expenses (transportation, insurance, losses, hired help), in order to show the friendship of the United States and win the gratitude and good behavior of the Indians. He could sell goods for money or peltry but was not to extend credit, however loudly the Indians might demand it, because credit would subvert the principle of the trade and would necessitate higher prices to make up for bad debts. The factor would have assistants to help in storing and packing skins by methods in which he would be instructed; and he might hire soldiers from the fort at one dollar a day to help handle the skins, make repairs to the building, and do other miscellaneous chores. He would be responsible for receiving the annual Creek stipend, then $1,000 in goods, which was to be kept separate from the trade goods. He would ask the commandant at Fort Colerain to provide whatever guards he thought necessary to protect the factory stock. He was to correspond regularly with the secretary of war on local conditions, with the purveyor to the factories on what goods were needed, and with the comptroller of the Treasury concerning accounts and receipts. He was to send skins to an agent of the government at Savannah, with an invoice to the storekeeper at the Treasury Department in Philadelphia. (From Savannah the skins were shipped to Philadelphia, where they were sold by a reliable merchant or at auction.) Although rum could not be absolutely prohibited at the store, the factor was charged with keeping the Indians as sober as possible while they were trading, "that they may know what they do and be satisfied that the trade is perfectly fair and honest, when they depart." He should firmly encourage them to go home as soon as their business was accomplished, and discourage them from hanging about and getting drunk; if they did get drunk, he must be especially cautious; and at all times he must treat them with candor, kindness, and friendliness.[6]

The instructions add up to a job requiring an agreeable personality, firmness, and tact, as well as a willingness to work hard and the ability to solve new problems and meet unaccustomed situations—and perhaps even personal danger—with cool resourcefulness. For all this the factor was to be paid $1,000 a year, plus food and lodging. His assistants would receive $300 each.[7]

The factor chosen for the Tellico store was James Byers, an honest, hard-working man whom Hawkins liked and trusted, and who gave Hawkins few problems. Unfortunately, Edward Price, appointed factor of the Creek store at Colerain in 1795, was a constant problem and a great strain on Hawkins's patience. A well-educated young Philadelphian, Price probably had never before seen an Indian and he seems to have had little commercial experience. He could correspond with Hawkins about philosophy and Dr. Benjamin Rush's medical theories, and could console his isolation with a few good books and his flute, but he had none of the qualifications required of a successful factor. He was not much of a storekeeper, squabbled with his assistants, and muddled his bookkeeping; he evidently preferred comfort, women, and a bottle to the boring and grubby work of Indian storekeeper; and worst of all, he had an infallible knack for creating factions among his associates, the officers and soldiers of the adjacent garrison.[8]

Price had arrived at Savannah from Philadelphia near the end of December 1795, and was delighted to find that on Christmas day he could sit by an open door in a room where green boughs "clustered with oranges" served as Christmas decorations. When after a three-day sail he reached Colerain, delight turned to dismay. The store was a makeshift wooden building, sixty feet by twenty-four. It was only partially floored and built on marshy ground. A partition divided it into two rooms shelved for merchandise, the back room for storage; the front one, with a long counter, was for trading. Next to the store was the fort, a crude blockhouse, surrounded by the shabby huts of suppliers and officers of the garrison. The troops had not even such amenities, but were housed in tents, their possessions afloat in muddy water whenever it rained. The situation was isolated; the mail from Savannah passed three miles from the post and had to be fetched from there. The only water supply came from the Saint Marys River, and food was limited to the staples that had arrived by then at the store, which was far from any farm or village where corn, vegetables, milk, or poultry might be bought. The few people who lived nearby, Price noted, "have a wretched appearance." Then and there, he decided that a better facility must be built in a more populous and salubrious location. Half a year passed before this was an accomplished fact.[9]

Within a week of Price's arrival, he was beset by a rough lot of private traders clamoring for goods on credit, specifically prohibited by his instructions. Creeks streamed in demanding gifts, led by a notorious beggar called Old Melithee. The Indians had quite possibly been put up to this annoying behavior by James Seagrove, to discomfort Price and especially Hawkins, who was vehemently opposed to giving handouts. Seagrove's former deputy, James Jordan, had been kept on to look after the store until Price's arrival, but he had taken himself off on an extended vacation before Price got to Colerain, leaving in charge another Seagrove man, Eleazer Bullard, who had followed the advice of his former boss to give the Indians presents, send them off happy, and avoid trouble.[10]

The welfare of the garrison was none of Price's business, but he was so moved to pity by the destitute condition of the soldiers that he shared his slim rations with them and wrote urgently to Tench Frances, the purveyor of supplies, telling him that they were sickly, starving, and almost naked. Nevertheless, although the soldiers were penniless—a private earned $4 a month, a corporal $7, and a sergeant $8—Price had great trouble finding any who would work for him at the authorized $1 a day to load wagons, make repairs, and do the weekly airing and beating of the deerskins, which was absolutely essential to prevent their destruction by maggots. The soldiers also ignored the factory rule forbidding them to barter with the Indians for provisions, and they complained bitterly when Price, carrying out his instructions, refused to sell store goods to them, a rule that was later relaxed.[11]

Price's chief trouble with the military seems, however, to have sprung from his own personality. By nature partisan, he struck up a close friendship with a light-hearted ensign, Sam Allinson, and wrangled with everyone else, right up to the commanding officer, Lt. Col. Henry Gaither, and his administrative officer, a Captain Tinsley. Within an amazingly short time, Price had fired Jordan and Bullard, was jailed on a charge by Bullard of appropriating government goods, got into drunken brawls in the store at night, suffered several attempts (probably by the military) on his life, and had an officer, a Captain Martin court-martialed for assault; he ignored pleas for funds by the girl he'd left behind him, who was bringing up his little daughter, and married another girl, Rachel, probably Indian, who bore him a son. He could not conduct business "with a class of people mostly the outcasts of civil society," Price wailed to Hawkins; "While I am deficient both in instruction and information all the wiles & cunning of natural and improved sagacity are displayed from all quarters to discountenance me." If matters did not improve, he wrote desperately, "I fear my crazy system will sink under the task. I think my intellect is affected a little."[12]

After months of frustrating delay, Price was finally able to move the factory goods and equipment from Colerain north to Fort Wilkinson, which had just been completed. He settled in there in July 1797. The accommodations were not much better than those he had left. During the move, maggots had done great damage to the deerskins. Supplies continued to arrive late, and often the most important items, such as gunpowder, were omitted. Price's living quarters were miserably poor; the colonel had appropriated the only room with a chimney, and Price considered dispossessing him.[13]

All these events and disturbances took place between New Year's 1797, and New Year's 1799. Yet trade did somehow go on, and the Indians were generally pleased with it, because they could buy at about half what the traders charged, and because the trade was run fairly, except for an occasional error resulting from the clumsy calculations of the "chalk" system.[14]

For many years the unit of currency of exchange in Indian country had been the chalk, representing one pound of deerskin, with a value of 25 cents. An Indian would bring his horse-loads of skins to the government store. As the skins were piled on the scales a chalk mark would be made on the ground for each pound that they weighed, and the storekeeper in his account book would credit the Indian with so-and-so-many chalks.

While throughout the lifetime of the factory system a pound of skin was worth twenty-five cents at the factories, the value of deerskin in Philadelphia and other markets dropped so much, and expenses such as cartage increased so much, that by 1810 an Indian actually received in trade only about fifteen cents per pound of skin. This devaluation was accomplished by manipulating the prices of the government store merchandise. Prices had to go up in order for the stores to break even, as they were obliged to do under their charter by Congress, but the Indians looked upon such changes with stern disapproval. In 1802, Efau Haujo demanded to know why store articles were higher then than they had been a few years earlier: "Can it be that they are small things growing out of the ground, and as such, we purchased them when we came, and they have now grown larger, and a price accordingly [larger] appears on the same things?" Perhaps Efau Haujo was simply being caustic, which he could be; but more likely, that was a straightforward question wittily put, because Indian culture provided no precedents for price fluctuations. A deer was so much food to be eaten, its skin was so many moccasins or so many chalks in the traders' books. These were eternal values; a deerskin as a commodity in fluctuating national and international markets was quite outside tribal experience. By 1808 the value of skins had sunk so low and expenses were so inflated that the factor was instructed, "The cost of goods should be figured as approximately 68 per cent advance over the marked cost."[15]

Chalks were written thus: O equalled 100 chalks; X equalled ten; I equalled one. Hawkins called the system clumsy, but too long in use to change. The necessity for multiplying by four in translating dollars to chalks led to errors. Hawkins himself on one occasion wrote a voucher for $125 as OXXIIIII chalks instead of OOOOO chalks, and the storekeepers made mistakes on a busy day. Not only skins but all produce that the Indians brought in for trade was credited in chalks, according to weight or measure, by a fixed system of values.[16]

The records of the Creek factory richly illuminate life at the agency. On one particularly busy day, following a dull period, the Indians brought in 1,210 pounds of deerskins, 53 pounds of beaver, one otter skin, 48 assorted small furs, and two small sides of dressed leather for shoes, totaling $366, or 1,464 chalks. In trade for these, they bought blanketing, chintz, bindings, calico, handkerchiefs, a saddle, a looking glass, vermillion, knives, lead, and two gallons of whiskey—and took their one dollar change in cash. Often, as the civilization program took hold, the Creek men and women drove in hogs or fat cattle to sell and brought other products of their husbandry and house-wifery. For example, in 1797 only a few bottles of hickory nut oil (traditionally made by Indian women and declared by Hawkins the equal of olive oil) were brought to the store for sale, although the store paid $0.75 a quart for it; a year later eight gallons were brought in, and the year after 30 gallons; in 1800, when Hawkins raised the price paid for the oil to $1.00 a quart, 300 gallons were brought in by the women. Other products sent to market by the women were corn (of which they were raising more and more), tobacco, cleaned cotton, fowls, eggs, butter, cheese, groundnuts, peaches, chestnuts, turkeys, venison hams and bacon, and a few manufactured articles, including coarse pottery, beaded garters, split-cane basket-sifters and fans, and—Hawkins's special pride—homespun cloth. The produce would be weighed or measured and its value marked down by the storekeeper; he used the standard avoirdupois weights and dry and liquid measures that Hawkins had introduced, instead of the former system of pricing by the basket, bundle, or other nonspecific quantity, a guesswork method "formerly fashionable here," as Hawkins put it. After selling their products, the women had the satisfaction of selecting from the store's stock articles that they needed or desired; perhaps earbobs at fifty cents a pair, sugar at five dollars a pound, or fabrics for clothing, from coarse osnaburgs for work clothes at one chalk per yard to humhums, a fine cambric, at three chalks or more per yard. The women were particularly pleased with the civilization program, Hawkins said, when they found that with a little labor they could clothe themselves from their own earnings. Hawkins commented that the Creek men, who considered women inferiors and treated them as such, were at first afraid that, when women found they could feed and clothe themselves, they would become "independent of the degraded state of connexion between them"; but, he added, the men soon discovered "that the link is more firm in proportion, as the women are more useful, and occupied in domestic concerns."[17]

At the end of a day of pleasurable trading, the Indians, with their tradition of hospitality, expected to be feasted and liquored. They thoroughly enjoyed lingering about the post, talking, teasing, joking, playing pranks, laughing, getting drunk and sometimes quarrelsome. They were very fond of games and betting; it was reported that the women sometimes at one of their ball games "bet with one another every rag of Cloathing they had . . . the Men Bet their horses, Guns, Jewelry." Doubtless, gambling contributed to the high-spirited revelry after a day at the store. Hawkins frequently warned the factors to clear the Indians off when their business was completed, but that was not easy to accomplish without hurting their feelings and perhaps starting real trouble. In any case, their recreations were exactly the same as those of the white civilians and military at the post at the end of a day's work.[18]

Except for the few educated men like Hawkins, there was little to do with leisure time but get in trouble of some sort. Hawkins had newspapers sent him and complained bitterly when they were delayed. He had a substantial library, and frequently ordered new books. Study of Indian culture and language was his pleasure, and he was also an enthusiastic, proselytizing gardener. At Coweta Tallahassee, or Old Town, Hawkins's own residence in the agency, he had "a garden well cultivated and planted, with a great variety of vegetables, fruits and vines, and an orchard of peach trees." After the attempt on his life by the young Creeks in 1798, it was here that he spent a recuperative day, puttering about. The garden was his pride and pleasure, and he gloated in a letter to Colonel Gaither that his seedlings had not been hurt by severe February frosts because "I had covered everything with cornstalks. I expect yours has suffered."

Yet even he craved occasional relaxation in agreeable company. For the uneducated majority on the frontier there were only gambling, whoring, drinking, and violence to break the tedium.[19]

Drunkenness was probably the most pervasively destructive factor on the frontiers and in Indian country, doing more damage than violence or plague. Ever since the introduction of spirits by the white men, drink had been the serpent in Eden. John Lawson, in his 1714 account of North Carolina, said drink and smallpox had killed five out of six Indians within 200 miles of the white settlements in the past fifty years. Another reporter of about the same time, Mark Catesby, said that despite good constitutions few Indians lived to old age, and named drink as the prime killer. Among those who plied Indians with drink were extremely respectable gentlemen, such as the Georgia commissioners at the treaty of Colerain who got the Creeks drunk to cheat them in forbidden private land purchases, as well as the rough soldiers of the Fort Wilkinson garrison who got the Indians drunk to cheat them in forbidden barter, the prestigious commercial house of Panton, Leslie and Company, as well as shifty little traders in Indian villages. The federal factories sold very little rum and whiskey to the Indians, though it appears that some spirits did pass under the counter at times when the factor was absent, and Price accused Colonel Gaither of handing out 200 gallons of whiskey to the Indians as gifts. No doubt the factories would have done a brisker business if they had sold unlimited quantities of spirits, but Hawkins was adamantly against it. All he would permit at the store was a small drink when the men brought in their skins, with lots to eat so that they would remain sober. When Jonathan Halsted was factor in 1805, he grumbled: "When an Indian brings in skins, ⅓ at least is taken to some other place to buy spirits. . . . They'll do it to get the drink."[20]

Many Indians liked to get drunk; so did many of the white man around them. A white observer one hundred years after Hawkins's time remarked that the greatest evil to the Choctaws, more of a menace than any disease, "was, is, and ever will be, Okahumma (red water or whiskey) which, when once formed into habit, seemed to grow to a species of insanity equal even to that so often exhibited among the whites." As a rule, it was Indian drinking that was stressed, and when both white and Indian drinking were mentioned, different terms were used for them. When Indians drank excessively, they were said to become noisy, rude, insolent, and violent; but when the garrison got drunk, gouging eyes and biting noses, Price characterized the brawl as a "drunken frolic." Price did, however, on one occasion write the secretary of war that he had "thought it prudent to retire for a short time (the officers generally being in a state of madness from the effects of our whiskey)." Hawkins tried to reform the hard-drinking John Galphin, but decided that he was "too far depraved to be reclaimed. . . . His passion for strong drink is not to be resisted by any present or future disadvantage." Even the exemplary Alex Cornells could, "forgetting himself," occasionally get drunk and disorderly. References, especially by name, to white men who drank too much are far less common. Timothy Barnard did name two such white men in a letter to Price in which he begged Price to watch over his half-Indian sons when they came to the factory to pick up some supplies; he asked Price not to let his sons visit these men and not to "give these young men of mine two much liquor wile there." The youngest, Barnard said, would not drink, and if the oldest wanted a drink, Price should "advise him against it by telling that a man that trades will neaver doe well if he drinks much liquor." When Barnard and his sons were older, however, a white man said of them, "Like all Indians, they are too fond of strong drink."[21]

Hawkins was angrily aware of the deliberate debauchery of Indians by whites either for pure villainy or in order to cheat them. When first Hawkins arrived in Indian country, he found that William Blount was defying his orders by giving whiskey to the Cherokee chief John Watts. Liquor was a usual accompaniment of treaties, although in some instances the Indians asked that it be withheld, altogether or until their business was finished. Hawkins changed the locus of a treaty in 1801 with the Choctaws from Natchez to a less populous place, because, he said, wherever there was a white settlement the Indians were corrupted. There are numerous records, from Bartram's time and earlier, that the southern Indians insisted in their treaties that no spirituous liquors be brought into or sold in their towns; and a circular was sent to all Indian agents by the War Department in 1802 at the request of some chiefs authorizing severe measures, even revocation of licences, to prevent traders from selling spirits in Indian country. It is perfectly clear that many Indians were aware of the destructive potential of drink and tried to protect their tribes from it.[22]

Traditionally, the Four Nations used no intoxicants, narcotics, or other consciousness changers except on a few ceremonial occasions. They had no experience of alcoholic drinks until white men introduced them. Lieutenant Timberlake, for example, found that even at a feast the Indians served only "water, which, except the spirituous liquors brought by the Europeans, is their only drink." On ceremonial occasions they did use certain drinks that may have produced a state similar to drunkenness. A decoction of a plant called "sou-watch-cau," given to boys at their initiation ceremony, was said by Hawkins to be "intoxicating and maddening"; and the war drink, "nuc-co-ho-you-e-jau," may also have been a stimulant. But the beverage brewed of button snakeroot, which was drunk at the annual boosketah, or green corn festival, and the "black drink" or "bitter drink," a tea-like infusion of cassine yaupon (*Ilex vomitoria*) that was passed about before any serious council or ceremony, were simply emetics, designed to empty the stomach of food so one would think clearly and soberly.[23]

The white man's magic, rum and whiskey—consciousness changers, pain killers, producers of craziness—became a craving of enough Indians so that drinking was known as an Indian "weakness." Indian addicts, like white addicts, had playful metaphors for their habit; whites might "wet their whistles" or "bend their elbows"; Indians called it "sharpening their hatchets," according to a report of treaty commissioners, who added that the Indians had done this so effectively they were "unfit for any business this day." There is no evidence that in the south in the early nineteenth century more red men that white men were drunkards, and a recent study finds no scientific foundation for the common belief that Indians have less tolerance for alcohol than whites. It is therefore impossible to prove the proposition that drinking was particularly a weakness of Indians, in regard to either desire or tolerance.[24]

The records and correspondence of the Fort Wilkinson factory bear ample witness to the drinking of white men in the factory and garrison while Price was factor. A yeasty brew of bored men, whiskey, and camp followers, heated up by Price's divisive personality, frequently blew the bung. Anything might start a quarrel. One night Captain Martin "lost a piece of his nose in a drunken frolic" at the factory. On another drunken, noisy night Martin gouged Price's eye, Price's Rachel got mixed up in a stomping melee, and the party turned into a general brawl. Another night officers and soldiers "with Bayonets guns swords clubs etc." threatened Price's life, and murder was barely averted in that "drunken freak" by the arrival of the commandant, Colonel Gaither, who according to Price was often as drunk as anyone else. But murder, it seems, finally did occur. Two weeks after his son's birth, Price made a will. A few weeks later he wrote Hawkins in desperation that he was sure the officers meant to remove him, and a few days later he was dead.[25]

Hawkins had been too occupied to lend any assistance. Through 1797 and 1798 he was almost constantly on the move, negotiating treaties and running treaty lines. When he was at the agency he was constantly beset by problems. When Gaither applied to him for advice about how to handle the disorders at the store, Hawkins reminded him that he had more serious business: "I am surrounded with difficulties . . . I have some white women and children who have been robed and striped of their clothing now depending on me for aid, and I meet some Spanish interposition. . . . I am surrounded with one hundred Indians daily; all of them with complaints, and my health is fast declining; yet with this pressure and my infirmities what I possess I give unto you." And he advised Gaither to cut off communications between factory and garrison and to protect Price until the secretary of war took matters in hand.[26]

That was in the spring of 1798, and it was not until December that Hawkins had any leisure at all, by which time Price was hopelessly entangled in his final quarrels. Hawkins urged him to end his bickerings with the officers, to try to be happy and help others be happy. In January he calmed Price, who by then suspected plots against himself in every quarter, assuring him that no one at the War Office knew of his troubles (not true) and that he was over the worst now because he knew what the officers were like, and adding firmly that he must "in future get the public business in an easy and regular train. You must on your part persevere, . . . report regularly, and complain not," because the president and secretary of war had more critical affairs to attend to. Hawkins was not only worried for the public business but was also annoyed with Price on his own account; in June he had complained to Gaither that his hopes of relaxing at Fort Wilkinson after two months of line-running had been so disappointed by the disagreeable state of affairs there that he had left as quickly as possible. Again, in December, when Price's affairs were at their worst, he wrote Gaither that the fort, which he had hoped would be a place to visit with pleasure, was now more disagreeable to him than the Indian life: "I am in a log hut surrounded by my red charges, and seem doomed to this tiresome life for some time to come." He does not appear to have been overwhelmed by grief when word of Price's death reached him.[27]

Literally the president's factotum in Indian country, Hawkins was busy all day every day doing the work of all three branches of government and, in addition, being foreign minister and official host—for a salary of $2,000 a year plus rations. As a diplomat Hawkins was charged with maintaining friendly relations with the Spanish governors of Louisiana and Florida, as required by the treaty of amity between the United States and Spain. This Hawkins faithfully did, although the Spaniards' vacillation in dealing with Bowles and the Seminoles infuriated him. Also, Hawkins was at the center of a vast intelligence network of Indians and whites and blacks; as the secretary of war said, without intelligence reports from Indian country "the United States can never be one moment secure, from the practices of spies and intrigues upon the Indians." The knowledge that Hawkins himself gathered as he traveled through Indian country was useful for trade and would be invaluable in case of war. Keeping friendly relations with the Indians demanded, especially in the light of Indian emphasis on hospitality, receiving them in numbers, day or night, be he well or sick; letting them crowd his house and vacuum his table, whatever the expense and however other business might press. Requiring particular tact was the task of refusing the hospitable offers of Indian women to become, or to have their daughters become, Hawkins's wives or consorts. His time was fully occupied:

> I am here in the midst of the Lower Creek towns, and I have been for a month on business with them. We begin to understand each other, we have black drink and talks in the day, and dancing at night. I go to bed about 12 and rise pretty early, the remainder of the time is claimed by the Indians, and I devote it to them. They will not be excluded even at meal times, they bring their private and public claims, I attend to them, and I am happy to find that by my exertions the benevolent views of the government have already taken so deep root that I may defy the malice of the enemies of it.[28]

Every kind of civil action in the agency had at some point to go through Hawkins's hands. He issued permits for hunting, horse deals, slave purchases and sales, and manumission. He examined travelers and, if their purposes were honest, gave them passports through Indian lands. He adjudicated claims of damages and losses, authorized and paid for return of stolen horses, and distributed public funds to persons in need or distress. He served as ombudsman in cases such as that of Hannah Hales, a contented white captive of the Creeks, whose relatives in Georgia were trying to make her come home; and of Polly Russell, a free black woman of South Carolina, who had been kidnapped by Creeks and sold by them back into slavery. Hannah Hales stayed; Polly Russell was given a pass to return home. Among the odds and ends of his job, Hawkins performed marriages and doctored the sick. Five hundred Creeks died of disease each year, Hawkins said. He claimed great success in treating the springtime malady, pleurisy, with carrot and snakeroot; for the autumn illness, which Hawkins called "the fever of the climate," he dispensed emetics and cathartics, saltpeter in water several times a day, and a sleeping potion of sassafras tea with twenty-five or thirty drops of laudanum.[29]

Although Hawkins pressed on with his hundreds of daily duties as Principal Temporary Agent to the Indians South of the

Ohio, his commission to that office actually ended in 1798, when the Mississippi Territory was established. Then the territorial governor assumed ex officio administration of the affairs of the Indians within that territory, mainly Choctaws and Chickasaws. When factories for them were built at Saint Stephens (in present-day Alabama), and Chickasaw Bluffs (the site of Memphis, Tennessee), they were under the charge of Governor Winthrop Sargent and, after 1802, of his successor Governor William C. C. Claiborne. But jurisdictions overlapped. For example, Hawkins continued as supervisor of Choctaw agent Samuel Mitchell. To make matters still more confusing, Gen. James Wilkinson, commander of United States troops in the territory, could supercede both Hawkins and the governor under a congressional authorization to handle special missions.[30]

An order issued by Secretary of War McHenry in 1798 compounded the confusion by giving the territorial governor responsibility for punishing Indian crimes against whites, while Hawkins was to retain "general superintendency" of Indian affairs. This arbitrary and impracticable partition of functions totally ignored one of the main points of the civilization program, which was to teach the Indians to punish their own criminals. Furthermore, the governor complained that subagents did not consult him, and that he ought to get more goods to give as presents to the Indians—another undercut of Hawkins's program. By the time Claiborne became governor, Hawkins was reduced officially from principal agent to all the tribes to agent to the Creeks only, the equivalent of Silas Dinsmoor's position as agent to the Cherokees. An old hand in government, Hawkins wisely ignored his title and stuck with his job.[31]

From his arrival in Indian country, Hawkins had lived among the Creeks and had concerned himself mainly with their affairs, because the Creek-Georgia and Creek-Cumberland frontiers were the worst trouble areas. But his civilization program was meant eventually to reach all the southern Indians, and could be effective only if it did. Hawkins called councils of all the Four Nations, and sent reports of them to the Seminoles, to achieve his goals throughout Indian country. In 1798 he called such a meeting to discuss again the need to punish troublemakers, pointing out again that the land speculators watched eagerly for Indian crimes as an excuse to seize their land. At that meeting Efau Haujo declared that the Four Nations must cooperate and communicate: "no one nation shall part with any of their land without the head men of the four nations are present and give their consent. . . . We make this talk that the whole nation may know that no individual can part with any of our land. . . . We have appointed one man in the Chickasaws, William Colbert, to remove the land speculators in their neighborhood." This was to be done peaceably, Efau Haujo said. Also, the chiefs of the Four Nations would guard their frontiers and try to prevent their young people stealing. As Hawkins was absent, his clerk Richard Thomas attended this meeting. Efau Haujo, an experienced negotiator, immediately after the meeting announced that he was going directly to Pensacola, where the Spaniards were said to have gifts waiting.[32]

To restrict Hawkins's jurisdiction to the Creeks only would have halted his efforts to foster a joint opposition to land speculators by the four tribes. Indeed, the speculators in devious ways may have been working toward that very end. Fortunately, Governor Claiborne at that time was content to leave Indian affairs to the agents, and the division of jurisdictions between himself and Hawkins was allowed quietly to lapse.

Price's death (early in 1799) created new problems for Hawkins, which seemed happily resolved when after three months Price's replacement, Edward Wright, arrived. Hawkins described Wright to the secretary of war as "a prudent cautious honest man" who would give satisfaction. Wright's early letters from the factory were censorious of Price's conduct of business, but within a very short time he was expressing the same complaints that Price had, and becoming more and more irritated with the situation: the most important items in his orders—gunpowder, flints, salt, and blankets—were omitted from shipments, although the hunting season was to start very soon; the store was unfit for business; the housing for his family was rough and small with no privacy or convenience. Wright was a cautious man and lived in fear of Indian attack on the fort, "which would be a disagreeable place for me to be in with my family, at such a time." Although there was no attack, Hawkins agreed that the shortages of needed items at the store made the Indians restless. Also, when Wright became factor, he was told that he might continue to pay a chalk a pound for deerskins, but that since the skins' market value had dropped considerably, he must make up the loss by raising the prices of factory goods. This was another cause of acute irritation among the Indians.[33]

By 1801, Wright, like Price before him, was having serious trouble with the officers. This time Hawkins intervened promptly, but he could not sooth angry feelings. Where Price perhaps had had too little caution and prudence, Wright seems to have had too much. Things went from bad to worse. Wright's nerves could not take it. By early 1802 he had quit, leaving the factory's goods and affairs in sad disorder. Fortunately, a very steady, experienced man, Jonathan Halsted, took his place, and the factory continued to function.[34]

Hawkins never ceased to believe that the factory system would inculcate the habit of trade instead of begging, would teach cash instead of credit buying, and would therefore encourage the Indians to produce trade goods, first by hunting and eventually by farming, stock raising, and home industries. Through the factories, Hawkins believed, he could accomplish the main goals of his mission: the Indians would learn to embrace white values of labor and private property, and develop the competence and confidence to live in peace in a white world.[35]

Within the plan for achieving the goals of the factory system, however, lay an irreconcilable contradiction. If hunting was to be the springboard from which the Indians were to leap into the modern world of trade instead of treats, cash instead of credit, work instead of begging, they had to have large hunting grounds with abundant game. Yet the United States government proceeded from treaty to treaty, each one shrinking the hunting grounds, and the newly acquired land was sold to settlers who, by clearing forests and ranging domestic cattle, chased the game away. Hawkins himself worked both sides of this inherently illogical proposition, urging the Indians to hunt and bring in skins, and also officiating at treaties that chipped away their ability to do so. Nothing in his character suggests that he was acting cynically. He firmly believed that, by the time game had become so scarce it would no longer support Indian needs, the civilization program would have changed the Indians from a hunting people to farmers, stock raisers, spinners, and weavers.

As early as 1797, when treaties had already somewhat contracted Indian hunting grounds, Hawkins was aware that the skin trade was on the decline, but he put the blame on Indian indolence and their ingrained habit of begging. Still, that year the Creek hunters had all gone into the woods by November, and were not expected back until March. Hawkins did all he could to make the hunt attractive and peaceable. Hunting parties with permits and responsible leaders were well treated at Fort Wilkinson, often invited to dine there and given supplies for the road home. Despite all encouragement, however, the Creeks did little hunting. An epidemic of distemper, or "yellow water," in 1797 killed many of the Indian horses. Game was already hard to find, and the wants of the Indians were increasing; but these men, "bred in habits indolent and insolent," Hawkins said, were "too proud to labor," so they had gone back to stealing horses, that major source of trouble on the frontiers.[36]

In 1799 half of the hunters were still in their villages in December. Hawkins knew that few skins would be brought in, and therefore the cash trading system so laboriously built up would be in jeopardy. Even the few respectable traders in the villages, who were permitted credit because they paid debts punctually, now could not pay because they had no skins left. There were about twenty debtor traders, who owed the factories an average of $500. As for the Indians, Hawkins wrote Edward Wright: "Their wants are increasing and their means are exhausted. They have as usual had recourse to beging." He kept telling Wright through that December that the Indians were poor, naked, and restless, which increased Wright's terror of an Indian attack.[37]

Yet Hawkins knew the hunt lagged for a reason other than indolence: the factory had no ammunition to sell the Indians. Price as factor had written again and again for powder and flints, and for salt to preserve the kill, and so did Wright, and so would Halsted after him. These more and more urgent requests for hunting needs were quietly ignored by the supply department, which instead poured out quantities of bindings, looking glasses, and knives, "more of that article on hand than can be disposed of in ten years," Halsted wrote disgustedly to the superintendent of Indian trade in 1805. By Halsted's time not only hunting necessities were omitted from shipments but also groceries such as sugar, coffee, and pepper, luxuries which the Indians had been taught to crave so much that they managed somehow to pay cash for them. The lack of these items, and the embargo on selling spirits except in small quantities, would certainly send the Indians to trade elsewhere than at the factories. They would have drink, Halsted wrote, "let it cost what it may."[38]

Sometimes Hawkins's anger overwhelmed his discretion, and he bluntly said why the Indians were poor and why they were reduced to begging; why they went elsewhere—to the "Dons" at Pensacola, on occasion—to trade or beg. His distress spilled over in a letter to Wright:

> The Indians are poor naked and restless. And it is a fact that the trade is not carried on agreeable to what I have been ordered to inform the Indians. By saying this, I do not mean to insinuate that you have not done your duty. —You have your orders, to sell what you receive, and . . . I have endeavoured to explain away the defect in the supplies, —but explanations are but a poor substitute for promises made them by order of the Secretary at War. The Chiefs at the national council, asked me how you expected to get skins for goods when you had no powder? How you expected to trade with Indians if you had no powder, salt, blankets or flints, and you would not receive any thing but skins?

Then he went on to what most deeply concerned the Indians, making them anxious, restless, and hostile:

> There is an opinion industriously circulated through this nation by the mischief makers, that the trading establishment is a deception, that there is but a few goods etc. suited to the trade, and that there exists no disposition to accommodate the Indians with such articles as they most need.[39]

There is good reason to believe that rumor correct; to suspect that by 1799 the strategy upon which the factories and Hawkins's entire civilization program were based had been changed.

Whether deliberately or not, Hawkins's job was made almost impossible to do. The cost of running the Creek Agency came to about $1,500 a quarter. All remittances, whether for Indian stipends, staff salaries, expenses, or bills were sent to the factory and distributed from there, but the money was always late arriving. Hawkins, lacking funds, wrote bills on the War Department to pay his interpreters, messengers, and other employees; to reward those who returned stolen slaves or horses; as gifts to the chiefs on special occasions; and for countless other expenses. If his bills were sent to the War Department, they were ignored. The nearest banker who would honor them was in Savannah, and he would take them only at discount. Hawkins, chronically desperate for cash money, told Wright near the end of 1799: "You must use the last means in your power to obtain with the least possible delay money for my bills." His assistants had only their salaries to live on; if his bills were not honored, Hawkins said, there would be trouble in his Indian agency before spring. Significantly, this bitter complaint was in the same letter in which Hawkins told Wright the Indians believed the factories were a deception, not intended to serve the Indians.[40]

Despite Hawkins's tremendous efforts, the Creeks remained a hunting people and the civilization program made slow progress against traditional ways. To officials Hawkins pretended an optimism he did not really feel. To Colonel Gaither and Governor Jackson, for example, he intimated that the Indians were disgusted with the poor hunting and were progressing in stock raising, agriculture, and handicrafts; but to Mathew Hopkins, acting factor at Fort Wilkinson after Price's death, he admitted more frankly that efforts to establish a substitute for hunting and the skin trade "are as yet feeble and but partial." Even that was an overstatement. The Creeks, Hawkins reported, had plainly told him that "they did not understand the plan, they could not work, it did not comport with the ways of the red people."[41]

Hawkins's ominous response to this plaint must have frightened the Indians, yet it could not budge them from their life as Indians. He told them bluntly: "The Game was gone Cattle and Hog would replace it" and "these aided by the Loom and agriculture would make them an independent people"; but if they rejected his plan of civilization and labor, and refused to respect the rights of their white neighbors, "I could assure them, the white people would find land enough to pay themselves for all the losses they sustained, and that the day of settlement was not distant."[42]

The factories were made the tool for achieving that settlement. Even before 1800 trade and the factories were acquiring a new function, that of luring the Indians into debt. This could happen only through a relaxation of the rule against giving credit, whose purpose was precisely to keep the Indians out of debt. A year and more after taking up his duties, Hawkins was still "an enemy to credit," which was a mistaken policy, he believed, but one that now, "as I am informed, has been sanctioned by the Secretary of War." In his instructions to Edward Wright in August 1799, Hawkins pointed out the evils of credit: "I find credit is unquestionably prejudicial to this Country. . . . it increases their extravagance while it lessens the Means of Supporting it. . . . If they were taught to provide the Means before hand for their support they would be vigilant careful and Econimical. But the contrary of this is Manifest. If a Man wants a keg of Taffia [rum] he will give a horse for it. . . . If he wants a whore he cloaths her in fine Calicoe with Gilt silver ware. If he wants a beef he gives 10 chalks a year for it. . . . The last want is the means, these are Credit, they are goods."[43]

Gradually more and more credit was permitted. What the Indians still possessed was the valuable asset of land, vast land. Little by little, treaty by treaty, the acre replaced the deerskin as the unit of trade.

PART TWO

Treaties

Under these views the purchase has been made, with the consent and desire of the great body of the [Cherokee] nation, although not without some dissenting members, as must be the case with all collections of men.

THOMAS JEFFERSON TO THE SENATE, 1808

CHAPTER 6

Tenants at Will

"We are a wandering people not from inclination but from Neces-
sity—where is the land we can say to our band, build your houses
strong, make your fences high, and raise a plenty of cows & Hogs,
our great father will protect us in our possessions? We know of no
such land."

PETITION BY A BAND OF SHAWNEES
TO THE PRESIDENT OF THE UNITED STATES

ALTHOUGH the government of the white settlers claimed title
to Indian land by right of discovery as far west as the Mississippi, which made a mockery of treaties, it was nevertheless
deemed appropriate for the United States to pay small amounts
bit by bit for territory that it already claimed, particularly since
such payments conformed to Indian custom and helped ensure
peace.[1]

To the frontiersmen who were to live on these lands, philosophical concepts of rights and title were of remote interest
compared with the proximate danger of an arrow in the back
from the bow of an Indian equally indifferent to such concepts.
What the frontiersmen wanted were firm agreements that white
men might move unmolested into such and such lands, and
that red men would exchange their rights to those lands for
such and such goods, money, protection, and services: in fact,
treaties.

Treaties, however, had little permanence, as both Indians
and settlers quickly became aware. Typically, a treaty included a
guarantee to the Indians of the rights "in perpetuity" of all

lands remaining to them after the cession made in that particular treaty, but Secretary of War Knox made it clear that a later treaty could extinguish the guarantees contained in earlier treaties without damage to the validity of cessions made in those earlier treaties. The Indians became wary, from repeated experiences of broken promises, so that when rumors spread of a treaty to come they became restless and hostile, anticipating demands for more land. "The Indians have constantly had their jealousies and hatred excited by the attempts to obtain their land," Knox wrote Blount. The frontiers were primed to explode into violence at the hot breath of rumor. An agent among the Creeks said, "It is in the power of an ignorant vagabond trader, at anytime, over a pipe and a cup of black-drink, to persuade them that the most solemn treaty is no more than a well-covered plot, laid to deprive them of their lands . . . and that the sooner they break it the better. This arouses their jealousy, which, with their insatiable thirst for plunder, will probably, so long as the white villains are among them, continually destroy the good effects intended by treaties." That comment was made in 1791, the year of William Blount's particularly obnoxious treaty of Holston, and the Indians had good reason for alarm. President Washington in his annual messages admitted the continuing outrages against the Indians, and in 1791 he called for "justice to the savages," but the Indians knew they were not getting justice, and the Creeks especially seemed ready to take the warpath.[2]

Indian mischief-makers contributed to the uneasiness and the dissatisfaction with treaties, Efau Haujo conceded. Some Creeks would go to the frontier, he said, pretending to be important chiefs, and after a few drinks with white settlers would grant them permission to range their cattle on Indian land, a promise of no force whatever, because no individual Creek, only the entire nation, could give such permission.[3]

As for the frontiersmen, whose intrusion onto Indian lands was acknowledged as the major cause of frontier violence by Washington, Knox, Pickering, Hawkins, and other informed authorities, why would they not have pushed out beyond each treaty line as soon as it was run, knowing that by the next treaty the Indians would perforce cede the land onto which settlers had intruded, although the previous treaty had promised that this land should remain Indian land forever?

In fact, if one peers around the impeccable Palladian facade of government disapproval of white intruders, concern for justice to the aborigines, and jealousy for the national honor, one catches a glimpse of shabby acquiescence by government in the principle of encroachment. If not for encroachment, how could the government have justified the succession of treaties? Secretary Knox in 1789 spoke harshly of "imbecile promises" to the Indians which were immediately violated, of "lawless whites [who] will ridicule a government which shall, on paper only, make Indian treaties, and regulate Indian boundaries"; it would reflect more honor on the United States, Knox said, and be more effective, were a "declarative law to be passed, that the Indian tribes possess the right of the soil of all lands within their limits," and that they cannot be divested of that land except by bona fide purchases by the United States. As early as the treaty of Hopewell in 1785 the Cherokees had been promised that anyone who intruded on their land must vacate within six months of the ratification of that treaty, or forfeit the protection of the United States, "and the Indians may punish him or not as they please."[4]

The question is, did Knox and the government as a whole really intend to prevent intruders? Francis Paul Prucha observes: "The federal government was sincerely interested in preventing settlement on Indian lands only up to a point, and it readily acquiesced in illegal settlements when they had gone so far as to be irremediable. The basic policy of the United States intended that white settlement should advance and the Indians withdraw. Its interest was primarily that this process should be as free of disorder and injustice as possible. The government meant to restrain and govern the advance of whites, not to prevent it forever."[5]

This being true, the epithets hurled by government at intruders could not have been sincere; only intruders who created disorder were deplored. Yet how could white men build their houses on Indian land or turn Indian hunting grounds into cattle range with any justice or in such a way as not to incite the Indians to violence?

Hawkins hoped to teach the Indians to use their land as white men did, so that they would be permitted to keep as much as they needed to survive as farmers and stock raisers. But thirty years after the beginning of Hawkins's work in the South, Indian superintendent Thomas McKenney was urging the Chickasaws to move west of the Mississippi, saying that only by giving up their lands in the East could they survive, "for the storm about Indian's lands is terrible indeed!"[6]

The American national conscience, a sense of moral responsibility for the welfare of other nations and peoples, was born with the nation. The concern expressed by the United States for the Indians, while it ingested their land like a benevolent earthworm, cannot be understood as plain hypocrisy. At the end of the War of Independence the nation was pratically beggared. In 1787, Hawkins and his North Carolina colleagues in Congress wrote their state legislature that the Union was "at the Eave of a Bankruptcy and of a total dissolution of Government."[7]

At that time of national crisis, and at other times to come, the United States did not act with justice, candor, or friendliness toward the Indians, although it continued to speak in the vocabulary of magnanimity. In fact, the Indian nations were regarded as enemies, witness their supervision by the War Department, and it was the intention of the United States to neutralize them and annex their lands by persuasion or force. The benevolent language of treaties therefore was meant to deceive both the Indians and the national conscience. A study of the treaties makes it difficult to concur with scholars who hold that justice and humanity were the keystones of policy toward the Indians; or with those who argue that it was United States policy, "repeatedly and consistently solemnized by treaty, to recognize the rights of the Indian tribes to the land, but the views of the settlers, as they reached the frontier where they came in contact with the Indians, was an entirely different thing."[8] Settlers who deliberately violated the line set by the Holston treaty, but who later claimed not to have known they were intruding on Indian territory and to have suffered loss and hardship when they were forced to vacate, were actually voted financial relief by a congressional committee.[9]

From the governmental foot-dragging on intruders, and from the pattern of treaties that one after another procured legalization of white title to lands illegally appropriated, emerges an interesting hypothesis: that the government used the intruders not only to encroach on territory that the United States meant in any case to acquire but also to provide a diplomatic and rhetorical whipping boy at treaties. Like the "wild" and "ungovernable" young red men upon whom the chiefs blamed all of the Indians' treaty violations, the "intruders" were the scapegoats of United States treaty commissioners. By resort to this diplomatic synechdoche, the negotiating principals on both sides were able to admit to misdemeanors and crimes and yet stand free of guilt; to make promises they knew would not be kept, but be innocent when they were broken; to voice and hear accusations without offending each other or putting each other in a position of no escape.

White technology, customs, systems, and values held many surprises for the Indians, but most strange and incomprehensible was the white man's relationship to land. At the core of Indian existence was the bond between human beings and the land. Bartram felt the glory and privilege of that bond as few white men did when he wrote, "This world, as a glorious apartment of the boundless palace of the sovereign creator, is furnished with an infinite variety of animated scenes, inexpressibly beautiful and pleasing, equally free to the inspection and enjoyment of all his creatures." The sixteenth-century English jurist Sir Edward Coke called the earth "the suburbs of heaven," meant for the habitation of man as heaven was the home of God. To the Indian the idea of owning a part of the land, in the white man's sense of property, was about as absurd as the idea of owning a part of heaven, whereas the white man, fully to enjoy land, had to own it.[10]

In view of the basic dissimilarity of Indian and white concepts, it is probable that when white men went among the southern Indians and sought to *buy* land, their intentions were not always fully understood. When Indians violated the terms of a sale or treaty cession of land, explaining that they did not understand what they had promised, they were accused of lying and perfidy; but it is likely, at least in some instances, that they really did not comprehend the terms they had accepted, even if they had been sober and not under duress when they made the agreement. How and by what right could a man dispose of a piece of the earth where the bones of his forefathers lay, a portion of the earth given to the tribe in trust by the Master of Breath to live and die on, and to preserve without harm for its children's children? From an Indian point of view, the idea combined absurdity and outrage; parting with any piece of land grew more and more repugnant as the tribal holdings shrank, forests and streams with their wildlife were lost, and finally, towns and villages engulfed.[11]

At last most of the southern Indians grasped what only a few of the wisest-such as Tassel of the Cherokees and Efau Haujo of the Creeks—had seen from the start, that whites were not mere interlopers to be chased off by an occasional scalping or killing, but masters of the land and of Indian destiny; and that to the masters the Indians were the intruders, suffered on federal land as tenants only, at the will of the landlord. The strongest hold of William Bowles on the Indians, aside from his liveliness and charm, was that he alone among white leaders confirmed, indeed insisted upon, Indian title to the lands of their nations, and he dared hamper Hawkins in running treaty lines that would diminish Indian lands. That was most likely why his picture hung in Indian huts and why the Indians resisted turning him over to the authorities; the land, which Bowles assured them would be restored to them, was far more precious to them than the money offered as a reward for arresting him.[12]

From 1790, when McGillivray of the Creeks was lured to New York by the flattering prospect of negotiating with the secretary of war, to treaties with the Choctaws in 1808, about thirty more federal treaties in which land was ceded were made with the southern tribes. By the later treaties some of the Indians, notably the Cherokees, had almost given up the struggle to hold onto their ancestral lands and had begun to migrate to the west side of the Mississippi; before 1810 about 3,000 to 4,000 Cherokees were settling the wild lands along the Arkansas River and contesting them with the extremely warlike Osages.[13]

In the mid-1780s it still seemed possible to keep both the In-

dians and the frontiersmen satisfied. Hawkins said at the time
of Hopewell treaty, "Congress is now the sovereign of all our
country. . . . They want none of your land, nor anything else
which belongs to you." But, he explained, "The commissioners,
in establishing the boundary which is the chief cause of all the
complaints of the Indians, were desirous of accommodating the
southern States, and their western citizens, in any thing consistent with the duty we owed to the United States." President
Washington had announced immediately after the treaty of
Paris that all Indian lands had been ceded by Britain to the
United States, and that the Indians could with justice be expelled (particularly since most of them had aided Britain during the war), but that the United States preferred to reserve
certain lands for them; and that as the tribes moved west their
lands could be cheaply purchased. Knox's just-war philosophy
had been embodied in Article 3 of the Northwest Ordinance of
1787, which promised the Indians that "their lands and property shall never be taken from them without their consent, and,
in their property, rights, and liberty, they shall never be invaded
or disturbed unless in just and lawful wars authorized by Congress." Following the logic of these statements, what would
make war just and lawful was the refusal of the Indians to continue giving by consent what was theirs.[14]

Within ten years President Washington's assurance of gradual, orderly absorption of vacated Indian lands was anach-
ronistic. White men were rushing the borders in a kind of
frenzy. Michael Paul Rogin says: "Whites signed treaties only to
move onto lands retained by Indians, and bought and sold land
in Indian country. Was the 'Savage Tribe that will neither ad-
here to Treaties, nor the Law of Nations' the Cherokees or the
American Scotch-Irish?" Twenty-odd years later, when President Monroe, returning from a tour of the frontiers, was asked
if he thought the Indians were still savages, he is said to have
replied: "The *worst* Indians I have seen in my travels are the
white people that live on their borders."[15]

The Yazoo speculations of the 1790s epitomized the land
frenzy. Speculators from within and outside Georgia formed
the Tennessee, South Carolina, Virginia, and Georgia Yazoo
companies. In 1794 and 1795 the companies procured, from

an almost entirely bribed Georgia legislature, laws promising to extinguish Indian claims and thus make possible the purchase of 35 million acres, a broad, fertile strip from Muscle Shoals on the Tennessee River to the mouth of the Yazoo River, about where Vicksburg, Mississippi, later rose.[16]

One of the many circumstances that indicate that the government deliberately blinked at the operations of this big land business, while chastising the encroachments of individual unruly frontiersmen, is that, although the Yazoo speculations involved so many people that they must have been an open secret for several years, the federal government did nothing to stop them. President Washington in 1791 had issued a proclamation threatening rigorous punishment of any violation of federal treaties with the Indians, which the Yazoo scheme certainly was, but no action was taken against the speculators. When the scandal broke in 1796, it was through the revelations of Georgia's Senator James Jackson. Then the Georgia legislature put a stop to Yazoo speculation by rescinding the act that had legalized it. Honest Georgians praised the legislature that thus defeated the speculators' "airy dreams of splendid palaces, and princely fortunes, erected on the ruins of their country." But division and turbulent passions continued, and Indian fear and distrust, and would continue even after Georgia at last ceded its western lands to the government in 1802, upon the government's undertaking to act to extinguish Indian titles to those lands with all possible expediency.[17]

There can scarcely have been a single event relating to the southern Indians from 1789 onward that did not reflect in some way the gigantic Yazoo gamble, which embraced the entire area from Blount's turf in southern Tennessee to the Spanish border. Consider, for example, the establishment of the federal factory system in 1795, with federal posts attached to the factories; the efforts to frustrate Hawkins by the Georgia commissioners at the treaty of Colerain; Hawkins's appointment as agent in 1796; the formation of the Mississippi Territory in 1798 and the choice of Winthrop Sargent, one of the few politicians unsullied by the Yazoo mess, as territorial governor; the activities of McGillivray and Bowles; the jubilantly greeted Pinckney treaty of San Lorenzo, by which Spain was committed to vacate forts and territory; and especially, all future treaties between the United States and the southern Indians, which had as their purpose the extinction of Indian titles from the Oconee River westward and from the Tennessee River south. The shadow of Yazoo overspread the whole era and area.[18]

Ironically, southern land became more valuable than it had ever been just as the Yazoo scheme exploded, because of the sudden ascendance of cotton as the great money crop of the South. Cotton had been grown successfully for some time in the fertile, well-watered "black belt" across southwestern Tennessee, western Georgia, and present-day Alabama, Mississippi, and Louisiana. The crop was so rewarding that the growing and processing of cotton was one of the anchors of Hawkins's civilization program, the other being stock raising. Hawkins found that, although black-seeded cotton did not do particularly well, the green-seeded variety, which matured earlier, throve throughout the area, and Sea Island cotton promised to do well in the more southerly parts. One of the first persons Hawkins came to know after arriving in the Creek agency was Robert Grierson, a prospering Scottish trader, stock raiser, and farmer, who lived with his Indian family in the Upper Creek town of the Hillabees. In 1796 when Hawkins met him, Grierson had two acres of his rich, moist land planted in cotton. By the 1797 harvest he had expanded his cotton culture and was employing enough women to spin 1,000 yards annually. A year later he employed "eleven hands, red, white and black, in spinning and weaving" the cotton made and cleaned by his Indian family and some other Indian women, all of whom, he believed, would eventually learn to spin and weave. The following year Grierson hired Rachel Spillard, a Georgia woman who had taught handicrafts in the Cherokee department of Hawkins's agency, to teach and superintend the manufacture of his cotton, at a salary of $200 a year. Hawkins advised Grierson on improved methods of cultivation, provided him with cotton cards to smooth and clean the staple, and procured spinning wheels and looms for his little factory. Grierson was doing well; good-quality cotton brought over thirty cents a pound in Philadelphia and Tennessee in those years.[19]

A most surprising development for that time, closely connected to the cotton boom, was the emergence of women as a "civilizing" influence and an economically important force in Hawkins's program. Indian women had always had an important role in southern tribal society, which was matrilineal, and they had always been the feeders and clothers of their families, using the flesh and skin of animals that their husbands brought in and the produce of their own gardens, orchards, and cornfields. Now the stimulation of a textile industry gave them gainful labor. They could work for Grierson or some other cotton grower for wages—not much, but they seemed pleased with his pay of half a pint of salt or half a pint of taffia or a few strands of wampum beads for each two baskets of cotton that they picked. If they would learn to spin and weave, they could save substantially by making their own homespun instead of having to buy homespun woven by the Indian countrymen.[20]

Unexpectedly, there were economic opportunities for white women, and probably for half-white women, in the country of the "savages," if they could teach textile skills to the Indian women. Rachel Spillard was not the only one. Timothy Barnard hired her sister to teach spinning and weaving at his home. In the fall of 1797, Hawkins provided Hannah Hales, the contented captive who declined to go home to Georgia, with all the appurtenances of textile production—harness, slay, and shuttle, and cotton cards—and he ordered a loom made for her at the agency's expense. With these to employ her time and interest, she was apparently quite happy to remain the wife of Far Off, a man of the town called the Fish Ponds, and was able to clothe herself and her family with the fruits of her loom. In the summer and fall of 1797 a male weaver was sent by Hawkins through Creek country to demonstrate the craft for Indian women, and he reported that many of them were determined to raise cotton and make their own thread and cloth. Then they, too, could go out and teach.[21]

In January 1798 Hawkins heard from his clerk, Richard Thomas, that the Indian wife of trader David Randon was spinning cotton: "The women approve much . . . and I have had several applications for cotton seed, cards & wheels. . . . Sookahoey brought two gallons [of seed] up, but will not spare to any of her neighbors a single grain; she is determined to plant the whole, & requests me to tell you not to forget the small wheel and cards." In February, Hawkins wrote the secretary of war with obvious gratification that two Creek girls had raised and spun fifty yards of "good 500 thread"; in the same letter he lashed out at Indian men as "this proud, haughty, lying, spoiled, untoward race." At year's end he wrote Price urgently: "Send me Eliza [Hollinger] to aid in the good work intrusted to the agency, she will be a powerful assistant." Cotton growing and processing, he felt, was precisely the kind of program to convince the Indians of the advantages of agriculture and technology over a precarious hunting existence.[22]

He would have to rely on the women, "who are the labourers in this land," to make a success of the civilization program, but he had great faith in them, and already had prize pupils like Hannah Hales, who within a couple of years of hard work had acquired a black slave, one or two horses, sixty cattle, and some hogs. Property gave Creek wives more independence than white wives had: "She [Hannah Hales] possesses the right of a Creek woman, and can throw away her husband whenever she chooses," Hawkins explained. Although he liked women and wished them well, he could not or would not accept their power in Creek social organization. The matriarchal system so outraged his white-male sensibilities, and the thought that "a whiteman by marrying an Indian woman of the Creek nation . . . becomes a slave of her family" was so repugnant to him, that he issued an order forbidding, on pain of dismissal, any of his assistants to marry a Creek woman. As a white gentleman, however, he deplored the domestic treatment of Creek women by their husbands, who to his thinking worked them like slaves. Through the civilization program—"this auspicious revolution," he said—Indian women had risen from being beasts of burden to a second level that women occupied in "nations civilized in their manners but not universally enlightened in their own opinions," where they were regarded as "the luxuries and idols of men." "We hope there is yet a third gradation in their destiny," he observed, "which the polished Virginian, as well as the untutored Creek, may hereafter ascend to." [23]

Through Hawkins's perseverance and the willingness of the women, the cotton industry made progress. The Choctaws, the most remote of the Four Nations from Hawkins's influence, were late acquiring cotton skills, but they were no less eager; at the Fort Adams treaty of 1801–1802 they asked for spinning wheels and for white women to come and teach the textile crafts, first to the half-Choctaw women, "and the thing will then extend itself; one will learn another, and the white women may return to their own people again," they predicted. Fifteen years later the Choctaws made enough cotton to think of sending it to market, and they asked to have a cotton gin built for them. [24]

The invention of the cotton gin had a tremendous impact on Indian life, and greatly speeded up, if it did not radically change, the destiny of the southern Indians. The gin made cotton culture boom, slave prices soar, and caused cotton land to be sought by fair means or foul. Daniel Clark, a wealthy merchant and speculator of New Orleans, brought the first cotton gin into the lower Mississippi country in 1795, and by 1800 the cotton crop was valued at $750,000 at the then current price of twenty-five cents a pound, replacing tobacco as the region's main crop. Lands in the Mississippi region were appreciating at the same time for the several other reasons already mentioned: the running of the treaty line between Spain and the United States in 1799, the formation of the Mississippi Territory, and the coming of American settlers and troops to protect them. In 1803 settlers could still buy Mississippi lands at $2 an acre; but ten or twelve years later bottomlands around Natchez and Tombigbee brought $10 an acre; the land, which had been acquired by treaty cessions during that interval, had brought the Indians an average one cent per acre. [25]

In a very direct way, the fate of black men was involved with the fate of red men in the land-and-cotton boom. The post-Revolutionary decade had trailed, like the tail of a meteor, some of the bright, pure light of liberty and justice, and benevolence had been extended to blacks as well as Indians. Manumission became more frequent, and deathbed emancipation of slaves. Abolition and recolonization projects were fashionable. Then, in 1793, Eli Whitney put into operation on a Savannah plantation his practical gin for separating cotton seed from the staple. By 1794 the cotton export business had increased more than tenfold. In 1796 the Georgia newspaper *Columbian Museum* carried articles extolling the merits of the wonderful new cotton gin, making it clear that cotton raising would become very profitable, and therefore field hands would be at a premium, the more so because slave importation might become unconstitutional in 1808.[26]

A field hand could produce 500 to 800 pounds of cotton a year. In the middle and late 1790s black field hands cost about $250 to $300; five or so years later the price of field hand was up to $500. Ed Price had paid $350 for a black woman in 1798; in 1805, Jonathan Halsted, factor at the government store, paid $900 for a black couple. As prices rose, manumission was prohibited by law in one state after another: South Carolina, 1800; Georgia, 1802; Mississippi Territory, 1805. By 1800 a large-scale business of kidnapping free blacks and selling them back into slavery was proceeding briskly. In 1811 Georgia began denying free blacks the right to trial by jury, which put the freemen in constant jeopardy. Slaves were still being imported into the United States, despite the efforts of George Mason at the Constitutional Convention of 1787. Alexander Moultrie, head of the South Carolina Yazoo Company, envisaged establishing on Yazoo lands a state that should be a center for the development of the slave trade.[27]

The fate of blacks became an inextricable strand in the rope that strangled the southern Indians. The Indians, especially the Creeks, had long been accustomed to make raids across their border to steal horses and slaves. Georgia protested vehemently, and the pursuit and return of slaves became one of Hawkins's most vexing problems. Every treaty with the Indians demanded the return to their masters of stolen or escaped slaves, but this term was generally ignored. Runaway or stolen blacks, once in Indian country, often remained slaves, passing through a number of hands so quickly and casually that it was very difficult to trace them. Sometimes they served as security for debts, and so might be moved from one master to another without a bill of sale; or, a black slave might be swapped for his market value in cattle or for another slave. Some of the stolen blacks, along with many others who had escaped from slavery, found their way to the lower Mississippi country and Florida, as far as they could get from the states, where they settled as freemen in relative security and prosperity. There was a black "factor," a trader, on the Chattahoochee; blacks on the Tombigbee, Hawkins was told by Polly Russell, lived in better style than whites on the Georgia border. In 1797 Hawkins assured the governor of Georgia that, for a reward of $12.50 a head, "I find no difficulty in obtaining restitution of . . . negroes who run from the state of Georgia" to the Creek Nation; but in truth, it was not so easy, even when the Creeks were willing to return the blacks. The following complaint filed by Robert Walton, a white trader among the upper Creeks, gives some idea of the difficulties of tracing and returning blacks:

> Robert Walton, a resident trader of Tuskegee, complains, on oath, that some time about three years past he left a negro fellow, his property, at the house of a daughter of Mr. Stradham . . . in care of Mr. Stradham's daughters for their use till he [Walton] should return and take him. After this, John Galphin applied to purchase the said negro and was refused; that after this, Galphin told Walton that Harrod had taken the negro and sold him to Kenard and taken one back which Mr. Durant sold Kennard; that since this, Walton says Harrod informed him that it was John Galphin who sold this negro to Kennard. Robert Walton, he purchased the negro of Mrs. Durant; she claimed him as the property of her father . . . and it is now said he is in the possession of some Indians at McCullee.[28]

By 1816, Hawkins was offering $50 for every escaped black slave in West Florida who should be delivered to him. Much difficulty arose from the claim of Georgia that the Creeks had committed themselves by the treaty of Augusta in 1783 to return black slaves, but the Indians denied any such promise, and the federal government did not recognize the Augusta treaty. In 1797, Hawkins told the Georgia governor that there was nothing in any treaty binding the Indians to such action, which was not quite true.[29]

To Georgians and citizens of other southern states, the boost given to cotton culture by the gin mandated relinquishment by

Indians of their lands and of the black labor that had taken refuge there; relinquishment by treaty was preferred, but if that failed, a "just war" might have to be resorted to. The factories were important not for the skins and pelts that the Indians traded but for putting the tribes in the mood to grant generous treaty terms.[30]

While he was still in the Senate, in 1792, Hawkins had vigorously opposed the policy of war with the Old Northwest tribes, and he had written Washington pleading for fair play toward those Indians. "During the war [for independence]," he had written,

> we acknowledged the Indians as brothers . . . urged them to be patient and declared that when success crowned our efforts, they should be partakers of our good fortune. They were then acknowledged to be possessors of the soil on which they lived. At the close of the war . . . we seem to have Forgotten altogether the rights of the Indians. They were treated as tenants at will—we seized on the lands and made a division of the same as possessing allodial rights allotted certain portions to the indians for hunting grounds and did not even think of offering them compensation. . . . This doctrine it might be expected would be disliked by the independent tribes. . . . from our conduct they conceived themselves deprived of what they deemed most precious.

He advised strongly against the threat or use of force. "I am for peace," he said.[31]

Even when the Old Northwest tribes had been offered compensation for their land, they had refused: "Money to us is of no value," the chiefs had said, ". . . no consideration whatever can induce us to sell the lands on which we get sustenance for our women and children." So the lands had been taken from them by force. What happened to those tribes makes it quite impossible to believe that the federal government's intentions toward the Indians were full of grace and light, and that the noble aims of official policy were set at naught by greedy, bloodthirsty frontiersmen. Greedy frontiersmen there were, but it was the United States government that made policy, in their favor.[32]

Benjamin Hawkins. From an engraving in Samuel Ashe's *Biographical History of North Carolina*. Courtesy North Carolina State Archives.

A detail of *General George Washington Resigning His Commission to Congress as Commander in Chief of the Army at Annapolis, Maryland, December 23d, 1783*, painted by John Trumbull, showing Benjamin Hawkins, center, and in the background left to right, Richard D. Spaight (North Carolina), Eleazer McComb (Delaware), George Partridge (Massachusetts), Thomas Jefferson (Virginia), and Arthur Lee (Virginia). Courtesy United States Senate Commission on Art and Antiquities.

Beautiful Savannah in the Pine Woods of Florida, painted by George Catlin in 1834–1835. Courtesy National Museum of American Art, Smithsonian Institution.

William Augustus Bowles, as painted by Thomas Hardy, circa 1791. From a private collection; courtesy Kennedy Galleries, New York.

Creek chief Hopohiethle Micco in 1790, the year of the treaty of New York. From an engraving by John Trumbull. Courtesy Smithsonian Institution National Anthropological Archives, Bureau of American Ethnology Collection.

Benjamin Hawkins's voucher for $125, a Creek town's stipend for 1800. He incorrectly renders that amount as OXXIIIII (125) chalks instead of 00000 (500) chalks, the exchange rate being four chalks to the dollar. Courtesy National Archives and Records Service, Record Group 75, Creek Factory Correspondence.

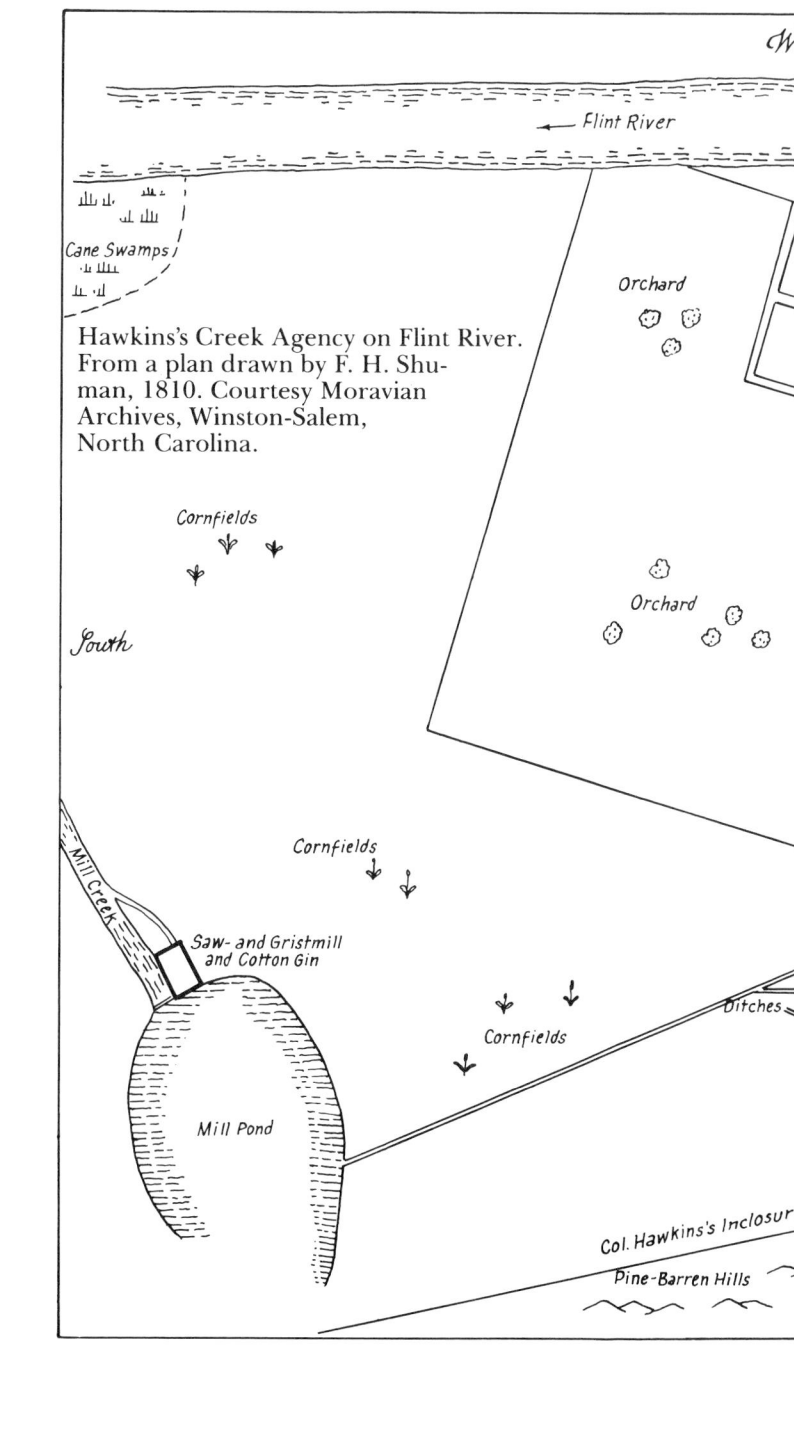

Hawkins's Creek Agency on Flint River. From a plan drawn by F. H. Shuman, 1810. Courtesy Moravian Archives, Winston-Salem, North Carolina.

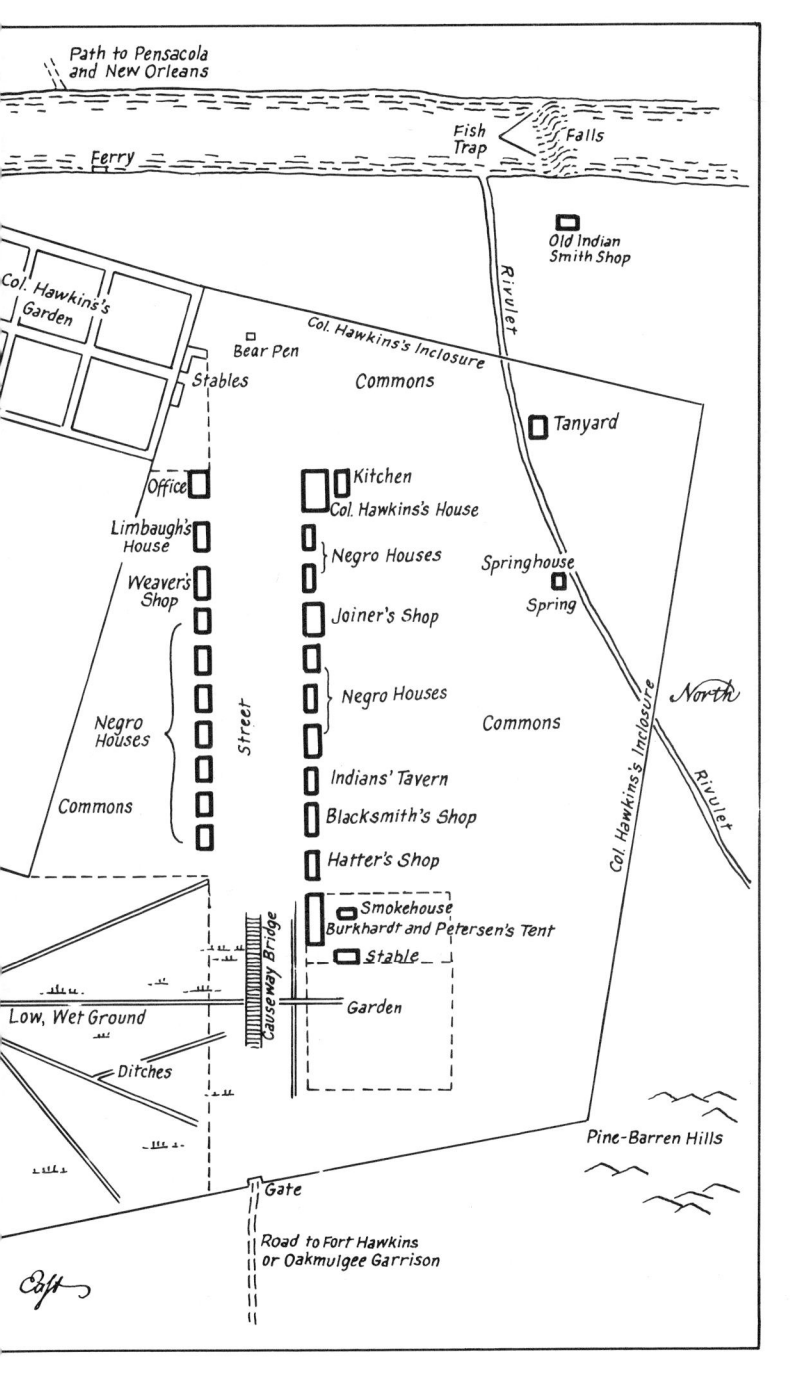

Path to Pensacola and New Orleans

Ferry

Fish Trap

Falls

Old Indian Smith Shop

Col. Hawkins's Garden

Col. Hawkins's Inclosure

Bear Pen

Commons

Stables

Tanyard

Office

Kitchen

Col. Hawkins's House

Limbaugh's House

Negro Houses

Weaver's Shop

Springhouse

Joiner's Shop

Spring

Negro Houses

Street

North

Negro Houses

Commons

Indians' Tavern

Commons

Blacksmith's Shop

Hatter's Shop

Col. Hawkins's Inclosure

Rivulet

Smokehouse

Burkhardt and Petersen's Tent

Causeway Bridge

Stable

Low, Wet Ground

Garden

Ditches

Pine-Barren Hills

Gate

Road to Fort Hawkins or Oakmulgee Garrison

Account of Andrew (alias Underlaw) of the Cussetas at the Creek factory, with items credited and debited on January 10, 1799. Note the one-half gallon of whiskey and the error in translating dollars into chalks. Courtesy National Archives and Records Service, Record Group 75, Creek Factory Daybook No. 2.

Friday November 8th 1799

House Expence Dr

For Cash paid Able Woods
his Acct for making
hinges & Staples for kit-
chen Door & Window 1.25

Sold for Cash
1 yard Brittanias @ 62½ — 62½
5/16 Gallons Whiskey @ 2.0 — 62½ 1 25

9th

Received of Indians Viz
1210 lb Deer Skins @ 25cts 302.50
53 lb Beaver @ 100cts .... 53.—
1 Otter Skin 1.50
40 small furs @ 12½ .... 6.—
2 small sides Seal Leather .... 3.—
$366.00

Bartered in payment Viz
2 Pieces Strouds @ 30dlls .... 240.—
23½ yards Strouds @ 150 .... 35.—
6 Pieces binding @ 1dll .... 6.—
28½ yards Ozinbrigs @ 25cts 7. 6½
17½ yards India Chintz @ 100 .... 17.75
3½ yards furniture Chintz @ 1/7½ 3. 6½
21 yards India Callico @ 50cts 10.50
5 fancy Handkerchiefs @ 150 .... 4.50
2 black silk Handkfs @ 125 .... 2.50
16 Romal Handkfs @ 50cts .... 8.—
1 Mans Saddle 13.37½
1 looking Glass 25
1 lb Vermillion .... 3.—
4 papers Vermillion @ 25cts .... 1.—
13 — 14 Inch Knives @ 50cts 6.50
4 — 10 Inch Knives @ 25cts .... 1.—
20 lb Lead @ 12½cts 2.50
2 Gallons Whiskey @ 150 .... 3.—
Cash .... 1.—
366.—

Edward Wright Dr
To 3½ yards yellow flannel @ 37½ 1 31¼
1 hank Thread ....
1 31¼

A day's transactions at the Creek factory, including payment for repairs and items bought for cash or bartered for furs and skins. Courtesy National Archives and Records Service, Record Group 75, Creek Factory Daybook No. 2.

Drinks the Juice of the Stone, a Choctaw Indian, in ball player's dress.
From an oil painting by George Catlin in 1834. Courtesy National Museum of American Art, Smithsonian Institution.

Timpoochee Barnard, son of trader Timothy Barnard and his Creek wife. Courtesy Smithsonian Institution National Anthropological Archives, Bureau of American Ethnology Collection.

The black drink used as an emetic before important deliberations, here by the Timucua Indians of Florida. From an early drawing by Le Moyne. Courtesy Smithsonian Institution National Anthropological Archives, Bureau of American Ethnology Collection.

William Blount, governor of the Southwest Territory. Courtesy Tennessee Historical Society.

Choctaw chief Pushmataha, from an engraving based on a painting by Charles Bird King during a visit by Pushmataha to Washington, D.C. Courtesy Smithsonian Institution National Anthropological Archives, Bureau of American Ethnology Collection.

Tenskwatawa, the Prophet, brother of Tecumseh. From an oil painting by George Catlin in 1830. Courtesy National Museum of American Art, Smithsonian Institution.

Part of the list of items sold from Hawkins's estate in the third week of October, 1816. The list of his books begins on line eight with "Constitution of Great Britain" and "Medical Companion," which brought fifty cents apiece. Courtesy Georgia Department of History and Archives.

A page from the appraisal of Hawkins's estate, dated October 24, 1816, showing a total worth of $6,599.17. The slaves who worked the agency's fields, gardens, and orchards accounted for a third of the total. Courtesy Georgia Department of History and Archives.

Believed to be the grave of Benjamin Hawkins. From a photograph made in 1928. Courtesy Georgia Department of Archives and History.

Eagle Tails and Anchovies

Brothers: We come not to ask lands from you, nor shall we ever ask for any unless you are disposed to sell, and your father will assist and protect you in the enjoyment of those you claim.—

GENERAL JAMES WILKINSON
TO THE CHOCTAWS, TREATY OF 1801.

You have heard us here; make your own fire and we will hear your answers. . . . Do not hurry yourselves, we have plenty of provisions for you here and for the path home.—

COLONEL BENJAMIN HAWKINS.

THE time of treaties, prior to Jackson's treaty of 1814, breaks down roughly into three phases. From Hopewell in 1785 to Tellico in 1798, the whites' goal was almost purely to acquire cessions of Indian land in return for payment by the United States in cash, goods, services, and annuities. Blount and his gang, very active in this period, had to be suppressed in order to restore Indian confidence to a level where the chiefs would consent to negotiate with federal commissioners, chief among whom was Hawkins.

About 1798 a new function of treaty negotiations emerged, and by 1801 it had become a major theme. The goal of acquiring land remained paramount, but in this new phase the Indians never laid hands on the quid pro quo when they made a cession; whatever the United States paid for the land—and payment was now almost entirely in money—was immediately applied to payment of Indian trade debts. Most Indians had only a rudimentary understanding of finance, their experience of trade until that time having been through barter, with the chalk as an intermediary symbol. Now, quite suddenly, they faced demands for payment of capital debts and interest; they paid with land, and to their way of thinking got a drearily negative return for it, the mere absence of debt. Their debts had grown into the tens of thousands of dollars, especially as the value of skins decreased and the cost of goods increased. By connivance between the United States and Panton, Leslie and Company (or its successor firm headed by John Forbes) treaties were made in which cash paid by the United States for relinquishment of Indian lands was at once turned over to Panton or Forbes. This system prevailed for about ten years.

Overlapping that second phase of the treaty era was one which foreshadowed the ultimate "just war." Treaty commissioners from the earliest treaties had had as one of their functions the gathering of information about how many warriors there were in such and such a tribe, and how they were armed, and the geography and topography of the region including towns, fords, paths, rivers, and soil. There are clear indications that such intelligence was valuable mainly for its usefulness in case of war. In 1803 the purchase of Louisiana created a new situation and new threats from the French, the Spanish, and the Indians under their influence. President Jefferson therefore pressed harder for cessions from the Choctaws and Chickasaws, encouraging the use of any device, such as the demands of Forbes for payment of Indian debts, to get land bordering the Mississippi. The president proposed to sell this land at once to settlers, because, as General Wilkinson explained, Jefferson was eager for "the formation of a barrior of Hardy Yeomanry on that Solitary frontier." Information was more vital than ever, and Lewis and Clark were dispatched by President Jefferson on a reconnaissance of the Mississippi and trans-Mississippi regions, where they would systematically record their findings.[1]

When, after 1805, Indian resistance to further "voluntary" cessions suggested that the United States might not be able to achieve its territorial imperative by peaceable negotiation, treaty commissioners were instructed to press harder for permission to build roads across Indian country. Purportedly these were to be "paths of peace," built at United States expense for the benefit of Indians as well as whites, to facilitate the postal service to outlying settlements and to make travel quicker and easier. But war was something in which the Indians had a long experience, and they understood that roads through their land would facilitate the transport not only of travelers but also of troops, guns, and wagons full of supplies. They opposed the roads, and when they were forced to permit some road building, they positively refused all "houses of entertainment," or inns, along the roads, aware that each added convenience would increase the number of travellers through their country, thereby increasing the incidence of thefts and murders by both whites and Indians. But as debts piled up, and Forbes threatened to cut off trade unless he was paid, treaty commissioners were able to buy most of the roads they wanted. Thus when Andrew Jackson bore down upon Creek country in 1813, he found the roads, fords, bridges, and causeways he needed for moving an army.

Considering the goals of treaties and Indian awareness of those goals, it is amazing that the tribes could be persuaded to attend treaty meetings. But it must be remembered that a treaty was an exciting occasion, on its lighter side a great big party, and the Indians liked a party as well as anyone. The chiefs were approached in advance, often several times. A great deal of trouble and expense went into treaty preparations, to make the event so attractive that Indians would attend. Care was taken to choose a favorable time. The period from autumn to spring was unsuitable, because the men were off hunting; and the *boosketah*, or green-corn festival, occupied a month or more of the summer. Hawkins advised that the best months to convene Indians were March and April, when they had returned "poor and hungry" from their hunting. At that time they would be glad enough to turn out for entertainment and free rations.[2]

Usually, in fact, many more Indians showed up than had been invited, often with wives and children. The government provided rations of beef, flour, and tobacco; also some whiskey unless the chiefs specifically prohibited it. These commodites were obtained through the factories, and the early factors, Price and Wright, arranged for most provisions through regular contractors. Jonathan Halsted, when he took over the Fort Wilkinson store, engaged "to furnish the rations on better terms than have ever been at this place heretofore," and this he was able to make good by having the factory itself provide the rations, on its nonprofit basis, rather than a contractor. Indeed, Halsted claimed to have provided the flour and meat needed to feed 961 Indians at the Creek treaty of 1802 at a cost of only $2,186, compared with the $10,000 it would have cost through a contractor. Apparently he was an extraordinarily shrewd and honest businessman, because he managed to supply the beef for this treaty at three and a half cents a pound, and the flour at three cents a pound, and to round up enough of these commodities to feed the 961 Indians for twenty days with one and three-quarter pounds of meat and the same of meal per day. A share of applause is undoubtedly due Hawkins's civilization program, which by 1802 was sufficiently advanced to enable Halsted to buy enough fat cattle from Indians and Indian countrymen not only for an occasional treaty but also to supply the garrison of the fort.[3]

In the light of many complaints by the War Office that too many Indians turned out for free food and presents at the treaties, it should be noted that, while each Indian cost the government only about ten cents a day to feed at the 1802 treaty, each treaty commissioner cost almost ten dollars a day, over and above salary. Not all the supplies the commissioners ordered were basic foodstuffs; for example, at the Colerain treaty, Hawkins and Pickens had required tumblers, wine glasses, tea and coffee pots, cups and saucers, and decanters, and professional items such as paper, sealing wax, inkpots, quills, pencils, mathematical instruments, parchment, and red tape, in addition to rather a lot of delicacies, including hams, chocolate, crackers, tea, rice, tongues, madeira, port, sherry, brandy, coffee, cigars, and loaf sugar. Secretary of War Henry Dearborn grew positively apoplectic over an expense voucher submitted by James Robertson and Silas Dinsmoor when they officiated at treaty negotiations in 1805. Wrote Dearborn: "The quantity and expense of the articles of highest luxury, such as could not have been intended for Indians, exceed all reasonable bounds. The amount of the most delicate spices, anchovies, raisins, almonds, hyson tea, coffee, mustard, preserves, English cheese, segars, brandy, wine, etc. etc. could not have been either necessary or useful. Many of the articles ought never to have appeared on a bill of expenses for an Indian treaty, especially in the wilderness."[4]

In addition to those operating expenses, treaty costs had to include gifts for the Indians, from trinkets for general distribution to quite substantial presents for important chiefs, usually given on a confidential basis.

The gifts became more generous and numerous in proportion to the difficulty of getting the cession being sought. At the 1805 treaty with the Chickasaws, allowances amounting to about $5,000 were privately bestowed on tribal leaders. Smaller sums were paid other Indians who worked as messengers and interpreters. Indians selected to accompany the federal commissioners when treaty lines were run earned two dollars a day. Other expenses attendant on marking boundaries could add up to as much as the costs of the treaty itself. In September 1797, and January and February 1798, Hawkins incurred considerable expenses in marking the Creek line. Costs included his own salary of four dollars a day, that of five Creek commissioners at one dollar a day, and the pay of various interpreters, pilots, escorts, packhorsemen, surveyors, chain bearers, and their assistants, plus the rations consumed by all these people. Hawkins's bill on the United States for those items came to $1,947.40, and he paid the Indian commissioners an additional $488.75 for "extraordinary expenses." In addition to the costs of transport, food, drink, gifts, and salaries, each treaty promised the tribe payment and annuities amounting to many thousands of dollars.[5]

However much Congress might grumble at treaty costs, the Indians had to be generously entertained to put them in the mood to swear away their birthright. They themselves, in a party mood, put on quite a show at the treaty meetings. There would assemble some 500 to 1,000 chiefs and warriors, in formal paint and dress; after two or three days in which they were wined and dined by the commissioners, they would begin an elaborate ritual as prelude to the business part of the meeting. The black drink and the pipe were essential elements of any conference, and at treaties these were accompanied or preceded by rituals that are said to have been adapted from tribal rites of condolence on the death of a chief—perhaps a manifestation of the ironic humor of the Indians. The eagle-tail ceremony was a regular part of the ritual, featuring eagle feathers carried in a dance and then waved above or across the heads of the white commissioners. Soft white deerskins were used as handkerchiefs to wipe the faces of the commissioners. Then arrows or other symbols of war were broken and buried, and commissioners and chiefs exchanged embraces of friendship. White deerskins were spread on logs or other seats for the chiefs and commissioners, and they sat, hand in hand, and drank the black drink together. At Colerain a gun salute from the ships in the river added panache. Then interpreters were called forth and admonished to correct each other's interpretations if necessary (a useful reminder that much of our information about Indian affairs is based on the translations of men who were not all literate or reliably bilingual). Finally, the pipe was smoked, and the opening speeches were made. Under a blue sky, in bright sunlight, all of this must have made an impressive spectacle. In opening speeches, the fair weather was often commented on by both white and red speakers as "emblematical of our intentions," and one suspects that these introductory ceremonies were synchronized to fair weather.[6]

It is essential to bear in mind that the treaties were seldom if ever acceptable to all the Indians of the tribes involved, and that those who had not signed or did not agree to the terms did not feel bound by them. Thus many of the Creeks, especially those of the Lower Towns where Bowles's influence was strong, repudiated the cessions made at New York by McGillivray; and regarding the same treaty, the Seminoles denied that McGillivray had spoken for them in agreeing to deliver to the United States black persons residing in the Creek Nation. Another source of frequent complaints and trouble was the claim by one tribe that another had by treaty ceded land that did not belong to it, or had granted the right to build roads through territory not its own. The Indians were used to intertribal quarrels arising from infringement on each other's lands, but this was a much more serious matter. The Creeks had bitterly resented a cession by the Cherokees at Augusta in 1783 of what they claimed as Creek territory, and they hotly contested a cession made by the Choctaws in 1805 of a stretch of land to the ridge dividing the Alabama River from the Tombigbee, claiming that the Choctaws had stolen that land from them. They were still fighting that cession in 1816, and at the same time the Cherokees and other tribes were protesting that the Creeks by the treaty of Fort Jackson had ceded lands that did not belong to them.[7]

Lines of demarcation between tribes, and between them and contiguous states, especially Georgia and Tennessee, often caused trouble by their ambiguity. For that reason McGillivray insisted that Cumberland settlers stay north of the Tennessee River, because "the river is a boundary that can't be mistaken or removed." Secretary Knox advised his treaty commissioners to ascertain carefully the boundaries between the states and tribal lands, and where there was a difference of opinion on these bounds between the states and the federal government, so to negotiate matters that "the states may not conceive their legislative rights in any manner infringed." The admonitions of McGillivray and Knox were wise, but they simply did not work. Border quarrels frequently arose and were exploited by Spanish and British agents and American speculators.[8] In fact, when intertribal differences of any nature came up, American speculators were quick to encourage them. Until late in 1795, Blount and his faction consistently endeavored to set Creeks and Cherokees and Chickasaws at each other's throats. Chickasaw leader James Colbert wrote Blount in 1792: "I have to inform you that the Creeks has killed one of [our] people. . . . Now Brothers the Days has come they have spilled our Blood." He hoped Blount would soon join him so that the Chickasaws can "give the lads Drubben for they have encroach on us this great while." The two tribes did send raiding parties against each other, but the full-scale war for which Blount hoped did not occur. Early in 1795, Blount wrote Robertson that "no person could be more pleased with the killing of the five Creeks by the Chickasaws than I am" because this latest aggression would surely bring Creek retaliation, and might at last persuade the president to send an army to destroy the Creeks. Blount hoped, however, that the Creeks would not march before the president was ready to send in federal troops. Troops were not sent, and the Creeks did retaliate; six months later Blount's agent John McKee reported to him that 3,000 Creeks had marched against the Chickasaws. But the Indians were keenly aware of the dangers of disunion, and the Choctaws sent talks begging the warring tribes to be reunited, because by division the United States hoped to take their lands from them.[9]

The incessant quarreling about boundaries, which challenged treaties, invited foreign interference, created violence on the frontier, and discouraged settlement by quiet, hard-working family people, was one very cogent reason for the eagerness of the federal government to remove the Indians from lands east of the Mississippi. The need grew more pressing after the purchase of Louisiana early in Jefferson's administration, an expansion that presented a whole new set of boundary disputes. A river, as McGillivray had pointed out, is an immovable, unmistakable boundary; and it seemed more and more that the only way to obviate disputes between tribe and tribe and between states and tribes was to put the Mississippi between the red men and the white. Later treaties squeezed the Indians into intolerably confined holdings with the hope that these hunting people, on the promise of big, open grounds west of the river, would be persuaded to migrate. Only thus could every disputed boundary line be erased from the map of the southern United States.

In considering any of the various dissatisfactions resulting from treaties and spawning encroachment and violence, the role of the young Indians, the so-called wild, ungovernable young men, must not be overlooked. Some of the most eloquent and moving statements by Indians concerned the responsibilities of elders to their children; the future of the children whose elders deprived them of the woods and streams by which they lived; the reaction of the young to having roads penetrate their wilderness homelands; and the loss of respect of these young people for elders who permitted such outrages.

"Cattle Hogs and Horses are put over and stray on our lands, some [white men] will be marking trees roads, paths   my young people being about will say our old people are crazy and do not look into our rights"—so wrote a Creek chief to President James Madison. Whether the youths of the tribes were the only Indians who violated treaties, or whether they were diplomatic scapegoats, there is no doubt of the love and, more significantly, the respect that Indian parents felt for their children. In no area of culture, not even in land ownership, was there a more profound difference between red and white people. The federal commissioners at Colerain expressed white sentiments about the parent-child relationship: "The young and ambitious must be taught to respect the decisions of their wise and old chiefs . . . they must be taught to respect the law, to acquiesce in its decisions, and not to attempt to be judges in their own case." On another occasion Hawkins asked a Creek elder: "Do your chiefs see there danger arising from the misconduct of their young men? . . . Do they see the wickedness of your young men, who even steal the horses of the agents who attend my orders, and are not punished? Do they see that they must help me or all is lost?" And again Hawkins stated, "Your young men must be attentive to their chiefs, and then you will be a great people." Hawkins was convinced, "their young men have been sadly corrupted, and there is not energy enough in any arrangement hitherto attempted to govern them."[10]

Hawkins had a better understanding of Indian life and thought than most of his colleagues, but he was incapable of construing the absence of child discipline as due to anything but a lack of effort. A recent study of Indians today found that they are reluctant to tell others what to do, and that they are permissive toward their children for fear of retaliation if they try to discipline them. Certainly retaliation was an active concept in Indian philosophy, and the Creeks did express a fear that, if they gave away land, their youth might revolt. Most Indian utterances suggest love and esteem for youth, however, rather than fear. At the 1802 treaty Efau Haujo said, "When a man has a child, he considers him, and is not willing to distress him and make him poor." In 1801 the Choctaws had asked that their young people, as well as the elders, be given a hearing at treaties. Hawkins was annoyed when young Creek warriors repeatedly hindered the running of a treaty line to which their elders had agreed, but the chiefs knew why their young people were obstructive. They explained that intrusions on their land and infringement of their rights to its timber and game "rendered their young men ungovernable" and was the real cause of their depredations. Hawkins knew that, but could not accept the Indian view that young people had the right to influence their own fate.[11]

Treaty terms in general varied little up to the Fort Jackson treaty in 1814, in spite of increasing discontent and opposition. The parties agreed to maintain eternal peace and friendship. The negotiating tribe or tribes agreed to acknowledge the protection and sovereignty of the United States; to restore white prisoners, escaped or stolen blacks, and any livestock, horses, or other property taken from United States citizens; to inform the federal agents of any crime or any plan inimical to United States interests of which they might learn; and to cede to the United States specified portions of land and assist in running the new lines established by such cessions. In return, the United States agreed to give for the ceded land certain payments in money, goods, services, equipment, and instruction and, in addition, an annuity to be shared by the tribe. Furthermore, it guaranteed to the tribe the integrity of all its territory south and west of the new boundary; it promised that any white intruder in such territory would forfeit the protection of the United States and that the Indians might punish him as they wished, and that any white person who committed a criminal act against an Indian would be punished as if the crime were against another white. Finally, the integrity of earlier treaties, except for changes now made, was affirmed; and it was stated that the treaty would become valid when ratified by the president with the advice and consent of the Senate. No allowance was made for ratification by the Indian nation involved.

Special terms made their appearance as the immediate goals of treaties changed. When the treaty was chiefly concerned with roads rather than territory, the nature, direction, landmarks, and destination of the road were specified. Where a cession was to be made so that the tribe might pay its debts, that purpose was stated in the treaty, along with the amount of money that the tribe would receive to turn over to its creditors, and some additional gifts or annuities for individual members of the tribe for their help—that is, bribes.

The Hopewell treaty, made in the early days of generous, democratic sentiments, contained one provision that gave Blount and other speculators a great deal of trouble: the Indians were given the right to send a deputation to Congress whenever they wished. Some of the early deputations had good reason for their visits, as, for example, the Cherokees who went to complain of the treaty that Blount had forced on them in 1791. These visits made for good feeling among the Indians, and for a time the government welcomed them, sending the guests home well pleased with their presents and entertainment and with stories to tell of their good treatment. But their glowing reports encouraged more visits than were considered necessary or desirable. Within a few years Secretary of War Pickering complained that "Six Indians, Chickasaws and Choctaws, have strolled to Philadelphia" for no apparent reason but to get presents. After they had been given clothes and guns and sent on their way home, Pickering advised Governor Blount, "I am desirous of discouraging such irregular and unauthorized visits." Pickering's successor, James McHenry, also tried to discourage mere junkets, as many of the Indians' visits seemed to be, because they were expensive and time-consuming. Hawkins, as a commissioner at Hopewell, had been at least partly responsible for the clause permitting deputations. In 1798 even he instructed the Choctaw agent that such visits were to be avoided in future; enough Indians had by now reported on the good treatment accorded them.[12]

But petitions to see the president continued, for at least one good reason: the president whom Indians had visited in 1792 was not the same man as the president they wanted to visit in 1798. "Your Father the President" was no longer Father Washington, whom they knew, but Father Adams, whom they had not met and probably wished very much to see. In 1801 there was yet another "father," President Jefferson. Although visits were ever more firmly discouraged, the Hopewell treaty obligation had to be honored if the Indians insisted on it. The presents to visitors grew more and more lavish, including, as recommended in 1812, a magnificent outfit of formal clothing, with gorgets and medals and gold-laced coats for each chief, and somewhat plainer suits for those of lower rank.[13]

Talk was an outstanding feature of treaties and other formal meetings, and treaty talk is about the only kind of Indian expression of which we have considerable records. There are no records, of course, of Indians communicating casually with one another, because they had no written language. A few informal conversations between Indians and white men were recorded by the whites, and we have some letters dictated by Indians to persons who could put their thoughts into English and write them down; but such letters are rare because so few in Indian country could write. Critical judgments of Indian talk therefore are based almost entirely on treaty speeches, a highly specialized mode of communication significant only in its particular framework.

Lieutenant Timberlake remarked of the Cherokees: "They have many of them a good uncultivated genius, are fond of speaking well, as that paves the way to power in their councils." The Creeks and other tribes were practiced speakers on important matters, since their government operated on principles of consultation and consensus at every level. The micco of a town sat with his counsellors and warriors every day in the town square to smoke a pipe and discuss town problems and the news. Evenings, the whole town or village met in what the traders called the "hot house," a public building kept very warm by a good fire, for dancing, singing, joking, games, and chitchat. Annual national councils of the Creeks, instituted by Hawkins, and occasional joint councils of the several tribes, gave the Indians further opportunities to exercise their skill in talking.[14]

They talked excessively, in the opinion of some contemporaneous and also some modern critics. John Innerarity, representing the John Forbes trading house at the Creek council of 1812, suffered extreme boredom, and in his diary he complained of the deliberateness and repetitiveness of the Indian speakers: "Big Warrior began an endless talk about all that had been told at the Hickory Ground to Mr. Forbes," he wrote; and again, "They had now been sitting three days exclusively on my business & had yet done nothing." He was quite exasperated by day-long arguments about business matters, in which the Creeks seemed designedly obtuse and insisted on going over the same ground again and again. But Innerarity was trying to explain to them that they owed to his company not only the capital sum of their debt but also interest on it for a number of years, and the chances are that the Creeks simply did not comprehend the concept of interest, for which they had no word in their language. Questions, complaints, arguments, and a resort to figurative language about concepts foreign to Indian life cannot be taken to mean that the prolixity and metaphor of treaty language characterized Indian speech in general.[15]

Timberlake had commented in a more tactful way than Innerarity that Cherokee talk was pretty tedious: "As the ideas of the Cherokee are so few, I cannot say much for the copiousness of their language." An informed scholar of today calls the Indians prolix to exhaustion, painstakingly careful in the unfolding of an argument of seemingly immense complexity, in speech larded with repetition and stereotyped metaphor. A more expanded view of Indian talk might note that at treaties the Indians were fighting for their lives; as defendants, they might be expected to argue their case at length, to repeat important testimony, to insist on understanding the charges against them, to be represented by counsel. When vital matters were at stake—perhaps the loss of thousands of acres of the land that fed them—meetings naturally went on for days, weeks, even months; different speakers were brought forth to present various facets of the argument, frequent recesses were called for consultation among the chiefs. Arguments were presented as persuasively as possible, through both direct and figurative speech.[16]

There were white commentators who found beauty and nobility in the formal language of Indians. Bartram, the complete admirer, wrote, "All the Indian languages are truly rhetorical, or figurative, assisting their speech by tropes; their hands, flexure of the head, the brows, in short, every member, naturally associate, and give their assistance to render their harangues eloquent, persuasive and effectual." The poetic speech of Chief

Logan of the Mingo tribe in Pennsylvania (who was possibly not an Indian at all), bewailing the massacre of his family in 1774, was extravagantly admired by many, including Jefferson, and became a favorite "elocution" piece of schoolboys. But Bernard Sheehan cites other authorities with different views: Abbé Raynal, who believed the imagistic quality of Indian [formal] speech resulted from the inability of the savage mind to comprehend abstractions; and Amos Stoddard, a historian of the time, who believed that the Indian languages were incapable of expressing abstractions. As in the matter of the quantity of Indian speech, so with its quality: one may expect any man to say what he can, with any embellishment of rhetoric that may make his argument clearer and more persuasive, when, as at treaties, he is fighting for his and his children's survival. In other situations, Indian communication could be quite literal, brief, and unemotive.[17]

At national council meetings, where Indians talked to each other and to Hawkins with a minimum of formality, the language was almost entirely direct. For treaties the Indians dusted off certain formal phrases that were as traditionally appropriate to the circumstances as their formal clothes, gorgets, and medals. White treaty commissioners used the same kinds of formal expressions, and there is no way of knowing with certainty who, in the distant past of Indian-white negotiations, had introduced them. Treaty conventions called for the use of symbols on both sides. The whites gave medals and gifts in token of respect and peaceful intentions; the sixteen-gun salute at the Colerain treaty was a polite, impressive, and quite meaningless ceremony of respect, because there is no sixteen-gun salute.[18]

Some of the objects produced by the Indians were true symbols: the stick, a concrete expression for the punishment of malefactors by beating or some more horrid use of it; the pipe and the broken weapons, symbolizing peace. Other objects sometimes produced by the Indians were practical as well as symbolic: a bundle of sticks served not only as a symbol for the period of time until a scheduled event but also as a calendar, because the time could be measured by breaking one stick each day; and the wampum belt symbolizing peace was also a mnemonic device, like the quipu of the Incas, which by its colors

and patterns enabled a trained "rememberer" to recall and repeat what had passed at a particular meeting, thus providing a
record for people who had no written language.

To form any reliable idea of Indian talk, one must listen to it.
The excerpts chosen for presentation here are from formal
treaty and council speeches, and from the much smaller body
or recorded informal communications, chiefly with Hawkins.
They are sometimes embellished with symbol, simile, and metaphor; or, when the situation demanded, they were starkly, urgently, plain. Sometimes a little joke would lighten a serious
matter, as in this address of Efau Haujo, Speaker of the Creek
Nation, to his fellow Creeks and Hawkins at the National Council meeting of 1798: "I will give you a little talk this afternoon as
a beginning, and we will then go on until we have accomplished
the business we have met on. The first thing I will mention is
relative to the cattle ranging on our lands. They cannot be re-
strained well; they do not understand stipulations relative to
boundaries; where they have once had good grass they will go
again."[19]

Next day Yeauholau Micco addressed Hawkins, showing a
belt of white wampum that the northern tribes, still subdued by
the terrible defeat that General Wayne had inflicted on them a
few years earlier, had sent to be circulated among the southern
tribes: "This belt you have seen and it has been explained to
you, and I have at this meeting explained it to the chiefs, and
now I call you to witness we take fast hold of the belt; it is usual
with us when we speak of peace, to hold this white emblem in
our hands, and this is the belt we use on such great and important occasions. This mode of transacting our business was
handed down to us by our forefathers; they are all dead and
gone and we, their descendants, are following in their ways."[20]

That evening Efau Haujo displayed another wampum belt,
this one of blue and white beads, to be sent to President Adams
"with a view to join the hands of the people of the United States
and the people of my land." This called for a metaphor, or as
Bartram nicely called it, a trope: "When you and we have done
all we can I hope we shall immitate a happy family who have
swept the yard and are siting down viewing the children who
are innocently playing in it." Then Efau Haujo at once ex-

pressed in abstract form: saying, "I wish to remove every obstruction to a happy reconciliation between the red and white."[21]

Symbol, trope, and abstraction all appear in the following excerpt from another speech by Efau Haujo, this one a message to the Seminoles describing a meeting of Creeks and Chickasaws: "We all met and agreed to bury all past grievances and settle all matters with our neighbors and friends, & in token of our everlasting friendship, we have cut up a large piece of tobacco, filled our pipes, and made a white smoke in token of friendship with all our neighbors, red and white, & as the smoke ascended to the skies never to return, so we hope to remain in peace with red and white as long as the sun rises."[22]

"They are silent except when land is mentioned," Hawkins observed of the Indians, "and the bare mention excites very disagreeable emotions." The treaties after Jefferson's election in 1801 mentioned land frequently and more urgently than ever before, and for a better understanding of the true scope, force, and general quality of Indian talk, the minutes of the treaty of 1802 with the Creeks at Fort Wilkinson provide excellent examples. The opening ceremonies of the treaty, at which General James Wilkinson was the senior commissioner, accompanied by Hawkins and Andrew Pickens, were particularly elaborate, and so were the opening ceremonial statements. On the part of the Indians, the sharp weapons were buried, the deerskins were spread, and the pipe was smoked. Then the clearness and brightness of the day were remarked upon, and a white staff was presented, before hands were joined for the drinking of the black drink. Wilkinson was more than a match in verbosity for any of the chiefs when he responded:

> I have received from your chief speaker this white staff; it is an emblem of peace; I shall lean upon it. . . . We have been appointed to brighten the chain of friendship between the red and white people of this country. . . . We have been pleased to see the bloody arrow and the tomahawk buried in the earth. . . . We view with you the blueness of the sky, the brightness of the sun, and serenity of the day, as emblems favorable to a happy issue of our negotiations.[23]

The speeches were friendly, but the chiefs had anticipated the meeting for several months with great agitation, knowing that they would be asked for large amounts of land. In April,

Georgia had ceded for $1,250,000 all of its western lands to the United States government, on the understanding that the federal government would expeditiously extinguish Indian rights in that territory. This, too, the Indians probably knew.[24]

Wilkinson began softly enough, asking the Creeks if it would not be wise to sell some of their more distant lands (the ones most wanted were those closest to the Mississippi) to provide for their old and poor by an immediate payment in part, and for their progeny by annuities in goods and money. This, he said, would defeat the mischief-makers "who lead your young men astray." But what Wilkinson was asking for, however softly, was land, and the Indians became disagreeably excited. Efau Haujo spoke for them:

> I was told by your beloved men, that the talk you have given us was straight, and that, before we parted, every thing would be straight on both sides. . . . The thing that was asked us to part with, was like asking us to cut ourselves in two, and take one half one way, and the other half the other way. . . . Upon the talk you gave us, we have considered much; it was some time before I could make up my mind upon it, but I have weighed it well, and am now going to give my mind upon it. When a man has a child, he considers him, and is not willing to distress him and make him poor. . . . We now give on paper (delivering the map) what we mean and intend; it is a map of the country we cede.[25]

What he offered was less than the commissioners had hoped for.

Efau Haujo went on to explain his fears that the new boundary, a land boundary west of the Oconee River, would not be as clear a line of demarcation as the river had been and would bring more whites and their stock wandering into Indian country. Yet he nevertheless agreed to the cession:

> This day the land under us we have given up, the trees around us, the water, fine for mills, and good land, and a great deal of it. The good that will arise from the land will have no end; in the summer there will be the grass for stock, and other things in the winter; I consider these things, and I have given them up. The way of the red is this; they are a poor people; if there be any oak trees, they get acorns from them, and from the hickory trees they get nuts, and the blackberries in their season.[26]

In the long and difficult negotiations that followed, the Indian speeches were remarkably succinct and unembellished. It was the commissioners who, now and then, talked figuratively to drive home a point. Hawkins, for example, warned that the Lower Creeks and Seminoles "have taken a white man, of the name of Bowles, made him a chief, and are, in his name, carrying on a war against Spain. . . . In this state of things, the Creek nation may be compared to a piece of spunk; that fire is struck in it, on the side of the Seminoles, and it is likely to burn up the whole nation, if not timely extinguished." [27]

For some reason the chiefs came next day offering a cession even larger than the commissioners expected or had asked, and that concluded negotiations. Possibly some chiefs had been bribed, but more probably they all realized that refusal would bring them only suffering and eventual, inevitable loss of what they refused. As Cherokee chiefs said a number of years later, when they were told they must vacate their homeland and move west of the Mississippi: "The theory upon which you have founded the principle of taking private property for public good, we are not fully capable of comprehending your excellency's ideas on that point; unless you mean that the public good requires the acquisition of this country, and that you are determined to seize it." [28]

Undoubtedly the Creeks at the 1802 treaty knew that settlers, speculators, and troublemakers would come pouring across the new boundary. Any doubts that the Indians of the South knew precisely and could express clearly and briefly the complex problems by which they were surrounded are dispelled by Hawkins's record of a conversation with Tustennugee Emautlau in 1797. Hawkins had asked the chief: "Have you heard any thing of the difficulties which surround the four nations, of Blount and his projects, or Cox and his, and other intruders on the Indian rights?" The chief had replied, in what Hawkins described as "a bold, candid, and intelligent manner":

> Yes, I was one who attended the meeting of the four nations; There I heard all about it; the Coweta Micco [Little Turkey] told us everything; the difficulties you had with the white and red people about the Cherokee line; that Fushe Micco and Chasse Tunne [Blount and Chisholm] wanted to get you out of the Indian country, that they might ruin the red people; that Cox, the leader of the Ecunnaunuxulgee [land-grabbers] was ready to seize upon the Muscle Shoals, but you and the officers of the government had disappointed all of them. He told us the difficulty you had with the red

people; that you set down with them at Tuskegee and talked to them as if you were their father; you told them their situation; that they must restrain their young men and make them leave off horse stealing and medling with the white people's property; that you did not once threaten them, but beged they would listen to your talks; that if they did not, they were a ruined people in spite of all you and the officers of government could do, and the Ecunnaunuxulgee would rejoice at it and get possession of their whole country.

"I certify the foregoing to be faithfully translated from the Creek," Timothy Barnard appended to the memorandum of this conversation. It would be difficult to improve on this précis of events during Hawkins's first year as agent, either for comprehensiveness, accuracy, or plain speaking.[29]

CHAPTER 8

The Dirt King, William Blount

To comprehend the troubles in the South, the restlessness and apprehensions of the southern tribes and the problems of Hawkins in protecting these Indians and their country, it is necessary to examine in some detail the ambitious plans of William Blount, which Hawkins was jeopardizing by his presence. "Can't Rogers contrive to get the Creeks to desire the President to talk Hawkins out of the nation," Blount urged one of his men, James Carey, "for if he stays in the Creek nation he can and will do great injury to our plan."[1]

A scheme of the magnitude of Blount's encompasses so many subplots, entwines so many lives in its coils, that it bears study from a hundred different angles. The purpose here is to expose its impact on the Indians, who had what the schemers wanted, and on Hawkins, who stood between the opposing forces. Hawkins's dilemma sprang from his double duty: to protect the rights of both red and white Americans. As he expressed it to a group of Cherokee chiefs: "You may depend upon my taking great care of your interests and those of the white people. I know no difference between you, you live on the same land and are intitled to equal rights, and must live as friends and brothers, and it is my particularly [sic] duty to see justice equally distributed among you."[2]

Hawkins not only guarded Indian rights but kept the Indians informed of what he was doing. Thus, he told the Chickasaws: "You have heard of an attempt of Zachariah Cox and Co. to settle the bent [bend] of Tennessee; he . . . applied to me for permission to come and trade among you, but as he stated his object fully, and as I am informed that the Indians . . . looked on him as the precursor of those who are represented as grasping after their lands . . . I have not consented to indulge Mr. Cox with the permission he applied for."³

A short time after that frank talk about Cox's intentions, Hawkins had the first startling news of Blount's much larger and more dangerous plot. Hawkins's letters to Blount, quoted in Chapter 2, plainly show that by 1797 he had entertained suspicions about Blount for ten years or more. When Hawkins went into Indian country, his suspicions were immediately reinforced. In a letter to a friend in 1797 he referred to Blount as "the man, my old friend . . . and untill the last year or two of my being a member of the Senate, deemed to be of the purest integrity."⁴

Far from being of "purest integrity" in the 1790s, Blount had been trading illegally in Indian lands since, at latest, 1783, when he entered into his partnership with James Robertson for the purpose of taking title to 100,000 acres of unceded Indian land.⁵ In 1785 at the treaty of Hopewell, Hawkins was a Federal commissioner and Blount a North Carolina observer guarding the interests of the speculators. Blount, finding that the new boundary did little more than reiterate the existing line, immediately protested the treaty, claiming that it infringed on North Carolina's legislative rights. Some of the lands left to the Indians, he said, had already been appropriated by North Carolina for its Revolutionary War veterans' bounties, and several million more acres had been sold by the state to the white occupants of those lands. Hawkins in his official report noted Blount's protest briefly and without comment, but privately to Jefferson he showed his feelings about North Carolina's refusal to agree to any line "between the Indians and the citizens, as they claim all the land westward according to their bill of rights and that the Indians are only tenants at will."⁶

In 1787, Spain showed its intention of prohibiting Mississippi navigation by seizing American vessels. During the same year Thomas Blount was in London, possibly putting out feelers to the British government in the interest of his brother William and other speculators in western lands. Unlike Sevier, Robertson, James White, and Daniel Smith, William Blount does not seem to have been flirting with a Spanish alliance at that time, or if he was he did not let his name appear. Such was the confusion in the West that Robertson in 1788, in addition to his overtures to Spain, also promised Bowles and McGillivray to support a British attack on Florida if they would halt Creek hostilities in the Cumberland area. According to the later testimony of William Cunningham, Blount was in on this offer to the British, along with Robertson, Sevier, and other speculators.[7]

In 1790 the Territory of the Southwest was organized, and Blount was appointed its governor by President Washington. Blount at once gained absolute control of the territory by filling important posts with family members and cronies. Thus his brother Willie and Hugh Lawson White became his confidential secretaries; John Chisholm was named a magistrate; Sevier and Robertson were made brigadier generals, heading the militias of the Washington and Mero districts respectively; Daniel Smith became secretary and surveyor for the territory; Andrew Jackson was chosen as attorney general for the Cumberland District; David Allison was among those admitted as attorneys in the territorial courts; lesser positions, and Blount's payroll, show the names of Alex Outlaw, James Carey, and Robert King. From John Steele in Congress to Sevier's son Jo, a trader and carter, Blount's entourage was hand-picked.[8]

Blount, now in a powerful position to advance the interests of speculators, sent Robert King to call the Cherokees to a meeting in May 1791, at the confluence of the French Broad and Holston rivers, to remedy the damage he and other speculators felt had been done them by the Hopewell treaty. In March, two months before the meeting, Hawkins wrote Blount very freely his thoughts on the rights of the Indians to their lands and the responsibility of white intruders for Indian hostilities. He strongly advised Blount not to try for the Tennessee River as the Indian line, as it was rumored he would. Stressing his own faith in Blount's integrity, Hawkins went on to give his views:

> If you should but attempt so enormous a grasp in the present situation of affairs as all the lands on the North side of the Tennessee, you will rouse the resentment of the Cherokees, give serious alarm to the Chickasaws and risk cause of suspicion to the Creeks and Choctaws, a part of those lands are considered as a sort of common property among the hunters of all these nations. —They will suppose you are favouring the great land companies who are aspiring to the possession of all their lands, and why do this when in my op-

nion no possible advantage can result from it? . . . You know how reluctantly the Indians part with their lands and when the Commissioners in 1785 labored to induce them to give up those lying between the fork of French broad and Holstein, they refused positively and appealed to the justice of Congress.

Later in this very long letter, Hawkins seems to have been trying to let Blount know he was aware of the machinations of the speculators:

I am very desirous that you should stand well with the southern tribes, and if you do but set out right you secure their friendship. You are their Superintendant and they will look to you for protection. —Our fellow citizens must be compelled to respect the plighted faith of their government, and the rights of their neighbours, hitherto all our acts of No Carolina seem to favour intruders, whenever the land office was opened special provision was made for intruders under the appellation of occupants, and however strange it may seem you well know that by violating a solemn treaty these people could acquire this *right of occupancy*.[9]

For all Hawkins's protests of confidence, one reads between the lines a stern disapproval of Blount's plans for the Holston treaty.

Immediately before the treaty meeting, Hawkins again wrote Blount, in a tone a shade more censorious:

I am apprehensive you will have great difficulty in accommodating the Indians and citizens, the latter I am told are, many of them, very desirous of your acquiring an immense territory for them. The former I take it are as desirous that you should not get one acre. . . . As far as I can judge you continue high in the estimation of those who are deserving of respect, and with whom you do business. I have seen many letters and all of them in which you are mentioned in a stile favourable to you, one excepted and that perhaps not intentionally. . . . Your appointment of attorneys is disliked by some on your side of the mountains and deemed unconstitutional.[10]

But Blount's plans for the treaty were well advanced when Hawkins wrote that letter. Blount's agent, Robert King, was not very successful in inducing Cherokees to attend, perhaps partly because of a rumor that when they assembled at the appointed place they would be slaughtered, but also because they knew that when the Dirt King summoned them they would be asked for land, a lot of land. Nevertheless, Blount, acting as sole commissioner for the United States, proceeded to negotiate the Holston treaty with the forty-one chiefs who came, and got from them a cession of the northern and eastern parts of Cherokee territory—land on which intruders were already living—as well as the right to put a road through Cherokee hunting ground connecting Washington District in the east with Mero in the west, and the right to unmolested navigation of the Tennessee.[11]

The treaty looked innocent enough on paper. Possibly on Hawkins's advice, the Indians did not appear to have been asked for great cessions. Still, Blount was enabled to open up lands west of the Tennessee River, an area where he held claims, although he did not acquire nearly enough territory to satisfy all the other speculators. Hawkins, on the Senate committee to study the treaty, recommended ratification in the belief that the boundary it set was nearly the same as the line of the Hopewell treaty. He had no accurate idea where the treaty line was meant to fall until some years later, when he was appointed a commissioner to survey it. The president approved Blount's treaty with the advice and consent of the Senate in November 1791.[12]

When the year after the treaty an "experimental" line was drawn by Blount's commissioners, the Cherokees were enraged to find that it struck the Holston River much farther south than they had expected and thus cut far more deeply than they had anticipated into their territory. They rejected the treaty to which only forty-one chiefs had agreed, and there followed a surge of Cherokee hostilities and Tennessee reprisals. Blount pressed on with documenting Cherokee crimes against whites. No white man suspected of any connection with the speculators was safe in Cherokee country, and President Washington feared for Blount's own safety. Hawkins, if ever he had been ignorant of Blount's design to liquidate the Indians, must surely then have been alerted. Hawkins was serving in the Senate when a Cherokee delegation led by Leonard Shaw, federal agent to the Cherokees, arrived in Philadelphia in the summer of 1792, and he heard the bitter Cherokee protests that the Blount treaty had cheated them, that intruders were settling on their lands, and that they could not cede the Muscle Shoals as demanded because they shared rights there with the other tribes. David Allison had written Hawkins before the arrival of the Cherokees that Governor Blount would be much obliged if Hawkins would use his influence to prevent Indians from going to Congress with complaints against the Governor, which might result in measures "which would destroy private property obtained under the sanction of the law"—more precisely, occupancy by whites of land not yet relinquished by the Indians.[13]

Hawkins answered Allisons' letter directly to his principal, Blount, and while still affirming that Blount had the president's confidence, he unyieldingly repeated his own interpretation of land rights in Indian territory:

> The doctrine here is, that those who hold tittles to lands within the Indian boundaries have only the right of preemption, and cannot be put into possession but by extinguishment of Indian claims. That the State possessed no other, and could give no other right. That this right is secured by the cession, and the only one the general Government feel bound to support. . . . To this it may be asked whether the general government have it in their power to keep [here the letter is torn] preemptioners from getting into the possession of their rights until it is perfectly agreeable to the Indians to relinquish their claims, and for the government [torn; not?] the individual claimants to purchase that relinquishment? The answer here is indisputably they have that right.[14]

The total opposition of the views of Hawkins and Blount is apparent in a letter Hawkins had written to President Washington a couple of months earlier. It said, in part:

> During the war we acknowledged the Indians as brothers, told them of our difficulties and embarrassments arising from our contest with Great Britain, assured them of our disposition tho' unable to furnish them such comforts as they had been accustomed to receive, urged them to be patient and declared that when success crowned our efforts, they should be partakers of our good fortune. they were then acknowledged to be possessors of the soil on which they lived.
> At the close of the war being anxiously desirous of paying to our officers and soldiers as much of their well earned dues as was apparently within the view of the government we seem to have Forgotten altogether the rights of the Indians. They were treated as tenants at will—we seized on their lands and made a division of the same as possessing allodial rights alloted certain portions to the in-

dians for hunting grounds and did not even think of offering them compensation for any claims they might pretend to have to those reserved for other purposes of the government. This doctrine it might be expected would be disliked by the independent tribes. It was so and was complained of by them. It is the cause of their hostility.

Those at the head of affairs to westward, Hawkins's letter to Washington continued, are for war, and war will be their harvest. As for himself, Hawkins said, "I am for peace. . . . As long as we attempt to go into their country or to remain there we shall be at war."[15]

Almost simultaneously with this letter of Hawkins's, Blount had sent to Congress his dossier of Indian crimes and the testimony of one of his men, James Carey, that the Cherokees had committed offenses against Cumberland settlers and were determined on war, and that no adjustment of the boundary would stop their murders of frontiersmen.[16]

Since the Indians had the right to take complaints to Congress, Hawkins could not, if he had so wished, oblige Blount by preventing them. Lawful means lacking, Blount seems to have taken other steps to keep the Indians from complaining of him. A Cherokee chief, Hanging Maw, in June 1793 assembled at his home a group of Indians for one of those visits to Philadelphia to complain of the land-jobbers, when suddenly Captain John Beard of the United States Mounted Infantry descended on Hanging Maw's house, wounded him, and murdered his wife Betty along with ten or eleven others present. It was claimed by Daniel Smith, who was acting governor during an absence of Blount at that time, that Beard's attack had not been authorized. The captain was court-martialed the following month, but instead of being punished for exceeding his authority he was promoted; by August he was being referred to as Major Beard, and was warmly commended to the secretary of war for his service in patrolling the Cumberland frontier. In 1794 the whites living south of the Ohio sent a memorial to Congress saying help was urgently needed by the "Southwestern frontier in general and Mero district in particular" against savage tribes.[17]

In 1793 and 1794 hostilities on both sides escalated. Creeks and Cherokees went on the warpath. Sevier and Robertson re-

taliated with raids deep into Indian country led by their lieuten-
ants Harrison, Beard, and Ore. Blount went to Philadelphia
and pressed for a vigorous punitive policy, which alone, he said,
would teach the Indians to respect treaties. He persevered in
demands for action by federal troops, backing up his stand with
his long lists of whites hurt, robbed, or killed by Indians. It
could not pain Secretary of War Knox more to read the bloody
catalogue, Blount said, than it had him to compile it. It proved,
however, he said, that Mero District must be guarded by federal
troops; as for the Creeks, he believed they could be cheaply
destroyed by some United States forces aided by Cherokees,
Chickasaws, and Choctaws. Blount's conduct seems to have
raised some doubts in Congress and the administration about
his disinterestedness in seeking the reliquishment of Indian
lands and the annihilation of the Creeks. A letter to Blount
from his ally in Congress, John Steele, warned against trust-
ing "the sunshine faces" that some of his enemies might assume; from Steele's disparaging references in the letter to "the
Secretary" and "the Major General"—probably Secretary of
State Jefferson and Secretary of War Knox—it seems likely that
Blount's integrity was in question on a high level.[18]

When the Southwest Territory was admitted to the union as
the state of Tennessee in 1795, its governor no longer retained
the function of superintendent of Indians; but the agents to the
various tribes, such as McKee to the Cherokees, had been
Blount choices. All other jobs of importance also remained
firmly in control of the ecunnaunuxulgee, the land-grabbers:
Sevier was elected governor, Blount was sent to the Senate and
Andrew Jackson to the House of Representatives, and Gen.
James Winchester became Speaker of the state senate. Whatever restraints upon his conduct Blount may have felt as an
officer of the federal government were removed when he was
territorial governor. His loyalty to his state took precedence, and
Tennessee became, in effect, a fiefdom of the land speculators.

Hawkins's career took a precisely opposite turn. His appointment to the federal office of principal temporary agent to the
Indians south of the Ohio relieved him of any lingering loyalty
to William Blount or to the interests of any man, group, or
state; his loyalty now was pledged to the nation, and his duty

was to protect it from harm. "I had not been two days on the frontiers of Tennessee before I suspected there was some thing in train of execution injurious to the United States," he wrote a friend; "Colonel Henley, Mr. Dinsmoor, Gen'l Pickens and myself spoke freely to each other on the subject, and we were induced to exert all our vigilance." Meanwhile, Blount's plans were moving forward in new directions, since his efforts to induce the tribes to kill one another off had failed, and likewise his campaign to persuade the federal government to liquidate them. Hawkins was in the way; his vigilance would have to be dealt with, and in dealing with it Blount finally overstepped the line between mere land speculation, endemic in the West, and crime. "A something crept into the State of Tennessee," Hawkins wrote, "which leaped over the bounds of decency and law, and determined to put the government to defiance."[19]

In the spring of 1797, Hawkins was a federal commissioner to run the line between Tennessee and Cherokee country as established by the Hopewell and Holston treaties, the first official line to be run since the United States had won independence. When he reported for that duty, he immediately sensed something "injurious to the United States."

The other commissioners were Andrew Pickens, whom Hawkins knew well and respected, and General James Winchester. Winchester had done his part in the effort to have the United States Army march against the Cherokees; he wrote to Blount, undoubtedly for the eyes of the War Department, that frontier citizens were living "like besieged garrisons" because of Indian murderers, and he expressed his belief that, "if Congress knew their deplorable situation . . . they would not suffer a banditti of merciless savages to murder the citizens of the United States continually, with impunity." Tim Barnard, who was accompanying Hawkins, had recently commented that he had never seen the Indians so peaceable, the more remarkable a circumstance, he said, because "the woods on this side the Oconee on the Indian land is swarmed with hogs, horses and cattle" from across the border.[20]

Early in April, Hawkins arrived at Tellico Blockhouse on the Tennessee River near the Cherokee border, in good time for his rendezvous with the other commissioners. He and Pickens waited and waited for General Winchester to show up. Finally Hawkins got word from the general that he had not received Hawkins's letters, had misunderstood instructions and believed it was the Creek line that they were to run, and therefore had not come because he knew nothing of Creek country. Hawkins was not deceived: "He must certainly know that Tellico Blockhouse is on the Tennessee . . . and that we could never be so absurd as to come from the Creek line two hundred and fifty miles here for the purpose merely of meeting him to accompany us back again." He wrote the secretary of war about Winchester's "very extraordinary" explanation, and said he believed the real purpose was to delay the line until intruding settlers could plant their crops, after which it would be much harder to dislodge them. More weeks went by, and Winchester still did not appear. The Indians were becoming apprehensive and restless with suspense about where the line would fall and how much territory they would lose. Captain Richard Sparks, commander of United States forces in Tennessee, had advised Ensign George Strother, commandant at Tellico Blockhouse, that the Indians were dangerous and that Strother was not to obey orders of the commissioners to protect the Indians from a rumored attack by "lawless persons." Hawkins and Pickens wanted to proceed alone, but Winchester insisted all three commissioners must be present. They received information that his dilatoriness was part of a plan of "some persons" to frustrate the running of the line. "We are well aware of the speculative pursuits of the General," Hawkins noted in a memorandum.[21]

Before the end of April, about 300 Indians had gathered at Tellico, far more than Hawkins had invited, determined to see for themselves that the line was run properly, and Hawkins held conferences with them for several days. White settlers in the area of the line also came to Tellico, to make certain the boundary would coincide with the experimental line that Blount had run and would not exclude their plantations. They demanded admittance to Hawkins's talks with the Indians, which he refused. In his talks, Hawkins explained to the Indians that, although they might be dissatisfied with the Holston boundary, they had agreed to it, and the president had signed the treaty, and no alteration was now possible. Reluctantly they accepted this and chose their own delegates to accompany the commissioners—without Winchester—in running the line.[22]

Blount had anticipated, and perhaps secretly helped to stage, the troubles attendant on marking the boundary. He did not wish in any way to be associated with it, and he had advised his agent, Carey, "not to be present at the running of the line, nor to have anything to do with it, as . . . it would be a troublesome business, and might occasion the Indians to reflect on me." He very likely had advised Winchester to stay away for the same reasons. While Hawkins was at Tellico, Blount, who was on his way to Philadelphia for a Senate session, wrote a letter to Carey dated April 21, briefing him on what were to be the final steps in an elaborate scheme of speculation and treason.[23]

The purpose of the scheme, Blount's supporters persistently claimed, was simply to gain the freedom of the Mississippi for Tennesseeans, but it seems that that purpose was to be gained by involving British, French, and Spanish officials in speculations in United States lands. The details and personae of the plot have never been completely revealed, but there is documentation of the involvement of Lord Grenville, British foreign secretary; Richard Liston, British minister to the United States; and John Simcoe, governor of Canada. The Marquis de las Casas, Spanish ambassador to Great Britain, and Count de Moustier, the pre–French Revolution minister to the United States, are said to have originated the plan. John Murray, earl of Dunmore, who was governor of the Bahamas, was allegedly included in the scheme, and also William Augustus Bowles. A complete roster would name in addition Dr. Nicholas Romayne, a trustee of Columbia University, and James Mountflorence, Blount's land agent in France. In the tremendous cast were members of Congress Hugh Williamson, John Steele, and James White; George Roulstone, publisher of the Knoxville *Gazette*; Gen. James Wilkinson and other United States Army officers; Blount's brothers; Blount associates Sevier, Robertson, and Chisholm; numerous important connections by marriage of the Blount family, and connections of those connections, including Andrew Jackson; entry takers in the local land offices and local surveyors; and so on through a host of bit players—

traders, Indian agents, Indian fighters—down to such lowly Indian countrymen as John Rogers and James Carey.[24]

What actions were to be taken, and what was to be accomplished, differ according to different accounts. Blount's supporters claimed the goal was simply free use of the Mississippi. Hugh Williamson said that Blount meant to help Britain seize Florida and Louisiana from Spain; this purely patriotic deed, Williamson declared, was to be accomplished by British forces in concert with American frontiersmen and a rebellion of Indians against United States authority. Romayne said that Blount's purpose was simply to get land and find investors, European and American. Blount himself said that westerners would see nothing but good in his plan, "for so I intended it, especially for Tennessee."[25]

In April 1797, when Blount wrote his incriminating letter to Carey, Romayne was preparing to go to London, where Blount was to join him in a short time. Without Blount's knowledge, Chisholm had already sailed for England, probably on his own initiative and for purposes of his own. Hawkins was occupied in running the Cherokee treaty line.

Carey was at the Tellico store when Blount's April 21 letter was delivered to him about May 20 by trader James Grant. "We went down to the creek side," Carey testified later upon questioning, "and when I read it I was uneasy." With Grant helping him over the harder words, Carey read: "Among other things I wished to have seen you about was the business Capt. Chisholm mentioned to the British minister last winter, at Philadelphia." Carey, who had been there with Chisholm and a group of Indians led by Cherokee chief John Watts, knew what "the business" was: "a plan for the reduction of the Floridas" to be sent to England, the reply of the British government to be despatched to Chisholm in Cherokee country or, in his absence, to John Rogers, an Indian countryman. Blount's letter went on to say "the business" would probably be attempted in the fall, in a very large way, "and if the Indians act their part, I have no doubt but it will succeed." Success here depended on Carey's good management and secrecy, Blount reminded him: "You must take care, in whatever you say to Rogers, or anybody else, not to let the plan be discovered by Hawkins, Dinsmoor, Byers, or any other person in the interest of the United States or Spain."[26]

The existence of a plot had been rumored, however, for several months past, possibly through John Watts, who had been invited to participate in "the business" and had refused absolutely to have anything to do with it. Hawkins had heard of it and had reported in March: "There has been a vile attempt to prevail on the Indians to thwart the measures of the government; but they, more wise than the author of it, have refused their cooperation."[27]

When Carey read Blount's letter he did not know how to proceed; and since Blount was already in Philadelphia, he could not be consulted. Carey was instructed to build up confidence in Blount among the Creeks and Cherokees and destroy their faith in Hawkins: "Any power or consequence he gets will be against our plan," Blount had written. Carey was to convey the contents of the letter to John Rogers, so that Rogers also could spread rumors against Hawkins. "I have advised you," Blount's letter read, "in whatever you do, to take care of yourself; I have now to tell you to take care of me too, for a discovery of the plan would prevent the success, and must injure all parties concerned." If the Indians objected to the Holston line, Carey must convince them that the fault was not Blount's but President Washington's. "Can't Rogers contrive to get the Creeks to desire the President to take Hawkins out of the nation," the letter went on, "for if he stays in the Creek nation he can and will do great injury to our plan; when you have read this letter over three times, then burn it."[28]

But Blount's error, his friend Williamson later wrote, was that "he trusted to a sot." Carey was perplexed and possibly turned to the bottle for illumination. He had recently gotten federal employment under James Byers, a strong Hawkins supporter, at the Tellico store, and had taken an oath of loyalty to the United States; Blount's letter smelled strongly of treason. Carey, perplexed, held onto it for several days. Then, perhaps addled with drink, he turned the letter over to Byers. Byers at once showed it to Colonel Henley; Henley sent a copy to Hawkins; Hawkins, receiving it on June 4 somewhere along the treaty line, instructed Byers to ride with utmost speed to Philadelphia and hand the letter over to President Adams. The president received it on June 20.[29]

Hawkins himself wrote the secretary of war, saying how fortunate had been the interception of the letter and the "exposure of those dirty intriguers and their villanous attempts to involve the government in difficulties and distress. . . . If Chisholm, or any other man of his character, in the present conjuncture of affairs, be wicked enough to come among the Indians, he must instantly be removed."[30]

While Hawkins awaited Byers's return from Philadelphia, James Robertson presented his resignation as agent to the Chickasaws, probably afraid of being caught in the Blount exposure. Hawkins accepted the resignation, to be effective immediately; he had a trustworthy man, Samuel Mitchell, who was agent to the Choctaws but would take care of Chickasaw affairs as well for the time being. Then Byers returned with instructions for Hawkins, who by July 6 was in Knoxville to conduct a preliminary examination of Carey before witnesses and a magistrate. Hawkins also investigated the part that Rogers was to have played, but he hoped that Rogers, a white man with an Indian wife and a large number of Indian children, could save himself from prosecution. It was while Hawkins was in Knoxville attending to these matters that Zachariah Cox made his attempt to seize Muscle Shoals, an attack very likely planned with Blount's knowledge to increase the confusion and disorder of the moment.[31]

While the rest of the Blount melodrama unfolded, Hawkins was back with the Indians, especially the perturbed Creeks, holding talks with them during October and November and trying to calm them. Meanwhile the furious Tennesseeans ran a revised version of Hawkins's line, more in accordance with their wishes. Byers called them "a *holly pack of insurgents* who report the lines imperfect—and Colo Hawkins a liar—A set of brutes as they are, to endeavor to injure the reputation of a man who has more sence, honor, and honesty, than the whole State of Tennessee put together—." Hawkins and Pickens defended the accuracy of their line, and in November federal troops came to their aid in removing, by force where necessary, loudly complaining settlers whose plantations proved to lie in land not ceded by the Indians at Holston.[32]

As after other crises in his career, Hawkins that November was stricken with a terrible attack of gout, which, he wrote Price, had made sleep impossible for several nights: "I can now hopple about in pain, and I strive to keep my mind above it [by studying the Creek language]. . . . But would you believe it, this attack on my foot makes everything acid my stomach and mind and temper, are equally affected. Enough of an old bachelor." The acidity of temper probably prompted a spiteful letter to Winchester on the same day as the one to Price, mentioning his affliction but remarking that "I find my mind disposed to buoy itself above the whole, and I find some amusement in the certain progress of the benevolent views of the government intrusted to my superintendency." It cannot have improved Hawkins's state of mind that, after all his labor and efforts to abort Blount's plans and Cox's aggression at the Shoals, he had not had a word from the secretary of war in two months.[33]

Through other sources, however, Hawkins must certainly have learned what happened after the incriminating letter reached Philadelphia. Blount had entered the Senate chamber on July 3 just as the clerk was reading aloud his letter to Carey. The chamber was in an uproar. Blount, though shaken, denied that he had written the letter—something he was never to admit. On July 7 a charge of impeachment was entered against him in the House of Representatives, and on the following day he was expelled from the Senate. That expulsion proved Blount's best defense through the many conferences and hearings of 1797 and half of 1798, as the senators debated whether they could impeach someone who was no longer a member of their body.[34]

Meanwhile Blount, having filed bond of $20,000, was safely back in Tennessee. He sustained heavy financial loss through the bankruptcy of David Allison and was endangered by the belated exposure of the vast land fraud of the 1780s in which Sevier had been a prime actor. Still, Blount remained a major power in Tennessee. He managed in October 1798 through a treaty at Tellico to get a still larger cession of Cherokee land, enough to ensure the illegal settlers continued possession of their "intrusion castles," to use a Hawkins phrase. This large cession, Blount wrote Robertson, was due more to the "good sense of the Indians" than to the work of the commissioners— suggesting bribery or coercion of the Cherokee chiefs.[35]

Hawkins was not appointed a commissioner for the Tellico treaty, and his friends were being removed from Indian country as quickly as possible. "Your enemies, by misrepresentation, induced [President Adams] to turn out Mr. Dinsmoor," Hawkins told the Creeks. Dinsmoor was replaced by a drunkard and womanizer, Thomas Lewis. Byers had already been replaced by James Worthington Hooker. Hawkins would have attended the Tellico treaty as an observer, but somehow his orders from the War Department arrived so late that the treaty was over before he could get there.[36]

Two months after Tellico, Blount's impeachment trial in the Senate began, presided over by Vice President Jefferson and probably influenced by his astute legal guidance. The case was argued on technical rather than substantive grounds, and on January 14, 1799, with the Senate voting that it did not have jurisdiction over an expelled member, the nation's first impeachment case was dismissed.[37]

There lurks behind the narrative of Blount's plot, exposure, and failed impeachment a suspicion that it could all have been anticipated and prevented if Blount had not been indirectly serving the purpose of federal Indian policy, which was, for the sake of national expansion and security, to dispossess the Indians from their lands in the East. Washington and Knox had had grounds to suspect years before that Blount posed a threat to peace and order in the South, but Blount was an active, capable, ambitious man, and Washington admired those qualities. Instance the case of James Wilkinson, who Washington had known for years, was an agent in the pay of Spain. Yet Washington praised his "zeal and ability" and supported this "lively, sensible, pompous and ambitious man" up to the rank of commanding general of United States forces in the West. When in 1806 Wilkinson extricated himself from involvement in Aaron Burr's plot by turning informer on Burr, Burr's counsel Edmund Randolph called Wilkinson a "mammoth of iniquity" and "the only man that I ever saw who was from the bark to the very core a villain." Still, Jefferson believed or claimed to believe Wilkinson innocent, perhaps because, like Blount, he was very useful to the government in prizing larger and larger land cessions from the tribes. In 1803, Jefferson was to write William H. Harrison that he was interested not in the method used to secure large Indian lands but solely in the result.[38]

The real sufferers from the Blount plot and crash were the southern Indians and Hawkins. For years to come, Hawkins was to fight Blount's legacy to Indian country of disorder, suspicion, cynicism, hostility, and unscrupulous men like John Chisholm. Somehow Chisholm, this "rattling, boasting kind of a man," had gained credence with British officials and was in London when Blount's plot came to light. Even before Blount's exposure the British government and the United States embassy in London had found Chilsholm rather smelly company, and after it became desperate to be rid of him. In August 1798, Chisholm returned home with a passport from Rufus King, United States minister to Great Britain. From Secretary of War Pickering Chisholm had obtained a letter recommending him for a permit to trade in Indian country, Pickering saying he had no doubt but that Chisholm could be useful in the Indian department, chastened as he must be by his recent experiences and now ready to be a loyal citizen. Chisholm got the permit despite Hawkins's stern warning that he should not be allowed to go into Indian country. Now calling himself John D. Chisholm, he established himself as a white chief among the Cherokees, although they detested him. He gave trouble for many years after.[39]

Most accounts of Blount, old and new, find his guilt balanced or outweighed by his service to the South and West. Although what Blount did may indeed have been for the good of Tennessee, it was surely not for the good of the Cherokees that he tried to shrink their land into nothingness, nor for the good of the Creeks that he strove for their extinction by the Army, nor for the good of the Choctaws, Chickasaws, and Creeks that he set them at each others' throats when it suited his purposes.[40]

If the United States could have survived by no other means than the extinction of the Indians in the South, Blount's immorality and inhumanity toward them might perhaps be judged as a regrettable necessity. But Hawkins saw other ways to ensure survival and security for his country. He regarded the Indians not as erasable blots upon a scene of dazzling richness but as an integral, if sometimes exasperating, part of that scene; as aboriginal possessors of the land with rights that could not be violated without violation of the principles upon which the republic was founded; and as fellow human beings to be helped to enter the world of European civilization. Although the latter idea may be obsolete today, it then seemed a viable alternative to expulsion and decimation.

Some months after Blount's exposure Hawkins wrote to a friend in North Carolina, "I have since I left you seen much of the western country, witnessed the downfall of a character I highly valued, . . . and seen a check given, I hope an effectual one, to a base system for the destruction of the four nations, by the Ecunnaunuxulgee (people greedily grasping after all their lands), and I have the happiness to know that I have contributed much to the establishment of the well grounded confidence which the four nations have in the justice of the U.S."[41] But Hawkins was here, as always, overoptimistic. The check proved ineffectual.

CHAPTER 9

The Death of Hope

Should any tribe be foolhardy enough to take up the hatchet at any time, the seizing the whole country of that tribe and driving them across the Mississippi, as the only condition of peace, would be an example to others.

PRESIDENT JEFFERSON
TO GOVERNOR WILLIAM H. HARRISON, 1803

WESTERN affairs were not of primary interest to President John Adams of Quincy, Massachusetts. In 1800, however, executive priority shifted conspicuously westward with the election of Jefferson and his appointment of William C. C. Claiborne of the Blount faction to replace Winthrop Sargent as governor of the Mississippi Territory. The long-feared retrocession of Louisiana to France by Spain had become fact by the secret treaty of San Ildefonso a month before Jefferson's election. Disquieting rumors of it spread quickly on the frontiers, although Jefferson did not receive official confirmation of the retrocession until over a year later.[1]

With good reason, westerners feared that France would again close the Mississippi to American shipping. Without river rights western agriculture and industry would stifle, land values would tumble, and a new wave of separatism would ensue, with frontiersmen disposed to carve for themselves. Hawkins saw the danger; his hope was that the threat of French aggression would make the frontiersmen cling to the United·States for protection from such a formidable enemy.[2]

To President Jefferson consolidation of American power in the West was a matter of first urgency. The Indians could not be allowed to stand in the way. His earlier feeling for the Indians, which, in general, had been one of concern for justice to them and to their rights as human beings, became buried under his responsibility for the national security. That, as he saw it, hung upon quick acquisition of Indian lands to the Mississippi and replacement of the Indian tenants by American settlers who would defend their property against aggressions by France or any other foreign power. He and Secretary of War Dearborn pressed all four tribes for cessions and more cessions, clear to the Mississippi; and after the river was secured by the purchase of Louisiana in 1803, Jefferson's interest extended to lands west of the Mississippi, foreshadowing the still farther westward removal of the tribes. In that year Jefferson wrote John Breckenridge: "When we shall be full on this side [of the Mississippi], we may lay off a range of States on the western bank from the head to the mouth, and so, range after range, advancing compactly as we multiply."[3]

The change of party with the election of Jefferson did not dislodge Hawkins from his agency. As he wrote Jefferson a few months before the national election: "I have been so much occupied with the affairs of this agency that very little of my time is taken up with the political occurrences alluded to by you. I shall never change my old friendships, nor the men of the times of my past acquaintanceship whom I esteem and venerate for new ones."[4]

To Hawkins, Jefferson was still the author of the "benevolent plan," a theme that Hawkins often and enthusiastically expounded, as in the following excerpt from a letter he wrote to William Bowles: "The plan of the Government intrusted to my agency is benevolent in the extreme: it is to introduce the wheel the loom and the plough, to turn the attention of the Indians to raising Cattle hogs and horses and to facilitate to them the means of procuring them; to promote Civilization among them and peace toward their neighbors."[5]

By the summer of 1797 there remained only one major problem in Indian country toward whose solution Hawkins had made no progress, and that was the disruptive presence of William Augustus Bowles. Bowles, having somehow escaped from captivity en route from Luzon to Spain, was again keeping the

Creeks and Seminoles in a ferment of opposition as Hawkins was engaged in running a boundary line between United States and Spanish territory.[6]

Until the Louisiana Purchase the cessions sought from the Indians were strips along the southern edge of Tennessee and the western edge of Georgia. Before the United States could reach deep into Indian country, the extent of its sovereignty had to be determined by the running of a line of limits between United States and Spanish territory as provided by the treaty of San Lorenzo in 1795. That treaty had stipulated that the boundary between the two powers was the thirty-first parallel of latitude from the Mississippi east to the Chattahoochee; there the boundary was to make a short drop to the south and then run due east to the source of the Saint Marys River (yet to be determined) and finally along that river to its mouth. Also by the terms of the San Lorenzo treaty, Spain was to cooperate in running the line, to abandon all Spanish posts north of the line, and to open the Mississippi to American shipping. After Spain acquired France as an ally, however, it was less concerned with maintaining friendly relations with the United States. Indeed, the Spanish government hoped, by delaying ratification of the San Lorenzo treaty to postpone opening the river until new separatist movements developed on the American frontier, by which Spain might annex western lands of the United States. Spain agreed, however, that pending ratification the running of the line of limits might begin early in 1797.[7]

That marking of the line began in an atmosphere of uneasiness. The commissioners were Major Stephen Minor for Spain and surveyor Andrew Ellicott for the United States. The Creeks, in conformity with the treaty of Colerain, were to assist the commissioners where a line went through their land, but when the Creeks were called upon in 1797 to fulfill their obligation, they resisted, claiming that they did not understand why such a line was needed. Cherokees and Creeks, very much on their guard because of recent experiences with Blount and Cox, were determined to reject any proposal that might further endanger their lands. The Chickasaws and Choctaws were equally willing to take the warpath to defend their territory. Hawkins explained to the Indians that the international line of limits had to do only with the respective sovereignties of the United States and Spain in certain areas, and that the boundary was not a property line and could not affect Indian claims north or south of it. The Indians either could not or would not accept this assurance, and events proved them correct.[8]

White Americans who had settled in the boundary zone were likewise uneasy, not knowing if their farms would fall on the United States or the Spanish side of the line. Some had been there since the end of the French and Indian wars, when Britain gave generous land grants to veterans. Many were families from Tennessee or Kentucky who had taken up Spanish offers of generous grants to migrants from United States territory, and who held Spanish titles to their land. These were people whose craving for land had been strong enough to lead them on the long, hard journey through Creek country, in danger of robbery, molestation, or death along the way or after arrival at their destination. At the time the line was to be run there were sixty families in the Tensaw settlement and forty in the Tombigbee settlement, besides a large number around Natchez, all holding Spanish titles to their land, although it would probably be on the United States side of the new line. Further to complicate the situation, there was also the old British line, where the land the settlers occupied was covered by old British patents. Many settlers were leaving Natchez because of the uncertainty of land titles and migrating farther south into territory that was unquestionably on the Spanish side of the line.[9]

The commissioners were to begin running the line in the winter of 1797, but owing to the general unrest and the resistance of Spain, which raised a loud outcry when Blount's plot to invade its territory was exposed, nothing could be done then. In the summer of 1798, when the Spanish had at last slowly begun to evacuate their Mississippi posts, another attempt was made, but this was halted by Spain when disparities were found between the surveying instruments of the Spanish and United States commissioners. As delay followed delay, the Indians grew more disturbed. Hawkins's assistant Richard Thomas believed that the Indians themselves were deliberately holding up the survey, hoping thus to ensure a regular supply of ammunition from Spain. It was rumored that the Spanish at Havana and Pensacola had guns and ammunition for the Indians, and that war was imminent. Alex Cornells corroborated that the Spanish urged war; they were telling the Indians, he said, that they did not want any line run, and that the Indians were fools to let the Americans do as they pleased with Indian land; Cornells said it seemed to him that "the Commandants of the outposts, and the Spanish interpreters and emissaries are secretly preparing the Indians for acts of hostility against the citizens of the U.S." Cornells was echoed by Efau Haujo, who feared that if the Creeks and Seminoles allowed Spain to involve them in a war, they would lose both lives and land. Rumors were abroad of preparations for a concerted attack by the four tribes, and a simultaneous strike by northern tribes in aid of their brothers in the South.[10]

This yeasty mash of uncertainty, anxiety, and anger, from the Mississippi to the Saint Marys, in both whites and Indians, provided William Bowles with a perfect culture for the growth of his own plan. Whether that called for establishing a sovereign Indian nation in the South or turning that region back to the British is uncertain. By 1797 or at latest 1798, Bowles had escaped from his Spanish captivity and was in New Providence, perhaps also in Florida. He was certainly responsible for at least part of the Indian opposition to the line of limits. The survey went ahead by fits and starts. Andrew Ellicott expected the party to reach the Tombigbee, about half way to the Saint Marys, in January 1799, but was overoptimistic. From the Tombigbee eastward, as Hawkins knew, the Seminoles might be expected to give trouble.[11]

Other duties and disabling attacks of gout had prevented Hawkins from taking an active part in the line running up to that time. The attempts on his life by angry young Indians in June 1798 were probably sparked by hostility to the line running. From reports of the friendly chiefs, Hawkins was able to warn the irascible and tactless Ellicott in April that "impressions unfavorable to your business were made to the Creek Indians during your halt on the Mississippi"; although Hawkins did not say who was responsible, Bowles was known to be telling the Seminoles that the line would not be run without violence.

Hawkins sent well-disposed Creek chiefs to the uneasy towns to calm them.[12]

Before going to consult with Ellicott and Minor in mid-April at their encampment on the boundary, Hawkins had arranged for two chiefs to be selected from each town, and a few other chiefs, to participate in marking the line through Creek country. Although he invited only ten other chiefs, 212 Creeks attended the commissioners. In early May, Hawkins was near Pensacola. Throughout the spring and early summer parties of Indians wandered into the commissioners' camp to visit and object to the line. By July the commissioners had reached the Chattahoochee, and Hawkins went back to his agency; in August he was at Fort Wilkinson helping the new factor, Edward Wright, put the affairs of the store in order. Before leaving the commissioners, Hawkins had warned them not to stay on the Chattahoochee beyond July and August, safe months when the Indians would all be enjoying the boosketah and would not be inclined to make trouble. The commissioners ignored his advice, and in September, when Hawkins rejoined them, they were still at the junction of the Flint and the Chattahoochee, a prime trouble spot.[13]

On the night of September 17 some Tallassee Indians led by their very hostile chief Hopoheilthle Micco raided the camp, insulted the commissioners, and, unopposed by Ellicott, stole horses and other property. More raids followed for the next couple of weeks. Hawkins insisted that the raiders did not represent the Creeks as a whole, but were rash individuals set on by Bowles. He was disappointed in the Indians, but also thoroughly out of patience with Ellicott and Minor, who had stayed too long in the wrong place and who were so encumbered with female companions and other unsuitable baggage that they could barely struggle through the woods: "The flat irons alone for the two commissioners are 150 lbs.," Hawkins complained, "and it takes 4 horses to move Mr. Ellicott's washerwoman." He was also very much annoyed with Ellicott for refusing to drive off the Indian raiders by force. At Hawkins's request his Creek friends immediately sent down warriors to protect the commissioners' persons and possessions, but the raids continued. Hawkins thought the wisest course was to ship Ellicott off by boat "with his unwieldy accumulation of baggage" as quickly as possible, to sail down the Apalachicola River (formed by the joining of the Chattahoochee and the Flint). Ellicott would then go around by sea to the Saint Marys River to find its source, which was to be the final point in the survey.[14]

Ellicott set off during the last week of September, shortly after Hawkins heard that Bowles was on his way back from a visit to England. "We shall soon know more about it," Hawkins said. So they did; the Seminoles became even more active in stealing horses, and the Creeks sent out to recover them reported to Hawkins that the Seminoles were inspired by news of Bowles's imminent arrival. There then followed a most curious meeting of Ellicott and Bowles. According to the accepted version of the story, the British ship *Fox* in which Bowles and some comrades had come from England went aground near Dog Island, off the mouth of the Apalachicola, on September 18, a few days before Ellicott's boat neared that place. Ellicott was hailed by the stranded Bowles, went aboard *Fox*, and stayed there for eight days. During the visit Bowles informed Ellicott that as head of the Creeks bearing a royal British mandate he intended to capture the Spanish fort at Saint Marks and seize William Panton's store there. Bowles told Ellicott also that there would be no more land cessions, and that he had forbidden the king of Spain to have the line run.[15]

Why Ellicott should have spent so much time with Bowles is not at all clear. The meeting may have been purely coincidental, and the reason for the lengthy visit a perfectly legitimate desire on Ellicott's part to probe Bowles's plans. But there are other curiosities in Ellicott's behavior. His conduct in running the line was inefficient and dilatory to a degree that raises questions about his trustworthiness. In other situations also, both before and after the boundary survey, Ellicott's behavior was so odd that he appears to have been another of those men, like Blount and Wilkinson, whom the government continued to employ despite improper and suspicious actions.

Several years earlier Ellicott had been responsible for inordinate delays in laying out the capital city of Washington. The other commissioners there had had a great deal of trouble with him and had complained angrily that he was untruthful, inefficient, inaccurate, and extravagant; that he laid the blame for his mistakes on others, and that he had quarrelled with Pierre L'Enfant, the designer of the city, in a way that "strongly pointed to a duplicity and ill intentioned conduct of Ellicott." Hawkins in 1798 heard from Sam Mitchell, agent to the Choctaws, some other allegations of misconduct on Ellicott's part, which he refused to credit although Mitchell was a trustworthy man; there was perhaps a connection with the Choctaw demand in 1800 for payment of $2,000, which they claimed had been promised them, apparently without authorization, by Ellicott. Still more curious, when Hawkins met with Ellicott and Minor at Pensacola on May 25, 1799, Ellicott handed Hawkins a letter dated 8 November 1797, signed by Secretary of War McHenry and enclosing $1,200 in bank notes, which was to be paid to certain Creek and Seminole chiefs "agreeable to the secret article of the treaty concluded with Alexander McGillivray at New York." Why was this money delivered a year and a half late? Yet despite all the unsatisfactory and questionable circumstances in which Ellicott figured, despite challenges of his integrity and Hawkins's fulminations concerning his extravagance and inefficiency, and despite his very odd eight-day visit with the shipwrecked Bowles, Ellicott continued in federal and state employment as a surveyor and ended his career respectably as a professor of mathematics at the United States Military Academy at West Point.[16]

Aboard *Fox*, Bowles seems to have impressed Ellicott with his threats against Spain and the United States, but to Hawkins this extraordinary man, who was styling himself "Director General of Muskogee," was merely a troublesome adventurer-player who had to be eliminated. Hawkins wrote Ellicott after the eight-day conference in what seems to have been rather short temper: "Hitherto I think the whole savours a little of chivalry, from the Royal mandate which sent him [Bowles], his conference with the forces of peace, the attention of admirals and governors, the loss of a Royal Schooner. . . . Here I will leave him for the moment, among the countrymen of Don Quixote." Hawkins wanted the Spanish to subdue Bowles, who, in fact, while he remained on Spanish territory, was outside Hawkins's jurisdiction; but Hawkins declared, "If Bowles comes again on this side of the Line of Limits I shall call on Colo. Gaither to send me the cavalry under his command and a company of Infantry and I shall go after him." [17]

Although Hawkins remained politely diplomatic to the Spanish governor of Florida, Vicente Folch y Juan, he was exceedingly annoyed that the "countrymen of Don Quixote" did nothing effective to stop Bowles. Bowles had established headquarters on land that the Seminoles had given him, inland from Apalachee Bay among the Tallassees and Miccosookees, his friends who had raided and robbed the commissioners' camp; and he had promised the Chattahoochee towns 3,300 pounds of powder as a reward for their disruptive actions. Hawkins could only bluster, and did, writing to Bowles that the Creeks repudiated him as the director general of their nation, and that if Bowles continued to interfere with the agent's work by spreading word that he, Hawkins, was a dangerous man, "I assure you I shall be extremely so, as I omit no opportunity to execute this plan [of civilization] with zeal and fidelity. . . . I hope it is a farce you have been acting, and not a Tragedy, that you have played the last act, made your exit, and returned to your employers [the British]. If you have not, it becomes my duty . . . to inform you that you are together with your aiders and abettors on or before the 25th of this month to quit the territory of the Creeks, and not to return again, under the penalty ordained by the Laws." [18]

Hawkins meant the laws he had that year persuaded the reluctant Creek chiefs to adopt, making the Nation responsible for the punishment of its malefactors. The chiefs did punish the Tallassees who had robbed the commissioners' camp.

Under the guidance and management of Alex Cornells, seventy-two chiefs had agreed on the punishment and had sent warriors, led by Tustunnuggee Hopoie, to administer it. According to their report, "They marched 33 miles through hilly and stoney land near the house of the head leader of the mischief makers and plunderers who visited the Commissioners on the 17 Sept and at daylight they surrounded his house . . . he defended himself, we pulled down and set fire to his house. We beat him with sticks, until he was on the ground as a dead person." The beating was followed by mutilation, and the stick was thrust up the victim's rectum. After this, the avenging warriors destroyed all the man's livestock and other property. Less severe punishment was administered to two of the other leaders. Several more escaped but the chiefs sent a messenger with orders "to raise the warriors of the towns above us to pursue these people, to beat & leave them naked. . . . Oche Haujo he was with us and gave a direction for all our movements. . . . The sticks are now in the hands of the warriors and they will not lay them down, till they punish every thief and mischief maker in the nation To fulfill the promise made to you, and to carry the Laws into effect." They sent Hawkins a stick in token that punishment had been administered.[19]

The chiefs feared that, should any of the victims die, the dead man's family might retaliate against those who had ordered and inflicted the injuries. Terror of retaliation, the traditional Creek method of punishment, was so acute that Oche Haujo begged Hawkins to take care of his family should the families of those punished retaliate upon him for carrying out his duty. This incident suggests the beginning of a split within the Creek Nation, with one faction willing to go along with the new system on which Hawkins insisted, the other clinging to its ancient tradition of retaliation. Hawkins himself was in gravest danger as the instigator of the punishments. Friendly chiefs advised him to quit the nation for a while, lest he be killed; but Hawkins was rigid in his sense of duty, and he answered, "I shall not leave my post, until the thieves and mischiefmakers are punished and compelled to submit to the Law of the chiefs."[20]

The punishment by the sticks, as decreed by law, was calculated to convince the chiefs that Bowles was a weak reed and could not protect them. Let mischief-makers and thieves listen to Bowles's talks, but "the great chiefs must listen to the President and his agents," Hawkins advised Oche Haujo. "There are 38 great towns in this nation and dos [sic] 20 rogues and mischiefmakers think that they can spoil the talks?" Hawkins demanded of this trusted friend; no, they must get the sticks, according to the will of the whole Nation, "and if they are killed by the Sticks that is their pay." The one thing that troubled Hawkins, a common occurrence under the old custom of retaliation, was that in this speedy pursuit and infliction of punishment the wrong men might suffer. He admonished Oche Haujo, "I must put you in mind of One thing   take care of the Innocent, dont let one innocent person complain, nor one guilty one escape punishment." What he asked required constitutional guarantees of due process, which perhaps he thought might come in another generation.[21]

Despite the punishment of a few leaders, many Seminoles and Lower Creeks clung to Bowles and his promise of an independent Creek Nation that would cede no more land to the United States, would be free of Spanish sovereignty, and would trade not with Panton or the United States factories but with the English house of Miller, Bonnamy from its base on New Providence Island. To discourage trade with the federal factory at Fort Wilkinson, Bowles's Indian friends spread the word that the factory had no goods to trade, which unfortunately was near the truth. Bowles set about building storehouses on a bluff above the mouth of the Apalachicola in anticipation of supplies to come from Miller, Bonnamy, but as time passed and no ships came from New Providence, Bowles's white fellow-adventurers became disillusioned and began to drift off. At last, the Spanish decided to take some steps against Bowles, and in February 1800 sent a small fleet of ships, with Pedro Olivar as one of the commanders, to seize him; Bowles, however, escaped capture.[22]

With cool effrontery Bowles called together the "Supreme Council of Muskogee" to declare war on Spain early in April 1800; and when some Spanish vessels convoying a shipment of goods for Panton's store arrived at Saint Marks, they found Bowles with a few remaining white comrades and some two or three hundred Indians in possession of the fort and store. This aroused Governor Folch of Florida enough to send out a naval force against Bowles in June. Still cool under cannonade by Spanish ships in the harbor, Bowles invited the Indians to take from Panton's store what they could carry off, and then they and Bowles made a safe retreat. He escaped to a secure refuge among the Miccosookees, who could not be prevailed upon to give him up.[23]

Hawkins was extremely exasperated with the Spanish for allowing Bowles twice to slip through their fingers, but Spain, now confident in its French alliance, no longer felt an urgent need to cooperate with the United States. If "Captain Liar," as Hawkins called Bowles, was to be caught, Hawkins now believed it would have to be through his efforts.[24]

Another very aggrieved man, who detested and feared Bowles, was William Panton. He had suffered losses of over $30,000 by Bowles's raids on his Saint Marks store, and Bowles had put the Indians in such an intransigent mood that Panton's company had little chance of collecting any of the debts owed it by the tribes, which by 1803 amounted to almost $175,000. All Panton could do was try to frighten the Creeks and Seminoles into paying him some of what they owed by threatening to cut off trade—but there was Bowles promising better trade from Miller, Bonnamy. Panton desperately cast about for some way of recouping his losses. The only Indian asset was land, and Panton pursued a hope that he had for some time entertained of acquiring some of it. The catch was that most Indian land came under United States jurisdiction, and Panton's earlier petitions to the United States government to acquire such lands, beginning in 1796, had led nowhere, although they had not absolutely been denied. Hawkins, since coming to Indian country, had kept up a friendly, diplomatic relationship with Panton, and at the time of dangerous Indian restlessness in the summer of 1798 he and Panton had each praised the other to the Indians as a man who was working for their good. When Panton expressed concern about trade competition from the federal factories, Hawkins assured him that the federal trade system was "intended as an instrument of peace without being a monopoly, and it will be my endeavour to make this instrument common and mutually beneficial to those trading under the authority of His Catholic Majesty and the United States of America." Nevertheless, Panton's business suffered severely after the establishment of the government factories, which, being noncredit and nonprofit, could undersell him.[25]

In the summer of 1799, Panton wrote Hawkins for help in obtaining a cession of the Indians' land in partial payment of their debts, asking Hawkins to intervene in his behalf with the president, because without the sanction of the United States he knew he could not treat with the Indians for land. In sympathetic response, Hawkins pointed out to the secretary of war that unless Panton were permitted to accept a cession from the Indians, he stood to lose two-thirds of what was owed him. There were pre-Revolutionary precedents, he added, where the British government had sought a cession of Indian land for settling private business claims. But President Adams was apparently cool to the idea, and six months passed before any notice was taken of Panton's request.[26]

In February 1800, Hawkins had encouraging news for Panton from the secretary of war. Couched in oblique governmentese, the message seemed to be that Panton might collect his debts in land, as long as the peace and tranquility of the United States was not imperiled. Panton did not live long enough to benefit by Jefferson's success in obtaining cessions from the Indians, but his partner and successor, John Forbes, was able to recover the Indian debt with the cooperation of a president whose aim was to promote in the Indians the inclination "to exchange lands, which they have to spare and we want, for necessaries, which we have and they want." For Jefferson to achieve that goal, and for Forbes to recover the debts owed his company, William Bowles had to be eliminated. As long as he was alive—delighting a great number of the Indians with his charm and impudence, promising a return to the old system of presents, guaranteeing them good British trade with all the guns and ammunition they could wish for, and especially, telling them that they would under his guidance regain their land and their freedom—Bowles could frustrate the plans of Hawkins, Panton, and even the president of the United States. The Indians so ardently desired what he offered that they "continue to hope as long as he continues to promise," Hawkins wrote Secretary of War Dearborn in 1801; as for cessions, Hawkins believed pressure would be ill advised "until Bowles is effectually removed and the ferment he has occasioned has subsided."[27]

White Americans had elected Mr. Jefferson, Hawkins told the Indians in 1801; "He is their President and your new father. . . . From such a man you red people have everything to hope and nothing to fear." Probably Hawkins believed what he said.[28]

Congress in 1800 had authorized treaty meetings with the four southern tribes to secure roads through their territory and, if possible, land cessions. Jefferson at once pressed for the treaties. The next few years were busy ones for Hawkins, serving as treaty commissioner in addition to his duties as agent. It was imperative that he spend a great deal of time among the Creeks. They were restless and disturbed, partly because of Bowles—the promises he made and did not keep, the hopes he raised and could not realize—and partly because, from the frontiersmen's exultation at the election of Jefferson, the Indians feared that he would act against their interests—a fear encouraged by Bowles. Still, there were some further signs of the success of the civilization program: "The indians about me grumble, scold, fence, plough, spin and weave," Hawkins was able to say. By the middle of Jefferson's first term, Hawkins could boast of four hundred fenced fields and two hundred spinning wheels in the agency, and more wheels requested. But at the same time, the Indians were confused and worried about the future.[29]

Hawkins himself had reason to be worried, because a main prop of his civilization program was tottering. The act establishing the factories had prohibited the extension of credit to the Indians, and Hawkins had insisted on that prohibition as the best way of motivating the Indians to hunt or raise stock and food as trade goods. He was uncompromisingly "an enemy to credit," which he believed would ruin the Indian trade, set the Indians back to undignified begging for handouts, and benefit no one. As early as 1798, Hawkins had heard intimations that official policy on credit at the factories was softening, but his own opinion remained unchanged, and in 1799 he wrote Secretary of War McHenry that credit was ruinous to both traders and Indians. At the end of that year he was explaining to the new factor at Fort Wilkinson, Edward Wright, how fortunate they were that credit was prohibited; but in fact, credit was by that time sufficiently prevalent that by 1801 the Creek factory was owed $20,980 and the Tellico factory $6,515.[30]

When trade faltered in the spring of 1799, Hawkins noted that the Indians were uneasy "and couple everything with the pressure on themselves for land." They had been put in a suspicious frame of mind by the running of the line of limits between Spain and the United States at that time, and if their usual sensitivity to danger signs led them to connect the credit situation with pressure for land, it did not mislead them. The secretary of war early in 1800 told the House of Representatives: "We ought also to recollect that were the Indians to become indebted for goods furnished them by the trading Houses, equal to the amount of their respective capitals, the United States must sooner or later be reimbursed therefore by a cession of land equivalent to the debt." No clearer statement could be made of the changed function of the factories, a scant five years after their establishment as a means of providing the Indians cheap, fair trade and stimulating in them habits of industry and thrift. Although the concept of land-for-debts is sometimes said to have dated from 1802 or 1803, when the retrocession of Louisiana to France was confirmed and the purchase of Louisiana became a national necessity, there is more than enough evidence that the policy predated not only the Louisiana crisis but also the election of Jefferson. The difference under Jefferson was that the policy became more deliberately and methodically applied.[31]

Treaties were to be held seriatim with the Four Nations by commissioners Wilkinson, Hawkins, and Pickens, partially in the hope of getting large cessions of land, but primarily for the right to run roads through tribal territory to connect the westernmost white settlements with the east. The commissioners were urged, however, to proceed with utmost tact and discretion, and to put the wishes of government not as demands but as propositions that they might "enlarge, restrain, or even suppress" according to the Indians' response. Above all, they were not to press any suggestion that was ill received by the Indians. Bowles was as busy stirring up hostility throughout the treaties as the commissioners were allaying it.[32]

Disquieting truths emerge from the instructions given the commissioners by the secretary of war and from their reports back to him, which are not apparent in the recorded treaties. The roads asked for were not solely "paths of peace" as represented, but potential avenues to conquest. The houses of accommodation asked for along the roads were to be not merely inns but settlements. Land acquired by the treaties was not always paid for, and liquor was provided in suspiciously large quantities, although the Indians feared it as much as they wanted it.[33]

The first treaty scheduled was with the Cherokees, beginning early in August 1801 at Southwest Point, a post situated at the junction of the Clinch River with the Tennessee. Hawkins managed to arrive punctually, although the preceding month he had suffered an attack of gout "that pearces me to the heart, and has almost taken my life by surprise." He had conveyed to the chiefs the treaty invitation, a flowery message from the secretary of war that read in part: "The chain of friendship is now bright. . . . We must prevent it from becoming rusty; so long as the mountains in our land shall endure and our rivers flow, so long may the red and white people dwelling in it live in the bonds of brotherhood and friendship."[34]

But the Cherokees were not in a friendly mood. They objected to everything about the treaty from the very start, even the time and place. They had always been pro-British, and Bowles's promises of rescue through British armed might and British trade fell on receptive ears. Besides, the chiefs were much alarmed, as Hawkins found on his way to the treaty, by rumors that they were to be asked for a large land cession. John Watts, Doublehead, and other cooperating chiefs warned Hawkins that some of the leaders would not go to Southwest Point but would hold their own meeting at the Cherokee town of Oosetenaulah. "There is a division now among ourselves; we have thought seriously of it, and it is right that you should know," they told Hawkins. Watts and Doublehead might be willing to oblige the white men, but other Cherokees remembered too well for friendliness the aggressions by John Sevier and by Cox, Ore, Beard, Doherty, and McFarland for the purpose of driving the Cherokees off their land. There, without doubt, lay the cause of the division and of a hardened anti-white-Americanism in this group of Indians.[35]

Secretary of War Dearborn, advised by Hawkins of the chiefs' fears, instructed the commissioners: "You will impress upon them the belief that the United States have no desire to purchase any of their land, unless they are quite willing to sell."

The Cherokees, however, were not persuaded. The splinter group at Oosetenaulah, led by Chief Glass, bade the commissioners hold their treaty at Tellico instead of Southwest Point, because Tellico was traditionally a treaty ground and was more convenient for them. Chief Glass was noted for his fierce and bloody resistance to white intrusion; he was not a man to do the bidding of the president of the United States or his representatives.[36]

The commissioners forwarded news of this impasse to the War Department, along with a disquieting rumor that a four-nation meeting was soon to be held at Wills' Town and would be attended by delegations from the northern tribes. "Col. Hawkins is of opinion," the commissioners wrote, "that this measure is produced by a panic terror, springing from the apprehension that they are soon to be pressed for further relinquishment of Lands."[37]

Finally, on September 4, about a month behind schedule, the commissioners proceeded with the chiefs who were present at Southwest Point. General Wilkinson's opening address stressed that all the United States wanted of the Cherokees was permission to widen and improve existing roads through their territory for the convenience of travellers and the postal service, and to place on the roads ferries and houses of accommodation as needed, which would benefit both red and white people. "You have heard that your father would press you for further concessions of land. . . . You will know, hereafter, how to listen to such thieves, liars, and mischiefmakers, and will treat them as they deserve," Wilkinson said. Doublehead, as chief speaker, answered on the following day, warning the commissioners not to listen to land speculators who would tell them that the Cherokees wished to sell; they did not wish to sell. Furthermore, they did not need or desire more roads; roads would only attract undesirable people. Therefore, except for the roads that had been previously consented to, from Clinch River to Cumberland, and the Natchez Trace, there were to be no more roads, and no more talk about them. After that speech the commissioners heard complaints about white intruders, especially a Colonel Wofford and his settlement of fifty or more families at the Currahee Mountain, who were still living there although the

Holston line run by Hawkins had long ago put them out of bounds; the Cherokees wished Hawkins to have them once more ordered off. After other complaints about Tennessee's unfulfilled treaty promises to return Indian captives and to punish murderers of Indians, the treaty reached an end, having accomplished nothing.[38]

Hawkins reported to the secretary of war that the total failure of the treaty was due to the chiefs' alarm at rumors from all quarters that they would be pressured for all Cherokee lands east of the Mississippi. Several chiefs had consulted him about the feasibility of emigrating west of the river, where a small band of their people, including about one hundred warriors, had already settled. Still, Hawkins believed that the civilization program would win back their trust; of all tribes the Cherokees had made the greatest progress in the program. Doublehead's firm attitude on land, Hawkins wrote, "his pathetic appeal to the justice and magnanimity of the government respecting the roads, and the pressing demands . . . for the fulfillment of existing treaties and for the reparation of injuries recorded in blood" made it useless to prolong the meeting.[39]

In hindsight it seems obvious that any compromise would have served the commissioners' goals better than their adamancy, which permitted the opposition faction to meet separately. A split within the tribe doomed the treaty, which was humiliating to the United States. In addition, the division among the Cherokees, like the Creek division over punishment by the nation versus retaliation, set a sinister precedent. Each departure from the Indian tradition of action by consensus brought closer the possibility of civil war within a tribe.

The commissioners proceeded at once down the Tennessee, the Ohio, and the Mississippi, in no happy mood and sick with the autumn "fever of the climate," to treat with the Chickasaws at Chickasaw Bluffs, site of present-day Memphis. It was a short and successful meeting, in the latter part of October. The commissioners were able to convince the Chickasaws that they would ask no land, only permission for widening and improving the road. This was granted, but the roadside rest houses were firmly denied, and the commissioners did not press for them because they felt that, once the road was in, settlers would provide such accommodations. After their recent experience with the unyielding Cherokees, the commissioners were delighted with the "amicable and orderly disposition" of the Chickasaws, "whose greatest boast is, 'that they have never spilt the blood of a white man,'" read the commissioners' report. The Chickasaws gained little by their cooperation, a matter of fifty gallons of whiskey, two hundred pounds of tobacco, and some assorted trade goods, amounting to about $700; but Major George Colbert, the particularly friendly chief who directed the Chickasaw deliberations and spoke for the nation, was granted a lucrative ferry concession on the new road.[40]

It was indeed a new road and not, as represented by the commissioners, an ancient Indian trail merely widened and improved. In fact, this road, the Natchez Trace, at Colbert's suggestion would pass through almost one hundred miles of Cherokee land, although at the treaty it was described as Chickasaw land and the commissioners so believed it to be. Across a map of the proposed road that was forwarded to Secretary Dearborn a short time later, someone, presumably Wilkinson, had scrawled, "this road being compleated I shall consider our Southern extremity [sec]ured, the Indians in that quarter at our feet, & the adjacent province la[id] open to us."[41]

After this heartening success the commissioners sailed on down the Mississippi to meet their engagement with the Choctaws at Fort Adams, which was situated on Loftus Heights, overlooking the river at a point just north of the line between Spanish and United States territory. No serious opposition was anticipated from the Choctaws, who were reputed to be "more tractable and less sanguinary" than the other tribes; but alarming rumors had been circulated among them that the other tribes had been asked for land, and since the Choctaws were determined to cede no land, some of their chiefs—possibly on the example of the Cherokees—refused to attend the treaty. Wilkinson opened the meeting with soothing statements: "We come not to ask lands from you, nor shall we ever ask for any unless you are disposed to sell." They were, in effect, asked for land and gave it, but the request was so shrewdly disguised as a suggestion to redraw the old British boundaries of Choctaw land, a welcome idea to the Indians, that they gave away without reimbursement about 1.5 million acres of land. This was a most flagrant deception and extremely profitable, because it put within the bounds of the United States a number of out-of-bounds settlements that were thinly scattered along the Mobile and the Alabama rivers in Choctaw territory. The Choctaws agreed also to permit a road through their lands to the Tombigbee River. It was needed to improve communications between the settlements there and those on the Mississippi, Wilkinson explained, "since the King of Spain has given up this district to the United States"—thus admitting what the Indians had feared, that the running of the line of limits had indeed affected Indian land. Like the other tribes, the Choctaws declined permission for travellers' accommodations along the road. All the tribe got for what they gave was $2,000 worth of presents.[42]

One objection the Choctaws raised against the road was that it might encourage irresponsible men "to introduce a trade of liquor amongst us, that may cause the death of red people, which has happened lately, at Natchez, for which we are sorry." Regarding liquor, one chief said, "We came here sober, to do business, and wish to return so, and request, therefore, that the liquor which we are informed our friends [the commissioners] had provided for us, may be retained in store, as it might be productive of evil." The commissioners mentioned this in their report not as evidence of the wisdom and self-control of the Indians but as a "singular fact"—because of its singularity having no impact on the drunken-Indian stereotype: "It is a singular fact . . . that this council should have requested that none might be issued before, during or after the Conference." The commissioners described the Choctaws as ignorant and sunk in sloth, although the gradual disappearance of game might make them hungry enough to accept the civilization program; yet a deputation of younger Choctaws at the treaty urgently requested farm implements and carpenters' tools, a wheelwright, and a blacksmith, because "we half-breeds and young men, wish to go to work," and they also asked for wheels, looms, and teachers to instruct the Choctaw women in their use. In reporting this zeal, the commissioners commended the rising generation for having "rent the shackles of prejudice," concluding that with the help of the government these people might be made happy and useful, and that thus "the United States may be saved the pain and expense of expelling or destroying them."[43]

When the Choctaw meeting broke up just before Christmas, Hawkins and Pickens set out on their long homeward journey—500 miles for Hawkins and another 280 for Pickens—on horseback and laden with camp equipment, through midwinter weather. Even a man of robust constitution would have found the march fatiguing; somehow Hawkins withstood it, and by May was at Fort Wilkinson for the last in the series of four treaties, that with the Creeks.[44]

President Jefferson's objectives had been pretty well achieved in two out of the first three treaties. From the Creeks more opposition was to be expected for several major reasons: first, because they knew they would be asked for a large land cession to fulfill the government's obligation once Georgia gave up its western lands; next, because Efau Haujo, Speaker of the Creek Nation, was an extremely intelligent, experienced, honest, and respected man; and most particularly, because the Creeks felt Bowles's influence more directly than the other tribes. Bowles had been very active during the year past, not only in spreading anti-American propaganda but also in acts of aggression against Spain. During the Choctaw conference Hawkins received an urgent plea from the wealthy planter Francis Philip Fatio of Saint Augustine. Fatio's prosperous plantation, New Switzerland, had been raided by Bowles's Miccosookee friends, who had made off with thirty-eight of Fatio's blacks. Since the Spanish authorities were doing nothing to help Mr. Fatio regain his property or to punish the plunderers, he appealed to Hawkins. Bowles had also instigated the murder of a number of Spanish subjects, and Hawkins received information from one of the traders in Creek country, James Durouzeau, that "the govanors of Pensacola has Told Some of the Indians, that they will not have a paece until thaer is full Satisfaction Given for the Murder of the Kings Subjects. He wants to haer from them and the Nation Wheather they will Deliver or Kill Bowles who has been the instigation of all these Troubles."[45]

Durouzeau added in a postscript: "The indions are a Little alarmed at Some Reports from the Georgians telling them they are to be cauld to a meeting at the Ocoeney this fall When the

Land is to be Demmanded as far as the Ocmulgee as they say they have been Told that [they] would never be asked for any more land." Three of the important chiefs of the Lower Creek towns sent Hawkins word that they were relying on him to put an end to the claims of Georgia, "as our hunting ground is got very small and at our last talk we were told never any more demand for land should be asked of us from the white people of America." Bowles's promises of British aid and Creek independence were more appealing than ever, and he boasted that he had ordered Hawkins to leave the Creek Nation or be taken prisoner. True, Bowles's chief strength was with the Seminoles, but as Hawkins pointed out, the Seminoles and Creeks were one people and would sympathize with and help one another. If the Spanish would not punish the Seminoles, the only hope was, as Durouzeau wrote, for the Creeks to apprehend or kill Bowles, not a very likely prospect.[46]

The opening of the Creek treaty meeting was put off day after day, to give the Georgia legislature time to enact its cession to the United States; but at last the commissioners could delay no longer and began the conference late in May 1802, with the Georgia cession still two weeks off and without any official observer for Georgia present. The rumors that had so alarmed the Creeks soon proved correct. According to their instructions, the commissioners were to acquire an area already organized into Tallassee County, although not yet ceded to the United States, and in addition, if possible, the very extensive lands in the fork of the Ocmulgee and Oconee rivers. A less important objective was to settle once for all whether the Creeks or the Cherokees owned the Currahee Mountain land where Wofford's settlement stood. The conflicting claims of the tribes caused much trouble and frustration in efforts to adjust the boundary.[47]

Hawkins was prepared for difficult negotiations. At the last meeting of the Creek National Council, a year earlier, he had broached to the chiefs the idea of selling some land to take care of their present poverty and future needs. Speaker Efau Haujo said that they took his advice as kindly meant, but could not do what he suggested, given "the temper of the nation." An increasing number of Creeks, he said, believed Bowles's story that the king of England would soon relieve their wants without asking for land; also, they were growing more and more angry at the daily encroachments of the Georgians. After this chilly reception, Hawkins proposed to call another meeting when the national mood might be more receptive, but he pointed out that, with the game gone and begging outlawed, he saw no other alternative for the Creeks "but to sell, steal, or starve." To this Efau Haujo retorted that there was another alternative: the Indians could reject the new order, throw out the blacksmiths and other purveyors of new ways, prevent whites from traversing Creek land, and let the horse thieves harass the frontiers for a while. This alternative, he said, was gaining support among both the old chiefs and the opposition group, because all were coming to believe Bowles's assurance that if they repudiated the civilization program, the government would change its plan and return to the old British system of giving presents for the sake of peace, and would "court, caress and accomodate their wants" (as Hawkins put it) the way the British had done. Hawkins sternly told them that in such case the American government would indeed change its plan, and the Creeks would pay for the change out of their lands. We all know, he told Efau Haujo, where the opposition originates; it must be resisted, and the Creeks must soon sell a portion of their land to meet debts and present needs. Then Efau Haujo admitted that "he believed this to be true."[48]

Such outspoken defiance did not promise much for the next treaty with the Creeks, and by the time that treaty took place in May 1802, Bowles's credit was even greater among the Seminoles and Lower Creeks, and the Creeks had carried out part of their threat by destroying a blacksmith's shop and refusing to touch farm tools sent them by the Quakers.[49]

On May 23 the Fort Wilkinson treaty opened before the largest gathering of Creeks that Hawkins had ever seen, although Bowles had persuaded some chiefs to go instead to Saint Marks to get presents. After days of ceremonial and procrastination Wilkinson made his introductory address, still without a representative of Georgia being present. He began with stern warnings against joining Bowles and the bad Seminoles, but the effect of his injunctions must have been considerably weakened when some days later he described the land the United States wanted to buy: "west of the Altamaha, and below the Oakmulgee rivers, as far as the St. Mary's river, and also the land between the Oconee and Oakmulgee rivers"—a total of five million acres. With the proceeds, the Creeks were told, they could pay their debts, support their aged and helpless, and leave something to their children. The following day, Efau Haujo answered emotionally that such a cession "was like asking us to cut ourselves in two . . . when a man has a child, he considers him, and is not willing to distress him and make him poor." He countered with an offer of a much smaller piece of land, west of the Oconee River but extending only to a land boundary, not nearly so far west as the Ocmulgee. This would leave the Indians little enough, he said, but still "we can lie down and enjoy what we have." Efau Haujo confessed he was not happy about setting a land boundary; now, he said, even with the Oconee River as the boundary, whites crossed over to fire-hunt and to range their cattle on Indian lands, so how much more likely that they would encroach if the boundary was a mere line of marked trees? However, he concluded, this was the best that could be done. For the land offered, Efau Haujo asked two dollars an acre, explaining that white people "do not spare in their charges for things that are not lasting, and therefore we ask a price for that which is lasting." If that was acceptable, Efau Haujo said, the Creeks would assist in running the line at once, in case, the commissioners reported, "that man (meaning Bowles) may do something to prevent it."[50]

The day's negotiations ended there. Efau Haujo, however, by his expressed distrust of boundaries less clear and unchanging than a river, encouraged hope in the commissioners that the Indians, "because they prefer strong natural boundaries," might end by selling all the land in the fork, to make the Ocmulgee River the line along its entire length.[51]

On subsequent days the Indians and commissioners aired various complaints and requests concerning matters other than land. The Creeks asked for more tools and objected to price increases at the factory. They begged a speedy end to the conference so that they could get home in time to save their crops. Hawkins summed up protests against Creek violations of the Colerain treaty and spoke particularly of the Spanish complaint "that the chiefs have taken a white man, of the name of Bowles, an American, made him a chief, and are, in his name, carrying on a war against Spain." More and more, the Creeks were being involved, he said:

> People from Coweta, Tallahassee, Apalachicola, Hitcheta, Uchee, Oseooche, Oconee, Eufaulau, and Oketeyocenne, have all joined this man in war against Spain. In this state of things, the Creek nation may be compared to a piece of spunk; that fire is struck in it, on the side of the Seminoles, and it is likely to burn up the whole nation, if not timely extinguished.

Hawkins said that the Creeks would have to do better to please the new president, who cared enough for the Indians to give them good agents, and to keep Hawkins on as agent in spite of the untruths that had been told about him to President Adams, "because I was an enemy to those speculative views of your enemies." If they would sell the land, he said, they would no longer be so poor that they would have to steal horses, the cause of so much trouble.[52]

On the following day pressure for the land cession increased. Wilkinson contemptuously answered an objection raised by the chiefs that they could not, if they wished, sell the land below and beyond the Altamaha River because it belonged to towns that were not represented at the treaty—the disaffected people of the lower Flint and Chattahoochee rivers, who were followers of Bowles—and that if they sold that land, blood would be shed. Wilkinson fulminated:

> Who are these people? If they be of your nation, they have heard the voice of your Father, inviting them to this meeting. They have turned a deaf ear to his voice. They have taken the talk of an impostor, a pirate, a common liar. . . . we call on you to declare to us, you who are the masters of your land, whether it be wise or good, that you should suffer a few mischief-making towns, to prevent you from doing a thing, which would oblige an indulgent Father, and provide for the wants of your nation?
>   Should you be afraid to exercise your own judgement . . . we rec-

ommend to you to call for the arm of your Father to assist and support you. His arm is as strong as a whirlwind, and, if it is raised, will level to the earth all your enemies and all those who may oppose your will.

Wilkinson pulled all the stops to achieve a cession from river to river, playing on the doubts Efau Haujo had expressed of the effectiveness of mere landmarks as a boundary, and making an implausible promise that, "if you make that river the line, it shall be guarded by troops from one end to the other. . . . and stock, *sent into your land,* shall be killed" (the emphasis is Wilkinson's). Father Jefferson would "hang his head" if they refused him "a small part of your land, necessary to his white children." If they would but give the right answer, everyone could go home. "Water lines being more plain, and more lasting, than marked trees, we advise you to make the Oakmulgee your boundary . . . for which we will agree to pay you six thousand dollars, in cash, every year, will give you ten thousand dollars in hand, and will pay all your lawful debts."[53]

The council recessed at that point, with nothing accomplished in nearly three weeks of argument. Later that night the chiefs of Coweta and Cusseta called on Hawkins to offer a compromise, larger than their first offer and with the river marking part of the line—a big piece of land, but not all that lay in the Oconee-Ocmulgee fork. The offer was accepted. For the ceded land they received not two dollars an acre but a little more than two cents an acre.[54]

Upon this partial success of a most difficult negotiation the commissioners congratulated themselves, reminding the government: "We had to combat not only the jealousies, distrust, & fears natural to the Indians, but also an apprehension serious and alarming to the old Chiefs, that if they ceded any part of their Country, their young Warriors might resist it and joining the partizans of Bowles, divide the Nation, wrest the Government from those who at present administer it and by some hasty and imprudent act involve their country in ruin."[55]

The treaties of the past year with all four tribes had snagged, the commissioners believed, on William Bowles. During the year Jefferson's policy of Indian land acquisition had grown firmer. In some manner, short of a major war with the Indians, Bowles had to be got rid of. The very best way, as suggested several times in the course of treaty talks, would be for the Indians themselves to take him, so that the anger of those who loved him would not turn against either the United States or Spain.

The deadline for eliminating Bowles was May 1803, when to President Jefferson's great gratification France was to sign an agreement to sell Louisiana to the United States, opening up a prospect of vast expansion. Preparations related to the purchase had been accelerating for months, in anticipation of action to be taken whether negotiations succeeded or failed. Military forces were ordered to Fort Adams, and mail communications to the West were speeded up. The president began planning a scientific and exploring expedition along the Mississippi and Missouri rivers. Efforts to persuade the Indians to content themselves with small portions of land, as farmers, were intensified. The factories were to be increased to win over the Indians more quickly to the comforts of civilized life, and factors were instructed to encourage leading chiefs to incur debts that they could not pay except through land cessions.[56]

A new series of treaties with all four tribes was to begin soon, designed to extinguish Indian claims, particularly in the Mississippi region. But, as Hawkins had said as early as 1800, it would have been unwise to press for cessions until Bowles was "effectually removed." Elaborate preparations were made for a meeting in the spring of 1803 with all four tribes for a preliminary discussion of terms to be proposed at the various treaties. They were to meet at the Hickory Ground, in Upper Creek country, which was revered as the most sacred spot in the Creek Nation. Behind the meeting lay a year of discussions between representatives of the United States government and John Forbes, Panton's successor. The government position was that, although the United States would not take responsibility for losses through Indian debts to the Forbes company nor permit a foreigner to acquire land in Indian country as payment for those debts, it could and would guarantee Forbes what was owed him out of the purchase price of cessions to the United States if Forbes would apply pressure to achieve those cessions. The Choctaws were to cede land in the fork of the Alabama and Tombigbee rivers; the Chickasaws, between Duck and Elk rivers; and the Creeks, the rest of the land between the Oconee and Ocmulgee. The top $173,141 of the purchase money would at once be skimmed off and handed over to Forbes. The Creek debt of $113,512 was overwhelmingly the largest; according to Forbes's calculations, the United States would have to pay the Creeks $268,000 for the desired cession in order to settle his claims and allow for a suitable Creek annuity.[57]

The nature of the events that occurred at the spring meeting, and particularly the presence of Stephen Folch, son of Governor Folch of Florida, indicate that Hawkins had planned the meeting as a trap for Bowles. The bait was the promised presence of all four tribes, which would give Bowles the opportunity to declare himself "king" of the whole Indian South. No white man was to spring the trap, because that might rally the Indians to Bowles's side. John Forbes, who was present at the meeting, noted in his diary that "it would be much preferable if he could be laid hold of by the voluntary exertions of the Chiefs, who it seems are inclined to do so if he comes to the ensuing meeting."[58]

Hawkins had been planning just that with the chiefs since November. He himself had conceived the final strategem of using the occasion of the spring meeting, working quickly from the time in April when he had learned that the "mischiefmakers" intended to oppose the old chiefs at the meeting and were confident that they would accomplish great things. Forbes was determined to get his money, Jefferson equally determined to secure land cessions, and Hawkins, with his recent experience of Lower Creek rebellion against the civilization program, had resolved not to tolerate any more interference by the play-acting adventurer. It was a formidable lineup of power.[59]

By May 21 chiefs of all of the tribes had assembled with Forbes, Folch, and Hawkins at the Hickory Ground, where they learned of new wild promises by Bowles that the British had landed troops and would soon show themselves. Two days later Alex Cornells brought word that Bowles and chiefs of the

Lower Towns, his Mithlogee and Miccosookee friends, were on
the path and only a day away. Forbes noted in his journal:

now for
bella horrida bella!

Next day runners from the Bowles party came into the camp
demanding to see where their people would be lodged. Forbes
noted in his journal:

The Plot Thickens.

The Singer, one of the old chiefs, showed them a place set aside
for them. Hawkins at once passed the news of the imminent arrival to his friend Hopoie Micco of the Upper Creek town of
Ackeaubofau. Hopoie Micco, Efau Haujo's appointed successor
as Speaker of the Creek Nation, was chairing this intertribal
meeting; Hawkins regarded him as an exceptionally wise, influential man. "I must know from you," Hawkins said to him,
"whether you can or will as you have assured me, apprehend
Bowles, or is it to depend on me. If you find you cannot I know
I can—but as the Semanolie chiefs are here and the effect on
them will be important in its consequences to the subjects of
Spain, . . . I am of opinion it should proceed from the chiefs
themselves, and from you as their head."[60]

Hopoie Micco answered that, after some disagreement, he
now had the support of the chiefs of all four tribes, and they
had a plan:

The Chiefs of the lower Towns, of Tuckabatchee & the Semanolies
are near us just over the hill—Bowles is with them—I shall send a
deputation to them to assign them their quarters; I shall place
Bowles and the Semanolies at my own house in the quarters prepared for the Cherokees. I shall invite him & them to sit down
there & eat. I shall then take the Semanolie Chiefs to a Council of
the four Nations, give them our determination, apprehend & con-
fine the mischief maker and do with him as I have assured you I will
do; you & your White people will remain about your House, and
you will attend the Square as usual.[61]

The Seminoles and Bowles arrived. Bowles, undoubtedly
resplendent in glitter and plumes for the great occasion, remained in his quarters. The first steps of the plan went smoothly.
The rub came when Hopoie Micco gave "our determination"

to the Seminoles in the council; they obstinately rejected it throughout an afternoon and evening of talk. Furthermore, Bowles announced to a Cherokee delegation who came to see him that he expected to be made "King of the Four Nations," a nonexistent position. The Cherokee chief Doublehead reported that Bowles, very haughty and confident, had hinted that those who plotted to catch him might find themselves caught in their own trap.[62]

Talks continued all through the next day, and Bowles became sufficiently alarmed to send the council an offer to show papers proving that the king of England had sent him to preserve their lands for the Indians. At first the Cherokees declined the offer, saying he could easily deceive ignorant people like themselves, but then Doublehead came and demanded that, if Bowles had papers, he must show them. There is no record that he produced anything convincing.[63]

With Bowles still sequestered, the council continued to sit all the next day, hearing the customary recapitulations of the talks of the Four Nations. Then Doublehead demanded unanimous action. Consensus was reached at about half past ten that night, but the verdict was kept secret from Bowles all through the following day until nighttime, when he was seized by the Indians and manacled with handcuffs that had been hastily hammered out by Hawkins's blacksmith—the blacksmith, personification of the new order, whom the Creeks had so reluctantly accepted, a symbol of all that Bowles defied in his struggle to keep the Indians Indian, for whatever motives.[64]

That was the end of Bowles. He was taken by the Indians to Pensacola and delivered up to Governor Folch, then removed to New Orleans and shipped to imprisonment in the Morro Castle guarding the entrance to Havana, where he died two years later.[65]

Bowles's death was really only a matter of expediency, not necessity, because he had been not a cause but an effect of the trouble in Indian country. If he had not existed, the Indians would have had to invent him—and perhaps, to a great extent, they did, because he was the bringer of the hope they desperately needed. He conjured up a vision of what they longed for, their old land and old freedom to live as their fathers had lived.

He could have been taken by the Indians a thousand times, but he was not. They needed him and loved him, although he may have been merely what Hawkins thought him, a common desperado whom they had endowed with virtue by their need. They continued to hope as long as he continued to promise. During his earlier captivity some of his Indian friends had implored the Spanish agent, "We wish that you would send for him that we may see him once more to revive our drooping spirits." Symbiotically, Bowles continued to promise as long as the Indians continued to hope. Up to the last moment, Hawkins noted, "he gos on reacting his former part of Director General, untill he was apprehended in the midst of his guards and adherents and at the end in imagination of being a king of the four nations, and quits the stage in Irons." The $4,500 paid by Governor Folch to the Indians for Bowles's capture was a poor trade for hope.[66]

CHAPTER 10

An End of Treaties

Some will be marking trees, roads, paths—my young people being about and seeing them will be killing and doing mischief—and our young people will say our old people are crazy and do not look into our rights.

—HOPOHIELTHLE MICCO, CREEK CHIEF, TO PRESIDENT MADISON, MAY 1811

AFTER the acquisition of Louisiana, Jefferson became more hardened in his long-developing conviction that the Indians must be sent across the Mississippi. In case it should be needed to legalize the Louisiana Purchase, the president drafted a constitutional amendment which specified that a good portion of northern Louisiana was to be reserved for the Indians against the time of their removal. The amendment, which never got beyond the draft stage, also made provision for trading and military posts in this new-found Indian land.[1]

From 1803 at latest, Jefferson ceased pursuing the "Chimera" that in his younger days he had described as a visionary effort to reconcile invasion of Indian soil with the principles of justice and the rights of man. He still voiced noble sentiments in his public pronouncements, such as his message to Congress in 1803: "In leading [Indians] thus to agriculture, to manufactures, and civilization; and in preparing them ultimately to participate in the benefits of their government, I trust and believe we are acting for their greatest good." Arrell M. Gibson commented that Jefferson contented himself with philosophical musings on the need for a just policy toward the Indians, while practically he was no less determined than Andrew Jackson to accomplish the national purpose of annexing their land. Arthur H. DeRosier said that Jefferson "never actually intended to allow his wiser and more humane policies to prevail." There is in some of Jefferson's letters an almost irresponsible inconsistency, as when he wrote to Governor Harrison of the Northwest Territory, "Our system is to live in perpetual peace with the Indians, to cultivate an affectionate attachment from them, by everything just and liberal which we can do for them within the bounds of wisdom"; and then went on to recommend that we "push our trading houses, and be glad to see the good and influential individuals among [the Indians] in debt, because we observe that when these debts get beyond what the individuals can pay they become willing to lop them off by a cession of lands." One wonders where wisdom put the bounds of justice and liberality.[2]

In his second inaugural address, although Jefferson expressed pity for the freedom-loving red men driven before the onrushing tide of white settlers, he also railed at them for spurning efforts to civilize them, for clinging to "the habits of their bodies, prejudices of their minds, ignorance, pride" which combated enlightenment; and he spoke contemptuously of jealous tribal leaders who, in fear of losing their power under a new order of living, "inculcate a sanctimonious reverence for the customs of their ancestors" and preach that reason is a false guide, ignorance is safety.[3]

These opinions come strangely from a man of scientific and inquiring mind, and they suggest that Jefferson's anger was whipped up against the Indians because they were to be victims, because he meant to chastise them with the most terrible punishment to them conceivable—he would make then lop off debts by lopping off the land that they thought of as part of themselves. For a father to chastise by amputation, he must be very angry indeed.

The charge that the Indians had rejected the civilization program fails under examination, reinforcing the suspicion that it served Jefferson only as a peg on which to hang his anger. The Indians, especially the Cherokees and Creeks, knew quite well how to make use of the program and to manipulate it for their own purposes. It is true that when they felt too provoked by

white encroachments on their land or life they retaliated by re-
jecting philanthropy and leaving the gifts of the whites to rust
and rot. On the whole, however, their progress in the adoption
of western tools and technology was remarkable, considering
the short time during which the program had been systematically administered—only seven or eight years from Hawkins's
arrival to Jefferson's second election. By 1801 there was already
competition between tribes and within tribes for ploughs,
wheels, cotton cards, and looms. At the Southwest Point treaty
of 1801, chiefs of the Upper Cherokee towns said other towns
envied them their large share of these implements, but the
reason, they said, was that they had taken up offers of them
promptly, and so "we have got the start of [other towns], which
we are determined to keep."[4]

In the summer of 1803 the Creeks ordered the unprece-
dented quantity of six dozen cotton cards, and by 1804 wheat
culture flourished so well that Halsted anticipated a bumper
crop, which would drop prices from $10 or $12 a bushel to $5
or $6. Stock raising, not a new pursuit among the Creeks, had
become so popular and methods so improved that by 1800 they
were able to provision treaty meetings with cheap beef, as when
at the 1802 treaty Creeks had supplied about 34,000 pounds of
beef at three and one-half cents a pound. Western political customs were more reluctantly accepted, it is true, but the annual
Creek National councils and the steps taken by them to punish
malefactors, as the Indians had done after the raid on the commissioners' camp in 1799, showed their acceptance of Hawkins's
innovations in that area.[5]

Hawkins in 1803 summed up with parental pride and exaggeration the progress in civilized manners made by the Indians
in just a few years. In a letter to James Madison, using, as was
his custom, the first person plural to identify himself with his
Indian charges, he wrote:

Tell Mrs. Madison we are all Quakers here in the Indian agency,
and . . . we are full as silent, as grave, and circumspect here as in
Philadelphia. We are under the guidance of reason, and they under
the light of the gospel. . . . We will exchange our *guide* for their
light, and subscribe to whatever they recommend, provided they
will assist us here, to preserve the birthright portion of the planet

we inhabit. . . . We have availed ourselves of the aid and instruction afforded us by the government, and already feel the happy effects, we are better clothed and better fed than heretofore, our little daughters have extended their petticoats from the knee to the ancle [sic], by their industry have clothed some of them, our fathers and mothers. Labour is no longer a disgrace in our land, and our men lend a hand. Hunting has become insufficient to clothe and subsist us, and will soon be resorted to as an amusement for our young men. We shall in future rely on stockraising, agriculture and household manufactures, our means for these objects are not commensurate with our wishes, but they increase annually by the comity of the government and our own exertions.[6]

Two years later Hawkins was still glowing about Creek progress. The Creeks were steadily advancing out of their old ways, and he believed their new way of living had arrested their loss of population, stabilizing the number of Creek warriors at about 4,000. Stock raising, he said, was still a favorite pursuit, and in the last year he had bought at least 170 pounds of butter and cheese from Indian women, who also raised cotton and wove it into good, firm clothing fabrics. Perhaps the most important advance of the Creeks, said Hawkins, was in "the sensibility of their nature and the refinement of their manners."[7]

If all of this, or even half of it, had been achieved in less than ten years, one might reasonably expect that a generation of steady effort by the Indians and by sincere Indian agents, and a curb during that period of time on white land greed, might have produced what Jefferson had at one time expressed a hope for, and still professed to Hawkins as a goal in 1803: "The ultimate point of rest and happiness for them is to let our settlements and theirs meet and blend together, to intermix, and become one people. Incorporating themselves with us as citizens of the United States, this is what the natural progress of things will of course bring on." But in the same year, Jefferson confided to Governor Harrison that the alternative to incorporation was removal beyond the Mississippi; with no cessation of white pressure upon the Indians for land—for the ground on which they lived and for which they had such a "sanctimonious reverence"—peaceful incorporation was obviously an impossibility. Thus the conditions for removal were established. As the years of Jefferson's administration went by, he pressed harder and harder to break through the "ignorance" and "bigotry" that stiffened Indians' resistance to changing their status from lords without title of boundless forests to peasants with a bit of paper proving them owners of a few circumscribed acres.[8]

Time and events, as well as their own desires, had worked against the Indians to make dire poverty or removal inevitable. The establishment of the line of limits between Spain and the United States, the purchase of Louisiana, and the cotton gin diminished white enthusiasm for sharing the wealth of the land with Indians, just as it cooled any inclination to free the black slaves who would produce a great part of that wealth from the cotton fields. Furthermore, the reports sent back by the Lewis and Clark expedition gave removal a sudden reality. Jefferson now knew a great deal about the land west of the Mississippi: the tribes, their numbers and languages, the furs and peltry they took, their allies and enemies; the land, its topography, climate, flora and fauna. Because of all this knowledge the land to the west was now a very definite, visualizable locus rather than a vague landscape, and because that was so, removal sharpened from a possibility to a firm plan. The Indians were to remove by their own consent, it was hoped, rather than by a war, however just. Jefferson kept pressing for more treaties and more cessions, the more inevitable to make their consent.[9]

During the next several years treaties with all the southern tribes were avidly sought. The mechanics of the treaties, the amounts of land ceded by them, and the prices paid are extremely important and will be examined. One other matter is at least as important, and that is, that in each tribe the United States had one influential friend or more who could be counted on to cooperate in the white man's efforts. Among the Creeks, for example, there was Alex Cornells; among the Cherokees, Doublehead; among the Choctaws, the formidable Pushmataha (sometimes called "Push"); and among the Chickasaws, George Colbert. Cornells and Pushmataha seem to have helped the federal treaty commissioners out of friendliness and loyalty; the friendship of Doublehead was almost certainly based on hope of profit, and that of Colbert was perhaps partly mercenary. Cornells, who was on the government payroll at $400 a year as

an interpreter and assistant to Hawkins, never got special remuneration in the treaty provisions; but the others did get gifts
and annuities, as the details of the treaties show. The payments
are difficult to characterize. Some were merely tokens of gratitude for friendship and legitimate aid, others were insurance
premiums for future good offices and peace, and probably a
few were outright bribes for specific services in persuading a
tribe to accept the government's terms. Payments will simply be
mentioned where they occurred in particular treaties, without
any attempt to characterize them—except in the case of Doublehead, whose own tribal brothers put a name to his gifts.[10]

The men charged by Jefferson with the chief responsibility
for getting Indian land cessions during his first two years in
office were Hawkins and General James Wilkinson. Wilkinson
had been more a liability than a help in the treaty making of
1801 and 1802. Hawkins was almost certainly aware of the activities of this fat, deceitful general who had ousted Anthony
Wayne from command of the United States Army in the West.
Wilkinson was in the pay of Spain, and yet somehow he continued in favor with Washington, Adams, and now Jefferson.
He never lacked for important friends, including at this time
Jefferson's secretary of war, Henry Dearborn, who either did
not know about Wilkinson's multiple schemes or was himself, as
seems probable, to some extent involved in them. The general's
schemes were so astonishingly impudent that it is hard to believe any knowledgeable politician could not have heard of
them. For example, Wilkinson improved the occasion of the
formal cession of Louisiana to the United States, which he attended as a federal commissioner, by persuading Governor
Folch that Spain ought to pay him $20,000 in back pension
money and resume payment of his retainer in return for intelligence services; and he added mystery to intrigue by insisting on
being known to his employers only as Number 13, and on the
use of cypher for all communications. These were sillinesses,
since his espionage activities were generally known; but what
possessed Jefferson to appoint this "mammoth of iniquity" governor when the Louisiana Territory was organized in 1804, is a
puzzler.[11]

Wilkinson eventually tripped on the tangled skein that enwound him. But when, a decade later, Hawkins was exhausting his small remaining energy in trying to salvage some shards of the smashed southern Indian life, Wilkinson was cheerfully peddling copies of his allegedly sensational *Memoirs*, "for which," he wrote an acquaintance to whom he was mailing an un-solicited copy, "you are better able to spare me $10.50 than I am to give you the Book." This villain from bark to core must have been an engaging creature, but an infuriating colleague for a man like Hawkins.[12]

Bowles's capture in May 1803 left Indian country sullen, as internal division rocked tribal unity. It was not a promising time for treaties, and none took place for the rest of the year. White people were all in danger. Wilkinson, running the line agreed to by the Choctaws in the treaty of the preceding year, reported to the War Office that feeling against Hawkins ran alarmingly high.[13]

In 1804, Hawkins and Congressman David Meriwether of Georgia were commissioned to hold a treaty with the Creeks, with the objects of having the earlier cession extended along the entire length of the Ocmulgee River and of securing permis-sion for a road through Creek country. As with every treaty from this time forward, John Forbes exerted pressure on the Indians to comply, on his clear understanding with the United States that part of the cession price would be handed over to liquidate Indian debts to his company.[14]

The Lower Creek towns, however, formed an opposition group and refused to attend the 1804 treaty. Although Bowles had been eliminated, they were no less hostile to negotiations with the United States and had held meetings separate from the rest of the tribe at Oosoochee. The Uchees and Oosoochees had still not forgotten what Hawkins had called "that mur-derous business of Harrison," and they were still retaliating by killing white men, plundering and harassing travellers, and spurning the civilization program, treaties, or any other contact with white Americans.[15]

Cornells explained to the commissioners that all the chiefs were greatly perplexed and fearful of some dreadful thing to come of the 1804 treaty. A group of Georgians, headed by

Elijah Clarke came to the treaty meeting at Tuckabatchee and told the chiefs they were going to enforce the old treaties of Augusta, Galphinton, and Shoulderbone. Hawkins assured the chiefs that those treaties were not valid and ordered the Georgians not to interrupt the treaty, but alarm spread nevertheless. Furthermore, Cornells said, a letter of Wilkinson's to John Forbes in Pensacola had been opened and read (through an interpreter) by Indians entrusted with its delivery, and from it they had learned that, after the land to the Ocmulgee had been ceded, Forbes was to press for a further cession to the Flint River for payment of Indian debts; "and then the white people would own all on the east side of that river. . . . The Indians were greatly disturbed at this business, they saw what the white people were driving at," Cornells explained to Hawkins. Hawkins retorted that some of the Lower Creek chiefs were privately negotiating with land jobbers for the sale of land below the fork of Flint River, for their own gain. The road and the Ocmulgee, Hawkins kept insisting, must be yielded if the Creeks hoped to keep the president's friendship and protection; the Indians must associate themselves either with the white people, becoming happy and civilized, "or [with] the wild beasts of the forest, and in the latter case we [Indians] must fly our country and go to the wilds in the west; we must swap some of our lands here for lands there." [16]

Creek Speaker Hopoie Micco talked unhappily about the recalcitrance of some of his people, not only youths but "some of their old chiefs who might know better," such as Hopohielthle Micco of Tallassee, a leader of the resistance. Reluctant to permit a split to occur, Hopoie Micco suggested that the treaty continue at Oosoochee, stronghold of the disaffected towns, with Hawkins and Meriwether present to explain "the Road and Ocmulgee," so that consensus might be reached by the whole Creek Nation. To Hawkins, however, the opposition group were mutineers, doing harm to the main group, and he refused to acknowledge them by meeting with them. They would only say no to the road and the Ocmulgee; there was no point in going to them and being insulted. Hawkins held to his policy of firmness, of meeting force with force. If "these wild sons of ours" wanted war, "the warriors must turn out against them," he insisted. So Hopoie Micco's statesmanlike plea for presenting the question to the whole nation and achieving consensus was denied, although only the whole nation could give up land. Hawkins told him he must somehow get consent to what the president asked, even at risk of his life: "I must repeat again you will be opposed, strongly opposed you will be threatened. I know one of their weapons they intend to pull on me, they intend to break up my establishment at Flint River, out of resentment for the loss of their favourite leader (Bowles); be it so, we can remedy that, we can take time and let it affect me as it may personally, I sacrifice all to the acquisition of Ocmulgee."[17]

Hawkins's adamant refusal to meet the insurgents, and his absolute command to the old chiefs to get "the Road and Ocmulgee" for the United States, show the pressures he himself was under from Jefferson and Dearborn. "We are all Quakers here," he had written to Madison a year earlier, but now he was acting more like a tartar; "we are under the guidance of reason," he had claimed, like a good disciple of William Godwin, but the refusal to meet and talk with those who disagreed with him was far from reasonable; he had wittily begged for white men's help "to preserve the birthright portion of the planet we [Indians] inhabit," but he now made plain that the alternative to giving up "the Road and Ocmulgee" was banishment.[18]

The sound judgment and moderate temper that Hawkins usually applied to problems seem in this instance to have been unbalanced by his extreme anger toward the opposition group. As a servant of government, he was angry because they rejected the president's demands; as a friend of the Indians, he knew quite well that the demands must be met to avert removal or war. As the man who had labored to make the civilization program effective, regarding it as an absolute necessity for Indian survival in some portion of their homeland, he was furious that a few men should endanger it. Much had been accomplished, but much remained to be done; and Hawkins anguished over any delay or hindrance. His plea to the chiefs was urgent and moving:

> One observation which I made the other day upon being told that two little girls had perished with hunger near us, has haunted my mind; these little girls are murdered, who murdered them? It is

you Colonel Hawkins and the old chiefs of the land, you know and they know how to prevent this. If a bear was about to murder them, if an Indian or white person was about to murder them, how willingly would you take your arms and at the expence of your own lives save their's, and yet you know this enemy called hunger, and you will not unite in destroying him to save many of our little ones from being murdered.[19]

Rather than let the dissidents ruin themselves and the whole Creek Nation, Hawkins said, let us "turn out our warriors and use force"; the assembled chiefs more wisely suggested one more effort to win back the opposition before abandoning them. Hope of conciliation dimmed when a message came from the Oosoochee conference demanding that Hawkins leave, because "they did not want him or any white person among them." And so the Tuckabatchee meeting broke up at the end of July on an ugly note, with nothing accomplished except an agreement for a continuance soon. In the meanwhile, Hopoie Micco would do his best to persuade the opposition to send representatives.[20]

When the chiefs reconvened in the autumn, the meeting place was Hawkins's headquarters near Flint River, and Hawkins was the sole commissioner. This time the most distinguished chiefs from the opposing Lower Towns, as well as the Upper Creek chiefs, were gathered; any agreement, therefore, might be construed as a commitment of the entire nation. The matters to be considered were so important that Hopoie Micco "came to me here on foot, being unable, from sores, to ride," Hawkins noted.[21]

The Indians had probably decided before the meeting what they would do. Hopoie Micco proved as firm in his demands as Hawkins in his, so it was a diplomatic battle between well-matched adversaries, with the attending insurgents contributing only angry and insulting side remarks. The two leaders first consulted in private, Hopoie Micco reminding Hawkins that "of all things, this of land selling was the most disagreeable to an Indian." The price that the United States would pay was to be a determining factor. Some Creeks visiting tribes in the North had learned, Hopoie Micco said, that the United States sold land to citizens at two dollars an acre, and if the Creeks could get something on that order for it, an agreement might be reached; but, Hopoie Micco warned, Hawkins must not press for the road as well as the land until the Creek Nation had met again and discussed the matter.[22]

The land the Creeks offered still fell short of what Hawkins had been instructed to buy, because the Creeks would not risk war with the Cherokees by having the line start in disputed territory at the source of the Ocmulgee River; the boundary would have to begin farther south. Still, that cession would amount to about two million acres, worth, at Hopoie Micco's price, four million dollars. Hawkins told Hopoie Micco his figure was an impossibility. In fact, only $30,000 had been authorized for the treaty cessions of all four of the southern tribes, and desirable as was the whole of the Ocmulgee as a boundary, no binding promise might be made in excess of the appropriated funds. Hopoie Micco, however, in open meetings subsequent to his private talks with Hawkins, insisted that the minimum acceptable price would have to be enough to settle Creek debts, mostly to John Forbes, of $100,000, plus annuities of $500 for each town. Throughout several days of negotiations, with the hostile chiefs opposing everything "with all the arguments as well as rudeness in their power," Hawkins reported to Dearborn, Hopoie Micco stood absolutely firm. If the price were met, Hopoie Micco believed he could get the opposition to agree; if not, the Indians would leave next day, and the next meeting would not be until the summer of the following year.[23]

As the Indians began to set out for home, Hawkins yielded. He agreed to a price of $200,000, although he warned that the Senate would probably not ratify such an expensive treaty. It would be paid not in cash or goods but in stock drawing 6 percent interest per annum, the interest to be remitted to them half yearly; in addition, they would get, as requested, two smiths, two strikers to assist them, and two sets of blacksmith's tools. In defending the high price of the treaty to the War Office, Hawkins pointed out that half the two million acres acquired was "unquestionably the best land in this country. I have done the best I could in this transaction, and I believe a delay to another year would not have benefitted us, and it would have greatly inconvenienced the views of Georgia."[24]

Hopoie Micco did not get his two dollars an acre; the United States did not get an acre for two cents, the going rate; no one was satisfied with the ten cents per acre represented by the $200,000. In communicating the treaty to the Senate, Jefferson mentioned the three previous failures to get the cession, and defended Hawkins's exceeding "the usual rate of compensation" on grounds of Georgia's pressures for relinquishment and "a despair of procuring it on more reasonable terms, from a tribe which is one of the most fixed in the policy of holding fast their lands." Nowhere in his message, however, did he strongly urge ratification, and predictably, the Senate refused to ratify.[25]

But Jefferson meant to have "the Road and the Ocmulgee" upon which his plan of expansion depended: a strong eastern frontier along the Ocmulgee, a line of posts and settlements along the Mississippi on land to be acquired from the Choctaws and Chickasaws, and to bridge the two a road—already agreed to in part—across tribal territory. The eastern and western settlements would squeeze toward each other, gradually compressing the Indians into such small compass that they would have to tolerate white neighbors peacefully or move west.

Near the end of 1805, on orders from Jefferson, Hawkins escorted six Creek chiefs and interpreter Alex Cornells to Washington for talks with the president and a "reorganization" of the 1804 treaty with Secretary of War Dearborn. Not since Alexander McGillivray's treaty with Secretary Knox in 1790 at the national capital had an Indian treaty delegation been courted with such flattering pomp, from which the urgency of the situation may be inferred. Hawkins was present as adviser and consultant, with Dearborn conducting negotiations for the same lands that Hawkins had sought the previous year, and paying more for them: annuities totaling $206,000 to be paid over periods of eight and ten years. But now the Creeks agreed to the road as well, the vital road. Jefferson presented this treaty to the Senate more enthusiastically, pointing out that to pay such annuities would require only $130,000 as a capital sum, which invested at 6 percent would fulfill the annuity commitments as they arose; the same bookkeeping could have been applied to Hawkins's $200,000 agreement, but had not been mentioned. What made Dearborn's treaty so much more attractive was the road, and on the basis of the road Jefferson sold this treaty to the Senate: "If, from this sum, we deduct the reasonable value of the road . . . a road of indispensable necessity to us, the present convention will be found to give little more than half of the sum which was formerly [by Hawkins] proposed to be given." The Senate ratified.[26]

The important question, however, was whether the Creeks would think themselves bound by a treaty agreed to by only a handful of chiefs,—an agreement that Jefferson might not have achieved had the meeting been held in the midst of the Creeks. The treaty signed at New York in 1790 by McGillivray and a few chiefs had been bitterly contested for years. If Hawkins disapproved of Dearborn's treaty or how it was brought off, he did not voice his feelings; he never swerved from his loyalty to Jefferson. The government, however, may have lost confidence in Hawkins as a treaty commissioner because he had gotten too little at too high a price; for whatever reason, he was not again appointed to treat with the Indians concerning land until a dozen years later. The main reason for keeping agents among the Indians, Jefferson asserted in a letter to Andrew Jackson, was to get Indian land, and an agent's value depended upon the benefits he could obtain for his government. By this criterion, Hawkins was a failure.[27]

Now that the intention of the United States to absorb all Indian lands was so obvious, not even Hawkins's influence could restore the Indian trust and friendliness of ten years earlier. Awareness was growing, and with it anger.

Many changes had occurred in the Indian department. Hawkins, although he still signed himself "Principal Temporary Agent to the Indians South of Ohio," in fact had authority over only one tribe, the Creeks. In the Cherokee agency, the unsatisfactory Thomas Lewis had soon been replaced by Return Jonathan Meigs, a distinguished veteran of the Revolutionary War, whose energy and efficiency Hawkins admired although he did not approve of Meigs's speculative interests in Indian land. Silas Dinsmoor had been rehired by Jefferson as agent to the Choctaws, and Samuel Mitchell, also high in Hawkins's esteem, was named Chickasaw agent by Jefferson in 1801. There were also, however, relicts of the Blount group, still active in speculative pursuits and therein potentials for trouble with the Indians. John McKee, for example, had been replaced by Dinsmoor as Choctaw agent but was still in Choctaw country carrying on some of the functions of an agent. Daniel Smith and James Robertson, two of Blount's closest associates, were also present. As for John D. Chisholm, he was back in Indian country posing as a "white chief," a plague to the Indians, who petitioned Hawkins to rid them of "This white man who calls himself (Chisholm) . . . he is a great injury to both Cherokees & Creeks,—and by way or means he ought to be driven out of the nation" because he and his partner, the Cherokee chief Doublehead, were selling out the Indians in the interest of their own private speculations.[28]

The populations of border states could no longer be contained within state lines. Between 1800 and 1810, Tennessee's population grew more than 100 percent, Georgia's about 55 percent, Kentucky's almost 85 percent, and Mississippi's 312 percent. Obviously, this westward-flowing flood would increasingly spill over into Indian land. Return Meigs did not believe the government should try to stop the overflow. He wrote to James Robertson expressing his reluctance to enforce treaty lines: "I removed 201 families off the Chickasaw lands, and 83 families off the Cherokee lands. . . . These people bear the appellation of intruders but they are Americans . . . in our new country every man is an acquisition—we ought not to lose a single man for the want of land to work on." Eventually that philosophy led Meigs into a confrontation with Hawkins, who never faltered in his conviction that intruders were the true cause of Indian anger and hostility.[29]

Return Meigs and Daniel Smith had been appointed commissioners for a treaty with the Cherokees in 1804, just preceding Hawkins's last treaty with the Creeks. Dearborn's instructions were to get as much more land as the Cherokees could be persuaded to cede within the state limits of Tennessee and Kentucky, and also to free by purchase the settlement of Wofford and his neighbors near Currahee Mountain, that long-disputed site. Meigs and Smith, in a treaty held at Tellico, got some thousands of acres at Currahee Mountain for $5,000 and a $1,000 perpetual annuity.[30]

They had less success, however, with requests for a 10,000-square-mile tract lying between East and West (now Middle) Tennessee, because of the clashing claims to that area of the Cherokees and Chickasaws. In the opinion of the commissioners: "The titles of these two nations, to the lands in question, are questionable, and they are both conscious of it—each is afraid the other will sell." Apparently Meigs was not able to put enough pressure on the Indians. Smith suggested another treaty with James Robertson (his associate in land speculation) as a co-commissioner. Smith and Robertson went back to the Cherokees and negotiated a more satisfactory treaty; for $14,000 in cash and merchandise and an additional $3,000 annuity they acquired a tract of about four million acres of land. For an additional $1,600 the Cherokees relinquished their claim to Southwest Point and gave permission for two new roads, one of which was to run from Tellico Blockhouse southwest to the Tombigbee settlement, passing by the agency on the Tallapoosa River.[31]

As white pressure for land increased, Indian resistance began to reach a peak. The tribes, with their efficient communication system, must certainly have learned of the trans-Mississippi explorations in 1805 of Lt. Zebulon Pike, by order of General Wilkinson, of the headwaters of the Arkansas and Red rivers. This news heightened the Indians' terror of expulsion from their tribal lands east of the Mississippi and stiffened their resistance to demands for any more of their land.

Jefferson's pincer strategy shifted the focus of interest from the Georgia and Tennessee frontiers to the land near the Mississippi, which required a new series of treaties with the Choctaws and Chickasaws. One part of his program was already moving along, the establishment of federal factories in that country for the purpose of running the tribes there into debt, as had been done with the Creeks and Cherokees. A factory was set up at Chickasaw Bluffs in 1802; and others were established at Natchitoches and at the Arkansas Post, both west of the Mississippi, in 1805; plus one at Fort Saint Stephens on the Tombigbee in 1807. Meanwhile, the eastern jaw of the pincer pushed the Fort Wilkinson factory on the Oconee westward by one river when it was moved to Ocmulgee Old Fields in 1808; and the Tellico factory shifted slightly to Hiwassee.[32]

The Choctaws and Chickasaws both owed large amounts to John Forbes, because the Panton company had had a virtual monopoly of trade in that Spanish-oriented area. No major negotiations had taken place with either tribe since the treaties of 1802. In the case of the Choctaws, the conference had ended not in a conventional land cession but in the agreement that the boundary between Choctaw and United States territory should be redrawn to conform with the old British line. Relations with the tribe had continued to be quite agreeable until, in the summer of 1803, while Hawkins was dealing with the emotions aroused by Bowles's capture, General Wilkinson as sole federal commissioner commenced the running of the old British line.

Wilkinson's arrogance and chicanery in marking the boundary were extraordinary even in the prevailing pattern of exploitations of the Indians. He had determined where he wanted the line to be, and he would listen to no Choctaw complaints of its inaccuracy. He had come, he said, to complete an agreed contract, and if the Choctaws listened to liars who told them not to permit the line "he would positively throw them away and they would soon become a lost people." This evidently so frightened the Choctaws that they withdrew their initial opposition, but Wilkinson's demands went further and further. He arranged with a representative of the Forbes company that, although the United States could not officially appear in the matter, if the company could prevail upon the Choctaws "to sell such land, as the United States desires to purchase, I do not think any objection would be made to [the Forbes company] appropriating such part of the proceeds as they might deem necessary to discharge their just debts," because the United States government profoundly wished "the formation of a barrior of Hardy Yeomanry on that Solitary frontier." By handing out a mere $179 in gifts Wilkinson managed to get valuable land beyond the agreed line, and he reported to the War Office ten days later, "If we can extend the Indian concession sufficiently, on the Tombigby & Alabama, and get possession of Mobile, this will become the preferable district of our whole country."[33]

By October, Spanish agent Number 13 was able to promise

Secretary Dearborn that the boundary would be stretched enough to take in all the settlements of intruders "by the agency and pressing demands of the House of Panton & Leslie," that is, Forbes, because the Indians were told that "the House [of Panton, Leslie] have determined to withhold all supplies this Season, unless they will agree to make the sale desired by us—." The terrified Choctaws, dependent on Forbes for necessities, agreed to sell not only their own land but also lands demanded by Wilkinson in the fork of the Alabama and Tombigbee rivers, whose ownership was claimed by the Creeks. Wilkinson freely admitted to the War Office that he had run the boundary far beyond the old British line, his motive being "zealous attention to the Interests and accommodations of our fellow Citizens and of our Country." Yet with the next dip of his pen, reporting the Spanish rush to cash in on Florida land which they were expected soon to sell to the United States, Wilkinson could piously fume: "Is such conduct chaste? Is it honest?"[34]

Whatever Wilkinson may have gotten out of his dishonest treaty line, Jefferson did not gain by it the desired land along the Mississippi. So in the spring of 1805, Silas Dinsmoor and James Robertson tried again. Whether by then the Choctaws were alarmed by rumors of Aaron Burr's plot and Zebulon Pike's explorations, or simply tired of giving up land merely to pay their debts, Dinsmoor and Robertson found them in a mood far from receptive to a small offer for a huge amount of land.

The same commissioners then proceeded to talk with the Chickasaws during the summer about their Mississippi lands. Exhorted to sell land to clear their debts, the Chickasaws in July agreed to a huge grant in south-central Tennessee (part of which the Cherokees also claimed) and in present-day northern Alabama, on the condition that no settlers were to be allowed onto the tract until three years after ratification—a prohibition that turned out to be unenforceable. The price was the usual two cents an acre where the Chickasaw title was clear, and somewhat less where the contesting Cherokees would also have to be paid. In all, the Chickasaws got about $20,000, approximately half of which George Colbert turned over to Forbes within the next year. In addition, Colbert and Chickasaw chief

O'Koy each received $1,000 for their help in getting the treaty accepted by the tribe, and the "king" of the Chickasaw Nation was granted an annuity of $100. But in this treaty as in the Choctaw treaty, the United States failed to get what it most wanted, the lands bordering the Mississippi; the proposal of a cession there was instantly and absolutely rejected.[35]

Back went the commissioners to the Choctaws in the autumn of 1805, with instructions to buy the Mississippi lands only. Again they failed. Under the pressure of their overwhelming debts to Forbes, and threatened again with a cessation of trade, the Choctaws offered five million acres farther to the east, including a vast expanse along the Florida border, but still excluding the urgently sought strip along the Mississippi. Dinsmoor and Robertson accepted the cession, since it was the best they could get, for an immediate payment of $50,500. The Choctaws would see none of this, because $48,000 went to pay their debts—without interest, which they refused to consider or understand—and the small remainder to John Pitchlynn, the official Choctaw interpreter, for a reason vaguely described as "compensation for losses." In addition, the tribe was to receive $3,000 annually in goods, and the three foremost chiefs, including Pushmataha, were awarded $500 each and annuities of $150. In addition to selling this state-size tract at something like a cent and a half an acre, the Choctaws granted what they had earlier refused, the establishment of houses of accommodation along roads through their country. President Jefferson, disappointed by the failure to get the Mississippi lands, held this treaty more than two years before asking the Senate to ratify. By the time he presented it, with a Spanish war again a lively possibility, the strip lying north of the Florida border had assumed greater importance as "a barrier of separation between the Indians and our southern neighbors," Jefferson pointed out. The Senate ratified.[36]

The clutch of treaties hatched since Jefferson's second election—in which, significantly, Hawkins played no part—ended with several minor agreements made with the Cherokees between 1805 and 1807. Only small amounts of land could now be purchased from that resistant tribe. An 1805 treaty gained an island in the Tennessee River and some privileges for mail and travellers passing through Cherokee country. In January 1806, Secretary Dearborn negotiated a somewhat more substantive treaty by the proven expedient of inviting Doublehead and sixteen other Cherokee chiefs to Washington. They, claiming to speak for their nation, ceded a tract contiguous to Chickasaw land and a strip on the north side of the Tennessee River that finally established the long-contested claims of settlers there. Excluded from the cession were the Muscle Shoals tract and a strip two by three miles on the Tennessee River's northern shore which was to be reserved for certain Cherokees who resided there, one of whom was John D. Chisholm, who probably had threatened to obstruct the accord unless he got his cut. For this cession the price was $10,000 in cash and annuities plus a gristmill and a cotton gin.[37]

When the body of the Cherokee Nation found out what conditions had been agreed to by the seventeen chiefs, they repudiated the treaty. Their fury focused on Doublehead, who was known to be involved in land speculation with the detested Chisholm and was suspected of having been bribed in Washington. In 1801, Doublehead had vigorously opposed cessions; now five years later he sang a different tune. Did he see that resistance was useless, or had he learned to agree, for a price? When Doublehead returned home he was assassinated in his lodge. Another of the seventeen chiefs, Taklonteske, not long afterward migrated across the Mississippi and became the head of the small but growing band of Western Cherokees. Chisholm went with him.[38]

The last of these late Jeffersonian treaties with the Cherokees, negotiated near the end of 1807 by Meigs, gained a piece of land six miles square that was said to be rich in iron ore but perhaps was important more because it lay on the south side of the Tennessee River. The price paid, over $1.30 an acre, was far higher than usual. The tribe received $2,500 in cash and the same in merchandise plus 1,000 bushels of corn, for a piece of land that was less than 4,000 acres; and in addition the United States was to set up an iron works for the use of both Indians and white settlers. In presenting this proposal to the Senate, Jefferson stressed that the agricultural Cherokees would be attracted by an ironworks, which would produce farm tools for them, and thus the treaty would make "a great and important advance toward assimilating their condition to ours."[39]

No such accommodating spirit prevailed in any other part of Indian country, north or south, by the end of Jefferson's administration. In the north Governor Harrison during the Jefferson years had pressed the northern tribes time and again for land. Intertribal delegations and couriers kept northern and southern tribes informed of events in each others' countries, and before 1810 both northern and southern tribes were absolutely refusing to cede land. The hope of an all-Indian confederation was ripening. There were always rumors abroad of northern Indians taking the warpath to help their southern brothers defend their homelands.[40]

Jefferson's second term suffered a plague of problems that threatened the security of the South. In 1804, France claimed that the land from the lower Mississippi east to Florida was not included in the sale of Louisiana, thus raising the old fear that the Mississippi would again be closed to American shipping. Westerners were alarmed. Separatism again flared in the West, fanned by both Spain and Great Britain. The outbreak of war between Spain and the United States was expected any day, and tense incidents gave fear substance.[41]

This was the atmosphere of uneasiness, anxiety, fear, and anger that inspired and nourished Aaron Burr's plot. In 1805, Burr set out for the West with a vague scheme, so it seems, to separate that region from the union by the joint action of disgruntled westerners and Indian mercenaries, with British support. The plan never reached fruition. Through the treachery of Burr's coconspirator, that "mammoth of iniquity" James Wilkinson, Burr was apprehended before any violence occurred; but the mere idea of such a plot, of the possibility of the use of Indians as mercenaries or allies at that time of rapidly accelerating friction between Indians and frontiersmen, was unnerving to settlers and the government. The opinion of William Blount two decades earlier that there would be trouble "while there is a tribe of Indians remaining on this side of the

Mississippi" gained credibility at the highest levels of policy-making. Hawkins's concepts of civilization and assimilation already belonged to a past era.[42]

The Indians, who as their lands shrank and the game vanished felt poverty sharpen their bones, began themselves to think of moving west across the Mississippi, whence many of their forebears had come a century and more earlier to escape Spanish domination. After the purchase of Louisiana an increasing stream of southern Indians, mainly Cherokees but also some Choctaws and Chickasaws, packed up and moved westward. Within a few years of the purchase Secretary Dearborn instructed Meigs to encourage major chiefs to take whole towns and villages across the river, as Taklonteske did, with the probably sincere assurance that no white settlements would ever be permitted on the Arkansas River. Some Cherokees visiting Washington in 1808 were urged by Jefferson to go west; they returned home to spread the glowing reports they had been given of the Arkansas River region, and within ten years the Western Cherokee Nation numbered 3,000. Voluntary removal was clearly the preferred solution for acquiring the lands of the Indians, sparing the government "the pain and expense of expelling or destroying them," as Wilkinson had once put it. In time, white righteousness in the person of Thomas McKenney, an Indian superintendent from 1816 to 1830, would promote the thesis that Indians who refused to migrate must bear the guilt for the destruction of their whole people, because only through migration could the red race survive.[43]

High on the list of excuses for Indian removal were the claims—ignoring Hawkins's considerable successes—that Indians would never become "civilized," did not want assimilation, and could not live among whites. Many Indians did, in fact, spurn the white way of living, and the Osage chief Big Soldier spoke for them: "Talk to my sons, perhaps they may be persuaded to adopt your fashions, or at least to recommend them to their sons; but for myself, I was born free, was raised free, and wish to die free. I am perfectly content with my condition." These alleged words of Big Soldier underline what is so important to bear in mind in reference to Hawkins's civilization program: that it had been actively administered for only fifteen or twenty years—less than a generation to change the culture of centuries—when it was adjudged a failure, leaving removal as the only alternative. If indeed it were a failure, Hawkins's life-work had been a waste; that it was not a failure makes Indian removal particularly poignant.[44]

A few months after Hawkins's death in 1816, his nephew Philemon, temporarily in charge of the agency, advised the secretary of war: "Most of the respectable part of the nation, seem to prefer the more sure and rational mode of livelihood the raising of domestic stock and the persuits of husbandry to the precarious and uncertain persuit of hunting." Fifteen years later a group of Creeks who had removed to the glowingly de-scribed Arkansas lands voiced their culture shock:

> We knew that we were coming to a land of strangers, and that our intended neighbors were red brothers, who had not received the advantage of civilization as we, and the rest of your red children, who had resided east of the Mississippi. These wild Indians depend almost altogether upon the chase for support, and their glory is war. We are anxious to pursue a different course. Our object is to cultivate the land, to support our families by our industry, and to preserve peace not only with our white, but with our red brothers.

For at least some Indians, Hawkins had succeeded all too well.[45]

During the time of increasing hysteria in seeking and resisting treaties, Hawkins plodded on with his efforts to turn the Creeks away from "their wearisome and precarious life of hunting," still with the encouragement of a government that was already pressing the Indians to go West, where they would have to re-vert to their ancient skills. By 1807, the Flint River agency was well established and thriving. Hawkins was living there in com-fort with Lavinia and a growing family in a substantial log house adjoining the agency office. His assistant, Christian Lim-baugh, had a good house just opposite. Among other buildings were ten or more slave cabins, shops for the blacksmith, hatter, and woodworkers, a sawmill, a springhouse, and a tannery where deerskins were processed by improved methods. Large orchards and cornfields, Hawkins's garden, and cattle grazed on cane and the grass of the common produced food for the agency population and bountiful hospitality for guests.[46]

With the steady, efficient Jonathan Halsted as factor at the store at Fort Hawkins, about thirty miles from the agency, trade matters occupied Hawkins less than they had formerly. Factory affairs continued to muddle along, with orders sometimes ignored or incorrectly filled with goods that Halsted could not sell to the Indians, and with a huge inventory of deerskins piling up at the store because Halsted had been ordered not to forward any more of them; Halsted was capable of handling almost all problems without help until 1812, when he became fatally ill. Hawkins seems to have intervened only in the matter of trying to get the government to authorize a store credit of $10,000 to the Creek account, an amount earmarked in a treaty for payment of Creek debts that was by 1808 long overdue.[47]

One incident that roused Hawkins into vigorous action had to do with a land speculation plot in April 1809. James McIntosh, a part-Cherokee, accompanied by four or five white men, took a big boatload of rum and gunpowder down the Tombigbee River for pretended purposes of trade. Their actual intention, it seems, was to make private land purchases from the Lower Creeks. Chisholm was deeply involved in the enterprise, and the evidence indicates that Cherokee agent Return Meigs had a finger in it. The party passed safely through Cherokee country by virtue of a passport issued by Meigs. When they were stopped at Turkey's Town on the Cherokee-Creek border by about a hundred menacing Creeks who at once confiscated the cargo of the boat, McIntosh presented a passport through Creek country signed "Benjamin Hawkins" which said that the party was carrying supplies down the river to Fort Saint Stephens by order of the president. The passport was false; Timothy Meigs, identified in documents as Return Meigs's clerk, had written it himself and forged Hawkins's signature. Tustunnugee Thlucco took the alleged passport to Hawkins, who repudiated it. The chief chided Hawkins for permitting the troublemaker Chisholm to be in Cherokee country; "His Copartner received his punishment, I mean Dobblehead," the chief told Hawkins, and the Indians would do the same to Chisholm except that they feared to harm a white man. A year later Return Meigs demanded the return of the condemned cargo or payment for it. Hawkins in a report to the secretary of war sternly rebuked Meigs and defended the right of the Indians to seize the merchandise for their own use, implicitly pointing out, by referring to Meigs as "agent to the Cherokees" and signing himself as "Benjamin Hawkins Agent for I.A. [Indian Affairs]," that he was Meigs's superior officer. Meigs had certainly acted improperly and insubordinately, but he does not appear to have paid any penalty for it. He was still agent to the Cherokees in 1816. Like Clarke and Cox, Blount, Wilkinson, and Burr, Meigs was swimming with the tide, which then was toward removal.[48]

The McIntosh affair, insignificant in itself, may have been that one additional unpunished intrusion on Indian rights which the Creek opposition party could not bear. Hawkins had insisted again and again that intrusion was the cause of unruliness among the Indians, that the Indians were *not* tenants at will but rightful claimants of their land, "and there is but two ways of ousting them, conquest or compact." Compact had failed, as evidenced by all the failed or grudging treaties since 1801. The time of treaties was past. The Indians would give nothing more, either of their free will or by coercion and corruption. The time for conquest in the "just war" had at last arrived, wanting only leaders to set it in motion.[49]

PART THREE

Entreaty

They say: "They have been faithful to their treaty stipulations with us, yielding whatever was demanded of them. . . . They are now in a manner naked, their hunting done, their resources destroyed by their civil war, and they are without the means of clothing their helpless people and themselves, and winter is approaching."

BENJAMIN HAWKINS TO ACTING SECRETARY OF WAR
JAMES MONROE, OCTOBER 5, 1814.

CHAPTER 11

Two Wars for "Paradice"

What did your father, the British, tell the prophets, the beginning of this war? Tecumseh, in the square of Tuckabatchee, delivered their talk. . . . Kill the old chiefs, friends to peace; kill the cattle, the hogs, and fowls; do not work, destroy the wheels and looms, throw away your ploughs, and every thing used by the Americans. Sing "the song of the Indians of the northern lakes, and dance their dance." Shake your war clubs, shake yourselves; you will frighten the Americans, their arms will drop from their hands. . . . Has this proved true? Go to the fields of Talledega, and New-yau-cau, and see them whitened with the bones of the Red Clubs.—

HAWKINS TO BIG WARRIOR AND OTHER CHIEFS, 1814.

THE young Creeks had engaged in hostilities against white America and its ways for at least fifteen years before actual war broke out. For any hope of success against the powerful United States the Indians had to have foreign aid—a foreign source of arms, ammunition, supplies, and perhaps military force. Hostilities could not ripen into war, therefore, until the United States was at war, or about to be at war, with a foreign power that would help the Indians. This was the situation in 1811, when the United States was on the verge of war with Great Britain.

All the tribes from the Great Lakes to the Gulf had learned by successive offensives against one or another of them by white Americans, and by cessions wrested from one or another of them by speculators or the government, that only joint resistance could save them and their land. Confederation had always been the objective of great Indian leaders of the North: Brant, Pontiac, and finally Tecumseh. Jefferson had pressed at least as hard for extinguishment of Indian land titles in the North as in the South, and William Henry Harrison had administered Jefferson's policy vigorously.

Unencumbered with scruples, Harrison used tricks, chicanery, and threats. He promised presents to northern tribes if they would come to a meeting at Fort Wayne in 1803, and most of them attended. The Shawnees, however, convinced that Harrison was simply after their land, bolted. From the other tribes Harrison then and for the next several years got what he was after. In 1803 the Kaskaskias ceded all their lands in the Illinois Territory; in 1804, the Sioux and Foxes ceded over 50 million acres, and the Delawares and Piankashaws agreed to large cessions between the Ohio and the Wabash; in 1805, the Miamis, Weas, Eel River Indians, and Potawatomis yielded huge areas. In 1807 and 1808, Governor William Hull of the Michigan Territory took over as Jefferson's muscleman, acquiring large tracts within Michigan from the Ottawas, Chippewas, Wyandots, and Potawatomis. In 1809, Harrison was at work again, negotiating treaties and separate covenants with most of the same tribes, by which were extinguished their titles to land east and south of the Wabash. In all, land in that region acquired by the United States from 1795 to this last series of Harrison treaties came to more than 109,844,000 acres.[1]

Only the Shawnees had repulsed the land grabs, under the leadership of Tecumseh and his brother Tenskwatawa, two of several children of a Creek mother and a Shawnee father. Before Tecumseh's birth in 1768 the family had lived in Creek villages in Alabama, but then migrated north to the Shawnees in Ohio. According to legend, Tecumseh was one of triplets and endowed with the magic powers associated by the Indians with multiple births. It was not Tecumseh, actually, but the younger Tenskwatawa who was one of triplets and who became an inspired—mad, to his derogators—mystic known as the Prophet. Among other Tecumseh legends, it was said that his father was part white, a claim often made about outstanding red or black persons to explain how they happen to be outstanding. Other Tecumseh legends, however seem born out by the facts; it is generally agreed that he had great military skill and courage, was humane to the vanquished, incorruptibly honest, and a compelling orator.[2]

Tecumseh had good reason to hate the white intruder. His father had been killed in battle during Pontiac's Rebellion, and his mother, after many hardships, had fled her home with one daughter, leaving her other children to grow up as they could. The Jefferson-Harrison pressure for land cessions hardened Tecumseh into an implacable enemy of white Americans; he listened eagerly to offers of help against them put out by the many British agents in the Ohio country. In 1810 war between Britain and the United States was already inevitable. With the British hemming in the Americans from Canada and their Spanish allies pressing from Florida, the Indians might just tip the scales against the United States. Tecumseh accepted gifts of arms and supplies from the British and was led to believe vague promises that, if he could form an anti-American confederacy of all the tribes, the British would synchronize an assault with an Indian uprising to drive out the common foe.[3]

When Indians committed, or prepared to commit, acts of aggression and hostility, Hawkins and other reasonable men knew what had changed the once friendly tribes. As John Randolph said, "It was our thirst for territory, our own want of moderation, that had driven these sons of nature to depredations, of which we felt the effects."[4]

The People of the Lakes, as the northern Indians were called, grew exceedingly agitated after Harrison's Fort Wayne treaty in 1809. Under British urging, Tecumseh in the spring of 1811 advised Harrison that his treaties were not valid because they had been negotiated with individual tribes who had not the power to sell what belonged to all the tribes in common; settlers, he said, would be forcibly ejected. Harrison retorted that if Indian depredations did not cease he would destroy the community at Tippecanoe. This utopian settlement had been established by the Shawnees after Tenskwatawa, cured of alcoholism by a vision, had conceived of a refuge where Indians could return to old traditional moral values and ways of life, and where whiskey, the white man's curse, would be outlawed. About a thousand Shawnees, Delawares, Wyandots, Ottawas, Ojibwas, and

Kickapoos were gathered at Tippecanoe, and Tecumseh was fiercely dedicated to its preservation. Harrison's threat may have strenghtened Tecumseh's resolve to draw the southern tribes into an all-Indian confederacy. Leaving Tenskwatawa in charge at Tippecanoe with orders not to be drawn into a premature confrontation with Harrison, Tecumseh went south in 1811.[5]

Crossing the Tennessee by George Colbert's ferry, Tecumseh appealed first to the Chickasaws, then to the Choctaws. The following is a speech he is said to have addressed to a joint council of Choctaws and Chickasaws, and although the words ascribed to him may not be precisely those he spoke, the thoughts are those that were disturbing all Indians.[6]

He began by asking, where now were the Narragansetts, Mohawks, and other once powerful tribes?

> They have vanished before the avarice and oppression of the white man. . . . Soon their broad roads will pass over the graves of your fathers. . . . The annihilation of our race is at hand unless we unite in one common cause against the common fate. . . . Sleep not longer, O Choctaws and Chickasaws, in false security and delusive hopes. . . . Are we not being stripped day by day of the little that remains of our ancient liberty? Do they not even kick and strike us as they do their black-faces? . . . Then haste to the relief of our common cause . . . lest the day be not far distant when you will be left single-handed and alone to the cruel mercy of our most inveterate foe.

But Colbert of the Chickasaws and Pushmataha of the Choctaws wanted no part in an anti-American coalition. In response to Tecumseh's plea, Pushmataha said that the Shawnees had evidently had different experiences than the Choctaws with Americans, who gave his people good and fair trade, provided wheels, looms, cotton gins, farm tools, and instruction, and who doctored the sick and fed the hungry. They have never violated their treaties with us, said the Americans' good and forgetful friend Push, and we must stand by our word. Choctaws are not afraid of war, but they are a peaceful people, Pushmataha went on: "If we go into this war against the Americans, we must be prepared to accept its inevitable results." Death, suffering, hunger, grief, and devastation would follow. "I deplore this war," he said. Again, the words may not be the very ones Pushmataha spoke, but they do reflect the Choctaw rejection of Tecumseh, which never changed. Hawkins's friend and disciple Silas Dinsmoor had evidently been a successful agent, and the gifts and annuities awarded Pushmataha by the 1805 treaty were not wasted. He took a vote and announced that the majority of the council was for peace. His finding is challenged, however, by Angie Debo, who says that the vote was in fact evenly divided.[7]

Lastly, in October, Tecumseh went to the Creeks. Word of his coming had probably been brought by couriers, and the Creek National Council was expecting him. He came, according to an alleged eyewitness report, with an impressive escort of twenty-four dignified and powerful warriors dressed in buckskin shirts and leggings, heavily hung with silver ornaments; they wore red and black face paint and carried rifles, tomahawks, and war clubs. Hawkins's good friend Tustunnuggee Thlucco chaired the council, and Hawkins, as usual, was present. The guests were welcomed ceremoniously and then shown to their quarters. For several days there were rituals and dancing, but Tecumseh said nothing until Hawkins, doubtless aware that his presence was unwelcome, packed up and left.[8]

Then the Shawnees, stripped for a flap and wearing black paint, performed some mysterious symbolic rites and gave their war cry. Finally Tecumseh addressed the council. The speech that has come down as his through the report of a white man who claimed to have been an eyewitness, frontiersman Sam Dale, cannot be literally ascribed to Tecumseh; in fact, the presence of a white witness is highly unlikely. The gist of the speech, however, is indeed the message Tecumseh left with the Creeks, an exhortation to join in restoring the ancient might of the Indian people under the protection of Tecumseh's magic powers:

> Let the white race perish.
> They seize your land; they corrupt your women; they
> trample on the ashes of your dead.
> Back, whence they came, upon a trail of blood, they must
> be driven. . . .
> All the tribes of the north are dancing the war-dance. Two
> mighty warriors across the seas will send us arms.
> Tecumseh will soon return to his country. My prophets
> shall tarry with you. They will stand between you and

the bullets of your enemies. When the white men
approach you the yawning earth shall swallow them up.
Soon shall you see my arm of fire stretched athwart the
sky. I will stamp my foot at Tippecanoe, and the very
earth shall quake.[9]

Tecumseh is then supposed to have given a bundle of red-painted sticks to Tustunnuggee Thlucco, one to be broken for each day until the last, the time set for an uprising synchronized with a British attack. This calendric device could not have proven very useful, however, because the British had never given a precise date when they would strike. The Shawnee chief, seeing that Tustunnuggee and others were skeptical of the magic he claimed to hold through the Master of Breath, bade the Creeks look for the sign he had promised upon his return to Tippecanoe: "I will stamp the ground with my foot, and shake down every house in Tuckabatchee." Some of the Creeks were impressed; and when, sometime after Tecumseh's departure but too soon for him to have reached home, an earthquake did indeed rock the Creek area, many more must have become believers. Not all agreed, however, that revolt as timed by the red sticks was the right course. William Weatherford, or Red Eagle (a nephew of the late Alex McGillivray and probably Alex Cornells's brother-in-law), had grave misgivings and feared Tecumseh's war plan would ruin the Creek Nation, although he eventually joined the movement hoping to exercise some control on events. Another part-Creek who attended Tecumseh's talk and seems to have been unconvinced was Sam MacNac, who kept one of the inns on the post road.[10]

But Tecumseh's plaints—rape of the land, desecration of ancestral graves, changes in the Indian way of life, threat of enslavement—had a powerful impact on the rebellious young Creeks. The Choctaws, more remote from the white frontiers, did not resonate with the Shawnee to the same degree, nor did the Cherokees, who had been the first to take white culture and who had found it advantageous. Also, Tecumseh's mysticism held a special appeal to the Creeks; they believed devoutly in the Master of Breath and in his priests, the Prophets, who could predict the result of a battle, foretell flood or drought, "and even assume the power of directing thunder and lightning,"

Bartram said. Tecumseh brought once more to the Creeks—his relatives—Bowles's gift of hope, and the prospect of venting their anger in violent action.[11]

To that extent Tecumseh's journey had been successful. But on his return to Tippecanoe he was greeted by total devastation. His brother Tenskwatawa, despite Tecumseh's warning, had apparently allowed himself to be drawn into a confrontation with Harrison. After a battle that left many dead on both sides, Harrison chased the Indians back to Tippecanoe and destroyed the town with everything in it, including British arms cached by Tecumseh against the great uprising. From that time onward Tecumseh was fighting for mere survival in the North.[12]

Andrew Jackson had suffered politically and financially by the exposure of Aaron Burr, with whom he had been involved. An Indian campaign, always popular on the frontier, could erase his losses, and since Burr's fall in 1806 he had cast about for an excuse to march his Tennessee militia against the Creeks. To win government approval, Jackson spread stories of Indian atrocities and of British agents infiltrating Indian country—although in fact the frontier was relatively quiet—but Jefferson refused to authorize a frontier war. The border continued quiet even after Tecumseh's visit; the young Creeks had been told they must wait for a signal to rise up, and they waited.

Hawkins's Flint River agency was prospering, although Hawkins himself became very ill with what he called pleurisy on New Year's Day, 1812. By the ninth of January he was thought to be dying. He called in all who lived on the plantation, whites and blacks, "shook their hand and said, 'I am going.'" His will was made, and he asked Brother Petersen, a Moravian missionary who lived at the agency, to marry him and Lavinia, thus legitimizing a relationship of nearly fifteen years and his children. "Unlimited tears flowed," wrote Br. Petersen, who watched the sick man through the night. But to the amazement of all, the fifty-seven-year-old Hawkins did not go. On January 23, as he was recuperating, the earthquake occurred that many of the Creeks took to be the signal that Tecumseh had arrived home.[13]

Before his illness Hawkins had reported good progress in the civilization program, but in April a hostile wind could be felt stirring. A white man, Thomas Meredith, was killed on the post road. Sam MacNac said it was an accident, but Meredith's son claimed it was murder, and the Creek chiefs promised justice. In May, when the United States was on the brink of war with Great Britain, the Lower Creeks assured Hawkins they would remain neutral, but they complained bitterly that intruders over the Ocmulgee line were building fish traps, ranging stock, cutting timber, and farming Indian land—so much for the clear, unmistakable river boundary—and that this was the real reason the young men were running wild. To this Hawkins, stern as ever, answered that Georgians were claiming damages which would be paid out of the Creek annuity; he certainly agreed that white encroachment caused crime, but, with war imminent, he suspected also that British agents were stirring up trouble among the Indians. Then another white man, Lott by name, was murdered, according to Alex Cornells without provocation. The Creeks hung back about punishing the killers of Meredith and Lott, although they accommodated Hawkins by whipping and cropping two Indians for the lesser crime of stealing furs from the factory.[14]

After President Madison declared war on Great Britain on June 19, 1812, crimes in the agency increased, and Hawkins stepped up his demands for punishment. In August the chiefs had six persons put to death for murders on the post road and punished seven lesser offenders by cropping and whipping. Meanwhile there had occurred a crime of a particularly horrid and enflaming nature on Duck River, an area of intrusion since William Blount's time. Creek Indians murdered two children and took their mother, a Mrs. Crawley, into captivity. Willie Blount, Sevier's successor as governor of Tennessee, who was no less eager than Jackson for an excuse to descend on the Creeks, demanded furiously that Secretary of War John Armstrong order a campaign to punish this outrage, claiming that Mrs. Crawley had been taken from village to village and exhibited naked to the Indians. According to less lurid accounts, the Creeks did nothing worse to Mrs. Crawley than make her cook for them, but her children had indeed been brutally murdered. Tennessee was enraged. The legislature called for troops to exterminate the Creek Nation, echoing William Blount's "kill or be killed"; a Nashville paper said the Creeks "have supplied us with a *pretext* for the dismemberment of their country" (my emphasis). Jackson ranted about "beloved wives and little prattling infants, butchered, mangled, murdered, and torn to pieces," and cried, "we are ready and pant for vengeance." A much more practical reason for avenging the Duck River violence by exterminating the Creeks was Jackson's speculative interest in that fertile area. Almost fifteen years earlier he had written his brother-in-law Robert Hays: "Therefore lands on Duck River, should the Tennessee become the line will be valluable. This is as much as to say to you keep all you have and get what you can."[15]

The secretary of war still took no action. Governor Willie Blount wrote him again about Mrs. Crawley (who soon escaped her captors), lashing out at Hawkins for not punishing the Creek Nation: "His delay creates much surprise, and, indeed, it savors strongly of neglect." Armstrong forwarded this communication to Hawkins and sent Blount a reassuring letter that Hawkins had written to the War Office in which he had said that the Creek National Council would readily comply with an order to punish the murderers. To this Governor Blount responded in a letter incoherent with rage at Hawkins's deliberate procedure:

> That that round about way of giving satisfaction, or reporting about its being done, and about to be done, in that way, would be considered such a prompt execution of justice, on the part of the Creeks, in compliance with the demand made by the Government, that the Creek nation should give those offenders up to the laws of the United States, that the necessity of a campaign, to be carried against them, would be, or was thereby, superceded.[16]

Hawkins had demanded satisfaction for the murders as insistently as he dared; with Tecumseh's Prophets still among the Creeks, an intemperate or hasty action might set off far worse trouble than any so far encountered.

Hawkins had gone to Florida on business with John Forbes, and was seriously ill there through October and into November. He wrote Secretary Armstrong: "I am so reduced by fevers I can with difficulty sit up to write you a small note." That illness prevented Hawkins from accompanying John Innerarity of the Forbes company to Tuckabatchee for a conference with the Upper Creeks on their indebtedness to the firm, with the usual purpose of making the Creeks amenable to another land cession. It was the first such meeting since Tecumseh's visit, and Indian intransigence showed the Shawnee's influence. Hawkins was badly needed.[17]

Innerarity's journey from Pensacola was plagued with difficulties and frustrations: a fall from his horse, flooded fords, lamed animals. It was an understandably weary party that arrived at last on October 23 at Tustunnuggee Thlucco's lodge in Tuckabatchee. Alex Cornells was there, and Timothy Barnard; also Christian Limbaugh, Hawkins's deputy. Innerarity, with a bad cold and a headache, craved rest, but for the first several days in Tuckabatchee his quarters were filled with the usual Indian visitors by day, and he could not sleep at night "as we were continually incommoded by drunken Indians." He had most likely provided what got the Indians drunk. A number of days after his arrival he was still complaining bitterly that he had not yet had a chance to talk of his business, the Creek debt of $40,000 plus interest. Instead, the house was full of company all day, with more Indians talking loudly outside the door, and his table had always to be shared with various warriors and chiefs. At last, after almost a week of socializing, Innerarity was summoned to the Tuckabatchee square, where a year earlier Tecumseh had talked of freedom, for a beginning of talks about money.[18]

He told them how much they owed, and Tustunnuggee Thlucco supported his claims. The chiefs said they would consult, and business closed for the day. In private, Tustunnuggee warned Innerarity he would meet opposition, telling him that "the chiefs would act justly with [the Forbes company] but we must not think of charging them with interest although it was the custom of whites, for the Nation would pay none," and would object even to paying the principal unless the company promised to reduce prices and pay more for skins. The mood was already sullen. Before Innerarity gave his talk, Limbaugh had read aloud some stern messages sent by the ailing Hawkins, charging the chiefs with unpunished thefts and murders. Chief William McIntosh of the Lower Creeks had countercharged that Georgians were cutting cedar on Indian land, and Tustunnuggee Thlucco reminded the chiefs of his forewarning that intrusion, thefts, and murders would inevitably result if they permitted a post road to be cut through the nation.[19]

When the council reconvened next day, many objections were raised. The Indians insisted that they owed only half what Innerarity claimed, and that the remainder was interest, which they did not understand and would not pay. They would consult together about the principal sum, "but they would not hear of interest—" and they pointed out that if Forbes had accepted some land they had offered him, there would be no interest due. In vain Innerarity argued that the longer they delayed the bigger the interest would grow; interest was everywhere the custom; "it was always considered as sacred as the principal." Finally he proposed a compromise: half the interest. The chiefs, however, would have nothing whatever to do with interest; they argued that "they were poor . . . they knew nothing about interest, about what it meant, it might be a custom, a law among us white people, but poor Indians did not understand it, there was no word for it in their language, we were the first who ever talked of such a thing to them." Then the meeting broke into disorder. Youths called out that they would pay no interest. Tustunnuggee Thlucco, exasperated, accused Innerarity of "entangling the talks." The exhausted Innerarity returned to his quarters, "which I found as usual full of visitors which I had to maintain."[20]

For three days the matter of interest was tossed back and forth. Innerarity renewed his offer to forfeit $10,000 of it; the Creeks said they would have to go naked for years to pay off the principal alone, and on top of that he wanted interest, "which would tear the very skin off their backs." Tustunnuggee told Innerarity the chiefs were getting angry and would not settle at all if there was further talk of interest. A general murmur of disapproval arose, "& the cry of pay no such thing as interest, Pay only the debt was reechoed from every quarter." Innerarity noted in his journal, "I was quite tired & sick of the business," and perhaps he was frightened as well; the atmosphere bristled with hostility. On the first of November he capitulated; he signed an agreement to accept from the Upper Creek towns, over a period of three years, the sum of $21,916.01½ in settlement of

their indebtedness. Since their stipend for the three years—
1812, 1813, and 1814—would come to $22,000, they would in-
deed go naked and hungry, with nothing to show for all the
land they had ceded to the United States, unless they sold yet
another part of their shrunken domain.[21]

The full account of this meeting exudes a bitter essence of
hopelessness. Even Alex Cornells, as loyal a friend as Hawkins
could hope to have, was disgusted and talked angrily, telling Innerarity that he was sick of the boastings of the Americans and
of their enmity toward the English; that he was the friend of
the Americans, would live and die so, and was obliged to remain
Hawkins's interpreter, but "would renounce the Nation & his
[white] friends to live in peace & tranquility & be out of the
way of the Americans."[22] Cornells, who had managed since
Hawkins's coming to live between two worlds, now wanted
neither of them. The meeting had been extraordinary in its
anger and disorderliness, quite unlike the Quakerish gather-
ings Hawkins had described to Madison. Hawkins's power with
the Indians and their respect for him had never been so clearly
demonstrated by his presence as it was here by his absence.

The winter of 1812–1813 was very severe. In March, Hawkins,
back in the agency, was still suffering from a bad cough and
rheumatism. He had returned to a restless Creek Nation where
even the old chiefs were full of discontent, complaining that
any lie told about them was believed, that they were blamed not
only for the mischief done by their young people but for anything that any "idle worthless vagabone" might invent to their
discredit. Hawkins felt a chilly warning of war, unless the chiefs
could gain control of the deteriorating situation. If they did not
or could not, Jackson with the Tennessee militia would be quick
to take control, as Hawkins was aware. He urged Cornells and
Tustunnuggee Thlucco to punish their murderers speedily and
to see that drunkenness and depredations stopped.[23]

But the angry young Creeks were maddening themselves with
the magic of Tecumseh and could not be disenchanted by edict.
The Shawnee Prophet Seekaboo, left behind by Tecumseh, had
been teaching them northern mystic rites, and Tecumseh is be-

lieved to have fortified his power over them by a second visit to the nation in 1812. In 1813 it was rumored that a party of Shawnees would again appear among the Creeks. Those who accepted Tecumseh's plan of confederation quickly came to be known as Red Clubs, or Red Sticks, and sometimes Prophets. The first to go over to Tecumseh were the Alabamas, described by Hawkins as "the most industrious and best behaved of all our Indians" until "this fanaticism." Quickly the "fanaticism" spread through both Upper and Lower Creek towns, as the Red Clubs grew more numerous and more determined in their nationalist crusade. The British, successful in northern land battles that first year of the war, encouraged the Red Clubs to create turmoil in the South, by promises of arms and supplies awaiting them at Pensacola.[24]

April brought an explosion of violence. There were more murders near the Ohio, and Hawkins ordered the chiefs to pursue and punish the murderers without delay. Up to that time the chiefs had tended (or pretended) to take an indulgent attitude toward the rebellious youths, referring to their aggressions as "frolics," "fooleries," or "a sort of madness and amusement for idle people"; but now, Hawkins wrote Secretary Armstrong, "The chiefs are more alarmed than I have ever known them to be before." An open rupture with the excited Red Clubs seemed unavoidable. Reluctantly and fearfully the chiefs set out to do as Hawkins asked and punish those guilty of crimes. The traditional system of retaliation upon any relation of the criminals would have been easier, but Hawkins said, as always, "It is not an equal number the white people want, it is the guilty; and they want no innocent person to suffer." By Creek standards this was unreasonable. Hawkins also seemed unreasonable in his insistence that the chiefs should report voluntarily and immediately on murders done by their young people instead of waiting for him to find out, by which time the culprits had usually made their escape.[25]

Little Warrior, or We-wo-cau, a leader of the Red Club murder party and often a courier between the Shawnees and the Creeks, was pursued on orders of the National Council by a group of warriors. The murderers, after taking refuge at the sacred Hickory Ground, did their war dance and fired upon their pursuers. After a fierce engagement until ammunition gave out, the house in which the Red Clubs had sheltered was set on fire. Tuskegee Warrior was burned to death in the house. Two who tried to get out were killed with tomahawks. Of two others who ran for it, one was caught and killed. All were young men; all called on Tecumseh as they fought, and warned that those who did not follow him were ruined, that the Creek Nation must unite behind him. Some, maddened or drunk or both, boasted frightfully of killing and eating white people, of disembowelling a white woman near the Ohio. Four were killed at the Hickory Ground, but Little Warrior had stayed that night on the other side of the river and so got away; among the chiefs' party, two were wounded. Then the warriors pursued two more of the murderers and killed them; in that engagement one of the warrior leaders was hurt. After that, two who had committed murder on the post road were caught and killed, and a woman who had precipitated the murders at Duck River by a false report of a raid by Tennesseeans was executed. The chiefs then sent three warriors out to find Little Warrior. They sighted him near the Coosa.[26]

"He knew he had to die," Alex Cornells and Tustunnuggee Thlucco reported to Hawkins. They prepared to shoot him, but they knew if he located them by the snap of a gun being cocked he would wound them with his arrows. Two moved off and covered the sound of the third gun being cocked by rattling their bullet pouches. The third man shot and killed Little Warrior. Cornells hoped Hawkins would be satisfied: "We have killed eight for the murder at the mouth of the Ohio; two for the murder at the Wolf-path; one for last year, for the murder at Duck river; in all eleven, since the 16th of this month [April 1813]." Hawkins was satisfied with the executions: "I think it will put an end to all cause of alarm in the agency." The chiefs begged him not to let the Shawnees come again among them, "for if they should come, it will not be for our good."[27]

Hawkins was wrong; and the chiefs were too late in banning the Shawnees. Tecumseh's voice and promises were in the ears of the Red Clubs. The magic formulas, the war medicine, and the Dance of the Lakes gave them an intoxicating hallucination of power.

Very secretly the Red Clubs were making converts and gathering in the fork of the Coosa and Alabama, dancing the war dances of the Lake people and preparing to attack. By summer, according to various guesses they numbered somewhere between 3,000 and 4,800. Their ultimate goal was simple and appealing: destruction of the plan of civilization and a return to "the wild Indian mode of living," as Alex Cornells expressed it. One important old chief had joined the young people, Hopohielthle Micco of Tallassee, who had led the resistance at the treaty of 1804 and, before that, the raids on the commissioners' camp in 1799. Peter McQueen of the same town was another leading Red Club.[28]

So covertly did the Red Clubs organize that no one suspected their strength. Hawkins in early June wrote Armstrong: "From the present disposition of the Creeks, there is nothing hostile to be apprehended of them." He categorically denied complaints of the governors of Tennessee and Georgia that hundreds of fresh white scalps had recently been seen in a Seminole town. Cornells, always knowledgeable and reliable, assured Hawkins he had heard of nothing hostile from any quarter, and believed that the Alabamas alone were taking instruction from Tecumseh's Prophets in the dances and rituals. "The chiefs are as well convinced as I am, that their existence as a nation depends on their observance of their treaty stipulations with the United States," Hawkins wrote in June to the secretary of war; he said that the punishment of the murderers had convinced the Creeks that the Creek national government was effective. Hawkins advised the governor or Georgia, "If my fellow citizens on the frontiers will withdraw their intrusions on Indian rights, and be honest, they have but little to apprehend"; and if they would cooperate with the officers of government, "we should go on very well, and ease the timid mind of a frightful load."[29]

June was a month when cultivating the corn crop was the major preoccupation of the Creeks, and so June started quietly. Before the month was out, however, the situation had taken an alarming turn. According to Tecumseh's schedule, the first stage of the uprising was to persuade all Creeks to unite for confederation, even Tuckabatchee of the Upper Towns and Coweta of the Lower, both of which were much under Hawkins's influence. Only after all were united, in the autumn probably (when the harvest was in) were they to destroy Hawkins and all who helped with his civilization program, and rise up against the whites. However, the punishment by the chiefs of the killers of whites—who, to the Red Clubs, had been heroes doing the work of the Master of Breath—so infuriated the insurgents that they could wait no longer for their revenge.

In mid-June the chiefs' party sent a friendly message to the Red Clubs, especially Hopohielthle Micco, saying, show us the visions you have seen, let us hear what you say the Great Spirit has told you, and we shall believe what you say you have seen and heard. "You have nothing to fear," their messenger was to say, "the people who committed murders have suffered for their crimes, and there is an end of it." The messenger sent was one of the warriors who had executed the murderers. The Red Clubs instantly killed and scalped him.[30]

They then descended upon the house of one of the friendly chiefs, Captain Isaacs, sacked it and executed two more of the warriors who had been involved in the punishment of the murderers. Cornells reported to Hawkins: "After this they gave out they would destroy Tuckabatchee and Coweta, with every person in them; then kill Mr. Cornells, Tustunnuggee Thlucco, Mr. Hawkins, the old chiefs who had taken his talks, and all half-breeds; after this war among themselves, they would be ready for the white people. They had power to destroy them by an earthquake, or rendering the ground soft and miry, and thunder." Furthermore, "If any towns refuse to aid the Prophets, they should be sunk with earthquakes, or hills should be turned over them," or they would be struck by lightning. On receipt of this news Hawkins had to revise his report to Secretary Armstrong, saying with obvious reluctance that "there seems to be another object coupled with [internal political strife], and that of hostility to us eventually"; military force, he admitted, might in time be required.[31]

The nation was tense and divided. Red Club sympathy was

strong in the Upper Towns. For a time the Lower Town of Cusseta wavered, but then Cusseta Micco chose the party of the old
chiefs. By late June one hundred and ninety friendly chiefs and
warriors of Upper and Lower Towns were gathered at Tuckabatchee, awaiting the threatened Red Club attack and sending
urgently to Hawkins for help, either federal troops from General Wilkinson or Georgia militia. A military presence, they believed, would discourage the Red Clubs from violence. "Making
peace here in this way, is making peace for our white neighbors
as well as for ourselves," they reminded Hawkins; "we are of
opinion, if the prophets cannot be crushed, they will bring ruin
on us, and war against the white people." By then, however,
crushing them would be no easy task. Sixteen Lower Towns and
five Upper Towns had opted for the chiefs' party; the Red
Clubs had won to their side twenty-nine of the Upper Towns,
and some Uchees, a majority of the Creek Nation but far from
all of it.[32]

The chiefs who were gathered at Tuckabatchee had sent to
the Cherokees for aid, but none had yet arrived. Tuckabatchee
was virtually under siege. The old chiefs were terrified. Many
other Indians were "astonished, alarmed, and timid at the sudden explosion of this fanaticism," Hawkins reported. Hopohielthle Micco, once more appealed to, announced that the Red
Clubs considered the chiefs' party as people of the United States,
so they would be destroyed: first Tuckabatchee, then Coweta,
and finally the white people. The chiefs sent word of this fright-
ening message to Hawkins, adding, "If we are destroyed before
you aid us, you will have the work to do yourselves, which will
be bloody." The British on the Lakes, they said, were clearly the
instigators. Still Hawkins insisted it was a civil war, and was reluctant to intervene beyond sending the chiefs a few rifles and a
little ammunition, which, with characteristic punctilio, he would
deduct from their annuity. He continued to hope for peace,
pleading with the Red Clubs and assuring them that "war with
the white people will be your ruin." He never ceased to regard
the nationalistic youths as mere fanatics and extremists in the
grip of a crazy and suicidal religious zeal, and he kept thinking
they could be brought to their senses in time to avert destruction. But the situation in July in besieged and starving Tucka-

batchee was so desperate that Hawkins was almost ready to ask Gen. Thomas Pinckney, commander of the Sixth United States Military District, for a detachment of mounted infantry, despite the danger that such intervention might escalate civil rebellion into full-scale war.[33]

The Red Clubs swarmed around Tuckabatchee, demanding the surrender of Tustunnuggee Thlucco and Tustunnuggee Hopoie, the Speakers of the Creek Nation and of the Lower Towns, respectively, as an essential preliminary to peace talks. Although Tuckabatchee was in great distress, Cusseta Micco spoke for all when he declared: "Before we lose the Big Warrior [Tustunnuggee Thlucco], we will all die for him." More than two hundred warriors marched from Cusseta and Coweta to the besieged town and escorted the occupants from there to Coweta, but they lost everything except what they could carry on their backs; Hawkins ordered for them a larger supply of powder, lead, flints, muskets, and rifles, again out of their annuity.[34]

Food, however, was extremely scarce, because in a new and still more frenzied phase of their rebellion, perhaps inspired by more messages from Tecumseh, the Prophets were ranging the countryside destroying cattle, hogs, fowls, and all other foods associated with the detested civilization program. They had abandoned the towns and taken to the woods, where they were dancing the Shawnee dances, practicing the trembling, jerking, convulsive motions that so excited them, and giving demonstrations, in which some of them died, of their alleged protective magic against bullets. In a feverish burst of violence, they killed five chiefs in Oakfuskee and slaughtered almost all the cattle. A Scotsman named Grayson who lived in the town lost all his blacks and everything edible on the place; his daughter-in-law, one of the teachers of weaving who had come to Creek country at the express request of the Indians, had her livestock and woven cloth destroyed and, when she fled to a nearby town, was stripped of everything she possessed, down to her underclothes. All the property of Sam MacNac, who had not joined the Red Clubs, was destroyed. The stench of rotting animal flesh hung in the air for miles around the towns attacked by the Red Clubs, who were carrying out with fervor their avowed aim to destroy everything received from the Americans, and all the chiefs friendly to white ways, and every man who would not join them.[35]

Hawkins ordered a stand to be made at Coweta, from which parties of warriors should make forays against the Red Clubs. To his great annoyance, however, the chiefs had elicited a promise of aid from Governor David B. Mitchell of Georgia and had at once decided to wait for help rather than fight by themselves. Finally, however, the promised Cherokee aid arrived, two hundred warriors, and some battle action commenced. There were five hundred warriors from sixteen friendly towns at Coweta on the fourth of August; they agreed that in twelve days they would go out and fight an estimated twenty-five hundred Red Clubs. Tustunnuggee Thlucco and Tustunnuggee Hopoie sent word to Hawkins to make haste and come with troops and supplies to help them. Hawkins sent food to Coweta, but he did not rush out into battle. For one thing, he had not sufficient war supplies, and for another, he said he had found that "the promise of aid, gratis, paralyzes their efforts." Hawkins should have been able, from his long acquaintance with the Creeks, to make a wiser and gentler judgment; the Creeks as a people did not enjoy killing of any kind, and obviously they could have no stomach at all for killing the youth of their nation. War parties did go out from Coweta, nevertheless, and inflicted considerable damage on the towns of the Red Clubs. They destroyed Tallassee, the town of Hopohielthle Micco and Peter McQueen, which was the Prophets' headquarters. After that the Prophets moved to Autossee, a poor little town on the left bank of the Tallapoosa, and there did their war dances.[36]

On August 4, Hawkins had a message from Tustunnuggee Thlucco that Peter McQueen, on his way with a party of Red Clubs to Pensacola to pick up some ammuntion the British had promised, had stopped at the house of part-Creek James Cornells, captured Mrs. Cornells, and severely beaten a white man and a black man who were there. While McQueen continued on his journey, a small army (or large posse) was organized, comprising the outraged James Cornells, one David Tate, and a number of other half-Creeks of the Tombigbee settlements under the leadership of Dixon Bailey, all of whom had been threatened or molested by the Prophets. They were joined by some

white settlers and members of the territorial militia of Mississippi, the entire group coming to about one hundred and eighty
men. McQueen was said to have three hundred and fifty in his
party and to be returning with a train of horses packing the ammunition. The avengers, led by militia officers, rode down the
Pensacola road to intercept McQueen. About one o'clock on the
afternoon of July 27 the scouts of the Cornells party reported
that McQueen and his men had encamped near Burnt Corn
Creek, a stream roughly paralleling the road, and were busy
cooking and eating a midday meal. The attacking party moved
quietly forward, dismounted, and charged the Red Clubs, who
retreated in confusion toward the creek after firing a few shots.
Some of the attackers chased them, but the majority set about
capturing the packhorses with their valuable loads. Seeing
how few came after them, the Red Clubs reversed course and
charged their assailants, who now were the ones in confusion
and disorder. It was, in fact, a total rout, with the Cornells party
and militiamen scattering in all directions, many on foot; some
lost their way and were later found starving. Five Indians and
one black in McQueen's party were killed. Of the attacking party,
two were killed and fifteen wounded.[37]

McQueen had planned to attack Coweta about the first of October as a preliminary to the expedition against the white frontiers. But the families of the Red Clubs killed and wounded at
Burnt Corn clamored for retaliation, so it was decided instead
to attack Mims' Fort in the Tensaw settlement on the lower Alabama, just a little north of the Florida line. Mims' Fort was
a stockaded one-acre plot, the home of a prosperous part-
Indian, Samuel Mims. After the alarming news of Burnt Corn,
as many as 550 persons gathered at Fort Mims, including 260
territorial militia stationed there by the Mississippi commander,
General F. L. Claiborne. The fort commander was a Major
Beasley. By some accounts, there were only 160 military and
somewhere between 115 and 275 civilians, of whom 100 were
children. The number of Red Club assailants is variously put at
from 400 to 1,000; Hawkins was told they included warriors
from 13 towns. Those who crowded into Mims' stockaded acre
included perhaps 100 black people of the many who had farms

in that area, besides white and part-white settlers; about 70 of the militiamen were of mixed parentage.[38]

The Red Clubs, led by Peter McQueen and the disapproving Red Eagle, silently drew near the fort at ten or eleven on the bright Monday morning of August 30, giving no alarm to the inmates, who were said to have been dipping into a newly arrived supply of whiskey and generally enjoying themselves. Major Beasley is alleged to have been drunk. One account says that James Cornells had brought in a warning of the approach of the war party, but that Beasley ignored it and did not trouble to have the gates of the fort secured. A black man in the Red Club party, Siras, cut down the pickets; Red Eagle, McQueen, and their men stormed through the open gate. What followed was dreadful carnage, a massacre in which all but 36 of the fort's occupants were put to death, most of them horribly, and the few survivors, none of them white, were taken captive. The Red Clubs are said to have lost between 36 and 50 dead, and many more wounded. By one o'clock the battle was over.[39]

By all accounts, including their own boasts, the Red Clubs behaved like demons, killing, dismembering, disemboweling, throwing living bodies into burning buildings, sparing neither women nor children. The hideous reports made perfect propaganda for war hawks like Jackson, whose earlier allegations of women and babes "butchered, mangled, and torn to pieces" were realized at Mims' Fort.[40]

In another attack a few days later on a little settlement in the fork of the Alabama and Tombigbee, a detachment of Red Clubs under Prophet Francis massacred two white families. An attack on another stockaded house was turned back. It appears that control had now passed out of the hands of reasonable men like Weatherford—who had argued against the attack at Mims' Fort on the ground that, once white people were killed, the United States would intervene—and into the hands of manic zealots like Francis, who offered emotional release and euphoria rather than political goals. The devastation at Mims' confirmed to the mystics "the boasted power of the Prophet to take American forts with bows and arrows, to know the secrets of their enemies," Hawkins said; ". . . the Master of Breath has permitted a conquering spirit to arise among them like a storm, and it shall ravage like a storm." Their determination to kill every Indian who would not join them "has given to many much terror, which nothing but the presence of our army will remove," Hawkins was finally forced to admit. In their frenzy, they were destroying all that he had so laboriously persuaded the Creeks to accept—the cattle were killed, the gins smashed, and the axes, hoes, and ploughs flung into the rivers to rust. Theirs was a starvation course, win or lose, because natural resources were by then so depleted that the Creeks could not feed themselves in their traditional way, and by destroying the tools and domesticated animals of the new way they lost their only means of survival.[41]

Fort Mims provided the provocation for which Willie Blount and Jackson had been waiting. A month before the event Jackson had written Blount that he expected to be asked to lead an expedition against the Creeks, whom he had no doubt were urged to hostilities by the British enemy. He would demand, he said, a force competent to defeat "the whole Creek nation" and their allies the Choctaws, ignoring the facts that almost half the Creek Nation wanted peace and that the Choctaws had not allied themselves with either Creek party. His 2,000 volunteers, disgruntled after an aborted campaign in Florida, were ready to march at a moment's notice; they, with 5,000 Tennessee militia, one United States Army regiment, and a brigade from Georgia, "would be amply sufficient to drive the Indians and their allies into the ocean."[42]

What was a long awaited opportunity to Blount and Jackson threw Hawkins into despair. For months he had been handling an explosive situation that threatened an end to everything he had been working toward. He had reported almost daily to Secretary Armstrong on the Creek civil strife, but his communications met with total silence from Washington. He was furious at Governor Mitchell of Georgia for making a private deal with the old chiefs who asked for help, and disgusted by the unceasing efforts of Willie Blount to march out the Tennessee militia. He must have been alarmed at Jackson's impatience to turn what he knew to be an internal Creek problem that they themselves must solve into a full-scale, devastating Indian war. As Robert V.

Remini summed it up: "Thus, it needs to be remembered that from start to finish the Creek War was essentially an Indian civil war. And, most important of all, that it was General Andrew Jackson who took supreme advantage of this internal strife. He . . . virtually annihilated the Creek Nation."[43]

But Blount scoffed at Hawkins's insistence that this was civil war between two almost equally divided Creek parties. "The much formerly talked of civil war, said, by the agent, to be raging among the Creek Indians" was, Blount jeered, "altogether fudge—a mere tub for the whale . . . a blind for the credulous." Fully 90 percent of the Creeks were Red Clubs, Blount claimed, and the only thing to do was to exterminate the entire nation, especially since the United States was at war with Great Britain, whose cause was abetted by the Spanish in Florida. Clearly Blount's objective was to wipe out all the Creeks, appropriate their territory, and then move on West Florida—Jackson's aims precisely.[44]

President Madison had been acquainted for many months with the plan of Blount and Jackson, but had not yet decided on a course of action. This possibly explains why Hawkins had heard nothing from the War Department. Also, the war in the North presented far more pressing problems. Finally, after repeated pleas for attention to his troubles, Hawkins wrote Armstrong in evident distress of mind:

> As I hear nothing from you relative to the communications I have made you on Indian affairs, I have judged it advisable to have an understanding with myself on my situation here. I have not been concerned directly or indirectly, in commerce, or speculations of any kind, to accumulate money. From all the savings arising from my appointment, I have not made three thousand dollars. I have considered my public standing with the Indians as public property, and to be used as such, under the orders of Government, and for no other purpose; and I believe the period is arrived, when it is essential to that interest. Yet, if the President can find a man, who can fill this office, in his judgment, more for the public interest or convenience than I have done, he owes it to his high standing, and to me, to send him on; in doing so he will do me no injury, or excite the least resentment. . . . This department has always been strewed with thorns. It was first assailed by the late Governor Blount and associates, in Tennessee, and the recoil on himself destroyed his public character. It was then assailed by the British, through their agent

General Bowles. . . . I sent him in irons to the Governor . . . at New Orleans, to answer for his crimes. The calumny which hovered around, and assailed the Indians and their agent, I disregarded, as it originated from base sources, filled by dishonest motives.[45]

Hawkins wrote on September 14, 1813, just three days after Capt. Oliver Perry's great victory on Lake Erie and his electrifying message, "We have met the enemy and they are ours." Small wonder the War Department could not be bothered with Hawkins's problems. On September 18, after news of the Fort Mims massacre reached Nashville, Tennessee, leaders were crying for a war to "exterminate the Creek Nation and Abettors," and Willie Blount called on his legislature for immediate action to "teach those barbarous sons of the woods their inferiority." Less than three weeks later Andrew Jackson was ready to move against the Red Clubs, and Tecumseh lay dying in Canada after the battle of the Thames. Hawkins's offer to resign was not taken up, but his power had been usurped. The Blount faction ruled.[46]

The real reason for Jackson's war was not so much the national interest as the desire to bring the enormous wealth of the Indian lands to the white people of the South; during the campaign Jackson starved with his troops because, as he wrote his confidant John Coffee, if supplies would only arrive, "we would soon reach the promised land that flows with milk and honey." Or, as Governor Willie Blount wrote General Flournoy, if the troops of Georgia and Tennessee act in concert with the United States troops, they and all the people of the South and West may "soon become the cultivators of the rich soil, which they may, in that time, soon become possessed of by their valor. . . . These objects once effected, each southern and western inhabitant will cultivate his own garden of Eden, and will, through the natural channels placed by a wise and just Creator, convenient to his use, export his own produce, and import such comforts as he may think desirable, by the shortest routes of communication with the ocean."[47]

No wonder that this was such a popular war, and that Jackson, conceived of as its hero, became so popular for winning it. Furthermore, it could be defended as a legitimate war, no mere raid on unoffending red men; the violence of the Red Clubs had convinced even Hawkins that only armed force could restore order. It was, in fact, Knox's "just war" come at last.

Ringing the Creek country, and all eager to take part in and share the spoils of the just war, were Tennessee, Georgia, and the Mississippi Territory. The Territory sent in its militia under General F. L. Claiborne; General John Floyd led the Georgia militia, Generals John Cocke and James White the East Tennessee militia, and Andrew Jackson and John Coffee the militia of western Tennessee; United States Army troops were under General Thomas A. Flournoy, commanding officer of the U.S. Seventh Military District, and under the overall command of General Pinckney. Pinckney's and Hawkins's problem was a lack of orders or any communication at all from Washington, despite a threatening situation that worsened daily. Late in September Hawkins wrote Secretary Armstrong that the Spanish, supporting the British enemy, had been offering arms to the Indians if they would all unite against the Americans. In the latter part of 1813 the British were winning victories in the North, and boasting that they intended to press the war in the South and seize New Orleans, Mobile, and probably Savannah. Alex Cornells had reported that the Red Clubs planned an attack on Tuckabatchee in a few days, after which they would go east towards the Savannah River, "and were determined to give Colonel Hawkins a chace and take him, unless he was on a fleet horse, before he got there." The friendly Lower Creek chiefs, such as those of Eufaulau, were by then so frightened that they hesitated to join the other chiefs at Coweta unless their white friends promised to come quickly; otherwise, "from their fears, they will be compelled to join the Red Clubs," they told Hawkins. The Uchees did join them. Once the Lower Towns began to defect, there would probably follow a stampede to the side of the Prophets, who were now rumored to have 4,800 gunmen. They were still declaring that, having destroyed Tuckabatchee and Coweta, they would "take the post road, enter Georgia, ravage all before us." The friendly chiefs were panicking, calling in their patrols.[48]

In early October, Hawkins again pleaded with Secretary Armstrong for instructions: "I can hear nothing from you." Hearing nothing, he hesitated to act.[49]

The army of western Tennessee was not so burdened by scruples. Within two weeks of receiving news of the Fort Mims massacre, Jackson, without any federal authorization, dispatched John Coffee with 500 mounted cavalry. He himself followed a few days later with 3,000 soldiers. It was here that the Creek civil war turned into Jackson's war, governed by the simple rule that all Creeks unwilling to fight the Red Clubs were the enemy.[50]

By late October, Hawkins was preparing to take action. General Floyd had 2,500 Georgians in readiness, 600 of whom had crossed the Flint and were fortifying a supply depot at the agency. The friendly chiefs were offering Floyd their cooperation. More of Floyd's men were arriving each day, and Hawkins expected regular army troops as soon as they could find beef. While these preparations were going on, the Tennessee forces were flung into action. Coffee's cavalry swooped down on the Red Club stronghold at Tallushatchee on November 3, indiscriminately shooting down warriors, women, and children. Davy Crockett, one of the party, is quoted as remarking, "We shot them like dogs." One hundred eighty-six Indians were killed, and five Americans. Eighty women and children survived to be taken as prisoners. Coffee boasted in his report of the battle that "not one of the warriors escaped to carry the news, a circumstance unknown heretofore." Lt. Richard Call wrote that half-consumed bodies were seen amidst the smoking ruins of cabins, and dogs were feasting on mangled corpses. Jackson wrote Governor Blount, "We have retaliated for the destruction of Fort Mims." Robert Remini calls Tallushatchee "a slaughter . . . a massacre." But Jackson the warrior had a sentimental side. When soldiers brought him an infant boy rescued from the clutch of its dead mother, Jackson himself fed the baby sugar water and had him cared for, and later sent him home to his wife to be brought up as one of the family.[51]

Jackson had paused to build a supply depot, Fort Strother, at Ten Islands on the Coosa, but that did not delay him long. Six days after Tallushatchee he attacked Talladega on the Coosa with 1,200 infantry and 800 cavalry troops. Talladega was a friendly town, under siege by the Red Clubs. The siege was raised; 300 or more Indians were killed, and 15 whites. In both battles the Red Clubs were greatly outnumbered. These slaughters so terrified other towns that the Indians of Hillabee made an offer of surrender to Jackson and were awaiting his decision.[52]

Jackson had pressed forward far and fast. If he had dared push his advantage immediately, as he wrote General Clairborne, the war would soon have ended; but his advance had taken him deep into Creek country, far from his source of supply. "There is an enemy whom I dread, much more than I do the hostile Creeks," Jackson said, "—you know I mean the meagre monster famine." Another hindrance was that he would be short of men when his volunteers went home at the end of their enlistment term in December. A few days after Talladega, however, General White of East Tennessee with about 1,000 men of Cocke's division marched up and attacked Hillabee, either not knowing or not caring that the town had offered to surrender, and without consulting Jackson who was nominally in command. At Hillabee on November 18 occurred the most inexcusable massacre of all. "We lost not a drop of blood, and Fort Mims was again avenged," White reported.[53]

Then the Georgia troops marched out, with Hawkins and a Creek contingent. Twenty miles above the junction of the Tallapoosa and Coosa was the Red Club town of Autossee. On November 29, General Floyd attacked it with 950 Georgians and 400 Creeks, including Efau Haujo of Tuckabatchee. The Red Clubs were taken completely by surprise; about 200 were killed, and the town was burned. Also destroyed were nearby Tallassee and Little Tallassee, Alexander McGillivray's birthplace. Each time a town was burned, its food stores went up in the flames; the Red Clubs who survived, and their women and children, came nearer and nearer starvation.[54]

The war front was edging toward the Hickory Ground, near the junction of the Alabama and Coosa, five miles above Little Tallassee. In December, while Jackson was helplessly pinned down by shortages of men and supplies, General Claiborne brought up his army to earn its share of victory and spoils. He had nearly one thousand men, a combined force of United States infantry and cavalry, territorial militia, and volunteers, and Pushmataha's Choctaw battalion of some 150 warriors. On the morning of December 23, Claiborne's forces were only two miles from the Hickory Ground, but the Red Clubs' scouts had seen them in time to send off their women and children. At about noon the fighting started, and the Red Clubs held their ground for half an hour; but, again hopelessly outnumbered, their lines broke, and a great many made their escape by way of the river. Among these was Red Eagle, who, it was said, in epic style jumped his horse from a bluff into the Alabama, swam it across, and escaped unhurt. After the brief battle the town was sacked and burned. The Americans had one man killed and twenty wounded; the Red Clubs lost thirty-three, including twelve black men, but the number of their wounded is not known because their comrades managed to carry them off. Claiborne's army continued the destruction of towns and countryside through Christmas Day as they marched toward home.[55]

While Claiborne triumphed, Jackson was still immobilized by a lack of supplies and men. When Blount advised him to come home to Tennessee and procure what he needed, Jackson snapped at the governor who had "bawled aloud for permission to exterminate the Creeks" and then gave no support. At the turn of the year some men and supplies arrived, and Jackson quickly pushed on again toward another Red Club stronghold, Tohopeka, in the Horseshoe Bend of the Tallapoosa, seventy-five miles south of Fort Strother. He had 900 Tennesseeans and a contingent of 200 Creeks and Cherokees. On January 22, at Emuckfau Creek, three miles from the Horseshoe Bend, he was attacked by 500 Red Clubs, who outfought him and drove him back in the first Red Club victory. They chased him, attacked hard again two days later as he reached the Hillabee village of Enitachopco, and again outfought him; but for the action of one detachment and the Indian contingent, the battle could have been a complete rout. Jackson nevertheless won praise and promotion for his firm leadership. Both sides had suffered severe losses. Jackson, back at Fort Strother, licked his wounds and lashed out at everyone, the soldiers who were leaving him to go home and the armchair generals back in Tennessee— "little yelping currs"—who dared criticize him and Coffee.[56]

Now it was Georgia's turn again. Floyd, having increased his army to 1,700 troops and 400 warriors, was marching along the Calabee valley on January 22 when he was ambushed by Red Clubs and driven back into the swamps. His campaign ended then and there. Thus Jackson was to have the opportunity to bring the war to a close.[57]

At last Jackson was sufficiently reinforced to make an offensive. Again, his objective was the Horseshoe Bend. There, on March 27, he joined battle with perhaps 1,000 Red Clubs, men of Oakfuskee, Neu-yau-cau, the Hillabees, the Fish Ponds, and Eufaulau, who made a desperate stand there. Jackson had about twice as many men: 1,400 white troops, 500 or more Cherokees, and 100 Creeks. The Red Clubs in their usual fashion had surrounded their position with breastworks; Jackson jeered that they had "penned themselves up for slaughter." Presumably, if their defenses were breached the Red Clubs thought to escape by swimming across the Tallapoosa. Sending Coffee and the Cherokees to the other side of the river to cut off that escape route, Jackson with the main body stormed the breastworks. The Red Clubs fought to the end. "They were proud, haughty, brave, and mad by fanaticism," the old chiefs later told Hawkins, with obvious pride. White casualties were few. Eight hundred Red Clubs died. "You have saved this country," Judge Harry Toulmin of Alabama wrote Jackson.[58]

From incomplete and probably unreliable casualty reports of the various battles, it appears that something like 1,500 to 1,600 Red Clubs had been killed in battle, and it must be presumed that others died later of their wounds. The chiefs said "they did not believe the hostile Indians were ready for peace," Hawkins reported, but probably not enough survived to continue fighting.[59]

Perhaps William Weatherford, the rebels' Red Eagle, one voice of reason throughout the fanaticism, helped persuade them to stop. When Jackson returned from the Horseshoe Bend, Red Eagle went to him and gave himself up, saying, according to tradition: "I am in your power. Do with me as you please. I am a soldier. I have done the white people all the harm I could; I have fought them and fought them bravely; if I had an army, I would yet fight, and contend to the last; but I have none; my people are all gone. I can now do no more than weep over the misfortune of my nation." Jackson was awed and impressed by Red Eagle, but he explained that the Indians had to give up, and on his terms, or there would be no peace. Weatherford said he wanted peace, and in any case was forced to surrender: "There was a time when I had a choice, and could have answered you: I have none now. Once I could animate my warriors to battle; but I cannot animate the dead. My warriors can no longer hear my voice: their bones are at Talladega, Emuckfaw and Tohopeka. . . . You are a brave man: I rely upon your generosity." He said he would insist that all obey Jackson's terms, and not "sacrifice the last remnant of their country" for the sake of revenge.[60]

It was not true that all the Red Clubs were killed, however. Many, including McQueen and Francis, had escaped toward the south, to fight Jackson again in a short time alongside the Seminoles in Florida. It is true that those who remained were literally starving, and they were Hawkins's main concern. He urged the Red Clubs to plant their fields while there was still time. At any other season the war might have limped on longer, but corn had to be planted by the end of April if the Creeks were not to starve the following year. Hawkins said as much: "The friendly Indians, as soon as they had put their families down to planting their fields, would be ready to join, and cooperate with our armies . . . and believed, with but little aid, would be able to destroy their enemy, and their fanaticism." But Hawkins told them enough blood had been spilled; in fact, peace terms had been decided on by the secretary of war, and were about to be offered by General Pinckney.[61]

CHAPTER 12

The Dispossessed

*All men must surely die
Tho' no one knows how soon,
Yet when the time shall come,
The event may be joyful.*

—A CREEK FUNERAL SONG

Hawkins and General Pinckney had been appointed commissioners to make a peace treaty with the Red Clubs. The choleric Jackson was outraged at being omitted; Tennesseeans raised a loud protest at having no voice in the treaty and insisted Jackson must be a commissioner, as if he and his western Tennesseeans had single-handedly won the war. In fact, the battle record shows Jackson and Coffee victorious in only three of the nine major engagements, but by sheer audacious clamor Jackson conveyed and left upon history the impression that he alone was the victor and therefore he alone had the right to dictate terms of peace. Although he had not won the war, he did win its final battle, and it has been conjectured that if he had not then broken the power of the Red Clubs, they would have cooperated with a British landing in the South and the United States might have lost New Orleans. In preparation for a southern campaign 14,000 seasoned British troops were sent to America in the summer of 1814.[1]

Armstrong's letter appointing Pinckney and Hawkins was written March 17, which suggests that the war had been winding down before the March 27 battle of Horseshoe Bend. In his letter Armstrong suggested terms he wished the commissioners to include in a peace treaty with the hostile Creeks, "so soon as they shall express a desire to put an end to the war." On March 20 the secretary followed up with another letter to Pinckney, very brief, saying: "Since the date of my last letter, it has occurred to me, that the proposed treaty with the Creeks should take a form altogether military, and be in the nature of a *capitulation* [underlined by Armstrong]; in which case the whole authority of making and concluding the terms will rest on you exclusively as Commanding General. In this transaction, should it take place, Colonel Hawkins, as agent, may be usefully employed." Pinckney replied that the arrangement suited him; he would accept the capitulation.[2]

Two weeks later, after the battle at Horseshoe Bend, Pinckney wrote Hawkins his thoughts on the capitulation they were to arrange. His tone was firm, but his terms were those of a humane man; he spoke of the defeated Creeks as "miserable people" who perhaps sincerely wished to atone. The terms he suggested included: the United States to take sufficient territory to indemnify for war losses, in the area that had been conquered; the right of the United States to establish military posts and factories as it saw fit, and to restrict Indian trade with Spain and Great Britain; its right to build and use roads and to navigate waters through Creek country; and the surrender of the Red Clubs and all other instigators of war. Concessions to the friendly Creeks and mercy to the hostile ones had not been mentioned by Armstrong, but figured importantly in Pinckney's plans. He told Hawkins to inform the friendly chiefs that the United States would not forget their fidelity; that in taking lands as indemnity, their claims would be respected, and chiefs who had distinguished themselves by their exertion and valor would also receive remuneration in the ceded lands. Hawkins was also to tell the friendly chiefs the roads by which the Red Clubs could travel unmolested to the posts to surrender; they would be forgiven, and Hawkins was to ensure provisions at the posts for them and their homeless families. Hawkins at once advised the chiefs of Pinckney's considerate terms and with their help laid out the safest surrender paths.[3]

Jackson's formidable choler rose when he learned that Hawkins, following the spirit of Pinckney's instructions, had permitted some of the friendly Indians to return to their homes. "I did tell [Hawkins] the Territory I had assigned to them," Jackson wrote furiously to Pinckney, although the War Department had not delegated him to make any such assignments. Immense pressure exerted by leading Tennesseans, who gave Jackson a frenzied welcome on his return to Nashville, perhaps changed Armstrong's mind about the treaty and who should negotiate it. Also, news of a massing of British forces at the mouth of the Apalachicola for a campaign into Florida may have convinced the president that this was an inappropriate time to snub the country's outstanding war hero, now commander of the Seventh U.S. Military District. For whatever reasons, only a week after Jackson's furious outburst against Hawkins, Armstrong in a deferential letter told Jackson of a change of plans which would make Jackson sole commissioner for the Creek treaty. Armstrong wrote in a positively obsequious manner to say that, should Jackson accept the president's appointment, "I have to suggest the wish of the President that you should proceed, without delay, to Fort Jackson, and consummate the arrangements committed to Major General Pinckney in relation to the hostile Creeks." An enclosure for Pinckney informed him that Jackson would proceed with the treaty in his place.[4]

The shift must have been highly alarming to Hawkins. Although in a letter to Armstrong he spoke of "the splendid victories of General Jackson," he would certainly have preferred the "correct, intelligent, and dignified" General Pinckney in charge of the capitulation. Hawkins's distress shows in the last paragraph of that letter to Armstrong, in which he said, "I hope the President will appoint a man to succeed me, as soon as it may comport with the convenience of the Government."[5]

Jackson triumphant proceeded at once to Fort Jackson and announced August 1 as the date for opening the treaty. Fort Jackson was a restoration of the century-old French fort, Toulouse, strategically situated on the Coosa a few miles from its confluence with the Tallapoosa to form the Alabama River. Toulouse was a well-known landmark to many early travellers through the southern Indian country. Jackson had chosen Toulouse as a suitable junction point for his supply lines from Tennessee and Georgia; after the Horseshoe Bend fight he had had

Toulouse restored, renaming it Fort Jackson, and had encamped his army around it.[6]

Earlier treaties, always affairs of pomp, ceremony, and festivity, had nothing in common with the miserable capitulation at Fort Jackson. The summons Jackson bade Hawkins issue was for all Creeks to come, friends and enemies alike, on pain of total destruction of the nation.[7]

The Creeks had received only part of their annuity for 1812 and none for 1813; four thousand had come to the posts and were drawing rations. They were hungry, frightened men, many doubtless ragged and sick or wounded, who gathered with their families to learn on what terms they might put their lives together again. There was no spirit for elaborate ceremonials, no time for deliberate talk, compliments, metaphorical rhetoric, all the traditional Indian accompaniments to negotiation. And yet, interestingly, it was the first treaty in which the Indians were dealt with in a manner consonant with Article I Section 8 of the Constitution, which, by implication at least, classifies the tribes not as dependent red brothers of other Americans but as separate political entities, like foreign nations. At Fort Jackson the Creeks were treated as a foreign enemy, a nation that has been whipped and humbled and must pay whatever price is to be exacted for peace. Jackson invoked the name "Brother," but in no spirit of brotherliness he demanded land from the chiefs who had fought at his side as well as from those whom they had helped him defeat. There was some protest, notably from Tustunnuggee Thlucco, but no bargaining, not even so much as Wilkinson had permitted at the 1802 treaty with the Creeks. Even Wilkinson, although he rebuked the Creeks as ungrateful children of a kind Father, had been willing to listen to their talks and to negotiate. Jackson simply stated what he wanted and took it. Hawkins was present, but totally powerless.[8]

Jackson had known precisely what he meant to get even before he was put in charge of the surrender. His idea was, winner take all. A month after Horseshoe Bend he had been writing Secretary Armstrong about surrender terms. The friendly Creeks, he said, would be glad to be left alive and grateful for any little area given them, say, a strip north of a line from the Georgia boundary to New-yau-cau on the Tallapoosa, and thence to the Coosa a mile or so above Fort Williams; Tustunnuggee Thlucco and his people could be granted a little extra land, if necessary. Early's map, drawn in 1818 soon after the Fort Jackson treaty, shows that the strip described by Jackson would lie in or on the edge of Cherokee country and would therefore be a problem to the Creeks rather than a gift. The day Jackson wrote to Armstrong, Hawkins was writing General Pinckney that he had conveyed to the friendly chiefs Pinckney's generous assurances: that in taking land as indemnity their claims would be respected; and furthermore, that individuals who had done outstanding service to the United States would be remunerated out of the ceded territory.[9]

Then in mid-May, Jackson had written his angry letter to Pinckney saying: "I did tell [Hawkins] the Territory I had assigned them. I did tell him that no Indians should settle west of the cosee or north of the allabama, and I am certain Government will not permit them to settle below the allabama." The strength of the frontier, Jackson said, depended on land settled by "thick and wealthy inhabitants, unmixed by Indians." Furthermore, he wrote Pinckney, he was convinced that the time had come to extinguish Cherokee and Chickasaw claims within the state of Tennessee. It apparently mattered little to Jackson that no legal grounds existed for such action; Hawkins had been opposing the seizure of those lands since he had run the Holston line seventeen years earlier, believing oppositely that Tennessee claims within Cherokee and Chickasaw lands must be extinguished if crime and violence were to cease. But Jackson was determined to acquire the lands of the Yazoo and Muscle Shoals speculations, just as William Blount had been. Jackson went on to assure Pinckney that his proposal could easily be justified; the Chickasaws could be told with perfect honesty that they had shown their inability to protect American citizens from theft and murder on the roads running through their territory—the roads the Indians had been reluctant to grant for this very reason. For the safety of the country and its citizens, Jackson insisted, the United States must extend its settlements to the Mississippi. Then he waved onstage the spear carrier who is always waiting in the wings to rush out and distract attention from a flawed script—national security:

> Our national security require it, their [Cherokee and Chickasaw] security require it. The happiness and security of the whole require this salutary erangement, it must be done, and they shall be indemnified either in money or land gained by Creek conquest. Now is the time to obtain it, and it ought and must be had.[10]

Jackson's speculations required it; and his popularity required that his soldiers and supporters, Tennesseeans, have priority in buying parcels of it. The time had not been right when Blount had tried for the same goals, but now the war he had wanted had been fought, the Indians were cowed, and there would never be a better time to take from them what white Americans sought.

Jackson communicated to Secretary Armstrong thoughts similar to those he expressed to Pinckney. While admitting that the lands west of the Coosa and north of the Alabama were sufficient indemnification, he pointed out that the hostiles had forfeited rights to all their lands, and that the friendly Creeks, while they might be allowed to keep their towns and farmed fields, should be made to give up a wide strip through the middle of their country, which would always keep them "peaceable and faithfull." By this the United States would gain land worth $12 million, by Jackson's estimate, on which the government should encourage settlement, giving preference to those who had conquered it. Six weeks before the Fort Jackson meeting took place, Jackson advised Armstrong that the boundary line should be surveyed immediately the cession was arranged, because the ideal time to get ample indemnification was "when the past is fresh in their minds." The best ink for signing a surrender is blood.[11]

The cession Jackson demanded and took was indeed ample; a huge slice of land, twenty to twenty-three million fertile acres, about half the former Creek Nation and some four million acres of Cherokee land, worth at least $40 million. The ceded land joined the Tennessee settlements with those in lower Alabama. It extended from Georgia to the Mississippi Territory, nearly half of it the homeland of the Lower Creeks, who had almost all remained faithful to Hawkins and the United States at peril of their lives. The ceded lands form one-fifth of present-day Georgia and three-fifths of Alabama; in addition, Jackson got a long, rich strip along the Florida line, from the Perdido River just west of Pensacola to the Pearl River—right through southern Choctaw country. No tribe was untouched by the seizure.[12]

The Creeks were shocked. Tustunnuggee Thlucco spoke for the nation: they had been assured that fidelity to the United States would be rewarded; where was the consideration promised by Pinckney's letter? Jackson said he was not empowered "to embrace, by treaty or capitulation, the promises contained therein"; in fact, he said, the United States would be justified in taking all their land from the Creeks "merely for keeping it secret, that her enemies were in the nation." Hawkins had scolded the chiefs during the war for not coming forward voluntarily with such information, as they were committed to do by many treaties, but his rebukes were not of the same order as Jackson's vitriolic attack. "Brother," Jackson addressed the thlucco,

> Listen—the truth is, the great body of the creek chiefs and warriors did not respect the power of the United States—They thought we were an insignificant nation—that we would be overpowered by the British. . . . They were fat with eating beef—they wanted flogging—they had no idea they could so easily be destroyed. They were mad—they had a fever—we bleed our enemies in such cases to give them their senses.[13]

None of this was true of "the great body of the creek chiefs," as Jackson must have known. An official record states that 32 Creek officers and 597 Creek privates had served under Jackson during the war. In addition, as already noted, at least four hundred Creeks had marched with Hawkins and General Floyd. An unknown number of friendly Creeks, probably several hundreds, had remained as defenders at Coweta, Tuckabatchee, and other towns. Without allowing for any loyal Creeks who were noncombatants, and some there must have been, the figures show that between 1,200 and 1,500 chiefs and warriors did not go over to the Red Clubs. Since by various estimates the total number of Creek fighting men could not have exceeded 3,000 to 4,000, Hawkins was quite possibly right in saying the

nation was divided approximately in half, and Jackson was un-
justified in condemning "the great body of the creek chiefs and
warriors." If they were in any way mad, it was with terror lest
the Red Clubs destroy them and the nation.[14]

Tustunnuggee Thlucco tried to move Jackson to pity. "We
are a poor distressed people, involved in ruin, which we have
brought on ourselves," he said. That approach gained him
nothing. Then the Speaker appealed to reason. If Jackson's
powers were restricted as he said to taking only enough land for
indemnification, the Creek Nation asked upon what principles
he took the lands eastward to Georgia, lands of the friendly Indians? He did it, Jackson explained, to form a buffer zone separating the Indians from the Spanish and English in the Floridas, for the good of the Indians as well as the United States.
Then, the Speaker asked, where would the hostile Indians be
placed, if all their lands were taken? You have room enough to
take them among you, Jackson answered. The frightful possi-
bilities of mingling bitter enemies in one narrow strip of land
did not concern Jackson.[15]

Hawkins noted Jackson's inconsistency: when it suited his
purpose not to recognize the claims and hopes of reward of the
friendly Indians, he insisted he was authorized only to take
enough land to pay his country's war costs, not to recompense
its Indian allies; yet he went far beyond such instructions in ar-
bitrarily seizing eight million acres from the Lower Creeks and
the whole of the hunting grounds in Upper Creek country. But
Jackson was consistent to his purpose. What he demanded was
prime cotton land, which would soon enormously enrich southern speculators and planters, especially if the blacks living with
the Creeks and Seminoles were returned to slavery under white
masters.[16]

No appeal could budge Sharp Knife, or Pointed Arrow, as
the Indians called Jackson. As Tustunnuggee Thlucco reported
later to the Creek National Council: "He threatened us and
made us comply with his talk. . . . I found the General had
great power to destroy me." Hawkins bitterly noted, "He marked
his line, and demanded their acquiescence." Hawkins advised
the chiefs to accept the line; rejection would certainly have

brought a renewal of hostilities, and perhaps a greater loss in the end.[17]

To Jackson, Robert Remini says, the logic of taking Creek land was simple and convincing: Indians, savage because their overabundant land encouraged a roaming life, would become settled and civilized if their living-space were more restricted; taking away their land would therefore serve the safety and welfare of the Indians. It can be argued, Remini says, that this logic is specious, but Jackson and other westerners believed in it as "a doctrine of incontestable truth." Jackson's expressed main intent, however, is hard to interpret as in any way altruistic. What he said he wanted was to annex "the land that flows with milk and honey," "the cream of the Creek country." He said nothing of teaching the Creeks animal husbandry and beekeeping. Still, as Frank L. Owsley, Jr., points out, Jackson's views reflected prevailing frontier sentiment, and his huge land grab entirely supported the philosophy of the frontier.[18]

The day before signing the capitulation, the Creeks escorted Jackson and Hawkins to the council square in their encampment, and Tustunnuggee Thlucco made the announcement that his people wished to present General Jackson three square miles out of the land left to them. The gift, said the Speaker, was a token of gratitude for saving their lives, "in remembrance of the important services you have done us." Jackson at first demurred, fearing Congress would think he had got the land by fraud; he would take it, he said, only if the Creeks would accept its value in necessaries. The chiefs that evening told Hawkins "they did not give to General Jackson the land today to give it back to them in clothing, and other things; they want him to live on it, and when he is gone (dead) his family may have it, and that it may always be known what the Nation gave it to him for."[19]

Considering Jackson's brutal capitulation terms, it is difficult to take the expressions of gratitude seriously. Creek character and culture suggest that the gift may instead have been an expression of disgust and ridicule, a wry practical joke typical of Indian humor and ability to laugh in the face of misfortune. As Vine Deloria says, "In humor life is redefined and accepted."

John Lawson had observed a hundred years earlier, "All their misfortunes and losses end in laughter" except where the loss was a life. Close under the laughter was pride. Creek pride and sense of superiority were spoken of by almost all white men who knew them, both detractors and admirers. To give satisfied a tradition of generosity and the sense of superiority; there would have been particular satisfaction in bestowing a gift on their conqueror.[20]

By the treaty the Creeks also gave land to Hawkins, an equivalent three square miles, and one square mile to each of the interpreters, white George Mayfield and Alex Cornells, one of their own. Earlier in the negotiations, Big Warrior had spoken of Hawkins with respect and affection: "There sits the agent sent among us. Never has he broken the treaty. He has lived with us a long time. . . . By his direction cloth was wove, and clothes made, and spread throughout our country." In presenting Hawkins with the gift of land, Tustunnuggee Thlucco's comments show no hint of ridicule: "He has been long among us, helping of us, and doing good for our nation, and is our friend. He and I met at Coleraine, and were young men, and are now old; his children are born in our land. [Let him take land where he chooses] and, if he dies, his children will have a place to live on." In the formal instrument signed the following day the Creeks reiterated their intentions toward Hawkins: "Our nation feel under obligations to Colonel Benjamin Hawkins, our agent, and to Mrs. Lavinia Hawkins, his wife, for the unwearied pains they have taken, both of them, for a long time, to introduce the plan of civilization among us, and to be useful to us." This gift, which Hawkins accepted, also may have satisfied Creek pride, but the citation that went with it rings with genuine affection.[21]

All private gifts, however, were eventually deleted from the treaty by Congress. Jackson lobbyists kept bringing the matter up for reconsideration for many years. Hawkins, accused of having arranged the gift to Jackson, gave oath that Jackson had not solicited it, nor had he, Hawkins, used his influence with the Creeks to get Jackson the land. Although he clearly disapproved of Jackson's conduct of the treaty and of its terms, he gave Jackson credit for having stopped the Red Club revolt; and with his scrupulous fairness he said in his deposition that much was owed Jackson by both the Indians and the country for services "all things considered which have never been excelled." But Congress would not consent to this private gift, and in 1826, when Jackson was preparing for his second and successful bid for the presidency, the question of honoring the Creek gift to him was again under consideration in the House of Representatives.[22]

It was August 9, 1814, when the treaty establishing Jackson's boundary line was signed. Hawkins witnessed the treaty, and its Indian signatories included many of his best friends, among them Tustunnuggee Thlucco, Tustunnuggee Hopoie, William McIntosh, Timothy Barnard's son Timpogee, Efau Haujo, Captain Isaacs, and Alex Cornells.[23]

But the treaty aroused Hawkins's indignation. He assailed the secretary of war with vehement protests against Jackson's treatment of the loyal Creeks, asking that Jackson be removed. The War Department, however, had more pressing business. At just this time the British captured and burned the capital. Secretary of War Armstrong had been replaced by James Monroe as interim secretary. Washington was in chaos. Jackson's treaty stood firm.[24]

Thus Jackson gained, on paper, the line he wanted. In the two years after the Fort Jackson capitulation came several subsidiary treaties in which either Jackson or his kinsman John Coffee were commissioners, to settle conflicting claims of other tribes to parts of the Fort Jackson cession: in September 1816, with the Cherokees for lands south and west of the Tennessee (the long-sought Great Bend and Muscle Shoals areas), for a payment of $5,000 and a $6,000 annuity for ten years; with the Chickasaws that same month, for lands north and south of the Tennessee (except a piece on the north bank reserved for Chief George Colbert) to extinguish Chickasaw claims in the Great Bend, for a payment of $4,500 and a $12,000 annuity for ten years; in October with the Choctaws for an area between the Tombigbee and Alabama rivers, for a payment of $10,000 and a $6,000 annuity for twenty years. At the end of 1816, Acting Secretary of War George Graham was able to write Jackson: "As all difficulties on account of conflicting Indian titles are now happily removed, every exertion will be made to complete the surveys, and bring the lands in the Mississippi Territory to market as soon as practicable." Also, he added, the new road from Tennessee to Louisiana, being built by the government at Jackson's urgent request, will "no doubt, have a considerable effect on the price of the land contiguous to the road." By that time the government could refuse Jackson nothing. He had roundly defeated the British at New Orleans—the only great American land victory of the war—and was the nation idol.[25]

The effect of the treaty of Fort Jackson on the Creek Nation was dislocating and devastating. The Creeks still had Hawkins among them, worrying about them, and worrying that these hungry, homeless, cheated people would turn against the United States; but the people were too dispirited, uncertain, and divided to revolt. Most of the Red Clubs had surrendered before the treaty, coming in to be fed at the forts and food depots, but a number had fled to the Seminoles in West Florida, between Pensacola Bay and the Apalachicola. Couriers delivered invitations to the friendly Creeks to go down to the John Forbes store at Apalachicola and get quantities of guns and ammunition. The British were trying to revive the Creek war, to bring Tustunnuggee Thlucco and his party to the hostile side, and—the great bugaboo—to arm the blacks, as General Flournoy warned Hawkins. These intelligences Hawkins at once forwarded to the War Department, commenting that in view of the hostile British intentions the government was unwise in alienating the Creeks by not paying them their annuities for the war years. In October 1814, two months after the treaty Hawkins again wrote the War Department of the chiefs' bitter complaints against the United States for withholding their annuities for 1812, 1813, and 1814:

> They say: "They have been faithful to their treaty stipulations with us, yielding whatever was demanded of them. . . . They are called on for warriors, for runners, and other purposes, without receiving pay. . . . They are now in a manner naked, their hunting done, their resources destroyed by their civil war, and they are without the means of clothing their helpless people and themselves, and winter is approaching."[26]

James Monroe was the acting secretary of war to whom Hawkins addressed that letter. Monroe's philosophy, as expressed a few years later when he was president, precluded any help to the Indians in resuming their traditional free way of living or in retaining enough land to live that way. He told Congress in 1817:

> The hunter state can exist only in the vast uncultivated desert. It yields to the more dense and compact form and greater force of civilized population; and, of right, it ought to yield, for the earth was given to mankind to support the greater number of which it is capable; and no tribe of people have a right to withhold from the wants of others more than is necessary for their support and comfort.[27]

"Of course, no people will sit and starve for want of land to work," John Sevier had said, "when a neighbor nation has much more than they can make use of." The president is "under no obligation to extend his cares to a people, who withhold from others what they cannot enjoy," said General Wilkinson. Jefferson had said the Indians must be encouraged "to exchange lands, which they have to spare and we want, for necessaries, which we have and they want."

The Creeks were doomed from the moment they became unable to control their own civil rebellion and called on the United States for aid, as many a small nation or colony in ancient times had signed its own death warrant by calling on Greece or Rome for help. Jackson transformed the civil rebellion into a just war of conquest, and his treaty smashed with the mailed fist of the conqueror.

No sooner was the treaty safely signed than Jackson hurried to Florida to guard against the threatened British landing. But he planned first to punish the Seminoles and also the Spanish, who, he claimed, had instigated Seminole and Red Club hostilities. There is more than a suggestion, however, that Jackson's Florida campaign had as its purpose not only revenge on the Seminoles, who were really not so much of a threat as Jackson pretended, but also conquest and booty; specifically, the rich booty of black bodies, free and slave, living with the Seminoles. Blacks were scarce by 1815 in Creek country; the federal factory could find almost none to hire as laborers, even as seventy-five cents a day; they were evidently fleeing farther south.[28]

The month of the treaty, Hawkins had told the Creeks that

the British were stealing slaves, and he offered $50 reward for every black turned in. But the tide was still flowing southward in February 1816, when Hawkins advised Secretary of War William H. Crawford that black slaves in Georgia and the Creek agency were being invited to go to the Seminoles and be free; eight, he said, had left Tim Barnard's plantation alone. By spring Hawkins was prodding the Creek chiefs to force the Seminoles to give up refugee blacks, and he chided them for permitting a fortified black settlement to be established on the Apalachicola instead of returning blacks to the United States as their treaty obligations required. Again a reward of $50 was offered for each black recovered from West Florida. The Creeks said they would see what they could do about it, but nothing happened.[29]

The rumor Flournoy had passed on to Hawkins in June, 1814, that the British were preparing blacks and Indians for a war on the United States, was true. That month the British ship *Orpheus* had arrived at the Apalachicola, and joined forces with refugee Red Clubs. While the treaty was taking place at Fort Jackson, Maj. Edward Nicolls of the Royal Marines had landed at Pensacola with his men and five hundred Indians, seizing cattle and taking prisoners. In September, Nicolls had attacked the American garrison at Fort Boyer in Mobile Bay, but being repulsed had gone back to Pensacola. Jackson, then at Mobile, had marched on Pensacola with 3,000 militia troops and a Choctaw contingent. After blowing up Fort Barrancas at the mouth of Pensacola Bay, the British had sailed off; refugee Red Clubs, when their British ally retired, had fled to sanctuary in Seminole country.[30]

After easily securing Pensacola, Jackson went back to Mobile, left some defensive forces there, and proceeded in December to New Orleans, where he fought off the British with his peculiar army of regulars, militia, Choctaws, United States Marines, and Jean Lafitte's pirates, emerging the victor of a furious and bloody battle on January 8, 1815, two weeks after the war had officially ended with the treaty of Ghent.[31]

After the war's end, after Jackson's resounding victory, Nicolls and some other British officers reappeared in West Florida and built Fort Nicolls near the mouth of the Apalachicola, often called the Negro Fort because of the numerous blacks who lived near it. These were the so-called Exiles, some of them recently escaped slaves, others the descendants of black families who had taken refuge there from slavery in South Carolina a hundred years or more earlier, before the colony of Georgia existed. Exiled forever from the United States, where they would at once have been reenslaved, these people had put down roots in Florida and extensively intermarried with the Indians of the area. The Fort Nicolls situation was most curious: a fort on Spanish territory, flying the British flag, and garrisoned by Exiles, Creek Red Clubs, and Seminoles, all of whom preferred death to capture. In May, 1815, Nicolls protested to Hawkins that the treaty of Fort Jackson had been nullified by the treaty of Ghent, which provided that the United States return to the Indians everything that had been theirs in 1811, before the war. Hawkins refused to deal with Nicolls and reminded him, in case he fancied becoming another white champion of the Creeks, what had happened to William Bowles. Leaving Fort Nicolls under the command of a black man named Garcia, Nicolls sailed off.[32]

For a time the Exiles in the fort's neighborhood were left to pursue their quiet lives, but Jackson and the War Department were determined on the destruction of the Negro Fort. A useful pretext for an invasion of Seminole country was the refusal of the Seminoles to honor the treaty of Fort Jackson, to which they had not been parties nor signatories, but by which nevertheless a portion of their land, called Fowltown, north of the Florida line, was declared ceded to the United States. As for the fort, Jackson spread inflammatory stories that its purpose was rapine and plunder, that it should be blown up and the Exiles returned to slavery. Gen. Edmund P. Gaines, an ardent expansionist who was then commander on the Florida border, in July 1816 ordered Colonel Clinch with 500 Creeks under Chief William McIntosh to blow up the fort. Clinch and McIntosh attacked, their artillery fire exploding the fort's ammunition magazine. The resulting destruction was terrible. Of 334 persons in the fort, most of them Exile families, 270 were killed and 57 injured. The few survivors of the explosion fought to the death rather than surrender and be reenslaved.[33]

The victory fell short of Jackson's intention to subdue all the Seminoles and capture all blacks who lived among them. In what is known as the First Seminole War, Gaines with his border troops and Jackson with his mixed force of whites and Creeks raided and took, one after another, the desperately defended strongholds of the Seminoles and Exiles; finally in May 1818 General Jackson declared the enemy defeated, the war at an end. He was, however, frustrated in his purpose of returning the blacks to slavery. The men died fighting, the women and children hid deep in the swamps; it is said that not one of the Exiles was taken alive.[34]

While Jackson was thus occupied in Louisiana and Florida, the line of the cession he had exacted at the Fort Jackson capitulation was being run. In the fall of 1815, more than a year before the series of treaties adjusting conflicting claims of other tribes to lands within the Creek cession, commissioners had been appointed, Hawkins among them, and were already at work. Hawkins had begun his last big job, his last effort to see the Indians treated fairly. In his usual scrupulous manner, he respected the treaty terms however much he deplored them. He was, however, determined to frustrate any fraudulent intentions of Jackson and Coffee to design a line that went beyond the treaty specifications, a line that would enormously enrich them and other speculators but would virtually destroy the tribes and reduce to zero the civilizing effects of his twenty-year labor. He was sixty-one years old, and his always delicate health wavered alarmingly during the line running; his determination to see the thing done honestly never wavered.[35]

Hawkins, Edmund P. Gaines, John Sevier, and William Barnett had been appointed to run the line, but Sevier died that September, 1815. By sheer brazen insistence John Coffee inserted himself as a commissioner, with the cooperation of Gaines, a fellow Tennesseean. Coffee's opportunity to accomplish this came in November when, as the commissioners with their assistants and armed escort were already proceeding with the boundary marking, Hawkins fell so ill that he was barely able to be moved along the line. "Should Col. Hawkins decline acting, no time shall be lost in sending to you your commission by Express," Gaines wrote Coffee. Later in the month, when the surveying party had progressed to about eighty miles east of Flint River, Barnett got sick and left. A few days later Hawkins took a turn for the worse and had to return to the agency. In this most fortunate situation Gaines took it upon himself to name Coffee to replace Hawkins. "I have not . . . seen him nor have I heard from him on the subject of his health or disposition to continue upon the line," he wrote Coffee; "It is understood however that he is not desirous to even if he were able, which is very doubtful. At any rate I have determined to send your Commission which you will receive herewith. . . . You will of course continue to be one of the commissioners even if Col. Hawkins should continue." It is difficult to believe that Gaines was a disinterested party. If Hawkins were to continue, there would be no reason for a supernumerary commissioner; if he were unable to, there would still be no reason to commission Coffee, because two commissioners could legally finish the job. There seems little doubt that Gaines, at that time a friend of Jackson's, wanted Coffee on the commission. Coffee, further to legitimize his position, wrote Hawkins in January, 1816, saying, "If from any cause, you have declined to act in that capacity will you kindly have the goodness to forward the letter to the Commissioners by express, and write me by return of the bearer hereof." Hawkins did not decline, but Coffee by then not only had intruded himself into the commission but also had run a good part of the line all by himself.[36]

Coffee was intent on completing the northern boundary, between his state of Tennessee and the Indians, without interference. It did not deter him to hear from Hawkins late in January from the agency, where he was still ill, that the president had instructed the commissioners to mark only the line of the southern limit: "The line from the Alabama to the former river [Chattahoochee] is the only part which is necessary for the surveyor Genl. at this time." Besides, Hawkins told Coffee he was consulting the other commissioners "to ascertain how we construe the powers vested in us," and he would let Coffee know their decision. Did their powers entitle them to mark boundaries of the Creek cession through territory still being claimed by other tribes, which claims would not be settled until Graham's series of treaties in 1816? When Coffee received this advice from Hawkins he was, in fact, about to run the northern line through land claimed by the Cherokees, as suited his purposes.[37]

Fifteen years earlier William Blount had run an "experimental line," illegally opening up land for sale and settlement. Coffee, in connivance with Blount's old associate Jackson, now tried the same technique. The two, knowing that Cherokees were going to Washington to protest seizure of their territory, planned together (as is clearly shown in their correspondence) to run the Tennessee-Cherokee line at once, if necessary by use of threat, bribery, and force. Coffee went out in February with surveyors to accomplish this goal. "I wrote you," Coffee informed the commissioners, ". . . that I would proceed to run an experimental line between the U.S. and the Cherokees, which would enable the Commissioners on their arrival to run the true line." By the time the commissioners arrived, the line would be an accomplished fact.[38]

Meanwhile, the Cherokees were voicing their complaints to Secretary of War Crawford. They spoke of the long history of intrusions on their land and unprovoked murders of their people by malicious and lawless frontiersmen, and of how they nevertheless had given proof of their loyalty to the United States by providing warriors against the Creek Red Clubs; yet now—

> General Coffee, it appears, is disposed to run the line inconsistent with justice towards our Country. We have pointed out to you the lands we justly claim and we hope you will no longer delay to make a definitive settlement thereof agreeably to justice, our legal right. . . . You have also applied to us for the lands on the North side of Tennessee River in behalf of the State of Tennessee, we also inform you that it is not desirable to our nation to dispose of it.

Six months later the Cherokees signed a cession of lands both north and south of the Tennessee, satisfying the Coffee-Jackson experimental line although the War Department had some doubts about its legality.[39]

Neither the Cherokee complaint nor Hawkins's warning not to exceed the powers of the commission hindered Coffee; he simply claimed not to understand what Hawkins was talking about. By mid-February, however, Hawkins was well enough to rejoin the likewise-recovered Barnett and General Gaines at Fort Strother, and the three agreed on the limitation of their powers to the southern line. Gaines wrote this to Coffee on the very day Coffee was writing him that, "not hearing from you, and being out of employment, I shall commence meandering the Tennessee river." His meander put the Muscle Shoals and Great Bend lands within the state of Tennessee. Within a few days of completing his northern line, Coffee joined Gaines and Barnett as they were running a part of the southern line of cession. Hawkins was probably not there at that time but back in the agency, suffering a "severe indisposition," as he informed the secretary of war. He returned to duty early in April, ready to continue running the line as soon as the matter of lands ceded by the Creeks but claimed by the Cherokees should be settled.[40]

By then, however, Coffee's line was all marked, and he had sent a plat to James Monroe, the acting secretary of war, along with a lengthy argument and specious documents to prove that he had not intruded himself on the commission but was a bona fide, authorized member of it who had, in marking the whole of the cession, merely been carrying out his duty. The task Jackson and Coffee had set themselves was accomplished; the line they wanted had been marked and registered at least a month before the commission proper finished marking its line. When early in 1818 the lands within Coffee's plat went on sale, Coffee was able to buy for himself and Jackson coveted Muscle Shoals property and to enter claims for himself to 16,000 choice acres in Alabama, valued at $76,000. The experiment had succeeded. Hawkins's final attempt to frustrate a greedy powerplay was a failure.[41]

Had Hawkins been twenty years younger and in good health, matters would probably still have turned out the same way. The United States was in a postwar boom, economically and psychologically. Opportunities for expansion seemed unlimited. Land values leapt; bottomlands bordering the Tombigbee brought $10 an acre in 1815, and desirable farms were worth $30 an acre. Cotton brought thirty-four cents a pound, as against twenty-five cents in 1800. The Indians who lived on land that would grow cotton had no chance of fair play. Besides, the leader in the great snatch of Indian territory was one of the most popular heroes the United States has ever produced. Even the righteous John Quincy Adams in 1818 was singing Jackson's praises for destroying the "motley tribe of black, white, and red combatants," the "parti-colored forces" of "the Negro-Indian banditti" in Florida.[42]

Ill and aging, poor and powerless except in his moral force, there was little Hawkins could do to protect the rights or ameliorate the fate of the Indians. He persisted in the hope that Pinckney's compassionate promises would be included in the Fort Jackson treaty by the Senate in ratifying it; he presented the claims of the friendly Creeks for war damages of about $100,000, which Pinckney had said would be reimbursed; and he asked that the damage claims be paid "by themselves and not by attorney or order, to prevent a speculation on them" by brokers who would offer to cash such paper for anything up to a one-half share, a game already being attempted.[43]

Hawkins's world was in ruins, his friends gone by defection or death. Tustunnuggee Thlucco, deeply embittered by the treaty terms, had headed a party of the formerly friendly chiefs who had challenged the commissioners when in November 1815 they started to run the line through Lower Creek country. The military escort of the commissioners' party had deterred any violence then, but the now hostile chiefs had declared they would resist any attempt to settle on their land. In the spring of 1816 they were no less angry, and Hawkins had lost control of the National Council meeting. Convening at Tuckabatchee, the chiefs had suspended ratification of the treaty, and were so angry, Hawkins reported, that he had "not been able to prevail on them to come forward and afford any aid, to enable me to execute the duties enjoined on me satisfactorily." One of Hawkins's duties was to collect their damage claims; Tustunnuggee Thlucco refused to submit his claim, naïvely believing that without it the Fort Jackson agreement would be incomplete and therefore null and void. Tustunnuggee Thlucco was no longer Hawkins's ally and friend. An even closer friend, Alex Cornells, was dead. He had died suddenly while riding to the Tuckabatchee council meeting. Hawkins was evidently shaken by it: "I shall be at a loss for some time how to fill his appointment, as we have not his equal among us." Other good friends were gone, too. Silas Dinsmoor had become so enfeebled by illness that he had been forced to resign during the war, leaving the position of Choctaw agent to the Blount-Jackson man, John McKee. Jonathan Halsted, the exceptionally honest and capable factor of the Creek store since 1802, with whom Hawkins had enjoyed such a cordial relationship, had died late in 1814 after years of intermittent illness. The busy, peopled microcosm whose affairs Hawkins had made his life was an echoing void.[44]

In contrast, the world of the schemers whom Hawkins had spent twenty years trying to frustrate was the busy, striving world of the postwar boom. They ran it, in Tennessee, Georgia, Mississippi, Alabama, and Louisiana. Jackson and the entire old William Blount faction pressed on to fame and wealth. John Sevier was a United States senator before he died in 1815. Even that minor character in Blount's bizarre international plot, John Chisholm, was doing all right for himself as a leader of the Western Cherokees in Arkansas; in 1817 Jackson, negotiating a treaty that would facilitate the Cherokee removal, reported, "We were compelled to promise John D. Chisholm the sum of one thousand dollars to stop his mouth and obtain his consent."[45]

That manifestation of Hawkins's philosophy of Indian relations, the civilization program into which he had put his whole trust, was buried in the junk of war wreckage, its purpose rusting with the ploughs and hoes that the Red Clubs had flung into the rivers. The factory system, an imperative in the civilization program, which had fought detractors and competitors from its beginning, had suffered with everything else during the war years; trade at the factories had dwindled almost to nothing, providing private businessmen an excuse to lobby Congress for their abolishment.[46]

Secretary of War Crawford, in a curious report on the factories to the Senate in March 1816—as the line of the Creek cession was being concluded—pointed out that trade with the Indians was based on the premise that the government wished to civilize them; if however, he wrote, the primary object of the government was to extinguish the Indian title and settle their lands as rapidly as possible, commerce with them ought to be entirely abandoned to individual enterprise, without regula-

tion, which would result in "continual warfare, attended by extermination or expulsion of the aboriginal inhabitants of the
country to more distant and less hospitable regions." But Crawford could not believe, he said, that this was United States policy: "The utter extinction of the Indian race must be abhorrent
to the feelings of an enlightened and benevolent nation." True,
he added, the Indians would have to embrace the concept of
private property; if all efforts to bring them to accept it should
fail, encouragement to intermarry with whites might convert
them. It would redound more to the honor of the United
States, he said, to incorporate "the natives of our forests in the
great American family of freemen, than to receive with open
arms the fugitives of the old world." But Crawford was out of
date. The cry now was for quick, harsh action, to eliminate, not
incorporate, the Indians. Even Return Meigs's proposal in 1819
to give nine million acres of Cherokee land to Georgia and Tennessee, leaving one and one-quarter million acres to the Cherokees, was flatly rejected by Congress as too moderate.[47]

The object of the government was indeed to extinguish all
Indian titles in the east and settle white Americans on Indian
land. When the factory system was legislated to a close on May
6, 1822, capitalist free enterprise replaced governmental nonprofit in the Indian trade. As Michael Paul Rogin observes, "Indian destruction defines for America the stage of primitive
capitalist accumulation." Because the Indians would not embrace private ownership of land, the bulwark of capitalism, they
had to be extinguished. General Jackson smashed the southern
Indians to bits; President Jackson swept away the shards by
Removal.[48]

Hawkins did not live to see the dispersal of the four tribes.
He was already dead when, in 1817, an act of Congress required Indian offenders to be tried in federal courts, thus setting at naught his great and perilous efforts to make the tribal
councils responsible for the punishment of their own malefactors. The national development, mandating a direction exactly
opposite the one implicit in Hawkins's instructions when he was
sent out to the Indians, left all his wise, humane, conscientious,
unsparing labor of twenty years a kind of antiquarian back-
wash. The fields he had had ploughed, the wheels he had set

whirring, the lessons he had given in the principles of Anglo-Saxon jurisprudence, the plots he had frustrated against the Indians and the United States—all are mere historical curiosities; the country's history swept on as if he had never been.

Hawkins died in the Creek Agency on June 16, 1816, leaving Lavinia, whom he married before he died, and seven children: Georgia, Muscogee, Cherokee, Carolina, Virginia, Jeffersonia, and son Madison. Even in giving names he seems not to have favored either the Indians or the states. His nephew Philemon, who had been for some time his assistant, briefly took charge of the agency. Within a year, however, he was displaced by a new Creek agent, David B. Mitchell, who resigned as governor of Georgia to accept the position. His appointment wrote finis to the scrupulously nonpolitical and unbiased stewardship established by Hawkins. An old speculator of Yazoo times, Mitchell accomplished further Creek cessions for a few years, until he was forced out of public office on possibly trumped up charges of smuggling Africans into the United States.[49]

If the Creeks missed Hawkins, there is no record of it. When the secretary of war told a Creek delegation visiting Washington about their new agent, Mitchell, they responded: "Brother, You say to us that you have appointed an agent to fill the place of Col. Hawkins and that he will assist us and that he will see justice done to us and if necessary he will call on the commanding officer of your Army to see that no white people shall intrude over the line. . . . Brother, It gives us much pleasure to hear this from you." No one present said of Hawkins what he had said of Alex Cornells: "We have not his equal among us."[50]

Hawkins died far from rich. Although opportunities for acquiring land had been limitless, the only real property he left was "3 fractions of land adjoining river in Jones [County] 368¾ acres at 3.00—1106.25." Cash assets amounted to $12,215.14¾, plus some accounts receivable including $6,000 to $8,000 owed him by the Quartermaster Department, possibly for money he had laid out to feed the starving Creeks after the war. The largest part of his estate was in slaves, seventy-four of them including some children and aged, valued at $28,800. These were left to Lavinia and his children and to his nephew William Hawkins, governor of North Carolina—as perhaps Benjamin might have been if he had stayed comfortably at home. His entire estate, including land, slaves, cash assets, cattle, horses, books, tools of all kinds, and household goods from a piano and silverware down to the last frying pan, was valued at $65,990.17. The amount does not suggest that he made a profit from being agent. Probably most of his money and possessions derived from his North Carolina background: There is no reason to doubt his statement that he had not accumulated more than $3,000 from his pay for twenty years as agent. Considering that John Coffee in one purchase out of the Creek cession by Jackson's treaty acquired land worth $76,000, Hawkins's estate was very small indeed. Many of the items sold at auction to settle his estate are reminders, however, that his years in Indian country had been rich in experience if not in rewards: ploughs, coulters, weights and measures, spinning wheels, smith's tools and iron—the list is a gloss on Hawkins's last twenty years of life.[51]

He left the Indians infinitely poorer than he had found them, in spite of his unceasing work. Then they had owned enormous lands; now almost all were gone, and they were to move out of their "Paradice," now Jackson's Eden. The 1817 removal agreement that Jackson managed to push through by paying off Chisholm speaks eloquently of the poverty and degradation of people who twenty years earlier, bejeweled with Bartram's forests, savannahs, and rivers, had met Hawkins as coequals:

> The United States do also bind themselves to give to all the poor warriors who may remove to the western side of the Mississippi river, one rifle gun and ammunition, one blanket, and one brass kettle, or, in lieu of a brass kettle, a beaver trap, which is to be considered as a full compensation for the improvements which they leave.[52]

As Hawkins had said, "They are now in a manner naked, their hunting done . . . and winter is approaching."

Notes

ABBREVIATIONS USED

APS680   Benjamin Hawkins. *Letter Book* (*May 1798–Sept. 1801*; *1802*; *1810*). Microfilm Publication no. 215, roll 680. Philadelphia: American Philosophical Society.

APS692   Benjamin Hawkins. *Journal of Occurrences in the Creek Agency* (*1802*). Microfilm Publication no. 214, roll 692. Philadelphia: American Philosophical Society.

ASPFR   *American State Papers: Foreign Relations*. Edited by Walter Lowrie and Matthew Clark. Washington, D.C., 1832–34.

ASPIA   *American State Papers: Indian Affairs*. Edited by Walter Lowrie and Matthew Clark. Washington, D.C.: 1832–34.

Grant, *BH*   *Letters, Journals and Writings of Benjamin Hawkins*. Edited by C. L. Grant. 2 vols. Savannah, Ga., 1980.

H-L   *Letters of Benjamin Hawkins. Collections of the Georgia Historical Society* 9 (1916). Reprint. Spartanburg, S.C., 1974.

LC-MsD   Library of Congress, Manuscript Division.

NA75   Records of the Bureau of Indian Affairs (Record Group 75), National Archives, including:
NA75:42, Correspondence of the Creek Factory, 1795–1814
NA75:43, Letterbook of the Creek Factory, 1795–1816 (Microfilm Publication no. 4)
NA75:44, 46, 47, Ledgers and Journals of the Creek Factory
NA75:53, Records of the Fort Wilkinson Garrison
NA75:SW, Secretary of War, Letters Relating to Indian Affairs, Received (SW/LR) and Sent (SW/LS); Microfilm Publications 271 (4 rolls) and 15 (6 rolls)

NASPIA   *New American State Papers: Indian Affairs*. Edited by Thomas C. Cochran. Wilmington, Del., 1972.

Sketch   Benjamin Hawkins. *Sketch of the Creek Country. Collections of the Georgia Historical Society* 3 (1848), pt. 1. Reprint. Spartanburg, S.C., 1974.

CHAPTER 1. Bear, Deer, Turkeys, and Indians

1. John R. Swanton, *Indians of the Southeastern United States*, 735; George D. Harmon, *Sixty Years of Indian Affairs, Political, Economic, and Dip-*

lomatic, 1789–1850, 41. Secretary of War Knox in 1789 gave the extent of the joint lands of the southern tribes as 53 million square miles (*ASPIA*, 1:39).

2. Samuel Cole Williams, *Dawn of the Tennessee Valley and Tennessee History*, 101; William Bartram, *Travels through North and South Carolina, Georgia, East and West Florida*, 345, 385; James Adair, *History of the American Indians*, 383–84.

3. Benjamin Hawkins, *Sketch of the Creek Country*, 23–24; Grant, *BH*, 55–56, Journal, March 27, 1797.

4. Hawkins commented that a hunter traversing the 300 square miles of Creek and Seminole country would have difficulty finding enough game to feed himself (*Sketch*, 24), but considering the number of deerskins the Indians brought in for trade, this seems an exaggeration. Bartram, *Travels*, 186; Louis LeClerc Milfort, *Memoirs, or A Quick Glance at My Various Travels and My Soujourn in the Creek Nation*, 53; Henry Timberlake, *Lieutenant Henry Timberlake's Memoirs, 1756–1765*, 47, 71; in his *Memoirs*, 61, Timberlake noted that he would have enjoyed the feast more if he had not been obliged, just prior to it, to smoke the peace pipe that had already been in many mouths, which, "considering their paint and dirtiness, are not of the most ragoutant, as the French term it."

5. Timberlake, *Memoirs*, 70 and 70n; *Sketch*, 21, 24; Bartram, *Travels*, 112–13, 129, 130; Milfort, *Memoirs*, 45; Timberlake, *Memoirs*, 71; Swanton, *Indians of the Southeastern U.S.*, 775, and *Sketch*, 69, are among the many writings of the time that mention the emetic, known as the black or bitter drink, used ceremonially by the southern Indians, which they made of the leaves, buds, and tender twigs of the medicinal *ilex vomitoria*, or *cassine yupon* (one of several variant spellings); *Sketch*, 21.

6. *Sketch*, 53; Timberlake, *Memoirs*, 69; Bartram, *Travels*, 166, 180–81.

7. Timberlake, *Memoirs*, 73 and 73n; *ASPIA*, 1:752; Williams, *Dawn of the Tennessee Valley*, 108; NA75:SW/LR, Chickasaw agent to secretary of war, Aug. 22, 1812; NA75:SW/LR, Showonees to the President, March 29, 1811; Grant, *BH*, 137, Journal, Nov. 20, 1797. David Corkran, *The Creek Frontier*, 5–6, quotes other tributes to the "almost idyllic" Creek land.

8. *ASPIA*, 1:675, treaty with the Creeks, 1802.

9. Timberlake, *Memoirs*, 68.

10. Gerald Littman, "Alcoholism, Illness, and Social Pathology Among American Indians in Transition," 1777; APS680, Hawkins to William Panton, Jan. 28, 1798.

11. APS680, Hawkins to Creek Council, June 24, 1798; *ASPIA*, 1:21, James White to secretary of war, April 4, 1787; *H-L*, 477, Richard Thomas to Hawkins, Jan. 28, 1798; W. C. Vanderwerth, *Indian Oratory*, 63–64; Michael P. Rogin, *Fathers and Children*, chapter 4, on the relation between the Indian and the land; Williams, *Dawn of the Tennessee Valley*, 390.

12. Rogin, op. cit., 126.

13. Alexis de Toqueville, *Democracy in America*, 1:356; Ora B. Peake, *History of the United States Factory System, 1795–1822*, 230.

14. See LC-MsD, Blount Collection, Box 163, concerning Abe, an Indian boy kept as a slave by Joseph Tipton, for one of a number of examples in the records of Indians in slavery; Lawrence Foster, *Negro-Indian Relationships in the Southeast*, 19; Vanderwerth, *Indian Oratory*, 64. On the

experiences of Indians as slaves from earliest times, Charles Hudson, *The Southeastern Indians*, 435–39.

15. A. P. Whitaker, "Alexander McGillivray, 1789–1793," 302.

16. *ASPIA*, 1:39, Secretary of War Knox's report, July 7, 1789; NA75: 43, 97.

17. Swanton, *Indians of the Southeastern United States*, 374.

18. NA75:SW/LR, Hawkins to secretary of war, Sept. 1, 1801.

19. U.S. Department of Commerce, *Historical Statistics of the United States*, 13; 3 out of every 8 people in the South at that time were black. Lyman S. Tyler, *History of Indian Policy*, 18, estimates the total number of Indians in the United States at 1 million in 1790, when the total white population was 4 million.

20. Sources vary in estimates of the total number of Indians and the number of warriors among them: *NASPIA*, 6, 46, and 47, estimate of the commissioners at the Hopewell treaty, 1785; *ASPIA*, 1:39, Knox report of 1789. Hawkins used the ratio 1 warrior to every 5 Indians.

21. Tyler, *Indian Policy*, 18; *Historical Statistics*, 13; *ASPIA*, I, 604; *The Palladium, A Literary and Political Weekly Repository*, Dec. 1, 1805. In United States law at various times, persons of one-half to one-sixth Indian ancestry were considered Indians; on the difficulties of the courts in defining an Indian, see Felix S. Cohen, *Handbook of Federal Indian Law*, 2–5.

22. Adair, *American Indians*, 305; Bartram, *Travels*, 515 (the Choctaws were therefore called Flatheads by the traders) and 481. All travelers concurred on the superiority of the Indian physique: Adair, *American Indians*, 5; Timberlake, *Memoirs*, 75, 77; Bartram, *Travels*, 482; Grant, *BH*, 165, Hawkins to Elizabeth Trist, Nov. 25, 1797.

23. Descriptions of dress are drawn chiefly from Adair, *American Indians*, 178–80; Swanton, *Indians of the Southeastern U.S.*, 465–67. Francis Paul Prucha, *Indian Peace Medals in American History*, 5–11, stresses the importance of gifts of "great" and "small" medals. For an explanation of the turban, see Chapman J. Milling, *Red Carolinians*, 7, also Adair, *American Indians*, 178–80, and Swanton, op. cit., 465–67. William Augustus Bowles affected a particularly gorgeous turban, shown in Elisha P. Douglass, "The Adventurer Bowles," facing p. 3.

24. Littman, "Alcoholism, Illness, and Social Pathology Among Indians," 1774, notes these characteristics. Of particular interest is the Indian indifference to speed, which contributed to the Indian reputation for laziness and, in the early days of psychological testing, led to the conclusion that Indians were of low intelligence, because they ignored the speed factor in taking intelligence tests (Otto Klineberg, *Characteristics of the American Negro*, 121–22). Mauelshagen and Davis, *Partners in the Lord's Work*, 22, 53.

25. On Cherokee warrior qualities, Timberlake, *Memoirs*, Intro., 13; Ramsey, *Annals of Tennessee*, 563–615; *ASPIA*, 1:532. On other Cherokee qualities, Timberlake, op. cit., 80, and Bartram, *Travels*, 483.

26. NA75:SW/LR, Hawkins to secretary of war, Dec. 18, 1801; Bartram, *Travels*, 515.

27. *Sketch*, 83; *ASPIA*, 1:651, commissioners report, 1801.

28. Swanton, *Indians of the Southeastern U.S.*, 153; *Sketch*, 24–66; *ASPIA*, 1:848, Hawkins to Armstrong, July 13, 1813; Swanton, op. cit., 153.

29. Swanton, *Indians of the Southeastern U.S.*, 127; William H. Gilbert,

Jr., *The Eastern Cherokees*, 348–53. According to tradition, the Muskogees came across the Mississippi from the north by way of the Red River, arriving in Georgia between 800 and 1000 A.D. (Corkran, *Creek Frontier*, 4). *Sketch*, 29–30, 59.

30. Swanton, op. cit., 86–87; Angie Debo, *History of the Indians of the United States*, 81, says that about the year 1800 some Alabamas, disgusted with Georgian encroachment on their lands, went back across the Mississippi. For movements of the Uchees and Oosoochees, see Swanton, op. cit., 169, 212–14; the characterization of the Uchees is from *H-L*, 462–63, 467, 471; NA75:43, 6; *Sketch*, 62; *H-L*, 170–74; Swanton, "An Indian Social Experiment and Some of Its Lessons," 372. Bernard Sheehan, *Seeds of Extinction*, 204, describes this Benjamin Harrison as a frontier character with a patch over one eye and a piece out of his nose.

31. APS680, Hawkins to Major Minor, Spanish official, May 2, 1799; Hawkins consistently spelled the name "Simenolies" rather than "Seminoles." Later in their history these Indians were included with the Four Nations as one of the Five Civilized Tribes (Lawrence P. Schmeckebier, *The Office of Indian Affairs*, 2). Foster, *Negro-Indian Relationships*, 20, translates the name Seminoles as "runaways" rather than "wild People."

32. Bartram, *Travels*, 484; Grant, *BH*, 177, Hawkins to secretary of war, Feb. 23, 1798; Grant, *BH*, 388, same to same, Oct. 28, 1801; Sheehan, *Seeds of Extinction*, 111; John H. Wheeler, *Reminiscences and Memoirs of North Carolina and North Carolinians*, 452; Adair, *History of American Indians*, 415–17; Swanton, "An Indian Social Experiment," 374; Rogin, *Fathers and Children*, 118, quoting Gov. Willie Blount; Bartram, *Travels*, 374.

33. Bartram, op. cit., 487–88; Swanton, "An Indian Social Experiment," 376.

34. Hawkins said, "I believe I have never lost a paper in the care of an Indian" (NA75:42, Document 515, July 7, 1801); Grant, *BH*, 167, Hawkins to secretary of war, Nov. 28, 1797; NA75:SW/LR, April 2, 1816.

35. John Innerarity, "Creek Nation, Debtor to John Forbes & Co. . . . a Journal of John Innerarity, 1812," ed. F. M. Greenslade, 78, 80, 84; Sheehan, *Seeds of Extinction*, 107.

36. Bartram, *Travels*, 488; Grant, *BH*, 157, Hawkins to secretary of war, Nov. 19, 1797; *Sketch*, 61; Innerarity, "Creek Nation, Debtor," 76–83.

37. Swanton, "An Indian Social Experiment," 376; Adair, *American Indians*, 462; Innerarity, "Creek Nation, Debtor," 70–73; Grant, *BH*, 13, Journal, Dec. 7, 1796; *Sketch*, 30; Grant, *BH*, p. 20, Journal, Dec. 16, 1796, and p. 42, Feb. 2, 1797; Grant, *BH*, 28–29, Journal, Dec. 16 and 27, 1796.

38. NA75:SW/LR, Creeks to the President, May 15, 1811; Grant *BH*, 68, Hawkins to Col. George Gaither, Feb. 15, 1797; Grant, *BH*, 138–39, Hawkins memorandum, Nov. 24, 1797, also 475–76, Minutes of treaty with Creeks, July 2, 1804, and 371, treaty at Southwest Point, Minutes of Sept. 5, 1801; APS680, Hawkins to secretary of war, Aug. 1, 1798. Toqueville, *Democracy in America*, 1:355; NA75:SW/LR, Return J. Meigs to secretary of war, Dec. 20, 1811; on Meigs, Thomas P. Abernethy, *From Frontier to Plantation in Tennessee*, 224.

39. Adair, *American Indians*, 444; Constance L. Skinner, *Pioneers of the Old Southwest*, 70–71. Excellent sources on the early traders are Skinner, op. cit.; S. C. Williams, *Early Travels in the Tennessee Country*; Adair, op. cit.;

Mary U. Rothrock, "Carolina Traders Among the Overhill Cherokees, 1690–1760." When Christian Gottlieb Priber threatened British influence with his plan of a utopian state in Indian country, Grant and Adair helped to capture him.

40. Martin Abbott, "Indian Policy and Management in the Mississippi Territory, 1798–1817," 162.

41. NA75:43, Price to Hawkins, Nov. 31, 1798; NA75:42, Doc. 383, Courtmartial Papers, 1799; APS680, Sept. 19, 1799, Hawkins to Ellicott from his encampment "near the black factor's," on or near the Chattahoochee, Lower Creek country; *H-L*, 168–74, memorandum giving names and characters of traders in 1797.

42. *H-L*, 379, Wilkinson to Cherokees, treaty of Southwest Point, 1801, denouncing traders as rumormongers.

43. *H-L*, 429 (n.d., no addressee); NA75:43, 182–83, Price to Hawkins, Jan., 1799. On signing by one's mark, NA75:42 passim; Clark Wissler, *Indians of the United States*, 251, on white men who preferred the "free hunting life." Abernethy, *South in the New Nation*, 174.

44. *Sketch*, 66. For the case of Polly Russell, see APS680, March 19 and July 11, 1799. NA75:SW/LR, Paul Smith to secretary of war, Aug. 1805, Smith claiming to be a free black impressed into slavery by Chief Doublehead. Foster, *Negro-Indian Relationships*, 20–22; Rogin, *Fathers and Children*, 194.

45. Grant, *BH*, 29, Journal, Dec. 25, 1796; Foster, op. cit., 19–21; APS680, March 19, 1799.

46. *Sketch*, 66.

47. NA75:SW/LR, Wilkinson to secretary of war, Sept. 8, 1801; *NASPIA*, 6:185, Hawkins report of Creek treaty, 1802; NA75:42, Doc. 441; Peake, *U.S. Indian Factory System*, 102, 140, 189, 248–49; NA75:53, Doc. 69; NA75:42, Doc. 20; NA75:42, Doc. 383, Court Martial Papers, 1799; NA75:43, 148.

48. Grant, *BH*, 341, Hawkins to Jefferson, July 12, 1800.

CHAPTER 2. "That Ingenious Gentleman, Benjamin Hawkins"

1. LC-MsD, Madison Collection, Hawkins to Madison, July 11, 1803. Note how Hawkins identifies himself with the Indians by saying "we" instead of "they."

2. Pound, *Benjamin Hawkins*, 1–3; Wheeler, *Reminiscences*, 450–52, gives Hawkins' birth date as 1754. In several letters Hawkins mentions his nephew William as assistant to him in the agency, and his nephew Philemon was briefly acting agent after Hawkins's death (NA75:SW/LR, Philemon Hawkins to secretary of war, Sept. 23, 1816).

3. Princeton University Archives, Alumni Files (nongraduate); Pound, op. cit., 4; V. L. Collins, *President Witherspoon: A Biography*, 2:207. Hawkins drove the carriage in which Witherspoon's family escaped to safety.

4. *H-L*, memorandum (n.d.), 13.

5. McPherson, "Unpublished Letters to Jefferson," 252; George Washington, *Writings of George Washington from the Original Manuscript Sources*, ed. John C. Fitzpatrick, 29:374, Jan. 10, 1788; Grant, *BH*, 162, Hawkins to Elizabeth Trist, Nov. 25, 1797; Grant, *BH*, 177, Hawkins to James McHenry, Feb. 23, 1798.

6. Collins, *Witherspoon*, 2:108. "I am out of paper" (*H-L*, 244, Hawkins to John Galphin, Nov. 20, 1797) was a chronic Hawkins complaint.

7. Georgia Department of Archives and History, Hawkins Papers, Estate of Benjamin Hawkins, Inventory and Sale. Hawkins had two copies of Jefferson's *Notes on Virginia*, one of which he had borrowed and neglected to return (NA75:42, Doc. 469, Jan. 12, 1801, Hawkins memorandum).

8. Pound, *Benjamin Hawkins*, 8, says Hawkins suffered ill health from 1780; in 1786 he was too ill to attend the session of the Continental Congress (Burnett, *Letters of Continental Congress*, 8:341, secretary of Congress to Hawkins, April 18, 1786); from 1796 Hawkins frequently mentioned acute attacks of gout (e.g., Grant, *BH*, 161, Hawkins to Faulkener, Nov. 25, 1797; Grant, *BH*, 182, Hawkins to Edward Price, April 16, 1798).

9. *H-L*, 430 (n.d.).

10. John H. Wheeler, *Historical Sketches of North Carolina from 1584 to 1851*, 2:427, says Hawkins was with Washington at Monmouth, 1779, and on other occasions. According to Pound, *Benjamin Hawkins*, 6–11, Hawkins was sued for personal liability in the capture of ships of a North Carolina merchant, but was cleared by the court. Grant, *BH*, Intro., x.

11. Grant, "Senator Benjamin Hawkins," 236 n. 10; Burnett, *Letters of Continental Congress*, 7:198–99, 314–15, 342–43.

12. References to these outstanding men occur frequently throughout Hawkins's communications in Burnett, op. cit., vols. 7 and 8. Hawkins corresponded regularly with Jefferson from as early as 1784 (see McPherson, "Unpublished Letters from North Carolinians to Jefferson").

13. Burnett, *Letters of Continental Congress*, 7:310, Sept. 26, 1783.

14. *Ibid.*, 7:313, Sept. 26, 1783; Harmon, *Sixty Years of Indian Affairs*, 7; Abernethy, *Frontier to Plantation*, 67.

15. Grant, "Senator Benjamin Hawkins," 236; McPherson, "Unpublished Letters to Jefferson," 159, Hawkins to Jefferson, June 10, 1784, and 162, Jan. 27, 1792; Pound, *Benjamin Hawkins*, 17.

16. Sheehan, *Seeds of Extinction*, 54–55; Thomas Jefferson, *Papers of Thomas Jefferson*, ed. Julian P. Boyd, 8:186; Burnett, *Letters of Continental Congress*, 8:552, 619, and 7:302, 354; *Washington*, ed. Fitzpatrick, 27:39–40, 84–86, 123–24. Grant, "Senator Benjamin Hawkins," explores Hawkins's increasing Republicanism, esp. 242–47.

17. Burnett, op. cit., 8:619; *Washington*, ed. Fitzpatrick, 27:39–40, 84–86, 123–24; Hawkins had previously served on a committee charged with preparing for the evacuation of British posts on the western frontier.

18. Charlton W. Tebeau, *History of Florida*, 89–90; Marjorie S. Douglas, *Florida*, 111–13; J. Leitch Wright, Jr., *Britain and the American Frontier*, 4–10, 27. See also Charles I. Bevans, *Treaties and Other International Agreements of the United States of America*, 12:1.

19. *NASPIA*, 6:18, commissioners to secretary of war, Nov. 17, 1785, saying McGillivray is a partner of Panton. *H-L*, 429, Hawkins memorandum (n.d., prob. 1800).

20. Milling, *Red Carolinians*, 320–24; Downes, "Creek-American Relations, 1782–1790"; Kinnaird, "The Rock Landing Conference of 1789," 415–17. Hawkins spoke well of Pickens's character, but in regard to land Pickens seems to have been typical of the westward-moving frontiersman;

see his petition to Congress to run the Long Swamp line, Milling, op. cit., 323–24.

21. Stevens, *Georgia*, 2:415–16; *ASPIA*, 1:15, Report of Secretary of War Knox, 1789; Bartram, *Travels*, 484.

22. Burnett, *Letters of Continental Congress*, 8:70, 152n; *ASPIA*, 1:15, Report of Secretary of War Knox, 1789; Downes, "Creek-American Relations," 150–51, quoting McGillivray letter of Sept. 5, 1785.

23. Downes, op. cit., 149, 151–52; Harmon, *Sixty Years of Indian Affairs*, 49; Abernethy, *South in the New Nation*, 193; Kinnaird, "Rock Landing Conference," 353; Foster, *Negro-Indian Relationships*, 22; Donald L. Mc-Murry, "The Indian Policy of the Federal Government and the Economic Development of the Southwest, 1789–1801," 24. Article 9 of the Constitution was interpreted and reinterpreted for many years; in 1832 Chief Justice Marshall stated: "All intercourse with [Indians] shall be carried on exclusively by the government of the Union." See Schmeckebier, *Office of Indian Affairs*, 6f.

24. Blount was in the Continental Congress with Hawkins in 1781, 1784, 1786, and 1787 (Marcus J. Wright, *Some Account of the Life and Services of William Blount*, 8). In the North Carolina Senate in 1788, Blount secured passage of a resolution making it illegal to grant Indians hunting grounds within the limits of the state, which gave title security to any citizen holding lands under state grants regardless of any treaty between the Indians and the United States (LC-MsD, Blount Collection, "North Carolina, In Senate, 29 November 1788").

25. A. P. Whitaker, "The Muscle Shoals Speculation, 1783–1789," 373; LC-MsD, Blount Collection, "Copy—Col° James Roberson [*sic*] to William Blount—Articles of Agreement, Oct. 30, 1783."

26. For the history of the Franklin movement, see Abernethy, *Frontier to Plantation*, chapter 5, "The State of Franklin"; for a more partisan account, see Samuel Cole Williams, *History of the Lost State of Franklin* (Johnson City, Tenn., 1924).

27. Tassel's map is in *ASPIA*, 1:40, Secretary of War Knox's report on the Cherokees, 1789, including treaty of Hopewell, Nov. 28, 1785.

28. For the Hopewell treaty, see Wilcomb E. Washburn, *The American Indian and the United States, a Documentary History*, 4:2272–77. McMurry, "Indian Policy of the Federal Government," 24; Whitaker, "Muscle Shoals Speculation," 372–73. On Indian deputations to Congress, see Herman J. Viola, *Diplomats in Buckskins: A History of Indian Delegations in Washington City*.

29. *ASPIA*, 1:49, Hawkins report, Dec. 30, 1785; Whitaker, "Muscle Shoals Speculation," 373n; McPherson, "Unpublished Letters to Jefferson," 252, Hawkins to Jefferson, June 14, 1786 (also quoted by Pound, *Benjamin Hawkins*, 52).

30. *Papers of Jefferson*, ed. Boyd, 10, Jefferson to Hawkins, August 13, 1786.

31. *ASPIA*, 1:48, Joseph Martin to secretary of war, Feb. 2, 1789; Martin seems to have been unaware that Outlaw worked for Blount (LC-MsD, Blount Collection, Payroll, 1791); *ASPIA*, 1:42, Hopewell treaty, Minutes, Nov. 26, 1785; Whitaker, "Alexander McGillivray," 194–95; Kinnaird, "Rock Landing Conference," 354; Burnett, *Letters of Continental Congress*, 8:477, 483.

32. *ASPIA*, 1:536, Blount to secretary of war, Nov. 10, 1794; *NASPIA*, 6:18, commissioners at Galphinton to Congress, Nov. 17, 1785, on McGillivray's character and his design to form an Indian confederacy.

33. Washburn, *The American Indian and the U.S.*, 4:2275.

34. LC-MsD, Hawkins Collection, Item 39, Hawkins to Caswell, July 10, 1787, on western rights; LC-MsD, Blount Collection, Hawkins to Blount, Aug. 9, 1790.

35. LC-MsD, Blount Collection, Hawkins to Blount, March 10, May 14, and Nov. 14, 1791, and April 24, 1792.

36. Whitaker, "Muscle Shoals Speculation," 374; *ASPIA*, 1:36–37, John Galphin to Henry Osborne, June 1, 1789; Burnett, *Letters of Continental Congress*, 8:143; Downes, "Creek-American Relations," 155–57; *ASPIA*, 1:15, Report of Secretary of War Knox, 1789; Downes, op. cit., 162–63.

37. *NASPIA*, 6:78, Instructions to commissioners, Rock Landing Conference, 1789, and 76–78; see also Kinnaird, "Rock Landing Conference," and Whitaker, "Alexander McGillivray, 1789–1793," 290–93.

38. Kinnaird, "Rock Landing Conference," 358.

39. Stevens, *Georgia*, 2:434–35; Kinnaird, op. cit., 361, 364; Whitaker, "Alexander McGillivray, 1789–1793," 290–93; Kinnaird, op. cit., 364.

40. Kinnaird, "Rock Landing Conference," 364.

41. Downes, "Creek-American Relations," 180–81; *NASPIA*, 6:18, Hopewell commissioners to secretary of war, Nov. 11, 1785; *Washington*, ed. Fitzpatrick, 31:20; Whitaker, "Alexander McGillivray, 1789–1793," 296 and 296n, reveal that Panton forwarded Hawkins's letter to McGillivray to Governor Miro, July 12, 1790; Stevens, *Georgia*, 2:438.

42. LC-MsD, Blount Collection, Hawkins to Blount, Aug. 9, 1790. Stevens, *Georgia*, 2:440–43, describes the journey and festivities; Downes, "Creek-American Relations," 182–84, the treaty and its implications; for the treaty text, see *ASPIA*, 1:81–82, and Washburn, *American Indian and the U.S.*, 4:2286–91.

43. On July 22, 1790, during the New York treaty, Congress passed an act "for the regulation of trade and intercourse with the Indians" (McMurry, "Indian Policy of the Federal Government," 25); Washburn, *American Indian and the U.S.*, 4:2290.

44. Grant, "Senator Benjamin Hawkins," 246.

45. LC-MsD, Blount Collection, Hawkins to Blount, March 10, 1791. Intrusion by white settlers on Indian lands had been going on since colonial times; in 1776 the Cherokees attacked settlers along the Holston River, and the frontiersmen struck back with extreme ferocity (Hudson, *Southeastern Indians*, 442–43).

46. Ramsey, *Annals of Tennessee*, 541–42, and for the traditional account, 554, 560; LC-MsD, Blount Collection, Holston treaty, June 14, 1791, receipted bill; *ASPIA*, 1:124, Blount treaty with Cherokees, July 2, 1790.

47. *ASPIA*, 1:135, Hawkins's report to the Senate, Nov. 9, 1791; LC-MsD, Blount Collection, Hawkins to Blount, Nov. 10, 1791; *Washington*, ed. Fitzpatrick, 32:105, Washington to secretary of war, Aug. 5, 1792.

48. *Washington*, ed. Fitzpatrick, 34:218–20, Washington's Preliminary Message to Senate on Colerain treaty, June 25, 1795; on steps leading to the treaty, *Augusta Chronicle and Gazette of the State*, May 9, 1795.

49. *ASPIA*, 1:587, Hawkins to Seagrove, May 13, 1796; Milfort, *Memoirs*, 28, 29–30; *Washington*, ed. Fitzpatrick, 34:219–20, Washington's Preliminary Message to Senate on Colerain treaty, June 25, 1795.

50. NA75:42, Doc. 61, Timothy Barnard to James Jordan, Aug. 29, 1796; *Columbian Museum and Savannah Advertiser*, July 15, 1796.

51. *ASPIA*, 1:589, Minutes, treaty at Colerain, May 25–June 1, 1796; *ASPIA*, 1:594, Minutes, June 9, 1796; *ASPIA*, 1:596, Minutes, June 15, 1796.

52. *ASPIA*, 1:598, Minutes, June 18 and 19, 1796.

53. *ASPIA*, 1:393, report of the David Cornells incident, June 30, 1793; *ASPIA*, 1:611, Minutes, treaty at Colerain, July 2, 1796, in which reference is made to the murder of David Cornells and restitution to his heirs recommended; Debo, *History of the Indians*, 57, identifies David Cornells as a cousin of Alexander Cornells; a letter of David's, Jan. 6, 1793 (*ASPIA*, 1:375), says he is a "younger brother of Al. Cornell"; *ASPIA*, 1:603, Minutes, June 24, 1796.

54. *ASPIA*, 1:604, Minutes, June 24, 1796. The "old British line" of 1763 was at 32°30' (Douglas, *Florida*, 101).

55. *Palladium*, Dec. 1, 1805, interview with Hawkins; *Sketch*, 31, Hawkins memorandum, Jan. 1, 1801; *H-L*, 462, Thomas to Barnard, May 12, 1797.

56. *ASPIA*, 1:604 and 605, Minutes, June 24, and June 25, 1796.

57. *ASPIA*, 1:602, Minutes, June 23, 1796; *ASPIA*, 1:612, Minutes, July 6, 1796.

58. Grant, "Senator Benjamin Hawkins," 246; Abernethy, *South in the New Nation*, 79; *Washington*, ed. Fitzpatrick, XXXV, 165, Washington to secretary of treasury, Aug. 5, 1796; *Washington*, ed. Fitzpatrick, 35:179, Washington to secretary of war, Aug. 12, 1796, and 195, Washington's "Talk to the Cherokee Nation," Aug. 29, 1796.

59. *H-L*, 13, Journal, Nov. 19, 1796: "I this day arrived at Hopewell . . . on my way to the Creeks as principal temporary agent." Viola, *Diplomats in Buckskins*, 44, says that Congress in 1793 authorized the president to appoint temporary agents, but that later the word "temporary" was dropped from the title. *Washington*, ed. Fitzpatrick, 34:165–67, "List of Government Officers" by states, shows Washington's concern that each state should have its proper share of appointments. APS680, Aug. 16, 1798, Hawkins to G. Lee, A. Miles, & others.

60. Grant, *BH*, 87–89, Hawkins to Elizabeth Trist, March 4, 1797.

61. *ASPIA*, 1:605, Minutes, treaty at Colerain, June 24, 1796; Tyler, *Indian Policy*, 39–42, and McMurry, *Indian Policy of the Federal Government*, 25, 34, give useful summaries of the various trade and intercourse acts from 1790 on; *ASPIA*, 1:610, Minutes, June 30, 1796.

62. Debo, *History of the Indians*, 81; John Mahon, *War of 1812*, 232; APS680, Hawkins to secretary of war, June 24, 1798.

CHAPTER 3. Separatists, Nationalists, and Adventurers

1. George D. Harmon, "Benjamin Hawkins and the Federal Factory System," 138–52.

2. On international boundaries: Abernethy, *South in the New Nation*, 2, 43–47; Lawrence Kinnaird, "International Rivalry in the Creek Country,"

59–85; Frederic L. Paxon, *History of the American Frontier*, 84; J. Leitch Wright, Jr., *Britain and the American Frontier*, 4; Douglas, *Florida*, 111–13; Ramsey, *Annals of Tennessee*, 523; *ASPIA*, 1:304, Seagrove to secretary of war, July, 1792. For descriptions of Natchez, see Abernethy, *South in the New Nation*, 161, and Jack Holmes, *Gayoso*, 15–26, 42.

3. Harmon, *Sixty Years of Indian Affairs*, 13–14; Abernethy, *South in the New Nation*, 45–47, 130–33; Abernethy, *Frontier to Plantation*, 92; Paxon, *American Frontier*, 84; Staughton Lynd, "Slavery and the Founding Fathers," 120–22.

4. Harmon, *Sixty Years of Indian Affairs*, 13.

5. Variant spellings abound in the records: Milfort, Milford, and Melford; Oliver, Olivero, Olivar, and Olivier. Grant, *BH*, 138–39, Hawkins memorandum of talk by Tustunnagee Emautlau, Nov. 24, 1797; Whitaker, "Alexander McGillivray," 303. The shifting pattern of Spanish policy and what is usually termed the Spanish Conspiracy are fully discussed in Whitaker, "Spanish Intrique in the Old Southwest," 155–76, and Abernethy, *Frontier to Plantation*, chapter 6, "The Spanish Conspiracy."

6. *H-L*, 429, Hawkins memorandum (n.d.).

7. Abernethy, *South in the New Nation*, 136.

8. Ibid., 102–126, for background and events of the Genêt affair; also Ramsey, *Annals of Tennessee*, 534–36.

9. Abernethy, *South in the New Nation*, 127, 130–33; Ira Berlin, *Slaves Without Masters*, 35–36, 49, 82. In the West, Jay was burned in effigy and his treaty denounced. Genêt married the daughter of Governor De Witt Clinton of New York and settled as a farmer on Long Island (Abernethy, *South in the New Nation*, 128).

10. Abernethy, *South in the New Nation*, 136, 150; See Harmon, *Sixty Years of Indian Affairs*, 14–15, for a helpful summary of shifting alliances of Spain, Great Britain, France, and the United States, 1793–1796.

11. For Sevier's land fraud: Abernethy, *Frontier to Plantation*, 174–76; Rogin, *Fathers and Children*, 93–94; Robertson, "Correspondence," 373–74, Sevier to Robertson, Nov. 8, 1803, and 374–81, letters and depositions concerning the fraud, 1802–1803. Grant, *BH*, 370–71, treaty of Southwest Point, Doublehead's speech, Minutes, Sept. 5, 1801; NA75: SW/LR, Return J. Meigs to secretary of war, Dec. 20, 1811.

12. The Creek term for land-jobbers (*H-L*, 250, Thomas memorandum (n.d., probably 1797).

13. *ASPIA*, 1:312, a huge order for presents placed by Seagrove in Oct. 1792, including such items as five hogsheads of rum, two barrels of sugar, two hundred pounds of coffee, fifty dozen scalping knives (used for skinning game), two hundred hats and feathers for them, and a thousand yards of cloth for leggings; *Sketch*, 27, 67; *ASPIA*, 1:662, treaty with the Choctaws, Minutes, Dec. 13, 1801, Robert McClure complains that the gifts were not fairly distributed.

14. *ASPIA*, 1:532, Doublehead to Blount, Oct. 20, 1794; Robertson, "Correspondence," 83, treaty at Tellico, Journal, Dec. 28, 1794; *ASPIA*, 1:605, treaty at Colerain, Minutes, June 24, 1795; Grant, *BH*, 128–29, 169, 168, 151, 93, and 185, Hawkins to secretary of war, Sept. 20, 1797; Hawkins to Maj. John Habersham, Dec. 20, 1797; Hawkins to Alex Cornells, Dec. 19, 1797; Hawkins to James Winchester, Nov. 9, 1797; Hawkins to Alex Cornells, March 8, 1797; Hawkins to Creek chiefs, May 27, 1798.

15. *ASPIA*, 1:680, commissioners [for Creek treaty] to War Department, June 17, 1802.

16. NA75:SW/LR, commissioners [for treaty at Southwest Point] to secretary of war, Sept. 1, 1801; Grant, *BH*, 85, Hawkins to secretary of war, March 1, 1797; APS680, Hawkins to secretary of war, April 15, 1799; *ASPIA*, 1:809, Hawkins to secretary of war, May 11, 1812.

17. *ASPIA*, 1:536, Blount to secretary of war, Nov. 19, 1794; Gilbert, *Eastern Cherokees*, 180–81, for specific Indian paths and where they led; Burnett, *Letters of Continental Congress*, 8:384, Rufus King to Elbridge Gerry, June 8, 1786; Burnett, *Letters of Continental Congress*, 8:383, Hawkins to Caswell, April 18, 1787; Ramsey, *Annals of Tennessee*, 599; LC-MsD, Blount Collection, Pickens to Blount, Sept. 12, 1792; Philip M. Hamer, "The British in Canada and the Southern Indians, 1790–1794," 111, 118–19.

18. Hamer, "British in Canada," 120–22; Ramsey, *Annals of Tennessee*, 551, 560.

19. Sheehan, *Seeds of Extinction*, 206–207, quoting John Heckewelder's "Account of the Indian Nations"; Swanton, *Indians of the Southeastern U.S.*, 773.

20. H. S. Halbert and T. H. Ball, *The Creek War of 1813 and 1814*, ed. Frank L. Owsley, Jr., 28–29, 153, 175–76, on William Weatherford; on McGillivray's lineage and family, John Tebbel, *Compact History of the Indian Wars*, 118, and Grant, *BH* 24, Journal, Dec. 20, 1796; on Charles Weatherford, Grant, *BH*, 187, Hawkins memorandum, May 28, 1798. The Hickory Ground was near present-day Wetumpka, Alabama (Abernethy, *Frontier to Plantation*, 44); on McGillivray's estates, Halbert and Ball, *Creek War*, 273.

21. McGillivray's birthdate is uncertain, but the year was probably 1759 (Whitaker, "Alexander McGillivray, 1783–1789," 181–82). Kinnaird, "Rock Landing Conference," 361–62, quoting David Humphrey; *NASPIA*, 6:18, commissioners at Galphinton treaty to secretary of war, Nov. 17, 1785; Stevens, *Georgia*, 2:438; Whitaker, "Alexander McGillivray, 1783–1789," 183–84; APS680, deposition of Rachel Walker, Feb. 4, 1799; Swanton, *Indians of the Southeastern U.S.*, 236, quoting the Belknap and Morse report of 1796.

22. Whitaker, "Alexander McGillivray, 1783–1789," 184–98.

23. Ibid., 198–99.

24. Ibid., 290.

25. For Bowles's early life, see Stevens, *Georgia*, 2:446–49, and Elisha P. Douglass, "The Adventurer Bowles," 3–7. Stevens says Bowles was born in 1764 and that he fought at the battle of Monmouth; if that is correct, he was a fourteen-year-old soldier. J. Leitch Wright, Jr., *William Augustus Bowles, Director General of the Creek Nation*, says Bowles was born in 1763.

26. APS680, Hawkins to secretary of war, Oct. 26, 1799; Douglass, "The Adventurer Bowles," 5, 13; *ASPIA*, 1:264, David Craig to Blount, March 15, 1792; Whitaker, "Alexander McGillivray," 303; Bartram, *Travels*, 488; Hamer, "Letters of William Blount," 119, Wellbank to McKee, Feb. 16, 1793.

27. J. L. Wright, Jr., *William Augustus Bowles*, 29–32; Douglass, "Adventurer Bowles," 9–10; Whitaker, "Alexander McGillivray," 200–201; Abernethy, *South in the New Nation*, 56–58; D. C. Corbitt and J. T. Lanning,

"A Letter of Marque Issued by William Augustus Bowles as Director-General of the State of Muscogee," 249–50.

28. Stevens, *Georgia*, 434.

29. Whitaker, "Alexander McGillivray," 296–97; *ASPIA*, 1:603–606, treaty at Colerain, Minutes, June 24, 1796, complaints of the Creek chiefs against McGillivray; *ASPIA*, 1:257, secretary of war to Seagrove, August 1792; Abernethy, *South in the New Nation*, 98.

30. This was the time of the Nootka Sound affair, an Anglo-Spanish confrontation over fur-trading rights on the coast of Vancouver Island; the dispute was settled without warfare by the Nootka Convention, Oct. 28, 1790.

31. Abernethy, *South in the New Nation*, 98; Whitaker, "Alexander McGillivray," 301–302; Corbitt, "Letter of Marque," 252.

32. LC-MsD, Bowles Collection, Oct. 26, 1791, no addressee or signature, but probably from Bowles to the secretary of war or the governor of Georgia or the president; also, written in the same hand on the same sheet of paper as the foregoing, is what appears to be a copy of a separate letter to one of the above.

33. J. L. Wright, Jr., *William Augustus Bowles*, 67–70.

34. *ASPIA*, 1:246, secretary of war to McGillivray, Feb. 17, 1792; Whitaker, "Alexander McGillivray," 303. Several John Millers appear in the records. One Tom Miller, described as a U.S. citizen living in Florida where Bowles was active, had a brother Jack Miller (Grant, *BH*, 428, Journal, May 12, 1802) who may have been the man Panton tried to hire to kill Bowles. There was also a man named Miller who lived not far from Pensacola, at whose house Hawkins sometimes stopped in his travels.

35. LC-MsD, Bowles Collection, Narrative; Lawrence Kinnaird, "The Significance of William Augustus Bowles' Seizure of Panton's Apalachee Store in 1792," 190–92; Whitaker, "Alexander McGillivray," 301–302; *ASPIA*, 1:303, Governor Quesada of E. Florida to Seagrove, June 14, 1792; Corbitt, "Letter of Marque," 253; Douglass, "The Adventurer Bowles," 16–17.

36. *ASPIA*, 1:302, McGillivray to Seagrove, May 1, 1792; Whitaker, "Alexander McGillivray," 304, 306; Abernethy, *South in the New Nation*, 98–99; *ASPIA*, 1:382, March 26, 1793.

37. Whitaker, "Alexander McGillivray," 295–96.

38. *ASPIA*, 1:251, Hammond (British minister to the U.S.) to Jefferson, March 30, 1792, denying British support of Bowles. Kinnaird, "Significance of Bowles' Seizure of Panton's Store," 177–92, quotes Cunningham's testimony under interrogation by the Spanish at New Orleans, April 2, 1792.

39. McPherson, "Unpublished Letters to Jefferson," Hawkins to Jefferson, March 8, 1787.

40. LC-MsD, Blount Collection, George Hogg to Blount, April 16, 1792; *ASPIA*, 1:264, David Craig to Blount, March 15, 1792 (Craig was one of the intruders who later gave Hawkins problems in running the Cherokee line); Hamer, "Letters of William Blount," 129, Blount to Daniel Smith, April 27, 1792; Corbitt, "Letter of Marque," 253–54; *ASPFR*, 2:77, Blount to James Carey, April 21, 1797. (See Chapter 8 below for Blount's Spanish connection.)

41. Wheeler, *Reminiscences*, pp. lix and 11.

CHAPTER 4. "Civilization"

1. Schmeckebier, *Office of Indian Affairs*, 3, quoting opinion of Chief Justice Marshall in *Graham's Lessee* v. *McIntosh*, 1823.

2. Ibid., *Fletcher* v. *Peck*, 1810.

3. Vine Deloria, Jr., and Clifford M. Lytle, *American Indians, American Justice*, 58–61; Tyler, *Indian Policy*, 33–34; Cohen, *Handbook of Federal Indian Law*, chapter 4, esp. 68–72, for the history of Indian legislation through Removal, and also Deloria and Lytle, op. cit., chapter 3, "Indian Country."

4. Harmon, *Sixty Years of Indian Affairs*, 54–55; Tyler, *Indian Policy*, 32; Harmon, *Sixty Years of Indian Affairs*, 55, quoting Secretary of War Knox, June 15, 1789; Jane F. Smith and Robert M. Kvasnicka, eds., *Indian-White Relations: A Persistent Paradox*, 254, comment of D'Arcy McNickle.

5. Tyler, *Indian Policy*, 23 and 48–49; *ASPIA*, 1:679, treaty with Creeks, Minutes, June 13, 1802; quoted by Abbott, *Indian Policy*, 159; quoted by Rogin, *Fathers and Children*, 77.

6. Tyler, *Indian Policy*, 48–49, on honorable national policy frustrated by settlers; Francis P. Prucha, *American Indian Policy in the Formative Years: The Indian Trade and Intercourse Acts*, 186–87; Arthur H. DeRosier, Jr., "Myths and Realities in Indian Westward Removal," 86; Ronald N. Satz, *American Indian Policy in the Jacksonian Era*, 2.

7. See Burnett, *Letters of Continental Congress*, 8:688–90, North Carolina delegates in Congress to the North Carolina General Assembly, Dec., 1787.

8. Sheehan, *Seeds of Extinction*, 167, 169.

9. Williams, *Early Travels*, 115–21, Cuming's report. James Adair devoted the first 220 pages of his *History of the American Indians* to the argument that Indians and Jews were kin; William Penn held that Indians were descendants of the Lost Tribes of Israel (Gary B. Nash and Richard Weiss, eds., *The Great Fear: Race in the Mind of America*, 9). On Priber, see Skinner, *Pioneers of the Old Southwest*, 66–71, and Williams, *Dawn of the Tennessee Valley*, 101–113.

10. NA75:43, 178; "Adair's history" and "Godwin's enquiry" (*The Inquiry Concerning Political Justice*, 1793) were ordered by Hawkins and sent by messenger, Dec. 21, 1798, to his residence in the Creek agency. Mauelshagen and Davis, *Partners in the Lord's Work*, 17, 18, 22.

11. The Indian character as an embodiment of white expectations explains the coexistence of the "murderous red savage" and the "noble red creature of the forest" (DeRosier, "Myths and Realities," 84); Wilcomb E. Washburn, "The Moral and Legal Justifications for Dispossessing the Indians," 20, 21; Nash, *The Great Fear*, 5, 6.

12. Nash, *The Great Fear*, 5–6.

13. Williams, *Early Travels*, "Francis Baily's Tour (1797)," 390, and "Chateaubriand's Travels (1791)," 324. Swanton, *Indians of the Southeastern U.S.*, 232.

14. Swanton's *Indians of the Southeastern U.S.*, 237 (from Antoine du Pratz, *History of Louisiana*, 1758).

15. Swanton, *Indians of the Southeastern U.S.*, 234–35 (from John Lawson, *History of North Carolina*, 1714).

16. Nash, *The Great Fear*, 2; Richard Van Der Beets, ed., *Held Captive by*

Indians, xiv–xxix; for a full analysis of the captivity stories, see Wilcomb E. Washburn, *The North American Indian Captivity*. Donald H. Mugridge and Helen F. Conover, *Album of American Battle Art*, pl. 9, pp. 10–12, for an engraving dated 1766 showing tearful farewells between Indians and their captives who are about to be restored to white society.

17. See Sheehan, *Seeds of Extinction*, 75–82, on the Buffon controversy. Winthrop Jordan, *White Over Black*, 162–63, makes the point that Indians may have suffered less than blacks from hate and oppression because whites believed Indians to be too lacking in sexuality to pose a threat to racial purity.

18. Washburn, "Moral and Legal Justification," 26; McPherson, "Unpublished Letters to Jefferson," 171, Hawkins to Jefferson, Nov. 4, 1798; *ASPIA*, 1:38–39, report of the commissioners at Hopewell treaty, 1785; Mauelshagen and Davis, *Partners in the Lord's Work*, 7.

19. *H-L*, 13, Hawkins memorandum, Nov. 19, 1796; *H-L*, 13–14, Hawkins to secretary of war, Nov. 22, 1796. R. S. Cotterill, *The Southern Indians*, says Hawkins was appointed in December, 1796; that, however, was when he arrived in Creek country, having been appointed earlier.

20. Grant, *BH*, 2–17, Journal, Nov. 26–Dec. 14, 1796, and 21–30, 33–52, Journal, Dec. 18, 1796–Feb. 25, 1797; Grant, *BH*, 151, Hawkins to Winchester, Nov. 9, 1797.

21. Grant, *BH*, 167, Hawkins to secretary of war, Nov. 28, 1797.

22. Grant, *BH*, 186, Journal, May 27, 1798.

23. Swanton, "An Indian Social Experiment," 368, 375; Swanton, *Indians of the Southeastern U.S.*, 392–93, 442–45, 448–53; Milling, *Red Carolinians*, 9; Bartram, *Travels*, 511.

24. Grant, *BH*, 174, Hawkins to Governor Jackson, Feb. 18, 1798.

25. McMurry, "Indian Policy of the Federal Government," 23.

26. Bartram, *Travels*, 510–11; Swanton, "An Indian Social Experiment," 374–75.

27. *NASPIA*, 6:66, Knox report, July 7, 1789; Tocqueville, *Democracy in America*, 1:351n, quoting Clarke and Cass Report, Feb. 4, 1829; Bartram, *Travels*, 496; Rogin, *Fathers and Children*, 126, quoting Lewis Cass, "Removal of the Indians," 1830.

28. Rogin, *Fathers and Children*, 116.

29. LC-MsD, Blount Collection, Hawkins to Blount, Nov. 14, 1791.

30. On traditional Creek civil government: Swanton, "An Indian Social Experiment," 374; *Sketch*, 68–72; William T. Hagan, "The Indian in American History," 4–5; Bartram, *Travels*, 492–95; and particularly on the war and peace towns, Gilbert, "Eastern Cherokees," 348–55. *Palladium*, Dec. 1, 1805, printed the description of Creek government and law as part of an interview with Hawkins. Bartram, *Travels*, 491.

31. *ASPIA*, 1:386, March 22, 1793, William Weatherford on the great confusion in the Creek Nation following McGillivray's death.

32. The count was made by the author. Chief among sources consulted: *ASPIA*, vol. 1; *NASPIA*, vol. 6; LC-MsD, Blount Collection; Grant, *BH*; NA75:42; NA75:43; *Washington*, ed. Fitzpatrick, vol. 34. Secondary sources included Ramsey, *Annals of Tennessee*, which can by no means be considered pro-Indian. Incidents were noted nonselectively as they occurred in the records. Indians predominated in horse thefts, but the re-

ceivers of the stolen animals were in many if not most cases white men, some as far east as Savannah. Sheehan, *Seeds of Extinction*, 201–206, on white murderers; *ASPIA*, 1:48, Joseph Martin to secretary of war, Feb. 2, 1789; Whitaker, "Muscle Shoals Speculation," 368, 371–72; Abernethy, *South in the New Nation*, 75, 89; LC-MsD., Blount Collection, Blount payroll, 1791.

33. *Washington*, ed. Fitzpatrick, 32:118; *ASPIA*, 1:459, Daniel Smith (then Blount's territorial secretary) to secretary of war, Oct. 1, 1793. Blount was out of the territory, possibly deliberately, when the Beard violence occurred; Beard was court-martialed, but seems to have been let off (*ASPIA*, 1:464, 467, 468). Ramsey, *Annals of Tennessee*, 583, 578, 619; John Sevier, "Executive Journal of Governor John Sevier," ed. S. C. Williams, 113, Sevier to secretary of war, July 20, 1796.

34. Robertson quoted by Ramsey, *Annals of Tennessee*, 619.

35. Sheehan, "Indian-White Relations in Early America," 269, quoting Washington to Pickering; on the Padgeeligau massacre, Grant, *BH*, 313. Harrison was one of Sevier's militia officers (Ramsey, *Annals of Tennessee*, 581); he may be the "Capt. Harrison" of Carr's Bluff who in 1792 had had six valuable horses stolen by Uchees (*ASPIA*, 1:309, Barnard to Seagrove, July 13, 1792). *H-L*, 469, Thomas to Hawkins, Aug. 26, 1797; Grant, *BH*, 120, Hawkins to Barnard, July 13, 1797. Like "Capt. Harrison," many white men (and a few Indians) called themselves by military titles. The few who were officers of the United States Army will be so identified in text or note; the others held their titles from Revolutionary War service, state or territorial militia service, or merely self-service.

36. LC-MsD, Blount Collection, David Allison to Blount, Oct. 16, 1791 (Cox was to represent Blount's interests in Muscle Shoals); Ramsey, *Annals of Tennessee*, 550; *H-L*, 190, Memorandum, Aug. 6, 1797; Grant, *BH*, 124, Hawkins to Cox, Aug. 6, 1797, and 148, Hawkins to Col. Thomas Butler, U.S. Army, Nov. 9, 1797. Cox fled to Natchez, was arrested there but escaped, and died in New Orleans soon after.

37. NA75:42, Doc. 134, April 20, 1797, Barnard to Price. Grant, *BH*, 146, Hawkins to Cornells, Oct. 31, 1797, in which Hawkins links "horse stealing, and this murderous business on the frontiers"; *H-L*, 315, Creek National Council, Minutes, May 27, 1799; *ASPIA*, 1:265, Blount to secretary of war, Dec. 20, 1792; Grant, *BH*, 169, Hawkins to Maj. John Habersham, U.S. Army, Dec. 20, 1797. Additional references to horse thefts occur throughout the records, e.g., Grant, *BH*, 146, Oct. 31, 1797, Hawkins to Alex Cornells; *ASPIA*, 1:35, Blount to secretary of war, Nov. 10, 1794; *ASPIA* 1:646, report of the President to Congress, Dec. 8, 1801.

38. APS680, April 15, 1799, Hawkins to Maclin, and Nov. 13, 1799, Hawkins to Major Lewis; Grant, *BH*, 130, Hawkins to Maclin, Sept. 20, 1797. Galphin's deposition, *H-L*, 231, Nov. 12, 1797.

39. Hamer, "British in Canada," 129, description of Efau Haujo by Wellbank, Bowles's aide; for more on Efau Haujo, see Whitaker, "Alexander McGillivray, 1783–1789," 194–96; *H-L*, 437, treaty at Tuckabatchee, Minutes, June 30, 1804; Grant, *BH*, 185, 190, Creek National Council, May 24 and 27, 1798.

40. APS680, Creek National Council, Tustunnuggee Haujo to Hawkins, Nov. 4, 1799; APS680, Hawkins to Tustunnuggee Haujo and chiefs. "Punishment by the sticks" is explained in Chapter 9.

41. Harmon, "Benjamin Hawkins and the Federal Factory System," 144; NA75:42, Doc. 125, Barnard to Price, March 27, 1797, and Doc. 134, Barnard to Price, April 20, 1797; Grant, *BH*, 178, Hawkins to Governor Jackson, Feb. 25, 1798.

42. *ASPIA*, 1:46, Joseph Martin to secretary of war, Jan. 15, 1789; *ASPIA*, 1:468–69, 486, Seagrove to secretary of war, Oct. 31, 1793, and May 16, 1794. Robertson, "Correspondence," 69–70, Barnard to Blount, Sept. 16, 1795, and 179–86, Pickering to Blount, March 23, 1795.

43. *ASPIA*, 1:536, Blount to secretary of war, Nov. 10, 1794. The Duke of Orleans in his journal of his 1797 tour of America spoke of the continual pillage of Indian lands (see in Williams, ed., *Early Travels*).

44. Governor Walton of Georgia, like Blount, had kept a tally of Indian aggressions, and he reported to federal commissioners in 1789 that Creeks had murdered 82, wounded 29, captured 40, and burned 89 houses (Stevens, *Georgia*, 2:444). *ASPIA*, 1:541, Blount to Robertson, Nov. 22, 1794; LC-MsD, Blount Collection, Pickens to Blount, Nov. 12, 1792; *ASPIA*, 1:437–39, Interrogation of James Carey by Governor Blount, sent to Congress March 30, 1793; for further Blount reports on Indian violence, *ASPIA*, 1:443, 448, 453, 466.

45. On Hawkins's illness: Grant, *BH*, 175, Hawkins to secretary of war, Feb. 23, 1798; Grant, *BH*, 181, Hawkins to Col. John Clements, March ?, 1798; Grant, *BH*, 184–85, Creek National Council, Minutes, May 26, 1798, talk of Efau Haujo.

46. Grant, *BH*, 186–89, Minutes, May 27 and 28, 1798; APS680, Hawkins to Robertson, June 5, 1798; *H-L*, 495, Thomas to Hawkins, Aug. 2, 1798 (probably); *H-L*, 477, Thomas to Hawkins, Jan. 28, 1798; APS680, Hawkins to secretary of war, June 24, 1798; APS680, Hawkins to William Panton, Jan. 28, 1799.

47. APS680, Hawkins to War Department, June 24, 1798.

48. APS680, Hawkins to Robertson and to Col. David Henley, U.S. Army, June 5, 1798, and Hawkins to Dinsmoor, Aug. 10, 1798.

49. APS680, Hawkins to George Walton, Aug. 25, 1798, and Hawkins to George Lee and other Georgians, Aug. 16, 1798; on the "proud, haughty . . . race," APS680, Hawkins to Colonel Henley, June 5, 1798; APS680, Hawkins to Dinsmoor, Aug. 10, 1798; APS680, Hawkins to Mitchell, June 22, 1798.

50. Hawkins had boasted of his accomplishments in the agency to Governor Jackson of Georgia (Grant, *BH*, 174, Feb. 18, 1798) and to George Walton (APS680, Aug. 25, 1798), among others. Hawkins was especially proud of Robert Grierson, who employed enough women to spin 1,000 yards of cotton thread a year under the instruction of Rachel Spillard, to whom Hawkins's department paid $200 a year as teacher (*Sketch*, 44); Grant, *BH*, 13–14, Journal, Dec. 9 and 10, 1796; NA75:42, Hawkins to Price, Nov. 19, 1798; *Sketch*, 56. Lavinia Downs was probably a white woman, the daughter of Isaac Downs of Hancock County, Georgia (APS680, Hawkins to Gaither, Dec. 17, 1798). Hawkins had six, possibly seven children by her, the last one born after his death in 1816 (Georgia Department of Archives and History, Hawkins Papers, Hawkins Will, and Lawsuit Papers). See also Mauelshagen and Davis, *Partners in the Lord's Work*, 36 and n. 21.

51. NA75:42, Hawkins to Price, Dec. 7, 1798. APS680, Hawkins to Walton, Aug. 25, 1798; NA75:43, 175–76 (probably Nov. 1798).

CHAPTER 5. Trade, Not Treats

1. *ASPIA*, 1:586, treaty of Colerain.

2. Tyler, *Indian Policy*, 40; *Washington*, ed. Fitzpatrick, 34:100, Washington to Edmund Pendleton, Jan. 22, 1795.

3. *ASPIA*, 1:543–44, Knox to Washington, Dec. 29, 1794; *NASPIA*, 6:64–66, Knox report to Washington, July 7, 1789.

4. LC-MsD, Blount Collection, James Holland to Blount, Jan. 23, 1796; William, ed., "Journal of Governor John Sevier," 131, Jan. 29, 1797, Sevier to Blount, Cocke, and Jackson; McMurry, "Indian Policy of the Federal Government," 36; "Journal of John Sevier," James Ore to Sevier, May 12, 1798.

5. Each trade and intercourse act was effective for only two or three years, then had to be renewed (Edgar B. Wesley, "The Government Factory System Among the Indians, 1795–1822," 490–94); *NASPIA*, 3:133, secretary of war to House of Representatives, March 22, 1800; NA75:42, Doc. 413, Hawkins to Wright, Christmas 1799; *ASPIA*, 1:601, treaty of Colerain; *NASPIA*, 3:130, report of Secretary of War Pickering, Dec. 12, 1795; Harmon, *Sixty Years of Indian Affairs*, 94–98; Harmon, "Benjamin Hawkins and the Federal Factory System," 143–47, 138n; NA75:43, Introduction. *ASPIA*, 1:583–84, discusses the choice of sites for factories in the South; Tellico was selected because it had a military post, and Colerain because goods could be shipped there cheaply by water.

6. NA75:42, Doc. 20, Instructions to the Factor—1795—Edward Price; *NASPIA*, 3:133, secretary of war to H of R, March 22, 1800; NA75:42, Doc. 20, Instructions to the Factor.

7. *NASPIA*, 3:133, secretary of war to H of R, March 22, 1800.

8. Grant, *BH*, 152, Hawkins to Byers, Nov. 9, 1797, and 162, Hawkins to Elizabeth Trist, Nov. 25, 1797, are among numerous evidences of the good relations between Hawkins and Byers; details of Price's character and life as factor were gleaned mainly from NA75:42 and NA75:43, *passim*.

9. NA75:43, 3–4, Price to Tench Frances, purveyor to the factories, Dec. 26, 1795; NA75:43, 6, Price to Frances, Jan. 11, 1796; NA75:43, 7, Price to Frances, Jan. 23, 1796; NA75:53, Doc. 69, n.d. (probably 1799), a record book on whose inside cover is sketched a building that roughly fits the description of the store.

10. NA75:42, Doc. 26, Seagrove to Price, Jan. ?, 1796; NA75:43, 40, Price to secretary of war, Jan. 24, 1796; NA75:42, Docs. 64 and 65, Seagrove to Bullard, Nov. 29 and Nov. 30, 1796.

11. NA75:53, Doc. 69 (probably 1799); NA75:42, Doc. 20, Instructions to the Factor; NA75:42, Doc. 376, Hawkins to Wright, April 24, 1799; NA75:43, 79, Price to secretary of war, Aug. 25, 1798.

12. NA75:43, 81–82, 86, 88, Price to Gaither, Aug. 27, 1797, Price to Allinson, Sept. 4, 1797, Price to Allinson, Sept. 12, 1797, and Price to secretary of war, Sept. 15, 1797; NA75:42, Doc. 24, Bullard to (page torn— possibly Seagrove), Feb. 5, 1798; NA75:43, Doc. 246, complaint of James

Jordan against Price, Feb. 5, 1798; NA75:43, 120, attorney general to Price, Feb. 22, 1798; NA75:42, Doc. 383, Papers Respecting the Court Marchal . . . . NA75:42, Docs. 211, 307, 350, Susannah Baker to Price, August 8, 1798, Price to Baker, Oct. 26, 1798, and Baker to Price, Nov. 22, 1797; NA75:43, 127, 182–83, Price to Allinson, March 5, 1798, and Price to Hawkins, Jan. 1, 1799.

13. NA75:43, 118, Price to Hopkins, Feb. 5, 1798. On Price's many efforts to get gunpowder, see NA75:43, 83, 91, 92, 104, 105. Later factors met the same frustration; possibly hunting needs were deliberately omitted to turn the Indians toward more "civilized" pursuits. NA75:42, Doc. 391, Hawkins to Wright, Aug. 2, 1799.

14. NA75:42, Doc. 391, Hawkins to Wright, Aug. 2, 1799.

15. The day-by-day transactions at the factories (NA75:44) provide price information. Carting charges were increasing rapidly, from about $1 per hundredweight in 1795 to as much as $3 in 1807 (NA75:43, 122–309 passim). The carters banded together "not to haul for the public but at their own price" (NA75:43, 122, Price to J. Meads, March 7, 1798). *ASPIA*, 1:676, treaty with Creeks, Minutes, June 11, 1802; Wesley, "Government Factory System," 499–500.

16. NA75:42, Doc. 643, Hawkins's voucher dated February 26, 1801. NA75:42, Doc. 369, shows an error in arithmetic by the storekeeper at the Fort Wilkinson store.

17. NA75:44, 16, Nov. 9, 1799; Swanton, *Indians of the Southeastern U.S.*, 297; *ASPIA*, 1:647, report of the President to Congress, Dec. 8, 1801; NA75:44, factory transactions, 1799–1816, passim; NA75:42, Doc. 412, Dec., 1798; for more on weights and measures, NA75:42, Docs. 391 and 392. Among Hawkins's possessions at his death were many weights, scales, yardarms, and other measuring devices (Hawkins Papers, Georgia Department of Archives and History, Estate Inventory and Sale). APS680, Hawkins to Dinsmoor, Jan. 6, 1799.

18. Gilbert, *Eastern Cherokees*, 303, and Swanton, *Indians of the Southeastern U.S.*, 677–85, on fondness of Indians for jokes, games, and gambling; also see Bartram, *Travels*, 506; Foreman, *Indians and Pioneers*, 30; NA75:42, Doc. 391, Hawkins to Wright, Aug. 2, 1799.

19. *Sketch*, 56; APS680, Hawkins to Gaither, Feb. 27, 1799. Hawkins wrote often and enthusiastically about his garden. He delighted in having in December turnips, beets, radishes, carrots, and 1,000 well-established strawberry plants, and in January lettuce and parsley big enough to transplant, and green wheat (APS680, Hawkins to Gaither, Dec. 30, 1798; NA75:42, Doc. 412 and 357, Hawkins to Price, Dec. 31, 1798, and Dec. 12, 1798). Hawkins's summer garden contained just about every English and Indian vegetable and a wide variety of aromatic herbs, as well as roses, wild flowers, and any unusual plant he had the luck to find, such as the Venus's-flytrap, seeds of which he dispatched to Jefferson (Grant, *BH*, 183–84, Journal, April–June 1798); APS680, Jan. 6, 1799, Hawkins to Dinsmoor; *Papers of Jefferson*, ed. Boyd, 15:506, and on Venus's flytrap, 10:240.

20. Swanton, *Indians of the Southeastern U.S.*, 786–90; Ferguson, "Confrontation at Coleraine," 3, 13; NA75:42, Doc. 306; NA75:43, 84, Price to Allinson, Sept. 4, 1797; NA75:43, 44, Price to Gaither, Feb. 21, 1797; NA75:43, 105, Price to Gaither, Jan. 2, 1798. NA75:42, Doc. 80, Thomas

to Price, Sept. 14, 1797; NA75:43, 278, Halsted to William Davy, Sept. 20, 1805.

21. Swanton, *Indians of the Southeastern U.S.*, 796. A recent study of the effects of drink on Indians mentions "crazy violence," suggesting that "species of insanity" which to the Indians seemed the normal consequence of drinking (Littman, "Alcoholism, Illness, and Social Pathology Among Indians," 1773). Another useful study of the stereotypical "drunken Indian" is Joseph Westermeyer, "'The Drunken Indian': Myths and Realities," *Psychiatric Annals*, Nov. 1974. NA75:43, Price to secretary of war, Apr. 30, 1798; Grant, *BH*, 26; APS680, Hawkins to Price, Feb. 27, 1799. NA75:42, Doc. 125, Barnard to Price, March 27 and 28, 1797; Timothy Barnard had three sons by his Uchee wife: Timpogee (or Timpoochee), Yawcoppee, and Falopee; in Swanton, *Indians of the Southeastern U.S.*, Pl. 36–1, is a portrait of "Timpoochee Barnard, Chief of the Yuchi Indians among the Lower Creeks." Mauelshagen and Davis, *Partners in the Lord's Work*, 43.

22. NA75:SW/LR, treaty at Southwest Point, commissioners to secretary of war, Aug. 2 (probably), 1801; Bartram, *Travels*, 490–91; NA75:42, circular letter from Secretary of War Dearborn, Sept. 14, 1802; on measures to prevent sale of spirits, see Abbott, "Indian Policy," 161.

23. Timberlake, *Memoirs*, 61; *Sketch*, 78. On the black drink, Bartram, *Travels*, 291, and Swanton, *Indians of the Southeastern U.S.*, 284, 775, and pl. 98; and Timberlake, *Memoirs*, 101.

24. NA75:SW/LR, Henry Drinker and others of a Quaker mission to secretary of war, Dec. 31, 1801; *ASPIA*, 1:835, Minutes, July 18, 1814. A study made at the Phoenix Clinical Research Center, reported in the *New York Times* (Jan. 7, 1976), found no significant difference in the metabolizing of alcohol by whites and Indians. Clark Wissler presents the thesis that to Indians the object of drinking was to get drunk, or "crazy," as quickly as possible, a state in which they were not responsible for their follies (*Indians of the U.S.*, 268). Edmond Atkin in his report of 1755 noted that the chiefs of every nation begged the colonial governors to forbid the sale of rum, "that bewitching Liquor," to Indians by traders (Atkin, *Indians of the Southern Colonial Frontier: The Edmond Atkin Report*, 26–27, 35).

25. NA75:43, 64, Price to Allinson, June 11, 1797; NA75:43, 130, Price to secretary of war, Apr. 27, 1798; NA75:43, 128, Price to Tinsley, Apr. 7, 1798; NA75:43, Price to Gaither, Apr. 7, 1798; NA75:42, Doc. 383, Papers respecting the Court Marchal, gives vivid details of the drunken brawling. The biting and gouging remind one of Milfort's description of methods of fighting by the Georgia "Crakeurs and Gaugeurs" (Milfort, *Memoirs*, 86–87). NA75:42, Doc. 370, Will of Edward Price, Jan. 14, 1799; NA75:43, 187, Price to Hawkins, Feb. 5, 1799; NA75:42, Doc. 381, Feb. 14, 1799, "after Mr. Price's death."

26. Grant, *BH*, 190–91, Hawkins to Gaither, Apr. 22, 1798.

27. NA75:42, Doc. 355, Dec. 7, 1798, Hawkins to Price; NA75:42, Doc. 364, Jan. 9, 1799, Hawkins to Price; APS680, Hawkins to Gaither, Dec. 17, 1798.

28. *H-L*, 351, Hawkins's accounts, 1798. Among Hawkins's many letters dealing with Spanish officials and their policy are APS680, Hawkins to secretary of war, Oct. 4, 1799, Hawkins to William Panton and others, May 14, 1800, Aug. 26, 1800, and June 9, 1800. *NASPIA*, 3:138, secretary

of war to H of R committee, 1800; Harmon, *Sixty Years of Indian Affairs*, 96; Grant, *BH*, 47–48, Journal, Feb. 16, 1797, and Grant, *BH*, 163–64, Hawkins to Elizabeth Trist, Nov. 25, 1797, on offers by women; Grant, *BH*, 148, Hawkins to Thomas Butler, Nov. 9, 1797.

29. For the Hales case, NA75:42, Doc. 336, Hawkins to Price, Nov. 19, 1798; also APS680, Hawkins to Col. Samuel Alexander, Jan. 21, 1799. For the Russell case, APS680, Polly Russell's deposition, March 19, 1799, and Hawkins's decision, July 11, 1799. NA75:SW/LR, Hawkins to secretary of war, Nov. 4, 1801; APS680, Hawkins to Dinsmoor, Jan. 6, 1799.

30. Wesley, "Government Factory System," 495; APS680, Hawkins to Mitchell, June 22, 1799; Abbott, "Indian Policy," 154.

31. Abbott, "Indian Policy," 155.

32. *H-L*, 491–94, Four Nations Council, Minutes, 1798; since Hawkins was absent, his clerk Richard Thomas attended this meeting.

33. APS680, Hawkins to secretary of war, Aug. 6, 1799; NA75:42, Docs. 395, 396, 441, 443, Wright to Harris, Sept. 3, 1799, Oct. 1, 1799, May 26, 1800, and June 2, 1800; NA75:42, Docs. 398 and 411, Hawkins to Wright, Oct. 26, 1799, and Dec. 12, 1799.

34. NA75:42, Doc. 477, Hawkins to Wright, March 12, 1801; NA75:42, Doc. 513, Wright to Hawkins, June 27, 1801; NA75:42, Doc. 698, Barnard to Hawkins, March 8, 1802; NA75:43, 219, Halsted to secretary of war, Apr. 3, 1802.

35. NA75:42, Doc. 20, Instructions to the Factor; NA75:42, Doc. 391, Hawkins's instructions to Wright, Aug. 2, 1799; Wesley, "Government Factory System," 499–500, Instructions to Factors, 1808, from John Mason, superintendent of Indian trade.

36. NA75:42, Doc. 158, Hawkins to Price, Oct. 23, 1797; Grant, *BH*, 156–58, Hawkins to secretary of war, Nov. 19, 1797; NA75:42, Doc. 391, Hawkins to Wright, Aug. 2, 1799. An earlier epidemic in 1791–92, which killed great numbers of horses, had created a large demand and high prices for stolen animals (*ASPIA*, 1:322, McGillivray to Seagrove, Oct., 1792).

37. NA75:42, Doc. 409, Hawkins to Wright, Dec. 10, 1799; NA75:43, 155, Price to secretary of war, Aug. 6, 1798; NA75:42, Doc. 409, Hawkins to Wright, Dec. 10, 1799.

38. NA75:43, 274, Halsted to William Davy, July 30, 1805; NA75:43, 318, Halsted to John Mason, Aug. 5, 1808; NA75:43, 278, Halsted to Davy, Sept. 20, 1805.

39. NA75:42, Doc. 411, Hawkins to Wright, Dec. 12, 1799.

40. APS680, expenses of the agency, July–Sept. 1799; *H-L*, 324–38 and 341–54, Hawkins's accounts for 1796–99, itemizing goods and services for which the agency had to pay; NA75:42, Doc. 411, Hawkins to Wright, Dec. 12, 1799.

41. APS680, Hawkins to Gaither, Feb. 27, 1799, Hawkins to Governor Jackson, Feb. 27, 1799; APS680, Hawkins to Hopkins, Apr. 15, 1799; APS680, Hawkins to secretary of war, June 24, 1798.

42. APS680, Hawkins to Mr. Foster, June (probably), 1798.

43. Grant, *BH*, 192, Hawkins to Hopkins, Apr. 22, 1798; NA75:42, Doc. 391, Hawkins to Wright, Aug. 2, 1799; Swanton, *Indians of the Southeastern U.S.*, 703, corroborates the existence of prostitutes among the

Creeks, adulteresses, and other outcasts, known by their painted faces. Not in the same category, but free sexually, were unmarried girls.

CHAPTER 6. Tenants at Will

1. Harmon, *Sixty Years of Indian Affairs*, 54–55.

2. Ibid., 365; Prucha, *American Indian Policy*, epigraph for chapter 3, Knox to Blount, Apr. 22, 1792; Swanton, *Indians of the Southeastern U.S.*, 232 and 230; John Marshall, *Life of George Washington*, 291; Tyler, *Indian Policy*, 38–40.

3. *H-L*, 314, Minutes, May 26, 1798.

4. *NASPIA*, 6:65, report of Secretary of War Knox, July 7, 1789; Deloria and Lytle, *American Indians, American Justice*, 61.

5. Prucha, *American Indian Policy*, 186–87.

6. McKenney, *Memoirs*, 328, talk to Chickasaw chiefs, Oct. 9, 1827; the government was still promising, through McKenney, that the new lands west of the Mississippi would belong to the Indians in perpetuity; see also in Harmon, *Sixty Years of Indian Affairs*, 374–77, a table showing the total of 442,866,370 acres of land that the United States acquired from various tribes, from the nation's establishment to 1840.

7. *NASPIA*, 6:65, Knox report, July 7, 1789; see also Tyler, *Indian Policy*, 39–40. Sheehan, *Seeds of Extinction*, 123, cites Pickering, Dearborn, and others to make the point that the policymakers were men of good intentions. Burnett, *Letters of Continental Congress*, 8:688, Hawkins and fellow N.C. delegates to Congress to the North Carolina General Assembly, Dec. 1, 1787.

8. Sheehan, *Seeds of Extinction*, 123; Tyler, *Indian Policy*, 48–49; Tyler's book was published under the aegis of the United States government.

9. *ASPIA*, 1:628, Dec. 1797.

10. Bartram, *Travels*, viii; Chief Justice Edward Coke, *First Part of the Institutes of the Laws of England*.

11. Harry Hoijer, ed., in *Language in Culture* (intro., v), discusses the theory of Benjamin L. Whorf that in the language of the Hopi Indians there was "a hidden metaphysics"; that is, that their language determined how they would think about the universe in ways different from the thinking of people who spoke English or other languages.

12. Some of the tribes could never accept the "tenant" concept; the Chickasaws, for example, as late as 1827, when they were about to be transported west of the Mississippi, still believed they could stipulate terms: "Understand," the chiefs told McKenney, "nothing is done, unless the country we go to look at suits; and not then, unless all we require is agreed to on your part" (McKenney, *Memoirs*, 328, Oct. 9, 1827).

13. *ASPIA*, 1:816–17, a useful but incomplete list of treaties; Donald Grinde, "Cherokee Removal and American Politics," 35.

14. *NASPIA*, 6:47, treaty of Hopewell, commissioners to secretary of war, Dec. 2, 1785; Grinde, "Cherokee Removal," 33; Harmon, *Sixty Years of Indian Affairs*, 11; Henry Steele Commager, *Documents of American History*, 131.

15. Rogin, *Fathers and Children*, 133, Andrew Jackson to McKee, Jan. 30, 1793; McKenney, *Memoirs*, 176.

16. *ASPIA*, 1:551–53, Georgia acts of Dec. 1794, and Jan. 1795; on the Yazoo speculation, Abernethy, *South in the New Nation*, 75–97, 136–67, and Stevens, *Georgia*, 2:461–96.

17. *Columbian Museum*, March 22, 1796; "country" as used at the time may have meant Georgia, not the United States.

18. President Adams had to withdraw the name of his original nominee, George Mathews, when he learned that Mathews (as well as former Secretary of War Pickering) was connected with one of the Yazoo companies (Abernethy, *South in the New Nation*, 158); just prior to the treaty of New York, McGillivray had been offered 400,000 acres of Yazoo lands to secure Creek cooperation with the speculators (Whitaker, "Alexander McGillivray, 1789–1793," 295–96); Bowles was said by his aide Cunningham to be involved with Blount and others in the Yazoo speculation.

19. *NASPIA*, 6:175, Hawkins report, 1801; Grant, *BH*, 13–14, Journal, Dec. 9 and 10, 1796; *Sketch*, 44; NA75:42, Doc. 331, Hawkins to Price, Nov. 19, 1798; NA75:43, Price to Grierson, Aug. 30, 1797.

20. Grant, *BH*, 14, Journal, Dec. 10, 1796; NA75:42, Wright to Harris, March 15, 1801, said the Indians bought five yards of local homespun to every one yard of calico.

21. NA75:SW/LR, Barnard to Hawkins, Oct. 10, 1801; see also *H-L*, 200, Hawkins memorandum, Sept. 18, 1797; *H-L*, 228, Hawkins to Grierson, Nov. 9, 1797. NA75:42, Doc. 336, Hawkins to Price, Nov. 19, 1798.

22. *H-L*, Thomas to Hawkins, Jan. 28, 1798; the woman trader was probably the one whose name is generally rendered "Sehoy," a member of the Weatherford family (Innerarity, "Journal of John Innerarity," 86); Hawkins to secretary of war, Feb. 23, 1798; NA75:42, Doc. 357, Dec. 12, 1798, when Eliza Hollinger was living at Fort Wilkinson, probably as an employee of Hawkins's department.

23. NA75:42, Doc. 412, Hawkins to Price, Dec. 31, 1798; *Sketch*, 48, for Hannah Hales's success story; APS680, Hawkins to Gaither, Jan. 21, 1799; APS680, Hawkins's order of Jan. 14, 1799; *Palladium*, Dec. 1, 1805. Hawkins employed women without racial discrimination, as for example, the black woman who served as his interpreter during his journey through the Creek Nation (Grant, *BH*, 5, Journal, Nov. 30, 1796).

24. *ASPIA*, 1:661, treaty with Choctaws, Minutes, Dec. 13, 1801. NA75:SW/LR, report of John McKee on the Choctaws, March 24, 1816.

25. Abernethy, *South in the New Nation*, on Daniel Clark, 47, 249, 266, and 447, 456–58 on cotton and land values; *ASPIA*, 1:750, Instructions to commissioners for treaty of limits with Choctaws, 1805.

26. *Columbian Museum*, issues of 1796. The Englishwoman Frances Wright in 1825 established the utopian colony of Nashoba on 300 acres of former Chickasaw land, to prepare blacks for freedom; assignees of Andrew Jackson were involved in the land purchase (Arthur E. Bestor, Jr., *Backwoods Utopias*, 218–29; S. C. Williams, *Beginnings of West Tennessee*, 239–43).

27. Abernethy, *South in the New Nation*, 447; *H-L*, 313, Hawkins memorandum, May 14, 1798; NA75:42, Doc. 441, Wright to Harris, May 26, 1800; NA75:42, Doc. 1354, slave bill of sale, Jan. 1, 1805, Benjamin Taliaferro to Jonathan Halsted; Berlin, *Slaves Without Masters*, 96–102.

28. Annie H. Abel, *The American Indian as Slaveholder and Secessionist*; Foster, *Negro-Indian Relationships*; and Berlin, *Slaves Without Masters*, help

to clarify the relationships among reds, blacks, and whites. Examples of complicated slave transactions: *H-L*, 309, Thomas Carr sues J. A. Sandoval, May 10, 1798; *H-L*, 339, suit concerning a black exchanged for cattle, Nov. 13, 1799. Many of the Hawkins papers describe the difficulty of tracing refugee black slaves in Indian country, e.g., *H-L*, 219, deposition of Joseph Thompson, Nov. 7, 1797, and *H-L*, 203, deposition of William McKenzie, Oct. 1, 1797. The situation was further complicated by the many marriages between black and red people in the area; at the time of Emancipation, slaves and probably also free blacks in Indian country were all lumped with Indians and placed under the jurisdiction of the Office of Indian Affairs (Schmeckebier, *Office of Indian Affairs*, 1). On black prosperity, APS680, March 19, 1799, deposition of Polly Russell; also Foster, *Negro-Indian Relationships*, 20–22; Berlin, *Slaves Without Masters*, 130–31. *H-L*, 245, complaint of Robert Walton, Nov. 20, 1797.

29. NA75:SW/LR, Hawkins to Creek chiefs, Apr. 2, 1816; *H-L*, 242, Hawkins to governor of Georgia, Nov. 19, 1797; Foster, *Negro-Indian Relationships*, 21–22. Indians had obligated themselves to return escaped slaves by the treaty of New York, Article 3, and by other treaties (Washburn, *The American Indian and the United States*, 4:2287).

30. McKenney, *Memoirs*, Appendix A, April 26, 1822, notes that southern deerskins "are a perishable article. They require to be sold immediately, else what the worms leave, the expenses [of packing, beating, etc.] are sure to devour"; and on furs, McKenney remarks that southern beaver "is little better than dog's hair." Despite these shortcomings, the government factories were set up in the South, because the United States was eager to compete there with the Spanish-supported Scottish-owned firm of Panton, Leslie and Company. In the North the government would be competing with John Jacob Astor's fur trading operations.

31. LC-MsD, Washington Papers, Hawkins to Washington, Feb. 10, 1792. The response to Hawkins's letter is in *Washington*, ed. Fitzpatrick, 31:491–93, "Communication of Sentnts. to Mr. Hawkins consequent of a lettr. of his [February 1792]," and bluntly disagrees with most of Hawkins's ideas; the style of this response suggests that it was drafted for Washington by some other person. The extraordinary freedom of Hawkins's expression to Washington confirms other evidences of a close relationship between the two men.

32. Harmon, *Sixty Years of Indian Affairs*, 31–32, Northern chiefs to Federal negotiators, 1793; the chiefs suggested, with what seems wry humor, that the proposed price be distributed among the poor frontier intruders so they could move elsewhere.

CHAPTER 7. Eagle Tails and Anchovies

1. NA75:SW/LR, Wilkinson to Dinsmoor, Aug. 19, 1803.

2. DeRosier, "Myths and Realities," 85–87; NA75:SW/LR, Hawkins and other commissioners for the Choctaw treaty to secretary of war, Sept. 6, 1801.

3. NA75:SW/LR, Hawkins and other commissioners for the Choctaw treaty to secretary of war, Dec. 18, 1801. On rations supplied by the factory: NA75:42, Doc. 515, Hawkins to Wright, July 7, 1801, Doc. 774, Clay to Halsted, June 25, 1802; NA75:43, 220, Halsted to secretary of war,

May 9, 1802; NA75:43, 223, Halsted to William Hill, Aug. 18, 1802; NA75:43, 222, Halsted to commissioners, May 28, 1802, and 253, Halsted to William Simmons, Dec. 3, 1803.

4. APS680, Hawkins to Commissioner Minor, May 2, 1799. NA75:42, Doc. 39, invoice of goods sent by order of commissioners Hawkins and Pickens for negotiations with Creeks at Colerain, Georgia, which had requested the treaty, reneged on its promise to pay a share of the cost when the treaty failed to achieve its objectives (*ASPIA*, 1:614, Colerain treaty, Minutes, June 28, 1796; also, *Columbian Museum*, July 15, 1796). *ASPIA*, 1:700, Instructions to the commissioners, March 20, 1805.

5. *ASPIA*, 1:700, Instructions to the commissioners, March 20, 1805; Washburn, *American Indian and the U.S.*, 2318; *H-L*, 343–44, "The U.S. in account . . . ," 1797 and 1798; *H-L*, 354, Hawkins memorandum, June 22, 1798; APS680, Hawkins to William Hawkins, his nephew, Sept. 21, 1799.

6. William N. Fenton, *American Indian and White Relations to 1830*, 23–24. For details of treaty ceremonies: *ASPIA*, 1:596, treaty of Colerain, 1796; *ASPIA*, 1:672, treaty with Creeks, 1801.

7. McMurry, "Indian Policy of the Federal Government," 24–25, and Harmon, *Sixty Years of Indian Affairs*, 27; *ASPIA*, 1:604–606, treaty at Colerain, opening speeches, June 24, 1796, and June 26, 1796; Foster, *Negro-Indian Relationships*, 22–23; NA75:SW/LR, Hoboheilthlee Micco to the President, May 15, 1811; NA75:SW/LR, commissioners for the Ft. Jackson treaty line to secretary of war, Feb. 9, 1816.

8. *ASPIA*, 1:322, McGillivray to Dinsmoor, Oct. 1792. *ASPIA*, 1:26, Secretary of War Knox to commissioners, Oct. 1787.

9. LC-MsD, Blount Collection, Colbert to Blount, Feb. 10, 1792; *ASPIA*, 1:557, Blount to Robertson, Jan. 20, 1795. Robertson, "Correspondence," 165, Blount to Robertson, Jan. 13, 1795, and 269, McKee to Blount, June 9, 1795.

10. NA75:SW/LR, Hoboheilthlee Micco to the President, May 15, 1811; *ASPIA*, 1:605, treaty of Colerain, Minutes, June 25, 1796; Grant, *BH*, 140, Journal, Nov. 24, 1797; Grant, *BH*, 146, Hawkins to Cornells, Oct. 31, 1797; NA75:42, Doc. 160, Hawkins to Price, Nov. 5, 1797.

11. Littman, "Alcoholism, Illness, and Social Pathology Among Indians," 1774; Stan Steiner, *The New Indians*, 136–43, cites a number of instances which suggest that Indians today retain their policy of noninterference with the freedom of thought and action of others. *ASPIA*, 1:680, commissioners for treaty with Creeks to War Department, June 17, 1802; *ASPIA*, 1:674, June 9, 1802; Grant, *BH*, 393–94, treaty with Choctaws, Dec. 13, 1801, remarks of Tuskonahopoie; Grant, *BH*, 157, Hawkins to secretary of war, Nov. 19, 1797; *ASPIA*, 1:809, Hawkins to secretary of war, May 11, 1812.

12. *ASPIA*, 1:203–204, Cherokee visit to President Washington, 1792; Robertson, "Correspondence," Secretary of War Pickering to Blount, Jan. 20, 1795; Robertson, "Correspondence," 275–76, Secretary of War McHenry to Blount, Feb. 27, 1795; APS680, Hawkins to Sam Mitchell, June 22, 1798.

13. NA75:SW/LR, to John Mason, with suggestions for Indian presents, March 3, 1812.

14. Timberlake, *Memoirs*, 80; Bartram, *Travels*, 488; *Sketch*, 71.

15. Innerarity, "Journal of John Innerarity," 78, 80, 83, 84. The Senecas likewise claimed not to understand the concept of interest (NA75: SW/LR, Dec. 9, 1811, Senecas to secretary of war).

16. Timberlake, *Memoirs*, 80; Sheehan, *Seeds of Extinction*, 107.

17. Bartram, *Travels*, 517; Sheehan, *Seeds of Extinction*, 107–108.

18. The sixteen-gun salute is reported in *ASPIA*, 1:596, treaty of Colerain, but gun salutes honoring ranks and titles are all in odd numbers, and there is no official significance to a salute of sixteen guns (*Naval Officers Guide*, 8th edition [Naval Institute Press]).

19. Grant, *BH*, 184, Journal, May 26, 1798.

20. Grant, *BH*, 185, Journal, May 27, 1798. Grant, *BH*, 194, Hawkins to Gaither, May 12, 1798, says that on May 7 Yeauholau Micco had read the belt in the public square; this was immediately following the young warriors' threat on Hawkins's life, so the message was particularly appropriate: "We have buried deep under a great lake our sharp weapons, and hope our young ones will grow up in peace and friendship with the children of our red and white brethren."

21. Grant, *BH*, 187, Journal, May 27, 1798.

22. *H-L*, 493–94, Aug. 2 (probably 1798).

23. APS680, Hawkins to Panton, Jan. 28, 1799; *ASPIA*, 1:672, treaty with Creeks, Minutes, May 24, 1802.

24. Grant, *BH*, 444 and 440, Hawkins to secretary of war, May 16, 1802, and May 2, 1802.

25. *ASPIA*, 1:673, treaty with Creeks, Minutes, May 29, 1802, and June 9, 1802.

26. *ASPIA*, 1:673, treaty with Creeks, Minutes, June 9, 1802.

27. *ASPIA*, 1:677, Minutes, June 12, 1802.

28. Washburn, *American Indian and the U.S.*, 2353, Cherokee protest against treaty of July 8, 1817.

29. Grant, *BH*, 139, Journal, Nov. 24, 1797.

CHAPTER 8. The Dirt King, William Blount

1. *ASPFR*, 2:77, Blount to Carey, Apr. 21, 1797.

2. Grant, *BH*, 115, Hawkins to Keanetuh, The Turkey, and Ocunna, The Badger, June 10, 1797.

3. Grant, *BH*, 112–13, May 21, 1797.

4. *Ibid.*, 163, Hawkins to Elizabeth Trist, Nov. 25, 1797.

5. LC-MsD, Blount Collection, Articles of Agreement, William Blount and James Roberson [*sic*], Oct. 30, 1783.

6. *ASPIA*, 1:48, treaty of Hopewell, Minutes, Nov. 24, 1785; *ASPIA*, 1:49, treaty of Hopewell, Hawkins's report to secretary of war, Dec. 30, 1785; McPherson, "Unpublished Letters to Jefferson," 252, Hawkins to Jefferson, June 14, 1786.

7. Burnett, *Letters of the Continental Congress*, 8:602, William Blount to John Gray Blount, May 30, 1787; Douglass, "The Adventurer Bowles," 8.

8. Abernethy, *Frontier to Plantation*, 117; Ramsey, *Annals of Tennessee* 543; Rogin, *Fathers and Children*, 72; Hamer, "Letters of William Blount," 126–27; LC-MsD, Blount Collection, Blount Payroll, 1791.

9. LC-MsD, Blount Collection, Hawkins to Blount, March 10, 1791.

10. *Ibid.*, May 14, 1791.

11. *ASPIA*, 1:124–25, the Holston (Blount) treaty of 1791; also see Ramsey, *Annals of Tennessee*, 554–56, and Abernethy, *Frontier to Plantation*, 119–20. For a full description of the treaty and its passage by the Senate, see above, Chapter 2.

12. Abernethy, *Frontier to Plantation*, 120; *ASPIA*, 1:135, Hawkins's report to the Senate, Nov. 9, 1791; LC-MsD, Blount Collection, Hawkins to Blount, Nov. 11, 1791.

13. *ASPIA*, 1:628–31, Report of the commissioners, Cherokee treaty line, Nov. 30, 1792; *Washington*, ed. Fitzpatrick, 32:129, Washington to secretary of state, Aug. 23, 1792; *ASPIA*, 1:203–204, Cherokee deputation to Congress, 1792; LC-MsD, Blount Collection, Allison to Hawkins, Apr. 20, 1792.

14. LC-MsD, Blount Collection, Hawkins to Blount, Apr. 24, 1792.

15. LC-MsD, Washington Collection, Hawkins to Washington, Feb. 10, 1792.

16. *ASPIA*, 1:437–39, Interrogation of James Carey, March 20, 1793.

17. *ASPIA*, 1:459, Acting Governor Daniel Smith to secretary of war, June 12, 1793; *ASPIA*, 1:464, 466, 467, and 468, letters of Daniel Smith to secretary of war in July, August, and September 1793; ibid., Memorial to Congress, Apr. 8, 1794.

18. *ASPIA*, 1:535–36, Blount to Knox, Nov. 10, 1794; LC-MsD, Blount Collection, John Steele to Blount, Jan. 31, 1792; that Steele was here referring to Jefferson is even plainer in LC-MsD, Blount Collection, Steele to Blount, Apr. 1, 1792.

19. Grant, *BH*, 163, Hawkins to Elizabeth Trist, Nov. 25, 1797.

20. *ASPIA*, 1:539, Winchester to Blount, Nov. 9, 1794; NA75:42, Doc. 125, Barnard to Price, March 27, 1797.

21. Grant, *BH*, 98, Hawkins to Dinsmoor, Apr. 6, 1797; Grant, *BH*, 99–100, Hawkins to secretary of war, Apr. 11, 1797; although Hawkins complained of Captain Sparks's action to the secretary of war and believed Sparks deserved court-martial, the captain continued in service and seems to have risen to colonel by 1810 (Grant, *BH*, 103, Hawkins to Colonel Henley, Apr. 16, 1797; Grant, *BH*, 106–107, Hawkins to secretary of war, Apr. 24, 1797; Ramsey, *Annals of Tennessee*, 342; Grant, *BH*, 79, Journal, March 16–Apr. 24, 1797, on Hawkins's difficulties with Winchester.

22. Grant, *BH*, 80, Journal, Apr. 25, 1797; Grant, *BH*, 106, Hawkins to secretary of war, Apr. 24, 1797; "Journal of Sevier," ed. Williams, 135, Sevier to Blount and Cox, June 6, 1797; Grant, *BH*, 83, Journal, Apr. 28, 1797; Grant, *BH*, 80–81, Journal, Apr. 25 and 26, 1797.

23. Wright, *William Blount*, 71; *ASPFR*, 2:76–77, Blount to Carey, Apr. 21, 1797.

24. Frederick J. Turner, "Documents on the Blount Conspiracy, 1795–1797," 574–606; LC-MsD, Blount Collection, Williamson account, 1808 (probably); Rufus King, U.S. minister to Great Britain, guessed or knew of a conspiracy connecting these individuals (Turner, op. cit., 395 n. 1); Abernethy, *South in the New Nation*, 172.

25. LC-MsD, Blount Collection, Williamson account; Wright, *William Blount*, 71; *ASPFR*, 2:76–77, Blount to Carey, Apr. 21, 1797; on Blount's land speculations, Abernethy, *South in the New Nation*, 172–73; Wright,

William Blount, 131, Blount to the People of Tennessee; Wright, *William Blount*, 39, Circular Letter, Blount to Friends in the West, July 26, 1797.

26. Wright, *William Blount*, 61, examination of James Carey; *ASPFR*, 2:76–77, Blount to Carey, the April 21 letter.

27. Wright, *William Blount*, 62; Grant, *BH*, 86, Hawkins to secretary of war, March 1, 1797.

28. *ASPFR*, 2:77, Blount to Carey, April 21, 1797.

29. LC-MsD, Blount Collection, Williamson account, 1808 (probably); Thompson, "Blount Conspiracy," 8.

30. Grant, *BH*, 113–14, Hawkins to secretary of war, June 4, 1797.

31. Grant, *BH*, 115, Hawkins to Robertson, June 14, 1797; Grant, *BH*, 126, Hawkins to Mitchell, Aug. 12, 1797; Grant, *BH*, 122, Hawkins to Rogers, July 16, 1797; Grant, *BH*, 118, Hawkins to secretary of war, July 5, 1797, saying: "I send you Carey's examination. . . ."

32. Grant, *BH*, 160, Hawkins to Pickens, Nov. 19, 1797; NA75:42, Doc. 161, Byers to Price, Nov. 14, 1797; Masterson, *William Blount*, 329.

33. NA75:42, Doc. 160, Hawkins to Price, Nov. 9, 1797; Grant, *BH*, 151, Hawkins to Winchester, Nov. 9, 1797; Grant, *BH*, 160, Hawkins to Pickens, Nov. 19, 1797.

34. Masterson, *William Blount*, 316; Abernethy, *South in the New Nation*, 186, 190; *Washington*, ed. Fitzpatrick, 35: Washington to secretary of state, July 3, 1797.

35. Masterson, *William Blount*, 319–33; Ramsey, *Annals of Tennessee*, 692–99; Abernethy, *Frontier to Plantation*, 171–76; *ASPIA*, 1:637–40, treaty of Tellico, October, 1798; APS680, Hawkins to Dinsmoor, Aug. 10, 1798; *ASPIA*, 1:677, Hawkins talk at Creek treaty, Minutes, June 11, 1802; Harmon, *Sixty Years of Indian Affairs*, 64, for the new Tellico boundaries; Robertson, "Correspondence," 370, Blount to Robertson, Oct. 1, 1798.

36. On Hooker replacing Byers, see NA75:42, Doc. 331, Hawkins to Price, Nov. 19, 1798; APS680, Hawkins to Colonel Freeman, Sept. 26, 1798; APS680, Hawkins to secretary of war, Oct. 5, 1798.

37. *Writings of Thomas Jefferson*, ed. Ford, 7:198, Jefferson to Monroe, Feb. 8, 1798. For steps taken by the Congress: *Journal of the Senate of the United States*, 2d. sess., 5th Cong., 435–37, Articles of Impeachment, Feb. 7, 1798; *Journal of the House of Representatives of the United States*, 2d. sess., 5th Cong., 151, Jan. 29, 1798; see also Ascher C. Hinds, *Precedents of the House of Representatives of the United States*, 3:644–80.

38. On Wilkinson, *Washington*, ed. Fitzpatrick, 30:252–53, and 252n, Washington to Thomas Marshall, March 27, 1789; 32:115, Washington to secretary of war, Aug. 13, 1792; 37:246, Washington to Hamilton, June 25, 1799; 31:511, Washington on characters of officers, March 9, 1792; 33:521, Washington to secretary of state, Oct. 6, 1794; Abernethy, *South in the New Nation*, 210, 214, 294 ("mammoth" was a comment on Wilkinson's bulk as well as his degree of iniquity). *Writings of Thomas Jefferson*, ed. Lipscomb and Bergh, 10:373, Jefferson to Harrison, Feb. 27, 1803.

39. *NASPIA*, 3:139, Chisholm to Pickering, Aug. 15, 1798; *NASPIA*, 3:140, Pickering to Chisholm, Oct. 29, 1798; *NASPIA*, 3:136, Pickering reports to Congress, March 22, 1800, and March 25, 1800; NA75:SW/LR, Hawkins to secretary of war, May 1, 1809, on Tustunnugee

Thlucco's complaints to Hawkins about Chisholm. Chisholm seems to have adopted the middle initial *D* while in England (Turner, "Documents on the Blount Conspiracy," 584–85); Kate White, "John Chisholm, Soldier of Fortune," 66n, states that John D. was John Chisholm's son, but evidence indicates that he was Chisholm senior.

40. Haywood, Ramsey, and Marcus Wright see little wrong in what Blount did. Among later writers, Isabel Thompson says he should not be censured too heavily, because he intended benefit rather than injury to the West ("The Blount Conspiracy," 20); Masterson's biography concludes that Blount was "a Federalist thwarted by Fate," not heroic but simply human (*William Blount*, 349–51); Abernethy finds Blount possibly the greatest force in the politics of the Southwest and regards James Byers, who rushed Blount's letter to Philadelphia, as a little man trying to play the part of a hero (*Frontier to Plantation*, 168, 184).

41. Grant, *BH*, 162, Hawkins to William Faulkener, Nov. 25, 1797.

CHAPTER 9. The Death of Hope

1. Mary P. Adams, "Jefferson's Reaction to the Treaty of San Ildefonso," 173–75; Abernethy, *Frontier to Plantation*, 179, and for the Blount-Claiborne connection, 167; Malone, *Jefferson and His Times*, 4:248.

2. APS680, Hawkins to secretary of war, Sept. 4, 1798.

3. Harmon, *Sixty Years of Indian Affairs*, 71; quoted by Arthur DeRosier, Jr., *Removal of the Choctaw Indians*, 127.

4. APS680, Hawkins to Jefferson, July 22, 1800.

5. APS680, Hawkins to W. A. Bowles, Dec. 10, 1799.

6. Corbitt and Lanning, "Letter of Marque," 253–54.

7. Abernethy, *Frontier to Plantation*, 132; Paxon, *American Frontier*, 85–86; Abernethy, *South in the New Nation*, 211.

8. Jack Holmes, *Gayoso*, 177; Robertson, "Correspondence," 336, Pickens to Robertson, Sept. 2, 1796; Robertson, "Correspondence," 341–42, unsigned letter to Robertson, Apr. 2, 1797; APS680, Hawkins to secretary of war, May 18, 1799. Virginia-born Stephen Minor had entered the Spanish service and had become adjutant of the Natchez post in 1781 (Holmes, *Gayoso*, 51).

9. Holmes, *Gayoso*, 12. Ramsey, *Annals of Tennessee*, 528–29, 533, *H-L*, 481–82, Thomas to T. B. (Timothy Barnard), Apr. 4, [1798], and *H-L*, 482–83, Thomas memorandum [April, 1798] are among many accounts of losses and sufferings of travelers; Grant, *BH*, 132–33, Hawkins to secretary of war, Oct. 23, 1797; Grant, *BH*, 33, Journal, Jan. 1, 1797; Abernethy, *South in the New Nation*, 161.

10. Turner, "Documents on the Blount Conspiracy," 591, Yrujo to Pickering, July 6, 1797; Wright, *William Blount*, 124; McMurry, "Indian Policy of the Federal Government," 28. On Spanish and Indian dilatoriness, *H-L*, 490, Thomas to no addressee (probably Hawkins), Aug. 6, ?1798; *H-L*, 485–86, Thomas to no addressee (probably Hawkins), July 1, 1798; *H-L*, 483, Thomas memorandum, Sunday the 8th [April, 1798]. The opinions of Cornells, *H-L*, 490, Thomas to no addressee (probably Hawkins), Aug. 6, ?1798, and of Efau Haujo, *H-L*, 492, Aug. 2, [1798]. *H-L*, 488, Thomas to no addressee (probably Hawkins), July 17, 1798.

11. APS680, Hawkins to secretary of war, Dec. 22, 1798.

12. On Ellicott, Holmes, *Gayoso*, 177. APS680, Hawkins to Ellicott, Apr. 5, 1799, APS680, Hawkins to secretary of war, May 12, 1799.

13. APS680, Hawkins to secretary of war, Apr. 15, 1799, Hawkins to secretary of war, May 8, 1799, same to same, Aug. 6, 1799.

14. *Sketch*, 26–27; Hoboheilthle and Hoboeilthle are variant spellings of Hopoheilthle. APS680, Hawkins to William Hawkins, Sept. 21, 1799, APS680, Hawkins to secretary of war, Oct. 5, 1799, complaining about Ellicott; Hawkins's letters to Ellicott (APS680, Sept. 24, 1799) and Major Minor (APS680, Oct. 1, 1799) refer to the same situation and events.

15. APS680, Hawkins to William Hawkins, Sept. 21, 1799; APS680, Hawkins to secretary of war, Oct. 5, 1799. Accounts of Ellicott's visit with Bowles are in Corbitt and Lanning, "Letter of Marque," 254–59, Douglass, "The Adventurer Bowles," 19–20, Wright, *Bowles*, 115–16, and Abernethy, *South in the New Nation*, 243–44. Hawkins reported Bowles's plans, APS680, Hawkins to no addressee (probably secretary of war), Oct. 30, 1799.

16. For Ellicott and the city of Washington, see NA42, Public Buildings and Grounds, commissioners Thomas Johnson, David Stuart, and Daniel Carroll to the President, March 23, 1794. APS680, Hawkins to Mitchell, June 22, 1798. APS680, Hawkins to secretary of war, Aug. 20, 1800; Secretary of War Dearborn, referring to the $2,000 present, wrote, "It was understood that they [Choctaws] had taken some expression of Mr. Ellicott's for a promise to this effect," and he said that it might be a good idea to give the present each year (*ASPIA*, 1:650, secretary of war to commissioners, July 3, 1801). APS680, Hawkins memorandum on receipt of the $1,200, May 25, 1799. *Dictionary of American Biography*, 3: pt. 1, "Andrew Ellicott," 89–90.

17. APS680, Hawkins to Ellicott, Nov. 3, 1799; APS680, Hawkins to secretary of war, Oct. 4, 1799.

18. LC-MsD, Hawkins Collection, Item 38, Hawkins to Governor Jackson of Georgia, Feb. 9, 1800; APS680, Hawkins to secretary of war, Nov. 6, 1799; APS680, Hawkins to Bowles, Dec. 10, 1799.

19. APS680, Tustunnuggee Haujo and Robert Walton to Hawkins, Nov. 4, 1799.

20. APS680, Hawkins to secretary of war, Nov. 6, 1799.

21. APS680, Hawkins to Alex Cornells, Dec. 5, 1799; APS680, Hawkins to Alex Cornells, n.d. (probably soon after Nov. 4, 1799).

22. APS680, Hawkins to Wright, Dec. 12, 1799; APS680, Hawkins to Governor Folch of Florida, Dec. 28, 1799; Corbitt and Lanning, "Letter of Marque," 250.

23. APS680, Hawkins to no addressee, May 14, 1800; APS680, Hawkins to secretary of war, June 11, 1800; APS680, Hawkins to secretary of war, July 10, 1800; APS680, Hawkins to John McKee, Aug. 26, 1800; APS680, Hawkins to Folch, Sept. 12, 1800. Micoosookee was near present-day Tallahassee.

24. APS680, Hawkins to John McKee, Aug. 26, 1800.

25. NA75:SW/LR, William Simpson, Agent, "Debts due to the House of Panton Leslie & Co.," Aug. 20, 1803; R. S. Cotterill, "A Chapter of Panton, Leslie and Company," 276–77; *H-L*, 488, Thomas to no addressee (probably Hawkins), July 17, 1798; Grant, *BH*, 194, Hawkins to Panton, May 20, 1798.

26. APS680, Panton to Hawkins, Aug. 11, 1799, and Hawkins to secretary of war, Sept. 10, 1799.

27. APS680, Hawkins to Panton, Feb. 3, 1800. The company carried on, but Panton himself died at sea March 26, 1801 (Cotterill, "Panton, Leslie," 278); on Forbes, see William Coker, "Entrepreneurs in the British and Spanish Floridas," 15. Malone, *Jefferson* 4:275, quoting Jefferson to W. H. Harrison, Feb. 27, 1803; APS680, Hawkins to secretary of war, July 18, 1801, APS680, Hawkins to Governor Jackson, Aug. 14, 1800.

28. Grant, *BH*, 364–65, Journal, Aug. 10, 1801.

29. NA75:SW/LR, commissioners to secretary of war, Sept. 6, 1801; NA75:42, Doc. 499, Hawkins to Wright, July 7, 1801; Forbes, "Journal of John Forbes," ed. Greenslade, 280.

30. Grant, *BH*, 192, Hawkins to Mathew Hopkins, Apr. 22, 1798; NA75:42, Doc. 355, Hawkins to Price, Dec. 7, 1798; APS680, Hawkins to secretary of war, Aug. 6, 1799. NA75:42, Doc. 409, Hawkins to Wright, Dec. 10, 1799; Harmon, *Sixty Years of Indian Affairs*, 117–19.

31. APS680, Hawkins to Mathew Hopkins, Apr. 15, 1799; *NASPIA*, 3:137, secretary of war to H of R, March 22, 1800.

32. *ASPIA*, 1:656, Jefferson to H of R, Feb. 9, 1802.

33. *ASPIA*, 1:651, commissioners to secretary of war, Oct. 25, 1801.

34. NA75:42, Doc. 515, Hawkins to Wright, July 7, 1801; *H-L*, 359–60, Hawkins memorandum, Aug. 4, 1801, notes Secretary of War Dearborn's message of June 18, 1801.

35. Oosetenaulah was the headquarters of Silas Dinsmoor when he was Cherokee agent, thus a town of importance (Grant, *BH*, 5, Journal, Nov. 29, 1796); Grant, *BH*, 364, Journal, Aug. 10, 1801.

36. *ASPIA*, 1:650, secretary of war to commissioners, July 3, 1801; NA75:SW/LR, commissioners to secretary of war, Aug. 2, 1801; NA75: SW/LR, The Glass to commissioners, Aug. 19, 1801; also, Grant, *BH*, 367–68, Journal, Aug. 24, 30, and 31, 1801.

37. NA75:SW/LR, commissioners to secretary of war, Sept. 1, 1801. Note that the commissioners attribute the opinion to Hawkins and do not expressly concur.

38. *ASPIA*, 1:656–57, treaty at Southwest Point, Minutes, Sept. 4, 1801; *ASPIA*, 1:657, Minutes, Sept. 5, 1801; Grant, *BH*, 370–71, Journal, Sept. 5, 1801, calls the road the Kentucky Trace, not the Natchez Trace.

39. Grant, *BH*, 379, Hawkins to secretary of war, Sept. 6, 1801.

40. NA75:SW/LR, Hawkins for the commissioners to the secretary of war, Nov. 14, 1801; *ASPIA*, 1:651, commissioners to secretary of war, Oct. 25, 1801; *H-L*, 389–90, the Chickasaw treaty signed Oct. 24, 1801; Richard H. Hulan, "The Natchez Trace Parkway: In Memoriam," 27.

41. *ASPIA*, 1:651, commissioners to secretary of war, Oct. 25, 1801; for the message written across the map, Hulan, op. cit., 28.

42. NA75:SW/LR, commissioners to secretary of war, Dec. 18, 1801, NA75:SW/LR, John McKee to secretary of war, Nov. 19, 1801; *ASPIA*, 1:660–61, treaty with Choctaws, Dec. 12, 1801. The goals of the treaty are explained in *ASPIA*, 1:659, instructions to the commissioners, June 24, 1801; *ASPIA*, 1:661–63, treaty with Choctaws, Minutes, Dec. 13–18, 1801; NA75:SW/LR, commissioners to secretary of war, Dec. 18, 1801. As explained in n. 16 above, the Choctaws would probably have received $2,000 in presents in any case.

43. *ASPIA*, 1:662, treaty with Choctaws, Minutes, Dec. 15, 1801; NA75: SW/LR, commissioners to secretary of war, Dec. 18, 1801.

44. Grant, *BH*, 403n, Hawkins to secretary of war, Dec. 21, 1801.

45. NA75:SW/LR, Mr. Fatio to Hawkins, Sept. 4, 1801; NA75:SW/LR, James Durouzeau to Hawkins, Sept. 26, 1801; Douglas, *Florida, The Long Frontier*, 108.

46. NA75:SW/LR, Durouzeau to Hawkins, Sept. 26, 1801; Cussetuh King, Little Prince, and Little Warrior to William Hill, Aug. 17, 1801; and Hawkins to secretary of war, July 18, 1801.

47. *ASPIA*, 1:651, instructions to commissioners, July 17, 1801.

48. APS680, Hawkins to secretary of war, June 1, 1801.

49. *ASPIA*, 1:678, Creek treaty, Minutes, June 18, 1802.

50. *ASPIA*, 1:674, Minutes, June 8, 1802; 674 and 675, Minutes, June 9, 1802; the parenthetical "(Bowles)" is part of the quotation.

51. *ASPIA*, 1:673, commissioners to secretary of war, May 30, 1802.

52. *ASPIA*, 1:675–76, Minutes, June 11, 1802; 677, Minutes, June 12. "Spunk" is touchwood, or tinder.

53. *ASPIA*, 1:678 and 679, Wilkinson's talk, Minutes, June 13, 1802. The emphasis is Wilkinson's.

54. *ASPIA*, 1:679, Minutes, June 13, 1802; Harmon, *Sixty Years of Indian Affairs*, 73.

55. *ASPIA*, 1:680, commissioners to secretary of war, June 17, 1802.

56. Paxon, *American Frontier*, 134; Adams, "Jefferson's Reaction to San Ildefonso," 174–77, 182; McMurry, "Indian Policy of the Federal Government," 114–16.

57. APS680, Hawkins to Governor Jackson, Aug. 14, 1800; Douglass, "The Adventurer Bowles," 21, and Rogin, *Fathers and Children*, 156, concerning the Hickory Ground; Cotterill, "Panton, Leslie," 278–81; NA75: SW/LR, William Simpson, Agent, "Debts Due to the House of Panton Leslie & Co.," Aug. 20, 1803; Forbes, "Journal of John Forbes," 279–80, entry of May 11, 1803.

58. Forbes, "Journal," 280, entry of May 11, 1803.

59. LC-MsD, Madison Collection, Hawkins to Madison, July 11, 1803; NA75:42, Doc. 963, Hawkins to Halsted, Apr. 12, 1803.

60. Forbes, "Journal," 282–83, entries of May 21, May 22, and May 23, 803. *ASPIA*, 1:670, Wilkinson and Hawkins to secretary of war, July 15, 1802, describing Hopoie Mico; Forbes, "Journal," 283–84, entry of May 24, 1803.

61. Forbes, "Journal," 284, entry of May 24, 1803.

62. Ibid., 285–86, entries of May 24 and May 25, 1803.

63. Ibid., 286–87, entry of May 26, 1803.

64. Ibid., 289, entry of May 27, 1803.

65. Wright, *Bowles*, 159–74.

66. Wright, *Bowles*, 17; LC-MsD, Madison Collection, Hawkins to Madison, July 11, 1803; Forbes, "Journal," 289, entry of May 27, 1803.

CHAPTER 10. An End of Treaties

1. Harmon, *Sixty Years of Indian Affairs*, 78–79, 74; McMurry, "Indian Policy of the Federal Government," 117.

2. Washburn, "Moral and Legal Justification for Dispossessing the Indians," 26; Arrell Gibson, *The Chickasaws*; DeRosier, *Removal of the Choc-*

taw Indians, viii and 25; *Writings of Thomas Jefferson*, ed. Lipscomb and Bergh, 10:373, Jefferson to Benjamin Harrison, Feb. 27, 1803.

3. U.S. Congress, *Inaugural Addresses of the Presidents of the United States*, 19, Jefferson, March 4, 1803. For more on Jefferson's change of attitude see Virgil T. Vogel, *This Country Was Ours*, 82–83.

4. Grant, *BH*, 364, Journal, Aug. 10, 1801.

5. NA75:43, 249, 222, 253; in 1803 beef cattle for rations were supplied at a charge of $2.50 per year of age of the animal, from two to six years of age (*H-L*, 432, Creek meeting, Minutes, June 26, 1803).

6. LC-MsD, Madison Collection, Dec. 9625, Hawkins to Madison, July 11, 1803.

7. *Palladium*, Dec. 1, 1805, interview with Hawkins.

8. *Jefferson*, ed. Lipscomb and Bergh, 10:362; U.S. Congress, *Inaugural Addresses*, 19, Jefferson, March 4, 1803.

9. Abernethy, *South in the New Nation*, 447; *ASPIA*, 1:705–742, Lewis and Clark Expedition, Journal and Observations.

10. Grant, *BH*, 68, Hawkins to Cornells, Feb. 10, 1797, on Cornells's salary.

11. See Abernethy, *South in the New Nation*, esp. 46–69, 192–216, for Wilkinson's involvement in various shady but profitable operations; Abernethy, *South in the New Nation*, 287, 261.

12. LC-MsD, Wilkinson Collection, Wilkinson to no addressee, March 17, 1815.

13. NA75:SW/LR, Wilkinson to Dearborn, Aug. 31, 1803.

14. Cotterill, "Panton, Leslie," 280.

15. *H-L*, 462–65, letters from Thomas to Barnard, Hawkins, Cornells, and Gaither of May and June, 1797, give details of some of the violent incidents; also *ASPIA*, 1:677, treaty with Creeks, Minutes, July 12, 1802.

16. Grant, *BH*, 474–75, 476, 477–79, Journal, July 2, and July 15, 1804.

17. Grant, *BH*, 473 and 478, Journal, June 30 and July 15, 1804. The parenthetical Bowles is part of the quotation.

18. Among the books that Hawkins from time to time asked Price to send him (NA75:43, Price to Hawkins, Dec. 21, 1798) was William Godwin's recently published *Inquiry Concerning Political Justice*, in which the faculty of reason is held to occupy the highest place in the pursuit of truth; the book was in Hawkins's possession when he died (Hawkins Papers, Georgia Department of Archives and History, Hawkins Estate, Inventory and Sale).

19. Grant, *BH*, 477, Journal, July 15, 1804.

20. Grant, *BH*, 479, 480, Journal, July 15 and July 30, 1804.

21. *ASPIA*, 1:691, Hawkins to secretary of war, Nov. 3, 1804.

22. *Ibid.*

23. *ASPIA*, 1:692, Hawkins to secretary of war, Nov. 3, 1804.

24. *ASPIA*, 1:691, a treaty concluded between the United States of America and the Creek Nation of Indians, Nov. 3, 1804. The striker was a blacksmith's helper, who wielded the heavy hammers when the smith was forging a large object.

25. *ASPIA*, 1:690–91, Jefferson to the Senate, Dec. 13, 1804.

26. *Palladium*, Dec. 1, 1805; *ASPIA*, 1:695, Jefferson to the Senate; also Harmon, *Sixty Years of Indian Affairs*, 76–77.

27. *Jefferson*, ed. Lipscomb and Bergh, 10:357–59, Jefferson to Andrew Jackson, Feb. 16, 1803.

28. NA75:SW/LR, Hawkins to secretary of war, Sept. 6, 1801; NA75: SW/LR, Tustunnuggee Thlucco to Hawkins, May 1, 1809.

29. Donald B. Dodd and Wynelle S. Dodd, *Historical Statistics of the South, 1790–1970*, 18, 22, 34, 50; Abernethy, *Frontier to Plantation*, 224, quoting Meigs to Robertson, June 25, 1809.

30. *ASPIA*, 1:699, Dearborn to Meigs and Smith, Apr. 4, 1804; ownership of the Wofford settlement was still being disputed in 1812 (NA75: SW/LR, Dec. 20, 1811 and Aug. 25, 1812, Meigs to secretary of war).

31. *NASPIA*, 6:282; for the whole Meigs-Smith treaty with Cherokees, 1804, *NASPIA*, 6:279–82; *ASPIA*, 1:699, treaties with Cherokees communicated to Senate by Secretary of War Dearborn, Dec. 21, 1804; *Palladium*, Dec. 1, 1805; Harmon, *Sixty Years of Indian Affairs*, 74–75.

32. Wesley, "Government Factory System," 494–95, and map, 497.

33. NA75:SW/LR, Wilkinson to secretary of war, Aug. 20 and Aug. 31, 1803.

34. Ibid., Wilkinson to secretary of war, Oct. 1 and Oct. 26, 1803.

35. *ASPIA*, 1:700, secretary of war, instructions to commissionrs Robertson and Dinsmoor, March 20, 1805; Harmon, *Sixty Years of Indian Affairs*, 77–78; Abbott, "Indian Policy," 165; Cotterill, "Panton, Leslie," 286.

36. R. David Edmunds, *Tecumseh and the Quest for Indian Leadership*, 147, mentions part-Choctaw Pitchlynn as pro-American, like Pushmataha, which may explain the "compensation"; Vanderwerth, *Indian Oratory*, 71, on "Push"; *ASPIA*, 1:700, secretary of war, instructions to commissioners, March 20, 1805; *ASPIA*, 1:748–50, President Jefferson to the Senate, Jan. 15, 1808; Harmon, *Sixty Years of Indian Affairs*, 77; Abbott, "Indian Policy," 165–66; Cotterill, "Panton, Leslie," 287.

37. Harmon, op. cit., 75. In 1817, when Andrew Jackson was negotiating removal of the Eastern Cherokees, he reported, "We were compelled to promise to John D. Chisholm the sum of one thousand dollars to stop his mouth & obtain his consent . . . without this we could not have got the [Cherokee] national agreement" (Foreman, *Indians and Pioneers*, 43–44); *ASPIA*, 1:703–704, Jan. 24, 1806.

38. NA75:SW/LR, Chisholm to Meigs, Jan. 25, 1807; Hulan, "Natchez Trace," 29 and 29n; Grinde, "Cherokee Removal," 35; Harmon, *Sixty Years of Indian Affairs*, 79.

39. *ASPIA*, 1:752, Jefferson to the Senate, March 10, 1808.

40. Gilbert, "Eastern Cherokees," 180–81, and Hamer, "British in Canada," 118, 119, and 119n, on intertribal communications; Harmon, *Sixty Years of Indian Affairs*, 30. Early expressions of fear of confederation: Burnett, *Letters of Continental Congress*, 8:384, Rufus King to Elbridge Gerry, June 8, 1786, and 8:583, Hawkins to Governor Caswell, Apr. 8, 1787; *ASPIA*, 1:39, Cherokee report of arrival of northern emissaries, 1785; also, *ASPIA*, 1:384, Alex Cornells to Seagrove, Apr. 15, 1793, and *H-L*, 488, Thomas to no addressee (probably Hawkins), July 17, 1798.

41. Abernethy, *South in the New Nation*, 330–32; e.g., the Sabine River incident, ibid., 276–78.

42. Abernethy, *South in the New Nation*, 296; Rogin, *Fathers and Children*, 137–38. For Burr's trial and others arising from it, see *Federal Cases*, bk. 25, 1–207 (the Burr story, 15–25).

43. Sheehan, *Seeds of Extinction*, 247; Harmon, *Sixty Years of Indian Affairs*, 79; Grinde, "Cherokee Removal," 35; Harmon, op. cit., 79; Sheehan, op. cit., 265.

44. Peake, *U.S. Indian Factory System*, 230, quoting Big Soldier.

45. NA75:SW/LR, Philemon Hawkins to secretary of war, Sept. 23, 1816; *NASPIA*, 9:198, Creek deputation to President Jackson, 1832. Jedidiah Morse, geographer, reported to the secretary of war in 1820: "To remove these Indians . . . into a wilderness, among strangers, possibly hostile, to live as their new neighbors live, by hunting, a state to which they have not lately been accustomed, . . . can hardly be reconciled with the professed views and objects of the Government in civilizing them" (Vogel, *This Country Was Ours*, 91).

46. Mauelshagen and Davis, *Partners in the Lord's Work*, 17, and plan between pp. 38 and 39.

47. Abbott, "Indian Policy," 167; NA75:43, 260–360, for events of Halsted's tenure as factor; NA75:43, 313–14, Hawkins to War Department, March 10, 1808.

48. NA75:SW/LR, talk of Tustunnuggee Thlucco to Hawkins, May 1, 1809; James McIntosh to R.J. Meigs, Jan. 22, 1810; Hawkins to secretary of war, Dec. 31, 1810.

49. Grant, *BH*, 148, Hawkins to Thomas Butler, Nov. 9, 1797.

CHAPTER 11. Two Wars for "Paradice"

1. Harmon, *Sixty Years of Indian Affairs*, 82–91.

2. Edmunds, *Tecumseh and the Quest for Indian Leadership*, 19, 136–37, 217–21; Edmunds, *Shawnee Prophet*, 29; Albert J. Pickett, *History of Alabama*, 241; Vanderwerth, *Indian Oratory*, 68.

3. Edmunds, *Tecumseh*, 22, 136–37; Edmunds, *Prophet*, 29.

4. Harmon, *Sixty Years of Indian Affairs*, the John Randolph quote.

5. Edmunds, *Tecumseh*, 122–24, 132; Edmunds, *Prophet*, 35–37. Tecumseh may have been one of the emissaries to the Cherokees as early as the Hopewell treaty (*ASPIA*, 1:39).

6. Vanderwerth, *Indian Oratory*, 62–66. See also Alvin M. Josephy, Jr., *The Patriot Chiefs* (reprint, New York, 1977), 131–73, on Tecumseh.

7. Vanderwerth, op. cit., 72–76; Debo, *History of the Indians*, 92.

8. Tecumseh's visit to the Creeks drawn chiefly from Klinck, *Tecumseh*, 94–97, quoting the report of Sam Dale as presented by J. F. H. Claiborne in *Life and Times of General Sam Dale*; also, Edmunds, *Tecumseh*, 146–47.

9. For the earthquake threat, Klinck, *Tecumseh*, 98, and Edmunds, *Tecumseh*, 220.

10. On Weatherford and MacNac, see Halbert and Ball, *Creek War*, 66, 96, 166.

11. Swanton, *Indians of the Southeastern U.S.*, 777; Bartram, *Travels*, 495.

12. Edmunds, *Prophet*, 104–116.

13. C. L. Grant and Gerald H. Davis, "The Wedding of Col. Benjamin Hawkins," 308–316; Mauelshagen and Davis, *Partners in the Lord's Work*, 66–67.

14. *ASPIA*, 1:809, Hawkins to secretary of war, Feb. 3, April 6, and May 11, 1812. Hawkins had some suspected British spies whipped out of the agency, Hawkins to secretary of war, June 9, 1812). *ASPIA*, 1:810, Hawkins to secretary of war, June 9, 1812.

15. *ASPIA*, 1:812, Hawkins to secretary of war, Aug. 24, 1812; Halbert and Ball, *Creek War*, 103–104; *ASPIA*, 1:813, Blount to secretary of war, June 25, 1812; Rogin, *Fathers and Children*, 147, quoting the *Nashville Clarion* and Jackson to Blount, July 10, 1812; and Rogin, *Fathers and Children*, 84, quoting Jackson to Hays, Jan. 25, 1798.

16. *ASPIA*, 1:813, Blount to secretary of war, July 26, 1812, and secretary of war to Blount, Aug. 7, 1812; *ASPIA*, 1:814, Blount to secretary of war, Oct. 14, 1812.

17. *ASPIA*, 1:812–13, Hawkins to secretary of war, Nov. 2, 1812.

18. Innerarity, "Journal of John Innerarity," 67–74, 76–78, 79.

19. *Ibid.*, 79, 75–76.

20. *Ibid.*, 80, 83, 84.

21. *Ibid.*, 85, 87.

22. *Ibid.*, 76–77.

23. *ASPIA*, 1:838, Hawkins to secretary of war, March 1, 1813; 1:839, Hawkins to Cornells, March 25, 1813; 1:839, Hawkins to Tustunnuggee Thlucco, March 29, 1813.

24. Debo, *History of the Indians*, 94; *ASPIA*, 1:842, Hawkins to secretary of war, May 3, 1813. The name Red Sticks may have referred to the calendric device of the "broken days," the bundle of red-painted sticks which Tecumseh was said to have left so that his supporters could count the days until the time of uprising. Hawkins consistently called them Red Clubs, and Debo, op. cit., 92, also says Red Clubs, perhaps because followers of Tecumseh painted their war clubs red; Arthur H. Hall, "The Red Stick War," 277, suggests that name was taken because Tecumseh carried a magical red stick or wand. On the Alabamas, see *ASPIA*, 1:846, Cornells to Hawkins, June 22, 1813, and 1:847, Hawkins to secretary of war, June 28, 1813. *ASPIA*, 1:842, Hawkins to secretary of war, May 3, 1813.

25. *ASPIA*, 1:843, Nimrod Doyell, Hawkins's assistant, to Hawkins, May 3, 1813; 1:845, Cornells to Hawkins, June 22, 1813; 1:839, Hawkins to secretary of war, Apr. 6, 1813; 1:842, Hawkins to Tustunnuggee Thlucco, Cornells, and McIntosh, Apr. 24, 1813.

26. *ASPIA*, 1:843–44, Doyell to Hawkins, May 3, 1813; NA75:42, Doc. 2998, Hawkins to Halsted, Apr. 26, 1813.

27. *ASPIA*, 1:843, Cornells and Tustunnuggee Thlucco to Hawkins, Apr. 26, 1813.

28. Halbert and Ball, *Creek War*, 91; *ASPIA*, 1:852, Hawkins to secretary of war, Sept. 13, 1813; *ASPIA*, 1:854, Hawkins to General Floyd, Sept. 30, 1813; *ASPIA*, 1:846, Cornells to Hawkins, June 22, 1813.

29. *ASPIA*, 1:844, Hawkins to secretary of war, June 7, 1813; 1:846, Cornells to Hawkins, June 22, 1813; 1:844, Hawkins to secretary of war, June 7, 1813; 1:846, Hawkins memorandum, June 23, 1813.

30. *ASPIA*, 1:846, Cornells to Hawkins, June 22, 1813.

31. *ASPIA*, 1:847, Hawkins to secretary of war, June 27, 1813.

32. *ASPIA*, 1:846, Cornells to Hawkins, June 22, 1813; 1:844, Hawkins to secretary of war, May 17, 1813, 1:846, Hawkins memorandum, June 23, 1813; Hall, "Red Stick War," 277.

33. Abbott, "Indian Policy," 157; *ASPIA*, 1:848, Hawkins to secretary of war, July 6, 1813; *ASPIA*, 1:847, chiefs to Hawkins, forwarded to secretary of war, July 5, 1813; *ASPIA*, 1:848, Hawkins to secretary of war, July 6, 1813, 1:848, "A Demand on the Fanatical Chiefs . . . July 6, 1813," and Hawkins to Pinckney, July 9, 1813.

34. *ASPIA*, 1:849, Cussetah Micco to Hawkins, July 10, 1813; 1:858, Hawkins to secretary of war, July 26, 1813.

35. *ASPIA*, 1:849–50, Hawkins to secretary of war, July 28, 1813.

36. *ASPIA*, 1:850, Hawkins to secretary of war, Aug. 2, 1813; 1:851, Hawkins to secretary of war, Aug. 10, 1813; 1:851, Tustunnuggee Thlucco and Tustunnuggee Hopoie to Hawkins, Aug. 4, 1813; 1:852, Hawkins to secretary of war, Aug. 23, 1813.

37. *ASPIA*, 1:851, Tustunnuggee Thlucco to Hawkins, Aug. 4, 1813. In 1799, Hawkins had hired an honest, truthful youth named James Cornells, as an interpreter for Edward Wright at the Creek factory (NA75: 42, Doc. 397, Oct. 20, 1799), but the Cornells were a large family and this may have been a different James. Hall, "Red Stick War," 279; Halbert and Ball, *Creek War*, 92, 130–42, an account of the battle that says the Creeks numbered fewer than 100.

38. *ASPIA*, 1:857, Hawkins to Judge Harry Toulmin, Oct. 23, 1813. The Mims Fort account is drawn chiefly from Halbert and Ball, *Creek War*, 143–76; also from Hall, "Red Stick War," 180, and *ASPIA*, 1, as cited. For the various estimates of the numbers involved: Hall, op. cit., 280; Halbert and Ball, op. cit., 144; *ASPIA*, 1:852, Hawkins to secretary of war, Oct. 11, 1813.

39. *ASPIA*, 1:853, Hawkins's report of the battle, Sept. 16, 1813, says 40 to 50 were killed.

40. *ASPIA*, 1:854, Hawkins to secretary of war, Sept. 26, 1813.

41. *ASPIA*, 1:854, Hawkins to Gen. John Floyd, Sept. 30, 1813; *ASPIA* 1:858, Hawkins to secretary of war, June 7, 1814.

42. *ASPIA*, 1:850, Andrew Jackson to Governor Blount, July 13, 1813.

43. Robert V. Remini, *Andrew Jackson and the Course of American Empire, 1767–1821*, 189.

44. *ASPIA*, 1:855, Blount to Gen. Thomas Flournoy, Oct. 15, 1813.

45. *ASPIA*, 1:852–53, Hawkins to secretary of war, Sept. 14, 1813.

46. Rogin, *Fathers and Children*, 148; Remini, *Andrew Jackson*, 190–91.

47. Rogin, op. cit., 153–54; *ASPIA*, 1:855, Blount to Flournoy, Oct. 15, 1813.

48. Halbert and Ball, *Creek War*, 269; *ASPIA*, 1:853, Hawkins to secretary of war, Sept. 21, 1813; *ASPIA*, 1:854, Hawkins to secretary of war, Sept. 26, 1813; *ASPIA*, 1:855, Hawkins to Captain Cook, commander at Ft. Hawkins, Oct. 3, 1813.

49. *ASPIA*, 1:855, Hawkins to secretary of war, Oct. 4, 1813.

50. Rogin, *Fathers and Children*, 148–51.

51. *ASPIA*, 1:857, Hawkins to Judge Toulmin, Oct. 23, 1813; *ASPIA*, 1:857, Hawkins to secretary of war, Oct. 25, 1813; Tebbel, *Indian Wars*, 122, for the Crockett quote; Halbert and Ball, *Creek War*, 269. Remini, *Andrew Jackson*, 193–94; although the Indian boy, Lycora, was well cared for, he died of tuberculosis at age seventeen (Remini, op. cit., 194).

52. Halbert and Ball, op. cit., 269–72; Rogin, *Fathers and Children*, 151.

53. Halbert and Ball, op. cit., 270; Rogin, op. cit., 151; Halbert and Ball, op. cit., 272.

54. Although Floyd reported success at Autossee, Hawkins claimed that he had been defeated at Autossee because he chose to use incompetent guides (*ASPIA*, 1:858, Hawkins to secretary of war, June 7, 1814).

55. A detailed story of the battle is given in Halbert and Ball, op. cit., 246–63.

56. Remini, *Andrew Jackson*, 209–11; Rogin, *Fathers and Children*, 153–54.

57. Halbert and Ball, *Creek War*, 274.

58. Grinde, "Cherokee Removal," 34, gives the number of Cherokees serving with Jackson as 800; Halbert and Ball, op. cit., 275–76; *ASPIA*, 1:858, Hawkins to Pinckney, Apr. 25, 1814; Rogin, *Fathers and Children*, 155, 156.

59. *ASPIA*, 1:858, Hawkins to Pinckney, Apr. 25, 1814.

60. Remini, *Andrew Jackson*, 218–19. Weatherford's speech to Jackson appears in very similar language in Virginia I. Armstrong, *I Have Spoken*, 47–48; Armstrong adds that according to tradition Jackson drank a cup of brandy with Red Eagle, shook his hand, and sent him off a free man.

61. Hall, "Red Stick War," 289; *ASPIA*, 1:858, Hawkins to Pinckney, Apr. 25, 1814; Remini, *Andrew Jackson*, 219.

CHAPTER 12. The Dispossessed

1. Harmon, *Sixty Years of Indian Affairs*, 143–44; Abernethy, *South in the New Nation*, 367.

2. *NASPIA*, 6:338, secretary of war to Pinckney, March 17, 1814; 6:338, secretary of war to Pinckney, March 20, 1814; 6:339, Pinckney to secretary of war, Apr. 8, 1814.

3. *ASPIA*, 1:858, Pinckney to Hawkins, Apr. 23, 1814; 1:858, Hawkins to Pinckney, Apr. 25, 1814.

4. Rogin, *Fathers and Children*, 157–58, quoting Jackson to Pinckney, and 159; Abernethy, *South in the New Nation*, 371; Rogin, op. cit. 156; *ASPIA*, 1:858, Hawkins to secretary of war, June 7, 1814; *NASPIA*, 6:340, secretary of war to Jackson, May 24, 1814.

5. *ASPIA*, 1:858, Hawkins to secretary of war, June 7, 1814; Remini, *Andrew Jackson*, 225.

6. R. Craig Ray, "Fort Toulouse of the Alabamas," 11–12.

7. Remini, *Andrew Jackson*, 225.

8. Harmon, *Sixty Years of Indian Affairs*, 146; *ASPIA*, 1:859, Hawkins to secretary of war, June 21, 1814, on the desperate poverty of the Creeks.

9. Grant, *BH*, 679, Hawkins to Pinckney, Apr. 25, 1814; Geography and Map Division, Library of Congress; *NASPIA*, 6:339, Jackson to secretary of war, Apr. 25, 1814.

10. Harmon, *Sixty Years of Indian Affairs*, 145, Jackson to Pinckney, May 18, 1814.

11. Grinde, "Cherokee Removal," 34; Harmon, op. cit., 144, and 146, Jackson to secretary of war, June 13, 1814.

12. Grinde, op. cit., 34; Remini, *Andrew Jackson*, 226; Harmon, op. cit., 147; Halbert and Ball, *Creek War*, map facing p. 32; Abernethy, *South in the New Nation*, 371–72, condones Jackson's harsh terms, claiming that the people of Middle Tennessee had always been the victims of Creek raids "whereas the settlers committed no aggressions against these implacable foes."

13. Remini, op. cit., 227; *ASPIA*, 1:857, transcript of letter from Pinckney to Hawkins, Apr. 23, 1814, forwarded by Jackson (n.d.) to the President; Rogin, *Fathers and Children*, 158, Jackson to Big Warrior at Ft. Jackson treaty, Aug., 1814.

14. LC-MsD, Indians, Miscellaneous Papers, Box 2630, "Names of

Creek Indians, Officers and number of men who served under General Andrew Jackson in the war of 1812—'The Redstick War.'"

15. Washburn, *The American Indian and the United States*, 4:2348; *ASPIA*, 2:115, Hawkins to acting secretary of war, Aug. 1, 1815.

16. Rogin, *Fathers and Children*, 159; Abernethy, *South in the New Nation*, 457.

17. Remini, *Andrew Jackson*, 227; Rogin, op. cit., 159; *NASPIA*, 6:341, Hawkins to Pinckney, Aug. 16, 1814; *ASPIA*, 1:837, treaty of Ft. Jackson, Minutes, Aug. 8, 1814.

18. Remini, op. cit., 226, 232; Owsley, *Struggle for the Gulf Borderlands*, 89.

19. *ASPIA*, 1:837; Rogin, *Fathers and Children*, 158; Remini, *Andrew Jackson*, 230.

20. Vine Deloria, Jr., *Custer Died for Your Sins*, 146–47; Swanton, *Indians of the Southeastern United States*, 234–35; Remini, op. cit., 230.

21. *ASPIA*, 1:837, treaty of Ft. Jackson, Minutes, Aug. 8, 1814; 1:838, Minutes, Aug. 9, 1814.

22. NA75:SW/LR, Hawkins to secretary of war, Apr. 16, 1816; on January 18, 1816, President Madison had recommended to the Senate that the gift to Jackson be permitted (*ASPIA*, 2:26), and Hawkins's statement was among those presented in support of the recommendation. *ASPIA*, 2 :676, President John Quincy Adams to H of R, Dec. 8, 1826, "Grants made by the Indians to Agents or Commisioners of the United States."

23. NA75:42, Doc. 340; a portrait of "Timpoochee Barnard, Chief of the Yuchi Indians among the Lower Creeks" appears in Swanton, *Indians of the Southeastern U.S.*, pl. 36–1; *ASPIA*, 1:838, treaty of Ft. Jackson, Minutes, Aug. 9, 1814.

24. Owsley, *Struggle for the Gulf Borderlands*, 90 and n. 90–91, states that these letters critical of Jackson survive only in summary form in the register of letters received by the secretary of war, and that the letters themselves were almost certainly removed deliberately. Another possibility, one would think, is that the letters were lost in the general chaos when Washington was burned by the British.

25. *ASPIA*, 2:92, Sept. 14, 1816, treaty with the Cherokees, and also Grinde, "Cherokee Removal," 34; *ASPIA*, 2:92–93, Sept. 20, 1816, treaty with the Chickasaws; *ASPIA*, 2:95, Oct. 24, 1816, treaty with the Choctaws, and also Abbott, "Indian Policy," 169; Harmon, *Sixty Years of Indian Affairs*, 152; *ASPIA*, 2:122–23, Graham to Jackson, Dec. 4, 1816; 2:119, Jackson to Butler, Aug. 14, 1816.

26. Sheehan, *Seeds of Extinction*, 214–16; *ASPIA*, 1:860, Hawkins to secretary of war, July 3, 1814; 1:860, Hawkins to secretary of war, July 13, 1814; 1:859, Flournoy to Hawkins, June 19, 1814; 1:859, Hawkins to secretary of war, June 21, 1814; 1:860, Hawkins to secretary of war, Aug. 16, 1814; 1:861, Hawkins to acting secretary of war, Oct. 5, 1814.

27. Harmon, *Sixty Years of Indian Affairs*, 148, Monroe to Congress.

28. Rogin, *Fathers and Children*, 160, 194–95; NA75:43, 363 (1815), on scarcity of black laborers.

29. Rogin, op. cit., 161, Hawkins's talk to Creeks, Aug. 30, 1814; NA75: SW/LR, Hawkins to secretary of war, Feb. 9, 1816; NA75:SW/LR, Hawkins to secretary of war, Apr. 2, 1816.

30. Hall, "Red Stick War," 289; Rogin, *Fathers and Children*, 161; Hall, op. cit., 290–91.

31. Abernethy, *South in the New Nation*, 373–98, on the last British campaign and the battle of New Orleans; E. H. Simmons, *The United States Marines*, 17, says there were U.S. Marines in Jackson's army.

32. Foster, *Negro-Indian Relationships*, 23–24; Abel, *American Indian as Slaveholder*, on free black communities among the Indians; Hall, "Red Stick War," 291–92; Rogin, *Fathers and Children*, 194; Owsley, *Struggle for the Gulf Borderlands*, 179, 181–84; Grant, *BH*, 732, Hawkins to Nicolls, May 28, 1815.

33. Rogin, *Fathers and Children*, 193; Foster, *Negro-Indian Relationships*, 25. James W. Silver, "A Counter-Proposal to the Indian Removal Policy of Andrew Jackson," 207–209, on Gaines's early career; Gaines had made powerful alliances through his marriages, first to the daughter of Judge Harry Toulmin, then to the daughter of William Blount, and finally to the daughter of Daniel Clark (*Dictionary of American Biography*, 4:93). Remini, *Andrew Jackson*, 344–45; Rogin, *Fathers and Children*, 195–96; Foster, *Negro-Indian Relationships*, 25–26.

34. On First Seminole War, Rogin, op. cit., 195–200, and Remini, op. cit., 351–64; Foster, op. cit., 27–28.

35. NA75:SW/LR, Hawkins to Meigs, March 8, 1816.

36. Grant, *BH*, 763, Hawkins to Graham, Sept. 22, 1815, and Hawkins to Gaines, Oct. 17, 1815; NA75:SW/LR, Gaines to Coffee, Nov. 4, 1815. Coffee's letter to Acting Secretary of War James Monroe, in which Coffee strove mightily to justify his appointment to the commission, suggests that the War Department had no enthusiasm for the appointment (NA75: SW/LR, Coffee to acting secretary of war, March 15, 1816). NA75: SW/LR, Gaines to Coffee, Nov. 4, 1815. In later years Jackson lost Gaines's political support because of a conflict on the policy of Indian removal, which, Gaines said, would "throw together twenty tribes speaking different languages where the most ferocious savages will cut the throat of the most civilized and orderly" (quoted by Silver, "Counter-Proposal to Indian Removal," 214).

37. NA75:SW/LR, Hawkins to Coffee, Jan. 28, 1916; Remini, *Andrew Jackson*, 322; Rogin, *Fathers and Children*, 171; NA75:SW/LR, Coffee to acting secretary of war, March 15, 1816.

38. Harmon, *Sixty Years of Indian Affairs*, 145, Jackson to Pinckney, May 18, 1814; 146, Jackson to Armstrong, June 13, 1814. Rogin, *Fathers and Children*, 170–71, cites substantial evidence of connivance in letters between Jackson (apparently the instigator) and Coffee. NA75:SW/LR, Coffee to commissioners, Feb. 18, 1816.

39. NA75:SW/LR, talk of Cherokee chiefs to secretary of war, March 12, 1816; *ASPIA*, 2:92, treaty with Cherokees, Sept. 14, 1816; Remini, *Andrew Jackson*, 324 and n. 11, and 466.

40. NA75:SW/LR, Gaines to Coffee, Feb. 18, 1816; NA75:SW/LR, Coffee to [Gaines], Feb. 18, 1816, suggests by its language that Coffee may have back-dated this letter so it would appear that Gaines's letter (of the same date) had not yet arrived; NA75:SW/LR, Hawkins to secretary of war, Apr. 1, 1816.

41. NA75:SW/LR, Coffee to acting secretary of war, March 15, 1816; Rogin, *Fathers and Children*, 176–77.

42. Abernethy, *South in the New Nation*, 457–58; Abernethy, *Frontier to Plantation*, 225; Abernethy, *op. cit.*, 447; Lynd, "Slavery and the Founding Fathers," 130, quoting John Quincy Adams to George William Erving, Nov. 28, 1818.

43. NA75:SW/LR, Hawkins to secretary of war, Apr. 1, 1816.

44. Hall, "Red Stick War," 292; NA75:SW/LR, Hawkins to secretary of war, Apr. 1, 1816; NA75:SW/LR, Hawkins to secretary of war, Apr. 2, 1816, on Cornells's death; Abbott, "Indian Policy," 156, NA75:43, 328–58 passim, contains many references to Halsted's illnesses.

45. Foreman, *Indians and Pioneers*, 43, quoting Jackson to secretary of war, July 9, 1817.

46. Some parts of the civilization program were carried forward, especially by Quaker missionaries (Sheehan, *Seeds of Extinction*, 157–59). For the decay and end of the factory system: Harmon, "Benjamin Hawkins and the Federal Factory System," 151; Harmon, *Sixty Years of Indian Affairs*, 122–25, 129–30; Hagan, "The Indian in American History," 11; Peake, *U.S. Indian Factory System*, 184–230; Katherine Coman, "Government Factories: An Attempt to control Competition in the Fur Trade," 373; Wesley, "Government Factory System," 505–510.

47. *ASPIA*, 2:27, secretary of war to U.S. Senate, March 13, 1816; Crawford's statement on Indian policy was used against him when he campaigned for the presidency in 1824 (*Dictionary of American Biography*, 2:529). Grinde, "Cherokee Removal," 36.

48. Rogin, *Fathers and Children*, 13. Charles Hudson thus sums up Jackson's attitude toward the Indians: "Jackson pretended to be a friend of the Indians, claiming that his removing them from the evil effects of exposure to white civilization was for their own good. . . . It soon became plain that Jackson was a friend of the Indians only so long as he needed them, as when the Cherokees helped him fight the Creek War of 1813–1814, and again when the Creeks helped him fight the Seminoles" (*Southeastern Indians*, 454).

49. Grant and Davis, "Wedding of Col. Benjamin Hawkins," 314–15. Jeffersonia, in a suit against Hawkins's other heirs in 1834, claimed as the only child born in wedlock the right to a larger share or the whole of his estate (Georgia Department of Archives and History, Hawkins Papers, Will and Lawsuit); Muskogee may not have been Hawkins's daughter, although brought up with the Hawkins children (Grant, *BH*, xxi and n. 41). C. M. Destler, "Correspondence of David Bridie Mitchell," 382.

50. NA75:SW/LR, Creeks to secretary of war, March 8, 1817.

51. Hawkins, Hawkins Papers, Estate of Benjamin Hawkins, Inventory and Sale, Georgia Department of Archives and History.

52. Harmon, *Sixty Years of Indian Affairs*, 150.

Bibliography

Abbott, Martin. "Indian Policy and Management in the Mississippi Territory, 1798–1817." *Journal of Mississippi History* 14 (1952): 153–69.

Abel, Annie H. *The American Indian as Slaveholder and Secessionist.* Cleveland, Ohio, 1915.

Abernethy, Thomas P. *From Frontier to Plantation in Tennessee.* Chapel Hill, N.C., 1932.

———. *The South in the New Nation, 1789–1819.* Baton Rouge, La., 1961.

———. *Western Lands and the American Revolution.* New York, 1937.

Adair, James. *The History of the American Indians. . . .* London, 1775. Reprint. Johnson City, Tenn., 1930.

Adams, Mary P. "Jefferson's Reaction to the Treaty of San Ildefonso." *Journal of Southern History* 21 (May, 1955): 173–188.

American Philosophical Society. See under Hawkins, *Letterbook*; Hawkins, Journal of Occurrences.

American Papers: Documents, Legislative and Executive, of the Congress of the United States. Edited by Walter Lowrie and Matthew Clarke. *Indian Affairs* and *Foreign Relations.* Washington, D.C.: 1832–1834.

Armstrong, Virginia I. *I Have Spoken.* Chicago, 1971.

Atlas of American History. New York: Scribners, 1943.

Abridgement of the Debates of Congress from 1789 to 1856. See under Benton, Thomas Hart, ed.

Atkin, Edmond. *Indians of the Southern Colonial Frontier: The Edmond Atkin Report and Plan of 1755.* Edited by Wilbur Jacobs. Columbia, S.C., 1954.

Augusta (Ga.) Chronicle and Gazette of the State.

Authentic Memoirs of William Augustus Bowles, Esq. London, 1791.

Bartram, William. *Travels Through North and South Carolina, Georgia, East and West Florida.* London, 1792. Reprint. Savannah, Ga., 1973.

Beard, W. E. "Colonel Burr's First Brush with the Law." *Tennessee Historical Magazine* 1 (1915): 3–20.

Benton, Thomas Hart, ed. *Abridgement of the Debates of Congress from 1789 to 1856.* 16 vols. New York, 1857–61.

Berlin, Ira. *Slaves without Masters: The Free Negro in the Antebellum South.* New York, 1974.

Bestor, Arthur E., Jr. *Backwoods Utopias.* Philadelphia, 1950.

Bevans, Charles I., comp. *Treaties and Other International Agreements of the United States of America, 1776–1949.* Vol. 12. Washington, D.C. 1974.

Brigham, Clarence S. *History and Bibliography of American Newspapers.* Vol. 1. Worcester, Mass., 1947.

Burnett, Edmund C., ed. *Letters of Members of the Continental Congress.* Washington, D.C., 1934.

Caughey, J. W. *McGillivray of the Creeks.* Norman, Okla., 1938.

Chappell, A. H. *Miscellanies of Georgia.* 1874. Reprint, 1928.

Cohen, Felix S. *Handbook of Federal Indian Law.* Washington, D.C., 1942.

Coker, William S. *John Forbes and Company and the War of 1812.* Pensacola, Fla., 1979.

———. "Entrepreneurs in the British and Spanish Floridas, 1775–1821." In *Eighteenth-Century Florida and the Caribbean*, ed. Samuel Proctor. Gainesville, Fla. 1976.

Collins, Varnum Lansing. *President Witherspoon: A Biography.* Vol. 2. Princeton, 1925.

Columbian Museum and Savannah Advertiser (Savannah, Georgia).

Coman, Katherine. "Government Factories: An Attempt to Control Competition in the Fur Trade." *Papers and Discussions of the American Economic Association* (1911), 368–88.

Commager, Henry Steele, ed. *Documents of American History.* 8th ed. New York, 1963.

Corbitt, D. C., and J. T. Lanning. "A Letter of Marque Issued by William Augustus Bowles as Director-General of the State of Muscogee." *Journal of Southern History* 11:246–61.

Corkran, David. *The Creek Frontier, 1540–1783.* Norman, Okla., 1967.

Cotterill, R. S. "A Chapter of Panton, Leslie and Company." *Journal of Southern History* 10:275–92.

———. "Federal Indian Management in the South, 1789–1825." *Mississippi Valley Historical Review* 20.

———. *The Southern Indians: The Story of the Civilized Tribes before Removal.* Norman, Okla., 1954.

Crane, Verner W. "A Lost Utopia of the First American Frontier." *Sewannee Review* 27:48–61.

Crowe, Charles. "Indians and Blacks in White America." In *Four Centuries of Southern Indians*, ed. Charles M. Hudson. Athens, Ga., 1975.

Cumming, William P. *The Southeast in Early Maps.* Chapel Hill, N.C., 1962.

Davis, Edwards. "The Mississippi Choctaws." *Chronicles of Oklahoma* 10:257–66.

Debo, Angie. *And Still the Waters Run*. Princeton, 1940.
————. *A History of the Indians of the United States*. Norman, Okla., 1970.
————. *Rise and Fall of the Choctaw Republic*. Norman, Okla., 1934.
————. *The Road to Disappearance*. Norman, Okla., 1941.
Deloria, Vine, Jr. *Custer Died for Your Sins*. New York, 1969.
———— and Clifford M. Lytle. *American Indians, American Justice*. Austin, Texas, 1983.
DeRosier, Arthur H., Jr. "Myths and Realities in Indian Westward Removal." In *Four Centuries of Southern Indians*, ed. Charles M. Hudson. Athens, Ga., 1975.
————. *The Removal of the Choctaw Indians*. Knoxville, Tenn., 1970.
Destler, J. M. "Correspondence of David Bridie Mitchell." *Georgia Historical Quarterly* 21 (Dec., 1937).
Dictionary of American Biography. New York, 1964.
Dodd, Donald B., and Wynelle S. Dodd. *Historical Statistics of the South, 1790–1970*. University, Ala., 1973.
Douglas, Marjory S. *Florida: The Long Frontier*. New York, 1967
Douglass, Elisha P. "The Adventurer Bowles." *William & Mary Quarterly*, 3d ser., 6 (Jan., 1949): 3–23.
Downes, R. C. "Creek-American Relations, 1782–1790." *Georgia Historical Quarterly* 21:142–84.
Drake, Francis S. *Life and Correspondence of Henry Knox* Boston, 1873.
Driver, Harold E. *Indian Tribes of North America*. Supplement to *International Journal of American Linguistics* 19 (1953).

Edmunds, R. David. *Shawnee Prophet*. Lincoln, Nebr., 1983.
————. *Tecumseh and the Quest for Indian Leadership*. Boston, 1984.
Edwards, Everett E., and Wayne D. Rasmussen. *Bibliography on the Agriculture of the American Indians*. See under United States Department of Agriculture.

Federal Cases. Book 25, National Reporter System, U.S. Series. *United States* v. *Aaron Burr* (Cases 14692a and 14692b). Saint Paul, Minn., 1896.
Fenton, William N. *American Indian and White Relations to 1830*. Chapel Hill, 1957.
Foley, John P., ed. *The Jefferson Cyclopedia*. New York, 1900.
Forbes, John. "A Journal of John Forbes, 1803." Transcribed by F. M. Greenslade. *Florida Historical Society Quarterly* 9:279–89.
Foreman, Grant. *The Five Civilized Tribes*. Norman, Okla., 1934.
————. *Indians and Pioneers*. Norman, Okla., 1936.
Foster, Sir Augustus John. *Jeffersonian America: Notes on the United States of America. . .* , Edited by Richard Beale Davis. San Marino, Calif., 1954.
Foster, Lawrence. *Negro-Indian Relationships in the Southeast*. Philadelphia, 1935.

Gibson, Arrell M. *The Chickasaws*. Norman, Okla., 1971.

Gilbert, William H., Jr. "The Eastern Cherokees." *Bureau of American Ethnology Bulletin* 133 (1943): 169–411.

Grant, C. L. "Senator Benjamin Hawkins: Federalist or Republican?" *Journal of the Early Republic*, fall 1981.

—— and Gerald H. Davis. "The Wedding of Col. Benjamin Hawkins." *North Carolina Historical Review*, July 1977.

Grinde, Donald. "Cherokee Removal and American Politics." *The Indian Historian*, 8, no. 3 (Summer 1975).

Hagan, William T. *American Indians*. Chicago, 1961.

——. "The Indian in American History." *American Historical Association*. Wash., D.C., 1971.

Halbert, H. S., and T. H. Ball. *The Creek War of 1813 and 1814*. 1895. Reprint, edited by Frank L. Owsley, Jr., University, Ala., 1969.

Hall, Arthur H. "The Red Stick War," *Chronicles of Oklahoma*, Sept., 1934.

Halliburton, R., Jr. *Red Over Black: Black Slavery Among the Cherokee Indians*. Westport, Conn., 1977.

Hamer, Philip M. "The British in Canada and the Southern Indians, 1790–1794." *East Tennessee Historical Society Publications* 2:107–34.

——. "Letters of William Blount." *East Tennessee Historical Society Publications* 4:122–33.

Harmon, George D. "Benjamin Hawkins and the Federal Factory System." *North Carolina Historical Review* 9:138–52.

——. *Sixty Years of Indian Affairs, Political, Economic, and Diplomatic, 1789–1850*. Chapel Hill, N.C., 1941.

Hawkins, Benjamin. Hawkins Papers. Georgia Department of Archives and History, Atlanta.

——. Journal of Occurrences in the Creek Agency . . . (1802). Microfilm Publication no. 214, roll 692. American Philosophical Society, Philadelphia.

——. Letterbook (May 1798–Sept. 1801; 1802, 1810). Microfilm Publication no. 215, roll 680. American Philosophical Society, Philadelphia.

——. *Letters (1796–1806)*. 1916. Reprint. Spartanburg, S.C., 1974.

——. *Letters, Journals and Writings of Benjamin Hawkins*. 2 vols. Edited by C. L. Grant. Savannah, Ga., 1980.

——. *Sketch of the Creek Country*. 1848. Reprint. Spartanburg, S.C., 1974.

Hemperley, Marion R. "Benjamin Hawkins' Trip from New York to Coweta Tallahassee, 1798." *Alabama Historical Quarterly* 33 (1971), nos. 3–4.

——. "Benjamin Hawkins' Trip through Alabama, 1796." *Alabama Historical Quarterly* 31 (1969), nos. 3–4.

Hinds, Ascher C. *Precedents of the House of Representatives of the United States*. Washington, D.C., 1907.

Hoijer, Harry, ed. *Language in Culture*. Chicago, 1954.

Holmes, G. K. "Aboriginal Agriculture—The American Indians." *Cyclopedia of American Agriculture*. 2nd ed. New York, 1909–1910.

Holmes, Jack D. L. *Gayoso: The Life of a Spanish Governor in the Mississippi Valley, 1789–1799*. Gloucester, Mass., 1968.

———. "Spanish Policy Toward the Southern Indians in the 1790s." In *Four Centuries of Southern Indians*, edited by Charles M. Hudson. Athens, Ga., 1975.

Honigmann, J. J., and I. Honigmann, "Drinking in an Indian-White Community." *Psychological Abstracts* 24 (1942).

Hudson, Charles M., ed. *Four Centuries of Southern Indians*. Athens, Ga., 1975.

———. *The Southeastern Indians*. Knoxville, Tenn., 1976.

Hulan, Richard H. "The Natchez Trace Parkway: In Memoriam," *The Indian Historian* 8, no. 4.

Innerarity, John. "Creek Nation, Debtor to John Forbes & Co. . . . A Journal of John Innerarity, 1812." Edited by F. M. Greenslade. *Florida Historical Society Quarterly* 9 : 67–89.

Jackson, Helen Hunt. *A Century of Dishonor: The Early Crusade for Indian Reform*. 1881. Reprint. Edited by A. F. Rolle. New York, 1965.

Jacobs, J. R. *Tarnished Warrior*. New York, 1938.

James, Marquis. *Life of Andrew Jackson*. New York, 1938.

Jefferson, Thomas. *Papers of Thomas Jefferson*. Edited by Julian P. Boyd et al. Princeton, N.J., 1950–.

———. *The Writings of Thomas Jefferson*. Edited by Andrew A. Lipscomb and Albert E. Bergh. Washington, D.C., 1903.

Jellinek, E. M. *The Disease Concept of Alcoholism*. New Haven, Conn., 1960.

Jordan, Winthrop. *White Over Black*. Baltimore, 1969.

Kinnaird, Lawrence. "International Rivalry in the Creek Country." *Florida Historical Society Quarterly* 10 (1931):59–85.

———. "The Significance of William Augustus Bowles' Seizure of Panton's Apalachee Store in 1792." *Florida Historical Society Quarterly* 9 : 156–92.

Kinnaird, Lucia B. "The Rock Landing Conference of 1789." *North Carolina Historical Review* 9 : 249–65.

Kinney, J. B. *A Continent Lost—A Civilization Won*. Baltimore, 1937.

Klinck, Carl F. *Tecumseh: Fact and Fiction in Early Records*. Englewood Cliffs, N.J., 1961.

Knollenberg, Bernhard. "John Adams, Knox, and Washington." *American Antiquarian Society* (1946):207–238.

Levine, Stuart, and Nancy O. Lurie. *The American Indian Today*. Rev. ed. Baltimore, Md., Penguin Books, 1970. London: 1802.

Life of General W. A. Bowles. Reprint. New York, 1803.

Littman, Gerald. "Alcoholism, Illness, and Social Pathology Among American Indians in Transition." *American Journal of Public Health* 60 (Sept., 1970): 1769–88.

Lurie, Nancy O. "Indian Cultural Adjustment to European Civilization." In *Seventeenth-Century America: Essays in Colonial History,* edited by James M. Smith. Chapel Hill, N.C., 1959.

Lynd, Staughton, "Slavery and the Founding Fathers." In *Black History,* edited by Melvin Drimmer. New York, 1969.

McKenney, Thomas L. *Memoirs, Official and Personal, With Sketches of Travels Among the Northern and Southern Indians.* New York, 1846.

McMurry, Donald L. "The Indian Policy of the Federal Government and the Economic Development of the Southwest, 1789–1801." *Tennessee Historical Magazine* 1:21–39, 106–119.

McNickle, D'Arcy. *They Came Here First: The Epic of the American Indian.* Philadelphia, 1949.

McPherson, Elizabeth G. "Unpublished Letters from North Carolinians to Jefferson." *North Carolina Historical Review* 11–12 (1934–35), no. 3:252–83.

———. "Unpublished Letters from North Carolinians to Washington." *North Carolina Historical Review* 11–12 (1934–35), no. 2: 149–72.

Mahon, John K. *War of 1812.* Gainesville, Fla., 1972.

Malone, Dumas. *Jefferson and His Times.* Boston, 1962.

Marshall, John. *The Life of George Washington.* Philadelphia, 1839.

Masterson, William H. *William Blount.* 1954. Reprint. New York, 1969.

Mauelshagen, Carl, and Gerald H. Davis. *Partners in the Lord's Work: The Diary of Two Moravian Missionaries in the Creek Indian Country, 1807–1813.* Atlanta: School of Arts and Sciences, Georgia State College, 1969.

Melton, Maurice. "War Trail of the Red Sticks." *American History Illustrated.* Feb., 1976.

Merriam, Lewis, ed. *The Problem of Indian Administration.* Brookings Institution Merriam Report. Baltimore, Md., 1928.

Milfort, Louis LeClerc. *Memoirs, or A Quick Glance at My Various Travels and My Soujourn in the Creek Nation.* Circa 1800. Reprint. Savannah, Ga., 1972.

Miller, John Chester. *The Wolf by the Ears: Thomas Jefferson and Slavery.* New York, 1977.

Milling, Chapman J. *Red Carolinians.* Chapel Hill, N.C., 1940.

Mugridge, D. H., and Helen F. Conover. *Album of American Battle Art.* New York, 1972.

Nash, Gary B., and Richard Weiss, eds. *The Great Fear: Race in the Mind of America.* New York, 1970.

New American State Papers, 1789–1860: Indian Affairs. Edited by Thomas C. Cochran. Wilmington, Del., 1972.

Owsley, Frank L., Jr. *Struggle for the Gulf Borderlands.* Gainesville, Fla., 1981.
———. "Benjamin Hawkins, the First Modern Indian Agent." *Alabama Historical Quarterly* 30 (1968), no. 2.

Palladium: A Literary and Political Weekly Repository (Frankfort, Ky.), Dec., 1805.
Paxon, Frederic L. *History of the American Frontier, 1763–1893.* Boston, 1924.
Peake, Ora B. *History of the United States Indian Factory System, 1795–1822.* Denver, 1954.
Pickett, Albert James. *History of Alabama, And Incidentally of Georgia and Mississippi from the Earliest Period.* Charleston, S.C., 1851.
Pound, Merritt B. "Colonel Benjamin Hawkins of North Carolina, Benefactor of the Southern Indians." *North Carolina Historical Review*, 19:1–21 and 168–86.
———. *Benjamin Hawkins, Indian Agent.* Athens, Ga., 1951.
Princeton University Archives, Alumni Files (Nongraduate).
Prucha, Francis Paul. *American Indian Policy in the Formative Years: The Indian Trade and Intercourse Acts.* Cambridge, Mass., 1962.
———. *Indian Peace Medals in American History.* Madison, Wis., 1971.

Ramsey, James G. *Annals of Tennessee.* Charleston, S.C., 1853.
Ray, R. Craig. "Fort Toulouse of the Alabamas." *Journal of the Council on Abandoned Military Posts* 8, no. 1.
[Reed, Andrew.] *No Fiction: A Narrative Founded on Recent and Interesting Facts.* Hartford, Conn., 1821.
Remini, Robert V. *Andrew Jackson and the Course of American Empire, 1767–1821.* New York, 1977.
Richardson, James H., ed. *Messages and Papers of the Presidents.* Washington, D.C., 1896–99.
Robertson, James. "Correspondence." *American Historical Magazine* 4 (1900):66–96, 163–92, 247–86, 336–81.
Rogin, Michael Paul. *Fathers and Children: Andrew Jackson and the Subjugation of the American Indian.* New York, 1975.
Rothrock, Mary U. "Carolina Traders Among the Overhill Cherokees, 1690–1760." *East Tennessee Historical Society's Publications*, no. 1, 1929.
Royce, Charles C., comp. "Indian Land Cessions in the United States." In *Eighteenth Annual Report of the Bureau of American Ethnology*, pt. 2, 521–997. Washington, D.C., 1899.

Satz, Ronald N. *American Indian Policy in the Jacksonian Era.* Lincoln, Nebr., 1975.

Schmeckebier, Lawrence F. *The Office of Indian Affairs: Its History, Activities, and Organization.* Baltimore, Md., 1927.

Schoolcraft, Henry R. *Historical and Statistical Information Regarding the History, Condition and Prospects of the Indian Tribes of the United States.* Philadelphia, 1851–57.

Sevier, John. "Executive Journal of Governor John Sevier." Edited by Samuel Cole Williams. *East Tennessee Historical Society Publication* 2, nos. 1 and 2.

Sheehan, Bernard W. "Indian-White Relations in Early America," *William and Mary Quarterly,* 3d. ser., 26 (April 1969): 267–86.

———. *Seeds of Extinction: Jeffersonian Philanthropy and the American Indian.* Chapel Hill, N.C., 1973.

Silver, James W. "A Counter-Proposal to the Indian Removal Policy of Andrew Jackson." *Journal of Mississippi History* 4: 207–215.

Skinner, Constance L. *Pioneers of the Old Southwest.* New Haven, Conn., 1921.

Smith, Jane F., and Robert M. Kvasnicka, eds. *Indian-White Relations: A Persistent Paradox.* Washington, D.C., 1976.

Steiner, Stan. *The New Indians.* New York, 1968.

Stevens, William B. *History of Georgia.* Philadelphia, 1859.

Stewart, Omer. "Questions Regarding American Indian Criminality." *Human Organization* 23 (Spring 1964): 61–66.

Swanton, John R. *Early History of the Creek Indians and Their Neighbors.* Bureau of American Ethnology Bulletin no. 73. Washington, D.C., 1922.

———. "An Indian Social Experiment and Some of Its Lessons." *Science Monthly* 31 (Oct., 1930): 368–76.

———. *Indian Tribes of the Lower Mississippi Valley and Adjacent Coast of the Gulf of Mexico.* Bureau of American Ethnology Bulletin no. 43. Washington, D.C., 1911.

———. *Indian Tribes of North America.* Bureau of American Ethnology Bulletin no. 145, Washington, D.C., 1952.

———. *Indians of the Southeastern United States.* Bureau of American Ethnology Bulletin no. 137. Washington, D.C., 1946.

Tebbel, John. *The Compact History of the Indian Wars.* New York, 1966.

Tebeau, Charlton W. *History of Florida.* Coral Gables, Fla., 1971.

Thompson, Isabel. "The Blount Conspiracy." *East Tennessee Historical Society Publication* 2 (1930): 3–21.

Timberlake, Henry. *Lieutenant Henry Timberlake's Memoirs, 1756–1765.* Edited by Samuel Cole Williams. 1927. Reprint. Marietta, Ga., 1948.

Tocqueville, Alexis de. *Democracy in America.* Edited by Phillips Bradley. New York, 1954.

Trennert, Robert A., Jr. *Alternative to Extinction: Federal Indian Policy and the Beginnings of the Reservation System, 1846–51.* Philadelphia, 1975.

Tucker, Glenn. *Tecumseh, Vision of Glory*. New York, 1956.

Turner, Frederick J. "Documents on the Blount Conspiracy, 1795–1797." *American Historical Review* 10 (1905):574–606.

———. "The Policy of France toward the Mississippi Valley in the Period of Washington and Adams," *American Historical Review* 10 (1905):no. 2.

Tyler, S. Lyman. *A History of Indian Policy*. Washington, D.C.: United States Bureau of Indian Affairs, 1973.

United States Congress. *Inaugural Addresses of the Presidents of the United States*. Washington, D.C., 1974.

United States Department of Agriculture. *A Bibliography on the Agriculture of the American Indians*. Edited by Everett E. Edwards and Wayne D. Rasmussen. Miscellaneous Publication no. 447. Washington, D.C., 1942.

United States Department of Commerce. *Historical Statistics of the United States*. Washington, D.C., 1960.

United States Department of Interior. *Biographical and Historical Index of American Indians and Persons Involved in Indian Affairs*. Boston, 1966.

United States House of Representatives. *Journal of the House of Representatives of the United States*. 5th Congress. 1st Session (July) and 2d Session (February), 1798.

United States Library of Congress, Manuscript Division. Papers of James Madison, William Blount, Benjamin Hawkins, James Wilkinson, William Augustus Bowles, Francisco de Carondelet.

United States Library of Congress, Map Division.

United States National Archives. Record Group 75, Records of the Bureau of Indian Affairs. Record Group 42, Records of Public Buildings and Grounds.

United States Senate. *Journal of the Senate of the United States, 5th Congress*. 1st Session (July) and 2d Session (February), 1798.

Van der Beets, Richard, ed. *Held Captive by Indians: Selected Narratives, 1642–1836*. Knoxville, Tenn., 1973.

Vanderwerth, W. C., comp. *Indian Oratory*. Norman, Okla., 1971.

Vogel, Virgil J. *This Country Was Ours*. New York, 1972.

Viola, Herman J. *Diplomats in Buckskins: A History of Indian Delegations in Washington City*. Washington, D.C., 1981.

Washburn, Wilcomb E., comp. *The American Indian and the United States: A Documentary History*. New York, 1974.

———, ed. *The Indian and the White Man*. New York, 1964.

———. "The Moral and Legal Justifications for Dispossessing the Indians." In *Seventeenth-Century America: Essays in Colonial History*, ed. James M. Smith. Chapel Hill, N.C., 1959.

Washington, George. *Writings of George Washington from the Original*

Manuscript Sources, 1745–1799. Edited by John C. Fitzpatrick. 1944. Reprint. Westport, Conn., 1970.

Watson, Thomas D. "Continuity in Commerce: Development of the Panton, Leslie & Company Trade Monopoly in West Florida." *Florida Historical Quarterly* 54 (1976), no. 4.

Wesley, Edgar B. "The Government Factory System among the Indians, 1795–1822." *Journal of Economics and Business History* 4, no. 3:487–511.

Western World (Frankfort, Ky.), 1806–1810.

Wheeler, John H. *Historical Sketches of North Carolina from 1584 to 1851.* Philadelphia, 1851.

————. *Reminiscences and Memoirs of North Carolina and Eminent North Carolinians.* Columbus, Ohio, 1884.

Whitaker, A. P. "Alexander McGillivray, 1783–1789," *North Carolina Historical Review* 5:181–203.

————. "Alexander McGillivray, 1789–1793," *North Carolina Historical Review* 5:289–309.

————. "The Muscle Shoals Speculation, 1783–1789." *Mississippi Valley History Review* 13:365–86.

————. *The Spanish-American Frontier, 1783–1795.* Boston, 1927.

————. "Spanish Intrigue in the Old Southwest." *Mississippi Valley Historical Review* 12:155–76.

White, Kate. "John Chisholm, Soldier of Fortune," *East Tennessee Historical Society Publication* 1, 60–66.

Williams, Samuel Cole. *Beginnings of West Tennessee: In the Land of the Chickasaws, 1541–1841.* Johnson City, Tenn., 1930.

————. *Dawn of the Tennessee Valley and Tennessee History.* Johnson City, Tenn., 1937.

————, ed. *Early Travels in the Tennessee Country.* Kingsport, Tenn., 1928.

Wissler, Clark. *Indians of the United States.* New York, 1940.

————. *Red Man Reservations.* 1938. Reprint. New York, 1971.

Woodward, Thomas S. *Reminiscences of the Creek or Muskogee Indians.* 1859. Reprint, Ala., 1939.

Wright, Marcus J. *Some Account of the Life and Services of William Blount.* Washington, D.C., 1884.

Wright, J. Leitch, Jr. *William Augustus Bowles, Director General of the Creek Nation.* Athens, Ga., 1967.

————. *Britain and the American Frontier, 1783–1815.* Athens, Ga., 1975.

————. *The Only Land They Knew: The Tragic Story of the American Indians in the Old South.* New York, 1981.

Index